Religion, Ritual and Ritualistic Objects

Religion, Ritual and Ritualistic Objects

Special Issue Editor

Albertina Nugteren

MDPI • Basel • Beijing • Wuhan • Barcelona • Belgrade

Special Issue Editor
Albertina Nugteren
Tilburg University
The Netherlands

Editorial Office
MDPI
St. Alban-Anlage 66
4052 Basel, Switzerland

This is a reprint of articles from the Special Issue published online in the open access journal *Religions* (ISSN 2077-1444) from 2018 to 2019 (available at: https://www.mdpi.com/journal/religions/special_issues/Ritual)

For citation purposes, cite each article independently as indicated on the article page online and as indicated below:

LastName, A.A.; LastName, B.B.; LastName, C.C. Article Title. *Journal Name* **Year**, *Article Number*, Page Range.

ISBN 978-3-03897-752-0 (Pbk)
ISBN 978-3-03897-753-7 (PDF)

Contents

About the Special Issue Editor

Albertina Nugteren (PhD 1991, Universities of Utrecht and Leiden, The Netherlands) is currently a Professor in the Department of Culture Studies and Digital Sciences at Tilburg University. Trained as a classical Indologist she now combines ethnography and textual studies. Through years of travel in South Asia as well as the shifting demands of academic curricula she also began to focus on contemporary issues such as Hindu communities in diaspora. Special research interests include religious rituals, rituals after disasters, material culture, and the 'green' environment (sacred trees, sacred groves, natural burial sites, the use of wood in open-air cremation, etc.). Her work is published widely, such as with Brill, Oxford University Press, Routledge, Equinox and Praeger/ABC-CLIO. She also published a novel on ancient India, and writes poetry.

Preface to "Religion, Ritual and Ritualistic Objects"

The idea for the present volume was conceived gradually during academic conferences, when receiving notifications of fascinating new series set up by well-known publishers, and while 'thinking through things' both in the classroom and during fieldwork. When I was invited to convene and guest-edit a Special Issue on ritual by the Journal *Religions,* I saw this as a thrilling opportunity to send out open invitations for an object-centered volume. I was highly curious to see what kind of ritualistic 'things' would come floating by.

I envisaged a wide range of contributions on material culture and ritual practices across religions. The primary focus was to be on objects: tangible material things as used in religious ritual settings. The response was promising, and the Journal's time schedule guaranteed a rapid production process. As often happens, some proposals were too broad and general, and submissions sometimes lacked originality or were not based on new ethnographic data gathered 'on the spot'. But what remained, and is proudly presented here, is an attractive collection of ten papers, most of them lavishly illustrated with pictures.

As editors, we would like to express our gratitude to all authors for sharing their fascination with the life of ritualistic objects with the readers. Also, we thank all the anonymous peer reviewers whose astute remarks and suggestions greatly enhanced the quality of each paper.

Albertina Nugteren
Special Issue Editor

religions

MDPI

Editorial

Introduction to the Special Issue 'Religion, Ritual, and Ritualistic Objects'

Albertina Nugteren

Faculty of Humanities and Digital Sciences, Tilburg University, 5000 LE Tilburg, The Netherlands; a.nugteren@uvt.nl

Received: 13 February 2019; Accepted: 25 February 2019; Published: 6 March 2019

If an object-centered volume on religious ritual is anything, it is a collection of contributions on material culture as a manifestation of structured symbolic practices (Fleming and Mann 2014; Grimes 2011; Keane 2008; Morgan 2008). Such practices are assumed to be endowed with signification and to be based on an interrelated set of ideas. Rituals may be taken to exist because they perform the function of establishing a common mood and thus assert social solidarity, but a ritual has a particular style, is part of a cultural and symbolic order. Its material dimensions, particularly its objects, may provide us with keys to meaning-making.

According to Hodder (1987, p. 1) the meaning in objects is threefold: (1) objects have use value through their effect on the world (a functionalist, materialistic, or utilitarian perspective); (2) objects have structural or coded meanings, which they communicate (their symbolic meaning); (3) objects are meaningful through their past associations (their historical meaning). Studying objects as transporters of meaning, as well as people's responses to such objects, especially in ritual contexts, thus becomes a study not merely of culture-specific materiality (or: materialization, when the processual character is emphasized) but also of the multiple interpretations that occur when people and objects move from one context to another.

We are fortunate that all authors in this Special Issue show a sensitive awareness of contexts and people's responses to objects, and do not limit themselves to iconography, style, or symbolism. Nor do they fall victim to 'the danger of a single story' (as the novelist Chimamanda Ngozi Adichie calls it in her TED-talk, (Adichie 2009)). The single story, according to Adichie, 'creates stereotypes. And the problem with stereotypes is not that they are untrue, but that they are incomplete' (quoted in (Buggeln and Franco 2018, p. xii)). Instead, all contributors present multiple perspectives and suspicion of single (or reductive) narratives, and thus allow their objects to come to life before the reader's eye, and shimmer.

This is not a collection of articles about rituals, but about the power of ritual objects. Some of those objects are found in museums; others are used within religious contexts and in daily life. Grimes: 'Ritual stuff is sometimes treasured and iconic, but sometimes it is not.' (Grimes 2011, p. 77) Cow dung is an example of the latter. In India it may be merely dirt; it may be scattered as fertilizer in the fields; mixed with straw and dried in the sun cow-patties may be used as fuel in simple ovens and furnaces; it may be the semi-fluid 'paint' with which the walls and floors of traditional rooms (temples and kitchens) were (and sometimes still are) ritually purified; and it may be the stuff from which divine figures are fashioned, as related by Catrien Notermans in her article on women's Govardhan festivities in rural Rajasthan.

1. Context

Things, objects, materiality: when they become saturated with religious meanings ((Morgan 2011, p. 140): 'a thing is an object waiting to happen') they appear to possess more power than people would reasonably allocate to them. What all contributions in this object-centered thematic issue share is the importance of **context**. The cow dung, mentioned above, in its normal appearance all over the world is 'nothing but shit', literally so. The object's existence, function, and potency depend on the context. A heap of cow dung on an Indian street may be smartly sidestepped by an urban lady passing by. She carefully hitches the borders of her silk sari for a minute. But what is dirt to the lady on her way to office may be precious to the urban scavenger. It can be collected, dried, and sold to the factory where it is made into granules of organic fertilizer used in gardens. In Notermans' article it is all this, and more. In her portrayal of cow dung's cognitive and relational specificity, she draws attention to rural women's intimate relation to cows and their dung in various contexts. Is it the multiple-day feast of Divali, not merely the single ritual, which makes cow dung stand out as the substance of fertility? Is it the specific context in which cow dung is not merely dirt—indeed, in the festive ritual situation it becomes the material from which divine figures are crafted and about which local stories are being told and re-told—or does its significance exist independent of the ritual and narrative context? Notermans shows that for the women the cognitive and imaginative relation may be heightened by the ritual context, yet the basis is found in their daily lives and ecologies.

One of the qualities ascribed to ritual (Bell 1992, 1997) is that rituals are an intensified form of participation and communication. If we take 'communication' here to have both social (for example, disciplinary, expressive) purposes and self-referring properties—women intensifying their pre-existing everyday relationships to both cows and their produce—we could state that the rural women around Udaipur have a matter-of-fact relationship to cow dung that becomes more dense when expressed through ritual, creativity, narrativity, symbolism, and a common mood (cf. Collins 2004). Cow dung, to them, is precious in a multi-purpose way. That the festive figurines made of cow dung are destroyed on the spot, then sun-dried, and at the right time carried out to the fields as fertilizer points at a lifeworld in which context is merely a matter of application, of use and deployment. Context does matter but in this case study it is transitional rather than sharply oppositional. That such precarious ecology—in terms of both lifeworlds and livelihoods—is under threat, such as by housing projects, fertilizer factories, and intergenerational change, is, literally, merely a footnote.

2. Form

Does **form** matter? The role that the shape or aesthetics may play in ritual efficacy is best illustrated and critically discussed through Walter van Beek's article on Dogon dance masks. Both in the production of the masks and the staging of the masked dance there are identities, there is personhood, there is agency, but there is also imitation, role-play, a masquerade. Dance is 'matter in motion' (as van Beek's title aptly states): 'Masks are matter in motion and symbols in context.' It appears that in this case study we need to consider both context and form, both objects and movements and places. The masks are to honor the dead and provide them with a means to become ancestors. Death itself is a major transition, marked by funerary rituals, but the major transition ritual—that of ritually transferring them, post-death, to the realm of ancestors—is essential. There is a reason why the dead are often referred to as 'the departed': they are somewhere else, not with us anyway, but they are still unsettled and for their own good and that of society they need to be firmly established 'elsewhere', as ancestors. Warning for over-interpretation of masks, van Beek rejects stereotypical significations attributed by outsiders, by whom masks are thought to represent ancestors, deities, spirits, or, in a different register: objects of art. The Dogon masks, van Beek cautions, are the entire apparition: costume, headpiece, and paraphernalia. They are a class of beings in their own right, and they come from outside the village. They are a presence rather than a representation: wild animals, sometimes humans. Their dances often mimic the particular animal the apparition refers to, but the apparition is the mask, not the person behind it. At the same time, masks show trends and fashions. At some recent point in time, the author notes, masks tended to become de-liminized, once some dancers started to write their own name on the headpieces, along with the year. In this process of masks becoming personal billboards, the ritual objects had crossed over into the 'real' world, of writing lessons in school, and of the international calendar.

One of the notions that is challenged in this article is the materiality of the masks, their 'objectness' (cf. Morgan 2011). In this particular case, the headpiece (commonly referred to as a mask when placed in an ethnological museum) may be an object, but it is not a ritual object at all. The ritual entity, in the staged context of the dance, consists of the material object(s) plus the costumed dancer. This implies that it is the combination of person, object, and act that is the real ritual agent, the ritual entity that moves and acts.

When we compare these insights about Dogon masked dances and masquerades to Andrea Nicklisch's processions and displays of seventeenth- and eighteenth-century ecclesiastical silverworks in the southern Andes, we truly cross over to another dimension of objectness and materiality. Although in van Beek's case we do find some intrusions of modernity—the European anthropologist, his camera, not to forget the billboard culture of individual names written on headpieces—in Nicklisch's study it is not the historical Spanish intrusion that determines the approach but the subsequent trans-cultural and inter-cultural processes. The silver objects are framed, by the author, as objects in their own rights, on their own non-verbal levels. This implies that the objects and images are studied from the perspective of the beholders. The degree to which, in the eyes of indigenous believers, the objects displayed before them may be interpreted as expressing continuity or discontinuity of indigenous or Catholic beliefs and iconographic vocabularies, is determined by the various angles. Nicklisch pays special attention to the angle that encompasses both belief systems, in the sense of a mutually transferred meaning. The objects are integrated into ritual acts in the context of church services and processions, yet in the ongoing cross-cultural and trans-cultural encounters there may be multiple readings of such images, objects, and rituals. The author uses the idea of 'contact zones' (Pratt 1991, p. 34), particularly cultural contact zones, as a sensitizing concept for indicating a (directly physical, spatial but also mental, intellectual) zone where cultures meet, clash, and grapple with each other.

A street shrine, framed in massive silverwork, hosts an image of the Virgin of Guadeloupe. Especially her cloak is covered with countless devotional gifts: precious stones, pearls, medals, coins and watches. It is this image of the Virgin—porcelain skin and sky-blue cloak—that is carried around in an annual procession. Pre-Hispanic worldviews and narratives shine through as mixed with Christian and possibly even pre-Christian European worldviews and narratives especially in the form of winged anthropomorphic beings. Much of this is made of local silver, or faced with silver, such as the tabernacle, candle banks, and altar. The author briefly discusses indigenous parallels, such as in the two silver plaquettes supposedly depicting Adam and Eve, as revealing a transfer of meaning. In the author's view, the indigenous system has instrumentalized a dominant system (Hispanic Christianity) as a vehicle and canvas for its own worldviews. By exploring processes as trans-cultural and cross-cultural transfer, she weighs related concepts such as cultural adaptation, acculturation, de-culturation, neo-culturation and trans-culturation. Is it possible, she wonders, to understand pictorial representations, in a colonial contact zone, directly, or at least beyond binary oppositions and exclusivities?

3. Figuration, Iconicity, Aniconicity

In Nicklisch's focus on historic objects made of silver, we may already have posed questions about **figuration, iconicity, and aniconicity** even when they were not accentuated or made explicit. Such questions were left out of both van Beek's and Nicklisch's presentation, but should be addressed here as a third connecting topic. The act of 'representation' may need to be distinguished from the notion of 'presence' (as van Beek did), but in most of the contributions there is no such distinction. Deborah de Koning, in her article on two annual rituals in Colombo, Sri Lanka, distinguishes two sides in the discourse and emerging cult around the god-king-hero-healer Ravana: the martial and the benevolent. She locates and temporizes these two main sides of his contemporary 'appearance' in two rituals: the ritual setting of a public street procession, and the low-key, low-profile rituals appealing to him as a healer, within the relative 'inner circle' of a Buddhist temple compound. Although the figure of Ravana has long been familiar throughout Asia through the Hindu epic *Ramayana* (and more popularly through plays and performances, and particularly televization), there is a recent upsurge of his popularity in Sri Lanka. Although the process of 'Ravanization' is still too young, too new, and too fluid for her to determine its reach and impact, the author acknowledges the multidirectionality and processual nature of Ravana's cult by consistently speaking of 'ritualization' (cf. Bell 1988, 1997; Grimes 1982, 2011) instead of rituals. Zooming in on two major ways in which Ravana is portrayed—his martial side and his benevolent side—she grapples with the inconsistency of binary categorizations. Yet, instead of the stereotypically monstrous, we find a warrior-king whose 'attributes' are presented in a spectacular display, ranging from a parade of 'jeweled' elephants to drum dances and *angampora* martial arts. Most stunning and disconcerting in its eeriness is the life-like statue of King Ravana himself as the center of the elephant procession. That Ravana is thus being hailed as a god-king refers back to (Sri) Lanka as the location of the epic war between Rama and Ravana. This direct (and highly imaginative) association between Lanka and Ravana—as Lanka's famous king in epic times—has gained new currency in today's nationalist sentiments.

The other, explicitly benevolent, side may be more puzzling to some: how could the same exalted figure, whose role combines the various personalities of royal adversary-warrior-epic king-founder of the nation be simultaneously a sage, a healer, a benefactor, a deity even, to those who participate in a ritual of participation, by imbibing his bathwater as medicine? Whereas the figure of the 'just ruler' may be a logical composition, the composite configurations we find in Ravana as a healer may need more crystallization before anything definite can be said about this aspect. Possibly, it is easier for us to understand a king's sword as symbolizing both his martial prowess and his role of dispensing or guarding justice. The warrior-king may have been previously demonized by his adversaries, but that this same god-king is now dispensing medicine and carrying the lotus as one of his emblems may be better understood and aligned with his martial side when seen in the perspective of a South Asian king's role in times of war as contrasted with his role in times of peace. There might be a fascinating sequence to this publication when the author would undertake an exploration of possible parallels with the *bodhisattva* figure; after all, these healing rituals take place within the precincts of a Buddhist temple.

From sword and scripture or lotus as attributes of a god-king, symbolizing his layered power, we move on to the symbol of the lotus in a completely different time and setting: ancient Egypt, the Levant and Mesopotamia, in an article by Andrew McDonald. Lotuses are widely dispersed—all they need is a little water, mud, and the sun's warmth—and so is the lotus motif. The lotus may have grown within everyone's reach in a wide area—from the Nilotic and other ancient river civilizations, such as those of the Euphrates and Tigris to contemporary ponds, marshes, and mud-holes throughout South and Southeast Asia. But the history of arts and artifacts is such that what has survived the rampages of time is often connected with royal dynasties, court deities, and priestly rituals. McDonald, in his study of Egyptian lotus symbolism, does not lose sight of the aquatic, biological, and botanical realities, but in studying surviving artifacts he is necessarily limited to the symbolism of 'high culture'. The lotus motifs he presents in his article are highly stylized, exquisite to look at, especially considering that some or most of the depictions must have been colored (blue and variations of yellow). Most of the floral and vegetative illustrations he uses are static images now kept in museums, but he also provides textual details and photographed botanic specificities to make his points: the time-tested role of water lilies in (royal or priestly) libation ceremonies. Such ceremonies are portrayed on the walls of tombs, on papyri, royal thrones, coffins, drinking cups, and vases. In ritualistic contexts on both sides of the Red Sea, a rite of passage involved a person's metaphorical transformation into a lotus flower, both in a ruler's inauguration and in his funerary rites. It should not surprise us that, in a circular worldview, a short-lived aquatic flower was so closely connected to the solar disc and the arc of the sky; by richly illustrating his article with well-chosen images the author discloses the associative logic of this floral symbolism.

Lotus symbolism, in McDonalds' presentation, is rich and layered. One of the keys to this symbolism is the plant's three-day life span, and the fact that new shoots arise before a flower stalk has finished the three days of anthesis. These three phases—as a bud, a half-open lotus with delicately unfolding petals, and a fully opened lotus looking like an aureole, indeed the solar disc—may seem extremely transient to some. Yet the lotus became a symbol of immortality, combining obvious fertility motifs, cycles of return, conceptions of immortality and aspirations to join the gods in the afterlife. In initiation rituals, 'lotus nectar' may even have been imbibed for its psychoactive effects. In the course of time (from 2500 BCE onwards) and through cultural diffusion as well as geographic expansion (Ancient Egypt, the Fertile Crescent, Levantine centers, Greece and onwards), distant human populations came to share these iconographic, mythic, and ritualistic conventions. Moreover, lotus symbolism began to collate crucial elements with sacred tree symbolism, and the occasional transition of the herbaceous plant into a sacral (lotiform) world-tree motif includes ancient winged entities, serpents, and solar orbs we may see referred to even today, such as in forms of both western and eastern esotericism. But on this point McDonald wisely restrains himself, and merely mentions a minor work by Ananda K. Coomaraswamy (1935).

Vegetative symbolism may use life-like floral and plant imagery, and in that sense its art may be called figurative, but plant symbolism can become so dense and stylized that the resulting compositions draw the beholder into complicated allegorical significances, especially in the ritualistic use of immortalizing plants. Can ancient Egyptian tableaus on coffins and tombs still be called iconic in the conventional sense of that term? When floral motifs become so stylized and juxtaposed with so many intricate motifs referring to eternal life, can we still speak of iconicity? Moreover, all persons and all vegetation portrayed there have been dead for millennia; how could we possibly link all that dead matter to biological and botanical reality? There seems to be an enormous gulf between the tombs of ancient Egyptian pharaohs and the next topic, pictures taken of children taking part in funerary rites for a dead parent in a contemporary Dutch family, but in fact there isn't. Laurie Faro introduces us to ritual-like mnemonic and coping practices of children in whose memories their dead father lives on, among other reminiscences, through a series of intentionally and purposely taken photographs. A striking detail of Faro's report is that the mother of the children, who, naturally, having lost her husband, herself is full of grief, carefully plans and initiates the entire event with the children's perspective foremost in her mind. While orchestrating the entire set of mourning activities, she is lucidly aware that she should create memories, good memories, for the children. In terms of academic studies on dying, death, and disposal, she is a prime example of the 'continuing bonds' and 'symbolic immortality' paradigms.

Today, post-mortem photography is rare. In this particular case, the children's mother decided not to have the deceased photographed, or at least not to have any photographs of him while lying in his coffin, to be included in the 'visual essay'. Photos of the dead, be they taken long before they actually died or on their death-bed, may function as tangible links between past and present (Zerubavel 2003), but most people choose to remember a lighter moment, the beloved person at his or her best. When the coffin had been positioned in one of the rooms in the family's home, they had surrounded it with flowers—indeed, in a way resembling the ancient Egyptians with their lotuses—as well as with some earlier pictures of the deceased among his family while still alive. Faro's article makes mention of some other objects, indicated as 'transitional objects', put into the coffin by the children, objects that the children considered to 'represent' or 'characterize' him. Although Faro does not discuss the 'absence-presence' predicament of death rites explicitly, there are clues in her article. For instance, the six-year-old boy imagines his father to now live on a little cloud (in the original Dutch it almost sounds as: on a cotton-ball fluff), and as on the way to a new life. Unexpectedly, bridging millennia, this is not unlike the imagery and promises of ancient Egyptian death rites.

Figuration, iconicity, and aniconicity are much more explicitly thematized in Albertina Nugteren's article on a Hindu god's footprint believed to have been left on a natural rock in Gaya, India. After a general introduction into the social facts of human feet and footwear in India, Nugteren zooms in on divine feet. The idea that the divine (deities, prophets, messengers, the numinously sacred in general) may leave footprints is widespread in the world, and India is particularly blessed by such visible-tangible 'traces'. Or should we say that human imagination proves to be so fertile that it finds traces of divine presence in both expected and unexpected places, and does not shy from exploiting such sites? Places of pilgrimage have often grown around such a gravitational point (Eck 2012), and so is the case in Gaya. A search for origins—what came first? How and with what object or story or event did this ritual center start?—is bound to lead contemporary scholars to frustration. Nugteren extricates various myths and local variations of such myths, but acknowledges that they may well be later—ex post facto—justifications, rationalizations, and embellishments. What remains is the object as such: a more or less clearly outlined imprint of a footstep (toes, and a hollow impression where both the ball and the heel of a foot may have slightly dented the surface) on a piece of natural rock.

In the temple's everyday reality, however, devotees are not particularly interested in the form. Instead, they cover the basin almost continuously with gifts of flower petals, sacred leaves, oil, clarified butter, and other ritual-sacrificial substances. Ritual gifts, naturally, are part of an exchange, and many prayers and wishes are said aloud or muttered inaudibly. Key to the ritual behavior in front of this divine footprint is a lively engagement with the god Vishnu's absence-presence: He was here, once, in primordial time, and subsequently left his footprint on a rock. Priests and devotees are now continuously filling the hollows his foot is supposed to have left on the stone. The dichotomies absence-presence and emptiness-fullness are thus ritually bridged, transcended, and transformed. From a more distanced and etic perspective, the cult around the footprint poses a question about the figurative nature of such a natural footprint: can we speak of an icon and thus of iconicity, or does such a 'natural manifestation of the divine' in the form of a trace of his presence, an imprint of his foot, belong to that other category, the aniconic (Gaifman 2017)? It cannot be called a relic, as this is not a foot, merely the alleged imprint of a foot; yet for the faithful it appears to be all at the same time, without the finer distinctions between concavities and convexities, or between presence and absence. What matters, really, is the god's grace, and the cultural heritage of narratives that ascertain that he once moved around in this world, and that his feet touched this spot. He may no longer be seen in his full form, but this is the place where one comes closest to his visible and tangible presence.

4. The Ritual Setting

As a fourth focal point, we trace the importance of **the ritual setting**. In an object-centered issue like this, some authors pay more attention to the ritual setting than others. With the jointly written contribution by Xiaohe Ma and Chuan Wang, we enter the domain of ritual manuals. Indeed, in some cultural situations rituals have to be performed 'by the book' and are highly stylized events. In ritual theories, especially those referring to events requiring adherence to time-tested traditional rules, stylization (or its concomitants, formalism, traditionalism, invariance and rule-governance) may be considered one of the crucial aspects of ritual performance (Bell 1992, 1997). Ritual manuals may have been newly constructed yet given the sheen of a long pedigree, but they also may have grown through long practice. Texts may become ritualized just as rituals may become textualized (Bell 1988). Such manuals may have been written down by one authoritative person, but in other cases an anonymous author may have merely compiled what had long been practiced and had been transmitted orally until the moment of compilation. Formalization may both produce and maintain tradition, and its efficacy may be partly due to the fact that a formalized ritual becomes a form of power and control. Another dimension of constructed tradition is that it may delineate group identity. This latter aspect becomes especially pungent in the case of Chinese Manichaeism, which in later Chinese history was often considered a potentially troublesome sect. One of its strategies was a continuous assimilation of Buddhist and Taoist terminology; it survived, in its later forms, as Religion of Light. The possession of a written collection of manuals for congregational worship may well have been a factor in both its precarious delineation and its vitality.

Although most religious scholars may be aware of Manichaeism (also spelled Manicheism) as a Gnostic movement that once stretched from the Atlantic to the Chinese Sea but has long been completely extinct, it may come as a pleasant surprise to hear that recent finds indicate that some material traces testify to its long survival in Buddhist or Taoist 'disguise' even today. This highly contested topic, however, is not what the two authors are concerned with; rather, they attempt to understand a collection of ritual manuals from Chinese Manichaeism in the perspective of a pictorial tradition in the form of a painting, and vice versa. The upper part of this painting, known as 'Diagram of the Universe', is generally said to portray 'Mani, the Buddha of Light'. It portrays Mani, the founder of Manichaeism who lived in the third century, as a Buddha. Not only was Manichaeism deeply sinicized on its entry in China, adapting to the Chinese cultural context, its basic tenets included a claim to universality, as the completion and fulfillment of all preceding religions. That its founder Mani was portrayed as a Buddha is not exceptional at all, considering both Manichaeism's claim to universality and its uneasy status as a sect. Ma and Wang, however, were puzzled about the lower part of the painting. In this article, they try to 'read' this lower part (of a half-devotional, half-didactic painting dated late 14th/early 15th century) by using the ritual manuals (of which the oldest parts may go back to the 9th to 11th century, but as a compilation may more or less be dated about the same period as the painting) as a clue or chiffre. Using the method of juxtaposition, by combining a written collection of rituals as a key to the lower half of a painted scroll, they hope to come to a deeper understanding of both objects.

Mahayana Buddhism in China had developed an extensive congregational cult, consisting of ritual activities such as worship (invocation of Buddhas, *bodhisattvas*, and even sacred scriptures), confession, and repentance, and chanting by the priests as well as the audience. For various reasons, Manichaean sects were, on and off, considered as potentially troublesome minorities, and this may partly explain why Manichaeism began to be practiced under 'the cloak of Buddhism', as Ma and Wang call it. The ritual compilation *Mani Buddha of Light* shows many parallel elements with Mahayana Buddhism, but the 'great ones' being invoked in rituals are the five Manichaean prophets (Narayaṇa, Zoroaster, Buddha Sakyamuni (the historical Buddha), Buddha Jesus and Buddha Mani). When the elaborate *Diagram of the Universe* is deployed as a kind of illustration of the rituals, or conversely but simultaneously, when the ritual manual is deployed as an illustration of the cosmology displayed in the scroll painting, an extremely rich and intricate image of Chinese Manichaeism emerges. Terms such as 'realm of Light', 'new paradise' and 'new Light world' not only indicate the salvationist and soteriological character of Chinese Manichaeism, but also present a fascinating parade of beings (humans, divine beings, monsters, animals) populating the various realms (or rings of existence) surrounding—indeed—mythical Mount Meru at the center of the cosmos.

Whereas the Manichaean pantheon and paradises of Light are overwhelming in their luminosity, there is a world of Darkness there as well. Manichaean views and practices in general may be known to most scholars of religion mainly through the works of anti-Manichaean polemicists, where Manichaeism tends to be presented as an arch-heresy. In a great leap through time and geography we now find ourselves, with Frank Bosman's article on the *Creed of Assassins* in the digital world of online games and encounter another cosmic dualism, another paradise, and another esoteric worldview: the battle for the Apples of Eden, between Templars and Assassins. Although the historical realities of these two name-giving associations do not entirely translate to the online identities, the names give a quasi-historic, quasi-mythic character to the game. The overall setting is the ongoing battle between two rival factions: the Assassin Brotherhood (modeled on the historical Nizar Isma'illis known from the Third Crusade) and the Templar Order (inspired by the historical order of the Knights Templar who had started as protectors of pilgrims in occupied Jerusalem). They compete over the possession of mythical artifacts, the Apples of Eden: power objects par excellence.

That the universal binaries—life and death; belonging and exclusion; state control and individual emancipation—are marked by in-game rituals may be expected. Initiation, the purpose of which is to accompany, produce, and announce a vital change of position, in this case of initiation into a fraternity, is usually classified as a rite of passage. The ritual of assassination—the victims belong to the competing faction—may be likewise characterized as a rite of passage: violence, human sacrifice, death. Political assassination is thus elevated and ritualized as one group's rite of belonging and identity for the good of the world ('We work in the dark, to serve the light. We are Assassins'). In the perspective of current extremisms, human sacrifice, in this series of games, is highly problematic, and Bosman admits that it may become palatable and justifiable only when ritualized, and when nothing less than World Order is at stake. Although 'it is merely a game', this latter aspect confronts us with another side of ritual and ritualistic objects. The ritual activity of sacrifice—from the perspectives of victims and perpetrators alike—has been studied by many academic disciplines, and the rich density of its meanings continues to invite theoretical reflections. The translation of online and in-game violence back into today's daily life-world, and vice versa, poses compelling questions about ritual refraction (Houseman 2011).

Violence, committed wittingly or unwittingly, is one of the subtopics in the co-authored article on stories told in the Alor-Pantar archipelago, Southeast Indonesia, by Francesco Cacciafoco and Francesco Cavallaro. The violence committed in various versions of the founding myth they study may be considered a sacrifice, it may be considered communion through food, but in its bare bones the story is about an innocent child. This child had lost its way and happened to trespass, i.e., it unintentionally passed into the supernatural world where some of the deities used to rest and meet with the Abui people. The child was taken hostage, dismembered, cooked, and served as food. Those who had been invited to the gruesome feast from the outside world only later discovered that the food that had been offered to them on a table was actually the dismembered body and head of the missing child. On request, the horrified dinner guests from the village were allowed to take the child's head with them.

The main story's composite configurations reflect a ritual setting in more ways than one. First, there is the ritual-like act of storytelling itself. Storytelling is not just a pastime, it is a ritual recreation of primeval times, and only the 'owner' of a story knows the story in its entirety. Gaps and inconsistencies should not be seen as flaws or errors; rather, they are the prerogative of the 'owner' of the story who leaves out certain parts or consciously makes leaps and bounds through the story. The rightful 'owner' of the story may even act as a trickster and put his audience on the wrong foot, intentionally, playing with his audience's misplaced rationality. Second, there is the ritual meal. The horrific dinner referred to above may reflect times when the Abui people were still cannibalistic head-hunters, and the head trophies—the skulls of people killed in war—were often placed and kept on altars in sacred places and fed with cooked rice. Remember that the child's head was ceremonially placed at the central table—as if on an altar—amidst the other cooked human meat! The altars with ritual stones surviving today may be directly linked with this past. Third, when contexts change or stories get juxtaposed with other narratives, or the same legend is being retold with shifting interpretations and shifting loyalties, the ritual-like activity of storytelling becomes a 'discourse': interlocking story motifs testify to intercultural contact, such as with the Portuguese and Dutch colonizers from the sixteenth century onwards. The authors not only relate an alternative (still unpublished) version of the same myth, they also attempt to make sense of the changing positions of the main deities, Lamoling and Latahala, in the light of Christian missiology and fragments of Platonic thinking and classical theology. Naturally, this results in clashes and paradoxes (cf. Ingold 2003). But by indicating the stratified character of the myth in its variations, the authors attempt a 'stratigraphy'. One of the outcomes is that one god, who used to be a companion of the people, eats with them, dances with them, and shares their everyday life events, begins to be gradually portrayed as demonic, constantly changing in form, unreliable—the epitome of the charms of animism (cf. Sprenger 2015) and the dangers of polytheism—whereas the other god is gradually elevated to a monotheistic rank where he is considered 'the only and true god'.

It is fascinating to notice how the authors, with their sociolinguistic backgrounds, are increasingly drawn into the narrative by their attempt to analyze and understand place names. One of the methods for tracing 'mythscapes' is the exploration of local landscapes in terms of place names: their semantic properties may define and delimit landscape categories, just as their features (plants, crops, but also vernacular names of typical landmarks in the topography) are situated by narration. Toponyms may testify to the traditional use of a place and may shed light on landscape as a religious category.

A toponym, explained either in a scholarly way or through local folk etymology, may also be a key to the ritual position of a particular location. Main places in this respect are Lamoling Beaka and Karilik, both 'gates' and 'portals' to the world of supernatural entities. Myths, like rituals, can be analyzed as 'situated practices' (Overing 2004, p. 71). Myth actually shapes the world and its landscapes. In a way, this represents the fourth aspect of the ritual setting in this article: they used to be indigenous cult places, now abandoned, but still honored as the sacred sites where the events reported in their founding myth had once taken place.

5. Conclusions

In a fascinatingly diverse way, people come to embody 'their' culture, a complex set of ideas, values, and practices. Whether they are religiously inclined or not, at cross-national, trans-national and inter-national levels, they are inescapably part of a world in which there may be religious dimensions to collective aspirations, such as for peace and justice, but also to tensions, violence, and conflicts. History shows that faith traditions may splinter into small groups. They may also merge, fuse, mix, co-exist, incorporate, compete, transcend, or fade away. In such processes, ritual calendars mark significant past events. What exactly is historic past, and what is mythic past, may easily get blurred, but particular moments, sites, and objects take on a particular importance in the group's hierarchy of time and place. Although all sacred occasions and sites are centers, some are believed to bring believers closer to the divine than others (Hassner 2009, pp. 29–30). The same may be true of sacred objects: 'ownership' of sacred objects has often given rise to violent conflicts. The individual rewards attributed to visiting such a site or possessing such an object vary from situation to situation, from culture to culture, and from religion to religion.

Instead of highlighting conflicts over such objects, in the sense of military, theological, political, or touristic clashes, the objects presented in this volume illumine subtler processes. Most of them are presented as modes of experiencing divinity, as making divinity (or the divinity of royal rule) sense-able. By studying them in their ritual setting, 'loops' are made between collective cultural practices and individual sensing (Howes and Classen 2014). An object may shine in all its exuberant materiality; it may come to life only through the ritual setting and its performative aspects; or it may exist merely for a moment, and then be intentionally eaten or otherwise destroyed. The use of religious objects involves not only the collective and individual's experience but also all those people who are involved in their production, ritualization, and maintenance. This broader context illustrates how religious acts and actors co-define material objects to suit changing times and audiences.

This brings us to the end of this introduction. In the final pages of this thematic issue of the journal *Religions*, on 'Religion, Ritual and Ritualistic Objects', the biodata of all authors are briefly introduced as well.

For me, acting as convener and academic editor, it has been a pleasure to work with them.

6. Contents (in Alphabetic Order)

- McDonald, J. Andrew. 2018. Influences of Egyptian Lotus Symbolism and Ritualistic Practices on Sacral Tree Worship in the Fertile Crescent from 1500 BCE to 200 CE. *Religions* 9: 256.
- Nicklisch, Andrea. 2018. Continuity and Discontinuity in 17th- and 18th-Century Ecclesiastical Silverworks from the Southern Andes. *Religions* 9: 262.
- Notermans, Catrien. 2019. Prayers of Cow Dung: Women Sculpturing Fertile Environments in Rural Rajasthan (India). *Religions* 10: 71.
- Nugteren, Albertina. 2018. Bare Feet and Sacred Ground: "Viṣṇu Was Here". *Religions* 9: 224.

7. List of Contributing Authors

Walter **van Beek** is professor em. in the Anthropology of Religion at Tilburg University, and senior researcher at the African Studies Center, Leiden University, both in The Netherlands. As a cultural anthropologist he has a long field experience among the Dogon of Mali and the Kapsiki/Higi of Cameroon and Nigeria. He has published extensively on indigenous religious aspects of both groups, such as in 2017, *Rites et religions dans le Bassin du Lac Tchad*, edited with Emilie Guitard (Karthala/ASCL); in 2016, *The Transmission of Kapsiki-Higi Folktales over Two Generations: Tales that Come, Tales that Go* (Palgrave-MacMillan); and in 2015, *The Forge and the Funeral. The Smith in Kapsiki/Higi Culture* (Michigan State University Press). At present he is engaged in a project of cultural heritage preservation in Mali, and a wide-ranging study of African masking rituals.

Frank **Bosman** is a senior researcher at Tilburg Cobbenhagen Center, Tilburg University, The Netherlands. He has published extensively on religion and popular culture, with a special focus on religion and video games. He plays a noticable role in the public discussions in The Netherlands on religion and society through multiple on- and offline media outlets. Game-related publications are: in 2018, Death Narratives: A Typology of Narratological Embeddings of Player's Death in Digital Games, *Gamenvironments* 9: 12–52; in 2017, The incarnated gamer. The theophoric quality of games, gaming, and gamers. In *Boundaries of the self and reality online. Implications of digitally constructed realities.* Edited by Jayne Gackenbach and Johnathan Brown (Londen: Elsevier, pp. 187–204), and soon to be published, his book *Gaming and the divine. A new systematic theology of video games* (London: Routledge).

Francesco **Cacciafoco** has a PhD (2011) in Historical Linguistics from the University of Pisa, Italy. He is a linguist and philologist with a focus on etymology and toponymy. He also works on anthropological linguistics and cultural anthropology applied to the documentation of undocumented and/or endangered languages and to the reconstruction of indigenous myths and legends. He joined Nanyang Technological University (NTU), Singapore, in 2013 where he is currently a lecturer in linguistics. Some of his selected publications are: in 2017, together with Francesco Cavallaro, The Legend of Lamòling: Unwritten Memories and Diachronic Toponymy through the Lens of an Abui Myth. *Lingua: An International Review of General Linguistics* 193: 51–61; and with the same co-author and František Kratochvíl, in 2015: Diachronic Toponomastics and Language Reconstruction in South-East Asia According to an Experimental Convergent Methodology: Abui as a Case-Study. *Review of Historical Geography and Toponomastics* 10: 29–47.

Francesco **Cavallaro** is an Associate Professor in Linguistics and Multilingual Studies and the Head of the Centre for Modern Languages, Nanyang Technological University, Singapore. His research interests are in sociolinguistics and the social aspects of bilingualism, especially of minority groups in multilingual contexts. His main research focus is the survival of minority languages and the factors that influence both language maintenance and shift. He has published on language maintenance and shift, the demographics of the Italian community in Australia, language attitudes in Singapore and on minority groups in South East Asia. In addition to the articles mentioned above, in co-authorship with Francesco Cacciafoco, he is the author of the book, published in 2010, *Transgenerational language shift: From Sicilian and Italian to Australian English* (La Trobe University, Melbourne).

Laurie **Faro** has been educated in the field of law and culture studies. Already as a young attorney she developed a strong interest in empowering the victim in the legal process. This focus remained when she switched to scientific research in the field of health law, care and patients' rights.

remained when she switched to scientific research in the field of health law, care and patients' rights. In 1990 she completed a PhD project on this subject, and in 2015 a second PhD on the experiences of people burdened with traumatic experiences in the past and the impact of their ritual commemoration practices. At present she is involved in the research project 'Children handling death: reality versus popular culture.' Related publications are, in 2015, *Postponed monuments in the Netherlands: Manifestation, context, and meaning* (PhD thesis Tilburg University); and in 2014, 'The Digital Monument to the Jewish Community in The Netherlands: A meaningful, ritual place for commemoration'. *New Review of Hypermedia and Multimedia* 20: 1–20.

Deborah **de Koning** graduated in the field of religious studies and is currently working as a PhD-candidate at Tilburg University in The Netherlands. She received a grant from the Netherlands Organisation for Scientific Research to conduct her PhD-research on the increased popularity of the mythological king Ravana among Sinhalese Buddhists in post-war Sri Lanka. Her main fields of academic interest are Buddhism and Hinduism in South Asia and Hinduism in diaspora, with a particular focus on contemporary developments and identity-issues. A related publication, in 2017, is 'Ravana: Once a demon, always a demon? Considering Ravana from a different perspective?', *Diggit Magazine* 30 March 2017.

Xiaohe **Ma**, a native of Shanghai, China, graduated from Fudan University (1982) and Simmons College, Boston (1997). He worked at *Yazhou Zhoukan* (*Asian Weekly*, Chinese version), Hong Kong (1993–1996) and East Asian Library, UCLA, Los Angeles, U.S.A. (1996–1999) before he came to Harvard Yenching Library, Harvard University, where he is currently librarian for the Chinese Collection. He is also a guest researcher of Fudan University and guest professor of Jinan University. Research interests include the history of Central Asia, the history of Sino-foreign relations, Manichaeism, etc. He is well-known for his studies on Manichaeism and research on the Xiapu documents, both in Chinese and English. A related publication in open access is 'On the Date of the Ritual Manual for the Celebration of the Birthday of the Ancestor of Promoting Well-Being from Xiapu', in *Open Theology* 1 (2015): 455–77.

Andrew **McDonald** is a plant systematist (evolution-based classification), floristic explorer of Southeast Asia and the Neotropics, conservation biologist and archaeo-ethnobotanist. He dedicates a large portion of his research efforts to understanding the role of plants in defining religious practices and values of civilized cultures. After having held research positions at the University of Texas-Austin, Harvard University and various federal botanical institutions in Mexico, Cambodia and Indonesia, he is presently a professor in botany at the University of Texas-Rio Grande Valley. Some related publications are: in 2016, Deciphering the Symbols and Symbolic Meaning of the Maya World Tree. *Ancient Mesoamerica* 27: 1–27; in 2012, together with J. Andrew and B. Stross. Water Lily and Cosmic Serpent: Equivalent channels of the Maya spirit realm. *Journal of Ethnobiology* 32: 73–106; and in 2002, Botanical determination of the Middle Eastern tree of life. *Economic Botany* 56: 113–29.

Andrea **Nicklisch** is a curator (department of ethnology) at the Roemer-und-Pelizaeus Museum in Hildesheim, Germany. She is one of the curators of the museum's considerable collection of pre-Columbian, ancient-Peruvian and early-colonial objects from Meso-America. For her PhD she studied ecclesiastical silverworks as objects illustrating the transfer of meaning and interpretation in early-colonial contact zones. One of the related publications is: 'The Seeming and the Real: Problems in the Interpretation of Images on Seventeenth-Century Silverworks from Bolivia'. In: *Image, Object, Performance: Mediality and Communication in Early Modern Contact Zones of Latin America and Asia.* Edited by Astrid Windus and Eberhard Crailsheim (Münster 2013, pp. 155–71).

Catrien **Notermans** is an anthropologist and associate professor at the Department of Cultural Anthropology and Development Studies at Radboud University, Nijmegen, The Netherlands. She did long-term ethnographic research in West Africa, Europe and India on the topics of lived religion, material culture, gender, kinship and migration. She co-authored two books on pilgrimage: *Moved by Mary: The Power of Pilgrimage in the Modern World* (2009) and *Gender, Nation and Religion in European Pilgrimage* (2012). Publications in the field of gender and material religion focus on ex-votos, pilgrimage souvenirs and religious remittances. Her most recent research is on people's spiritual relationships with nature, which led to (international journal) publications on sacred groves in South India and people's bathing rituals in the Ganges in North India.

Albertina **Nugteren** has an academic background in South Asian languages and cultures. She works as a Religion-and-Ritual specialist at Tilburg University, The Netherlands. Current research topics include: (1) the nexus Nature-Culture-Religion (recent example: 'Sacred Trees, Groves and Forests' in *Oxford Bibliographies in Hinduism*, 2018); (2) funerary rituals, particularly environmental aspects (recent examples: 'Consolation and the 'poetics' of the soil in natural burial sites', 2019, and 'Wood, Water and Waste: Material Aspects of Mortuary Practices in South Asia', 2017); (3) Critical discourses on the 'greening of religion' (recent example: 'A Darker Shade of Green? An Inquiry into Growing Preferences for Natural Burial', 2015); (4) Object-centered studies of ritual and material religion (recent example: guest editorship of this Special Issue on 'Religion, Ritual and Ritualistic Objects').

Chuan **Wang** is a native of Taiwan. She graduated from Chinese Culture University, Taipei, Taiwan. She worked part-time at Chinese Culture University before being transferred to the Department of Applied Chinese at Ming Chuan University, Taiwan, where she is currently a professor. She was also a visiting scholar at Harvard University (2010) and Peking University (2018). Her research interests are: Dunhuang Studies, Buddhist Confession Rituals, Manichaeism, etc. Main publications: *Studies in Ritual Texts of Dunhuang Manuscripts* (Dharma Drum Culture Press, Taipei, 1998); *Studies in Unearthed Texts of Buddhist Confession Rituals between Tang and Song Dynasties* (Wenjin Press, Taipei, 2008) and many articles concerning Buddhist history and culture.

Conflicts of Interest: The author declares no conflict of interest.

References

Adichie, Chimamanda Ngozi. 2009. *The Danger of a Single Story*. TEDGlobal. Available online: https://www.ted.com/talks/chimamanda_adichie_the_danger_of_a_single_story?/language=en (accessed on 20 February 2019).

Bell, Catherine. 1988. Ritualization of Texts and Textualization of Ritual in the Codification of Taoist Liturgy. *History of Religions* 27: 366–92. [CrossRef]

Bell, Catherine. 1992. *Ritual Theory, Ritual Practice*. New York and Oxford: Oxford University Press.

Bell, Catherine. 1997. *Ritual: Perspectives and Dimensions*. New York and Oxford: Oxford University Press.

Buggeln, Gretchen, and Barbara Franco. 2018. Introduction. In *Interpreting Religion at Museums and Historic Sites*. Edited by Gretchen Buggeln and Barbara Franco. Lanham: Rowman & Littlefield, pp. xi–xiv.

Collins, Randall. 2004. *Interaction Ritual Chains*. Princeton: Princeton University Press.

Coomaraswamy, Ananda K. 1935. Review of Walter Ernst Andrae, Die ionische Säule, Bauform oder Symbol? *Art Bulletin* 17: 103–7.

Eck, Diana L. 2012. *India: A Sacred Geography*. New York: Harmony Press.

Fleming, Benjamin J., and Richard D. Mann. 2014. Introduction: Material Culture and Religious Studies. In *Material Culture and Asian Religions: Text, Image, Object*. Edited by Benjamin J. Fleming and Richard D. Mann. New York and London: Routledge, pp. 1–17.

Gaifman, Milette. 2017. Aniconism: Definitions, Examples and Comparative Perspectives. Introduction to Thematic Issue on Exploring Aniconism. *Religion* 47: 335–52. [CrossRef]

Grimes, Ronald L. 1982. Defining Nascent Ritual. *Journal of the American Academy of Religion* 50: 539–55. [CrossRef]

Grimes, Ronald L. 2011. Ritual. *Material Religion. Journal of Objects, Art and Belief* 7: 76–83. [CrossRef]

Hassner, Ron E. 2009. *War on Sacred Grounds*. Ithaca and London: Cornell University Press.

Hodder, Ian, ed. 1987. *The Archeology of Contextual Meanings*. Cambridge: Cambridge University Press.

Houseman, Michael. 2011. Refracting Ritual: An Upside-Down Perspective on Ritual, Media, and Conflict. In *Ritual. Media and Conflict*. Edited by Ronald L. Grimes, Ute Hüsken, Udo Simon and Eric Venbrux. Oxford and New York: Oxford University Press, pp. 255–84.

Howes, David, and Constance Classen. 2014. *Ways of Sensing: Understanding the Senses in Society*. London and New York: Routledge.

Ingold, Tim. 2003. Three in One: How an ecological approach can obviate the distinctions between body, mind and culture. In *Imagining Nature: Practices of Cosmology and Identity*. Edited by Nils Ole Bubandt, Kalevi Kull and Andreas Roepstorff. Aarhus: Aarhus University Press, pp. 40–55.

Keane, Webb. 2008. On the materiality of religion. *Material Religion, Journal of Objects, Art and Belief* 4: 230–31. [CrossRef]

Morgan, David. 2008. The materiality of cultural construction. *Material Religion, Journal of Objects, Art and Belief* 4: 228–29. [CrossRef]

Morgan, David. 2011. Thing. *Material Religion, Journal of Objects, Art and Belief* 7: 140–46. [CrossRef]

Overing, Joana. 2004. The Grotesque Landscape of Mythic "Before Time", The Folly of Sociality in "Today Time": An Egalitarian Aesthetics of Human Existence. In *Kultur, Raum, Landschaft: zur Bedeutung des Raumes in Zeiten der Globalität*. Edited by Ernst Halbmayer and Elke Mader. Frankfurt am Main: Brandes & Aspel, pp. 69–90.

Pratt, Mary Louise. 1991. Arts of the Contact Zone. *Profession/Modern Language Association* 91: 33–40.

Sprenger, Guido. 2015. Animism. In *Religion in Southeast Asia: An Encyclopedia of Faiths and Cultures*. Edited by Jesudas M. Athyal. Santa Barbara: ABC-CLIO, pp. 7–10.

Zerubavel, Eviatar. 2003. *Time Maps: Collective Memory and the Social Shape of the Past*. Chicago and London: University of Chicago Press.

religions

MDPI

Article

Matter in Motion: A Dogon *Kanaga* Mask

Walter E. A. van Beek

Department of Cultural Studies, Faculty of Humanities, Tilburg University, Warandelaan 1, 5037 AB Tilburg, The Netherlands; W.E.A.vanBeek@uvt.nl

Received: 6 August 2018; Accepted: 29 August 2018; Published: 6 September 2018

Abstract: Dogon masks have been famous for a long time—and none more so than the *kanaga* mask, the so-called croix de Lorraine. A host of interpretations of this particular mask circulate in the literature, ranging from moderately exotic to extremely exotic. This contribution will focus on one particular mask situated within the whole mask troupe, and it will do so in the ritual setting to which it belongs: a second funeral, long after the burial. A description of this ritual shows how the mask troupe forms the constantly moving focus in a captivating ritual serving as second funeral. Thus, the mask rites bridge major divides in Dogon culture, between male and female, between man and nature, and between this world and the supernatural one. They are able to do so because they themselves are in constant motion, between bush and village and between sky and earth. Masks are matter in motion and symbols in context. Within imagistic religions such as the Dogon one, these integrative functions form a major focus of Dogon masks rituals—and hence, to some extent, of African mask rituals in general. In the Dogon case, the ritual creates a virtual reality through a highly embodied performance by the participants themselves. Then, the final question can be broached, that of interpretation. What, in the end, do these masquerades signify? And our *kanaga* mask, what does it stand for?

Keywords: mask; Dogon; funeral; performance; symbol; embodiment

1. The Glory of Masks

The 16 May 1989 is full of high expectations in the village and feverish activity in Amani, for this is the day when the masks perform not just for the village but for the 'strangers' as well, meaning visitors from neighbouring villages.[1] At the various dancing places throughout the village, groups of masks, each from its own ward, perform for their own appreciative neighbours and family members. Domo Pujugo, one of the youngsters of Amani, carefully prepared his *kanaga* mask long before the start of the dances a week ago, and he is proud now to show off with all the other dancers wearing this particular mask, and exerts himself as the antelope that this particular mask represents (see Figure 1, below). After this local performance the spectators move with masks and drummers to the houses where people have died in the previous years, because after all is danced and done, the masks are to honour the departed and provide their means to become ancestors. Everywhere the dancers are eagerly welcomed and, after the dance, hosted with large quantities of millet beer.

1 The data for this article come from personal fieldwork of the author in the Dogon area, starting in 1979 and lasting till 2016, a total of two years of field experience. The particular ritual described happened in 1989, and the author was involved in the proceedings as one of the visitors from the neighbouring village of Tireli. As the mother of his host was born in Amani, his adopted family had a front seat in this particular *dama*.

Figure 1. The mask of Domo Pujugo.

In the meantime, the visitors from the other villages arrive, first at the compounds of their friends or distant relatives, and are also received with ample beer. Their presence in the village and their assistance at the upcoming afternoon, which forms a crucial part of the whole mask festival, is absolutely essential; they have to 'shield' the masks when they emerge from the plains. In particular, the ones whose mothers came from Amani are in front, because as 'sisters' sons' of the village, they are in the perfect relationship to give ritual assistance at the high times of *dama*—the word for the mask festival in fact means 'taboo'.

The remainder of the morning is spent in what is, for the boys, one of the highpoints, a series of performances that together form a sort of dancing contest. The boys form groups, usually per ward, and go on to the other village squares for the remainder of the morning. There, they dance, as they have done in the past week; and when the drums grow silent at noon, the various crowds disperse, having come to some consensus as to who is the best dancer of the village. As this is Dogon, there is no prize and no proclamation, just the recognition of being the most agile dancer—which will undoubtedly help the winner later with the many admiring girls.

This particular day in the long sequence of the *dama* festival is called *manugo sugo*, 'descent[2] from the plains', and is one of the absolute highlights of the whole month of rituals. In the early afternoon, the old men gather on the square, discuss the proceedings of the day, and move down to the village rim, taking the drums with them. They seem nervous now, wary of any infractions on the liturgy,

2 The floor of the scree, where the dance is held, is the lowest point in the landscape.

when they mark out the dancing ground at the foot of the scree. The *yasigine*, women who accompany the masks, come down also—aided by some co-wives who help them carry pots of beer—and install their brew at the rim of the grounds, sporting their long calabash spoons that define them as 'sisters of the masks'. They form the exception to the rule: masks are for men, and are taboo for women; these particular women, however, have been initiated into the masks, either by choice (and investment) or by birth.

Around three in the afternoon, the initiates come down, emerging from all over the village. Yelling, the masks shout '*hé hé hé*', and run down the slope as 'naked masks' without any head covering. As such, they are all dressed more or less the same, as without headpieces, it is difficult to distinguish between types of masks. Without giving bystanders a glance, they pass the people at the grounds and run full speed into the dunes, halting just over the first one. Three elders, one with a drum, follow them into the bush, as they have to head the procession later on. The other men set out the perimeter of the dancing ground by walking in a single file along the rim, forcing the spectators aside. By now, quite a crowd has assembled. Women keep their distance and just watch from the houses near the grounds, but from this elevated position, they have a splendid view of the proceedings. The men, who are initiated and do not have anything to fear from the masks anyway, come closer and circle the grounds, while young boys climb the trees lining the spot.

The sun is lower at 16:30, when the sound of drumming comes from the dunes. The elders at the rim make a last nervous round to make sure the dancing ground is spotless and free of people (i.e., of young boys) and then join the crowd, who all look toward the dunes. From afar, a long, dark line of masks slowly nears the village, following an S-shaped route that gradually brings them to the dancing ground. At some distance, they gather the headpieces they had left at the start of the dunes and don them. Those with plaited tops place them at the back of their heads and remain 'naked' for a while longer, meaning they show their faces. For those with heavy wooden headpieces, like the *kanaga*, this is not an option and they don them completely. The 'foreigners' now join them, men from Yaye in the east and those from Tireli on the western side, and walk along with them, while praising the masks in the ritual mask language, *sigi so*, see below Figure 2, for the western side.

Figure 2. Men from Tireli accompanying the *kanaga* section of the Amani masks, 1989. Note the 'naked' masks in front.

The rationale for this arrangement is indeed protection: the two neighbouring villages shield the masks from the envious glares of villages farther away and less friendly; well, the shielding, evidently, is ritual.

The three elders in front with the drums show the whole column the way and move aside when they reach the main dancing ground at the foot of the cliff, where all dancers adjust their headpieces. There is tension in the air, for this is the time for the large dance, the time for a great performance with everybody watching. It is still a time of taboo (*dama*); indeed, it is the peak of the collective taboo, and the elders in charge stay on high alert.

The dancing ground has been marked off near a cone-shaped altar, with the mask pole, the *dani*, erected next to it. This is the ritual centre, and the masks will dance toward it with the drummers positioned next to it. The elders keep patrolling the grounds, chasing away anyone who does not belong here, such as women or small boys; but no woman dares to come near anyway, for they are genuinely frightened now—just some daring young boys who want to show off, dash over the grounds, barely keeping out of reach of the sticks of the elders.

This is the first time that all of the masks show up in one dance. As usual, the *ɛmna tiû* (tree masks) lead the way, and with eight of them, it is a small walking thicket of trees—a dancing forest, in fact. The five-metre-high headpieces are difficult to manoeuvre, and any dancer who can pull this off is highly regarded indeed, so they all sway their contraption up and down, in front and behind, and swing the 'trees' around, with the audience at a respectful and wise distance. Sitting on a house near the grounds, the *ɛmna tingetange* tie on their stilts and come in next. They always have to perform early in the programme, as fatigue would make their dance dangerous. They represent water birds, and their dance on stilts shows this: stepping daintily along the crowd, (see Figure 3, below) even standing on one leg and tapping the two stilts together, a feat highly appreciated by the onlookers. If one falters, all men rush to the rescue to catch the dancer; it sometimes happens, but rarely.

The large group of *kanaga* masks then makes its appearance, and only now does one see how popular this mask is. There are more than twenty of them. They have already made quite an impression in earlier appearances, but now they dominate the general dance: dancing, prancing, and sweeping their 'horns' through the dust. The old men are everywhere, beating the earth with their sticks while shouting at full force in *sigi so*: 'Dance, dance well, be strong. If a woman shows up, beat her!' This mask, topped with a *Croix de Lorraine*, features on all the tourist brochures and formerly on Mali's banknotes, and it has become the icon of Dogon masquerades. It is popular among the Dogon youth—who are free to choose their own main mask—as it is quite a showy one, while still being rather easy to dance in, compared with the first two at least. The *kanaga* line up and, following their specific drum rhythm, cavort on the stage of the *tei*, shaking their torsos, jumping and twirling. After some contortions, they bend over and swing the horns of their headpieces over the ground, stirring up dust, see Figure 4, below. While the drums go full throttle, the old men keep shouting in *sigi so* that they have to dance well. They perform in small lines of about four dancers, meaning that each of them has enough stage time to wipe the dust off the dancing floor and show his prowess at this dance; they can prove themselves real *sagatara*, strong young men, which is why this mask is so popular.

Then it is time for the other types of masks, in no particular order. Three young dancers in *goû* (hares) masks appear, and the drums switch to a slower beat to accompany this more youthful performance. One of the elders from the audience joins in with a spear and acts as the hunter, spotting the three hares and dancing after them. The three masks look around, see the hunter, and flee to the rim of the *tei*, continuously watching for other dangers as well. Thus, an amusing hunting scene is played out, and the agile hares just manage to escape the wily hunter. Young initiates are expected to dance a hare, an amusing piece of theatre that is appreciated by the admiring crowd. The hunter may well be represented by a mask also, *ɛmna dananu*, a fierce-looking human, a real man of the bush—but this time, no such mask appears and one elder happily joins in this play of the masks.

The hares have hardly left before a gazelle mask, *ɛmna wiru*, bursts onto the scene at great speed, his long horns pointing backwards, running fast to the rapid beat of the drums. His is not a play of hide and seek, but a demonstration of speed and agility, fleet-footed and fast. He is usually alone; this is a mask that demands a good runner to dance with it. Other masks follow, depending on the composition of this ward's troupe—in this case, it is an *ɛmna jojongunu*, a healer's mask. Slowly walking with his headpiece crowned with four human figures, the mask does not really dance but slowly perambulates among the audience. From time to time, he halts, kneels down, takes some medicine stuff from his pouch, and hands it to an onlooker, who is then expected to thank him and give some money. This is a doctor making his rounds, a role for an older dancer in fact, less forceful and vigorous, but demanding good judgement and some theatrical skills.

Some masks embody the gentle jokes of the Dogon to pull on their former masters, like the Fulbe and the white man, the *anjara*. The Fulbe man is pictured on a hobby horse and never manages to stay on top of it, continuously stumbling and falling, while his wife is always scooping up cattle dung; they are hardly the severe slave raiders they used to be in the nineteenth century. The white man's mask, *ɛmna anjara*, is also suited for an older man, in European trousers just strolling around with his huge red, bearded head and long flowing hair. His 'dance' resembles the one of the healer: he walks around, writes out notes, and then collects some coins—the colonial officer raking in taxes. Two recent versions are even more to the point. In one, the mask sports a wooden camera and bends over backwards to take a beautiful shot, shoving other masks aside to get a perfect angle for his photo: the tourist. The most pleasant variant, however, just sits on a stool, with two Dogon on the floor next to him, and brandishes a notebook while asking the most stupid questions imaginable: the anthropologist! In fact, the last *ɛmna anjara* I collected was made in my own likeness, (see Figure 5, below) and my host Dogolu smilingly acknowledged: 'That one is you!'

Figure 3. *Tingetange* performing.

Figure 4. *Kanaga* dancing, Tireli 2008.

Figure 5. This is, thus, more or less the author.

The other masks take their turn performing, coming on stage in small groups by genre: the bull, two gazelles, two hyenas, a monkey, the marabout, the healer, the *waru* antelopes, the *sadimbe*, mother of the masks, and one pupil mask, *bɛjɛ*—they are all there to be admired for their performance. As they perform in smaller groups, the other masks join the spectators and sit down on the stones that line the dancing place, so the masks dance for both the regular audience and their own colleagues.

The dance routines vary, up to a point. Three dance routines are performed by all masks; when they show up as one whole troupe, as they will do at the end of the dance and during the next day, they all perform this set of routines. Additionally, each mask has its own dance, its proper steps and drum rhythm, often mimicking the movement of the animals or people it represents: the bird picking the earth, the hyena jumping to look at its prey, the antelopes fleet footed. Some basic steps appear in all of them, as each dance is a variation of a general theme. The drums lead and follow the dances; they introduce the three general ones and then follow closely the movements of the individual masks, underscoring the specific steps and movements that mark the identity of the *ɛmna* in question.

The liminality of the performance becomes evident when small accidents happen. One of the trees breaks, a fairly common problem with these long contraptions of light, soft wood. Immediately, all the men in the audience start yelling and the elders swarm onto the dancing ground, running toward the mask in question and dancing around it, effectively shielding the damaged mask from the eyes of the audience—in particular, of course, from women. Surrounding the mask, they carefully lead it to the entrance of the dancing grounds and whisk it away to change into a new headpiece. It will be repaired later. When the *kanaga* wipe the soil, one of them may break off a 'horn', and they are treated the same way: masks have to be perfect. Carefully, the elders take away the broken parts, as no part of a mask may remain at the dancing place. As dancing is fierce and quite competitive during the peak of the *dama*, such mishaps are to be expected. Yet, when a whole mask stumbles, perhaps inevitable given the athletic prowess needed for a good performance, the reaction is one of mild amusement, and the dancer simply has to regain his feet on his own.

After the first round of dancing, the drums stop, and the masks crouch in a large circle around the mask altar, where Yedyè—the village speaker—addresses them, (see Figure 6) lauding their performance and exhorting them to keep up the good work: 'God bless you, keep up the good work. This is not a thing of ourselves; it is a thing of old, a thing found. You have danced well, this which we could not do. You are the force in the village that can dance.[3] May God bless you, give you many children.' At intervals during his long speech (with as many repetitions as it should have), the dancers stand up, wave their horsetail, and shout the mask cry, '*hé hé hé*.' The whole address is in *sigi so*, the mask language of the Dogon.

Figure 6. Yedyè, the ritual speaker, addressing the masks of Amani. The *dani* is on the left, the altar is in the centre behind the elder in black. The mask headpieces are shoved back.

3 Such an expression of dependence of the old on the young inside rituals is quite standard in Dogon communal rituals.

For about two hours, the masks dance constantly, in groups or individually. In the end, when dusk is gathering, they end the masquerade in a final show in which all of them participate. Now, the long line of masks performs as one, dancing one round; and finally, when nearing the entrance, each mask type runs into the village—the last ones, the hares, leaving the dancing ground empty in the falling dark. As a final farewell to this great day, the four *yasigine* form a group and slowly dance along the whole perimeter of the grounds, with their calabash spoons in one hand and with the other hand trailing their steps with their long *soû duro*, the fly whisks made of horse tails, the same many masks use. Thus, they symbolically erase their own tracks, as well as those of the masks—an act called *jaramu* (purification) by the Dogon—thus lifting the taboo from the dancing ground.

2. Apparitions from the Bush

A *dama* is a spectacle one never forgets, and 16 May 1989 is just one day out of a whole month of rituals. However, it is the most important one, this large-scale arrival of the masks at the scree-side. For what did we just witness, other than a captivating spectacle?

Religious studies, the craft that investigates some of mankind's deepest expressions of 'otherness', is based on observations such as we just have described, but observations that are always encompassed in interpretative frameworks (Grimes 2014; Bell 1997; Steward and Strathern 2014). To observe is to interpret, especially when it concerns 'things', such as these masks who are in fact strange objects. Coming from a western culture that is extremely 'thingy', and where each individual lives in an environment saturated with objects, we have a definite classification of 'things'. The bulk of our western objects are functional—or have been functional in the past, as a walk on one's attic might attest—and may carry remembrances or other associations, but are not highly symbolic in themselves. On the other hand, we do have symbols, but in our culture, these are a separate class of objects, which have changed their utility function into a purely symbolic one, such as the cross, a candle, or a flag. Evans-Pritchard once remarked about the Nuer of Sudan, that all their 'things' could bear a considerable symbolic load simply because there were so few of them, such as their spears (Evans-Pritchard 1956, p. 233); in this materially austere pastoral culture, each of the few objects in their possession formed the nexus of a relational and symbolic network, which obfuscated the distinction between a symbolic object and an everyday thing. When we are confronted with 'things in rituals', our first level of interpretation is that these are 'symbolic things', symbols, so doused with meaning beyond any functionality. With masks, that seems a foregone conclusion, for they are, indeed, special things, made for the occasion—even for one particular *dama*—and are used only in ritual, kept away from prying eyes beyond liminal times. So our first analytic question is to the meaning of the masks, expecting a symbolic signification of 'things in action'. Symbols are objects that do not refer to themselves but are 'thrown together'—the literary meaning of the word: form and meaning are not intrinsically connected (Grimes 2014, p. 344). Usually, they are polysemic and multivocal, signifying a host of meanings at the same time; in Ndembu culture Turner's example of the *mudyi* tree, with its white effusion, is paradigmatic (Steward and Strathern 2014, p. 54; Bell 1997, p. 40).

So for our interpretation, a preliminary question should be whether these masks are symbols. Are they? The inherent 'strangeness' of the masks presents a challenge for our analytic acumen, an offer we cannot refuse; these are obvious pathways of interpretation for western observers, and both lead to over-interpretation. Studies of individual masks routinely assume specific significations attributed by the 'West': masks are thought to represent ancestors, deities, and spirits, or more exotic, cosmos or creation. A different tack of western interpretation is that they are 'art', another category of objects without function in our culture; in essence, this definition frees the analyst from attributing any meaning at all, because 'art' exists for and in itself. These are stereotypical European interpretations, which do not fit very well with emic insights gleaned from the field. It is impossible to make a general case for African cultures, but at least in the Dogon example, the idea that masks refer to deities, ancestors, or creation is not correct (Van Beek 1991b). Also, though Dogon do express aesthetic appreciation quite easily, their language does not have a word that corresponds with the western notion of 'art'. Given these differences, what would be a more fitting interpretation of masks?

So let us see what these masks mean for the Dogon themselves. First of all, what we call masks and the Dogon call *imina* or *ɛmna*, are not just the things the boys wear on their heads, but the whole apparition, the dancer clothed in his costume, topped with the carved headpiece and with the paraphernalia in hand, such as the horsetails. The African equation runs as follows: mask = costume + headpiece + paraphernalia. It is this whole, undivided, and complete being that the Dogon call a mask—in fact, this is similar to all African masking groups—and we follow them in this. The costume, with its red and black fibres and the long blue trousers, defines the whole as a mask; and the headpiece stipulates what specific kind of mask is meant. This is by no means peculiar to the Dogon *ɛmna*, but holds for the great bulk of African masks. For the Dogon themselves masks, are, first and for all, masks, *ɛmna*, a class of beings in their own right.

These masks, therefore, are not so much symbols as apparitions, a presence instead of a representation; they signify themselves as a category: a mask is a mask is a mask. To some extent, they have an iconic side. For a large part, the masks portray animals from the bush, wild animals, very seldom domestic ones—such as antelopes, water birds, hares, monkeys, and gazelles, and sometimes also crocodiles, buffaloes, leopards, and hyenas. Another section concerns humans, because we see in the masks healers, Fulbe, hunters, shamans, and the odd European. There is no association with deities or ancestors, and only an indirect one with spirits from the bush. The latter is much stronger in masquerades in other parts of Africa, but is hidden in the Dogon *dama*. Portrayal, though, does not imply representations, the masks 'are' not animals, they rather portray the idea of the animal in question; if Africans want to portray an animal as such, they are perfectly capable of doing so in quite direct and recognizable ways.

If the performing masks mainly refer to themselves, any search for a more encompassing meaning has to be at a higher echelon, of the mask ritual as a whole. Ritual objects attain their meaning not from what they are, but what they do inside ritual. However, as Harvey Whitehouse's modes of religiosity theory indicates (Whitehouse 2004), this is a highly imagistic ritual inside a religion dominated by imagistic processes. Whitehouse's main distinction is between high frequency rituals with limited emotional investment but subject to elaborate systematic exegesis, on the one hand, the doctrinal religiosity, and on the other, an infrequent ritual with a large visual appeal that bears little explanation—the imagistic religiosity. For the latter, there is no authoritative exegesis, no authority to 'explain' things, and the main challenge is to participate—and participate correctly—instead of a deep understanding; this is exactly what is found for the participants in the Dogon masquerade, and most exegesis is spontaneous, on the spot. But whatever its association with death, for the young boys who are dancing, the *dama* is a feast, and feasts need no explanation.

Yet, the liturgy does give some pointers for an overall interpretation. The name of the day we witnessed is *manugo sugo*: descent from the plains. The core of the *dama*, the whole complex mask ritual, is in the arrivals in the village: from the four directions the masks enter the village, from each direction on a consecutive day, and the last the one we just saw, from the plains. On the previous days, they came from the mountainside and alongside the cliff from the north-eastern side. At the end of the *dama*, the masks leave again, toward the south-west. Even if it is organised by one village only, the ritual links a string of villages along the cliff. So the first interpretation is that the masks represent the bush coming into the village. African thought attributes specific powers to the bush, as well as the Dogon. From the bush stems wisdom, power, and fertility to be used inside the human village, and the animals from the bush represent that power and wisdom. Masks are—and here, the Dogon are typical—'things from the bush'. Masks are often associated with bush spirits, though not so much in Dogon; but then again, the implication is 'bush' first and spirit later. Myths of mask origin routinely stress the provenance from the bush.

This distinction between bush and village is surprisingly stable in African masking in general, whatever the specific ecological conditions of the various groups, from Senegal's coast to the eastern border of Congo, and from the Dogon here in Mali to the Zambian Ndembu, the nature of their 'bush' varies greatly, but the dichotomy remains the same. It is an opposition that is 'good to think', in Levi-Straussian terms.

So in the ritual, the masks cross the border between bush and village, a crucial opposition in their worldview; they are not imitations of animals but 'fusions of worlds', a mix of the human and the animal world, the village plus the bush. The masks share human and animal characteristics, they are 'therio-anthropic' (Fardon 1990, 2007). They bridge these two separate realms not by being there, but by movement, by journeying between the two worlds. The main thing a mask does is 'to appear', as when we saw them come from the bush; the village waits motionless for a moving mask, walking, dancing, or running at full speed. A mask is only a proper *ɛmna* when it appears, when it dances, when it performs, and when it leaves again into the bush shouting its characteristic cries. A headpiece in a museum may look good, but it is not a real mask—for two reasons; the first is the lack of costume, and the second is the fact that it just hangs on its spot without any movement. To analyse such a static mask is the same as analysing a ballet by focusing on a description of the ballerina's shoes.

Masks do not just walk, travel, and run; they mainly dance, they perform—the second aspect of movement, and the most spectacular one. Each mask in Dogon shares with all masks three standard dances with their respective drum rhythms, while each individual mask also has its own proper dance and drum rhythm. These dances often mimic the animal, like the high-stepping water birds, the shy hiding of the hares, and the light-footed running of the gazelles. When they rest, the masks sit at the rim of the square, watching their colleague-dancers perform, and then they are audience, not masks, as they do not move.

The second major border is between the genders, and here, the opposition-cum-mediation is more complex. It begins with the myth. As among many African groups, in the Dogon myth of the mask arrival, it is a woman who found the masks first—which originated among bush animals, in particular, among red ants according to the Dogon—and who danced with it, later to be appropriated by the men. This reflects a dominant aspect of masks: they are heavily gendered. Masks accentuate the line between the genders; all African masks do. The public secret, kept 'hidden' from the women, is that there are men inside these weird apparitions. Of course, the emphasis here is on 'public', as each woman knows this perfectly well, and they usually are well aware of who is dancing what mask. Nevertheless, these *ɛmna* do form a threat for the women, especially for their fertility, and they avoid any direct contact or close encounter. The reason is in the symbolic logic of the mask rituals.

A major interpretation of the whole liturgy of the Dogon *dama* states that this whole complex ritual, with the masks at its very core, is a ritual way for the men to generate life out of death (Van Beek 1991a). This is not too farfetched in a second funeral, wherein the dead have to become ancestors. For instance, babies born after the *dama* are deemed to represent of the deceased and carry their name; the circle of life is short among the Dogon, and it is the masks that close that circle. So the *dama* 'produces' life, because through their masks, the men appropriate the powers of life. Another clue for this interpretation resides in the feminization of several masks. In Figure 2 the stilt dancers, who represent wading water birds, sport 'breasts' made of baobab fruit halves—as is clearly shown on the close-up photo below of Figure 7—while quite a few masks show a hairdo that is definitely feminine, or wear feminine jewels. Also, the Dogon think that after the *dama*, many children will be born. So in the *dama*, the masked men have ritually appropriated the sources of life, and thus during this short liminal moment fertility, is transferred from the wombs of the women into the dance of the masks.

Now, fertility is not always the issue in African masks, but the Dogon masquerade operates in a different ritual environment from usual. Most mask rituals elsewhere are about the initiation of boys, but the *dama* functions as the second funeral in the first place. Almost immediately after death, the corpse is buried in one of the caves that dot the cliff side. Depending on the person who died, the first funeral can then be held either straight away or within a year; this is the so-called *yu yana*, a major complex of rituals lasting five days and nights. This first funeral does feature some masks as one of its many components, but in these rites, other elements—such as guns—dominate, not masks. However, in the second funeral, the *dama*, masks are everywhere and the link between death and fertility comes into full focus (Van Beek 2006).

Figure 7. A stilt mask, having a smoke while resting.

So the opposition man–woman runs deep and incorporates the border between death and fertility, a very fundamental one, and masks cross that border running at full speed. But here, the virtual reality of the ritual and the mundane reality of biology contradict each other. Evidently, the ritual self-sufficiency in male fertility is a chimera, just recognizable as a symbolic undercurrent in liminal times, while the women are perfectly aware that they are the ones who actually create the new generations. The wishful fertility of the men stands perpendicular to the real fertility of those excluded from the masking. As these two fertilities are at odds with each other, masks are indeed dangerous for female fertility, and that concern of the women makes perfect symbolic sense; the power that arrives from the bush is inimical to the actual source of procreation. The 'sisters of the mask', the *yasigine*, provide an ironic subtext—because even as masks, men have to drink and eat; and their very definition of masculinity, and surely of masking masculinity, fully prohibits them from doing these mundane tasks themselves. Masks may help men to gain procreative ascendancy, but that fleeting moment of male glory lasts for just one month, once every twelve years—and then only by force of that essential outsider: the mask.

3. Materiality, Performance, and Embodiment

Thus far, we have looked at the overall interpretation of the *dama* complex, featuring bush, death, and fertility, but for the individual performant, this elevated and, inevitably, constructed view need not to be relevant at all. For the observer, this is a spectacle with symbolic associations and interpretative clues; for the dancer, the performer, or even the audience, this need not to be the case. The young men dancing with the masks are 'inside' the ritual in a completely different way. They have to change into the mask, they are the ones who dance in the thick costumes with heavy headpieces, in the blistering heat of the afternoon, staying alert during the performance in order not to trip, as they see very little of their surroundings when dancing. Ritual is always embodied, but these performances take embodiment to a next level. As part of the *dama*, the young men change into masks, and thus we did not speak of dancers or 'maskers' as sometimes is done in art circles, but simply of masks, *ɛmna*. What appears are 'masks', not persons. The very material exigencies of the costumes and headpieces, the driving rhythm of the drums, the constant exhortations of the elders in the ritual language, the yelling colleague-masks, and the high ululations of the admiring women and girls all come together in a new embodied persona for the performer. His very exertions identify him with the ritual setting, aided by the long preparations, and his extensive practicing of the dancing skills that have led to this moment. Thus, the 'culturally in-skilled embodied schemas' (Vásquez 2011, p. 318, Steward and Strathern 2014, p. 119) converge in a crowning moment of glory.

Performance theory gives an additional angle into the masquerade, as two joined elements are added, aesthetics and judgment. In many ritual contexts, masks may aim at shocking or frightening their audience, but in this part of the *dama*, the mask performance is to be admired, liked, and emulated. A mask means a correct, convincing mask, and dancing means dancing well, just as the whole collective performance has to go well; Steward and Strathern call this 'felicitous performativity' (Steward and Strathern 2014, p. 93). Ritual performance is judged. The village aims at a 'good *dama*', the individual performer tries to stand out in his performance, in the gentle competition that is part of the masquerade and is one of its motivational engines.

From this vantage point of performative embodiment, we now go back to Domo Pujugo; he has danced well between all the other *kanaga*, just as he has danced other mask types too, as most youngsters have done. However, we also mentioned that he wrote his name on his mask top, as did several of his age mates that year in Amani—either their name or the year. A second example is the following (Figure 8):

Figure 8. Another *kanaga* of 1989. Note the year on the base of the headpiece.

The boys saw this as enhancing their performance, their personal standing out. Schooling in this part of the Dogon area came rather late; in neighbouring Tireli, the first school was founded in the 1970s, and some years later in Amani. So the boys of 1989 were among the first initiated who were schooled, and they were proud of it—hence the writing of their names. I bought this particular mask from Domo himself at the end of the *dama*. Masks are used only once for real *dama*, and after that may be sold; some rituals objects have to be fresh and new, not old. At that moment, I thought the writing on masks would be a new trend, which in itself is a normal feature of masquerades because they change constantly, with small adaptations to new circumstances.[4] But the elders of Amani were not so pleased, because they immediately realized that not just boys could read and write, but girls as well, if not now, then in the immediate future. There were probably already young women among the public who could read who were 'inside' that *kanaga*; the public secret was out, for these women were now forced to 'really know' and could no longer profess ignorance; and surely they would talk about it, the one thing a public secret aims to avoid. Not just dances have to be performed, but public secrets demand performance as well, by all parties.

So after the *dama*, the old men came together and issued a ruling that henceforth no one should write his name or anything else on the mask; there was to be just the mask and no text, and this was to be the case not only for the *kanaga*—which is well suited for writing—but for all headpieces. And, indeed, this rule was followed in the later masquerades, as well as in other villages, which do not at all fall under any jurisdiction of these particular elders. For instance, in 2008 in Tireli, with many more schooled participants and a huge outpouring of *kanaga* masks, no writing appeared on any mask.

After all, the mask we started out with, the one of Domo Pujugo, has become quite unique—in fact, it is a time piece, as it highlights a point in Dogon history where basic schooling had just started and, for a short moment, could be used as a distinction. Only at this time could the schoolboys think they were the only ones who could read and write and could stand out as such. They thought they had found another way for the gentle competition that runs inside the masking festival, a notion that could not have surfaced earlier. In itself, such a change fits well into the open system that masks are in Dogon culture; masks show trends and fashions.

However, this novelty turned out to be a contradiction in itself, as they wrote their own name on the mask, and the year—1989. Through their writing, the ritual object became part of another world, not of the virtual reality of a funeral (Kapferer 2004, p. 46; Van Beek 2008), but of the real one of the school and daily life. By the simple act of writing, the mask was 'deliminalized'. A *kanaga* with a name on it is not a mask but a personal billboard, endangering the construction of meaning of the whole masquerade. The mask elders of Amani were thus completely justified, and their reaction shows their very awareness of the essence of the mask festival, of the borders that should not be crossed, and of the paradoxes involved in masking. Their well-reasoned rejection of this novelty showed how much they were aware of the basic tenets of the mask ritual, how much they were intent on patrolling the borders of the virtual reality, by safeguarding these moving objects as the *raison d'être* of the complex ritual.

Embodiment and performance presuppose materiality (Vásquez 2011), as especially in imagistic religions, the material expressions are absolutely essential for any productive interpretation. Dogon religion is very much a 'religion of things', just like many indigenous African religions with their roots in imagistic processes; things ranging from guns to broken pottery, and from hoe handles to stools. But few rituals are as 'thingy' as a masquerade, those apparitions coming from the bush into the village, in a wonderful show that is a delight for the eyes while threatening for the women.

However, these mask-things generate one more reflection: they are not just a prime support for our interpretation, but they also challenge our notion of a 'thing', of an object. Ingold (2011), in his ecological approach, challenges the dichotomy between nature and culture, matter and mind, and he does find the *dama* at his side. The first photograph shows the headpiece of Domo's mask, very much

4 For an analysis how mask dances intertwine with village dynamics, see (Van Beek 2012).

an object and very much what we in the global North would call a mask; this is what we find in a museum—or now in my collection. But for the Dogon, this may be an object, a thing in itself; but it is not a mask, not a proper *ɛmna*—and as such, it is not 'a ritual object' at all. The ritual entity, the one that moves and acts, is the material object plus the costumed dancer, and none of these elements can stand on its own. It is the combination of man, object, and act that is the real ritual agent; so the material side of religion is another fusion of worlds, those of matter and of man, inanimate and animate. Materiality is a precondition for an embodied performance, and as such can bridge the divide between the world in which we live and the 'other side', the final border crossing.

Funding: The overall research on the Dogon was financed by WOTRO (Netherlands Foundation for Tropical Research, grant W 52-112), the field stay of 1989 by a travel grant of WOTRO (W 52-142) and by Utrecht University, Faculty of Social Sciences.

Conflicts of Interest: The author declares no conflict of interest.

References

Bell, Catherine. 1997. *Ritual. Perspectives and Dimensions*. Oxford: Oxford University Press.

Evans-Pritchard, Edward Evan. 1956. *Nuer Religion*. Oxford: Clarendon Press.

Fardon, Richard. 1990. *Between God, the Dead and the Wild. Chamba Interpretations of Religion and Ritual*. Edinburgh: Edinburgh University Press for the International African Institute.

Fardon, Richard. 2007. *Fusions: Masquerades and Thought Style East of the Niger-Benue Confluence, West Africa*. London: Saffron Books.

Grimes, Ronald L. 2014. *The Craft of Ritual Studies*. Oxford: Oxford University Press.

Ingold, Tim. 2011. *Being Alive. Essays on Movement, Knowledge and Description*. London: Routledge.

Kapferer, Bruce. 2004. Ritual dynamics and virtual practices: beyond representation and meaning. In *Ritual in its own Right*. Edited by Don Handelman and Galina Lindquist. New York: Berghahn Books, pp. 35–54.

Steward, Pamela J., and Andrew Strathern. 2014. *Ritual: Key Concepts in Religion*. London: Bloomsbury.

Van Beek, Walter E. A. 1991a. Enter the Bush: A Dogon Mask Festival. In *Africa Explores; 20th Century African Art*. Edited by Susan Vogel. New York: Prestal Munich & Center for African Art, pp. 56–73.

Van Beek, Walter E. A. 1991b. Dogon Restudied: A Field Evaluation of the Work of Marcel Griaule. *Current Anthropology* 32: 139–67.

Van Beek, Walter E. A. 2006. Boys and masks among the Dogon. In *Playful Performers. African Children's Masquerades*. Edited by Simon Ottenberg and David A. Binckley. New Brunswick and London: Transaction Publishers, pp. 67–88.

Van Beek, Walter E. A. 2008. Heeft ritueel dan toch betekenis? *Jaarboek voor Liturgie-Onderzoek Yearbook for Liturgical and Ritual Studies* 24: 23–49.

Van Beek, Walter E. A. 2012. To dance or not to dance: Dogon masks as an arena. In *African Hosts and their Guests. Dynamics of Cultural Tourism in Africa*. Edited by Walter E. A. van Beek and Annette Schmidt. Oxford: James Currey, pp. 37–57.

Vásquez, Manuel A. 2011. *More than Belief: A Materialist Theory of Religion*. Oxford: Oxford University Press.

Whitehouse, Harvey. 2004. *Modes of Religiosity. A Cognitive Theory of Religious Transmission*. Walnut Creek: Altamira Press.

religions

MDPI

Article

'Requiescat in Pace'. Initiation and Assassination Rituals in the Assassin's Creed Game Series

F. (Frank) G. Bosman

Department of Systematic Theology and Philosophy, Tilburg University, 5037AB Tilburg, The Netherlands; F.G.Bosman@uvt.nl

Received: 16 April 2018; Accepted: 18 May 2018; Published: 21 May 2018

Abstract: The Assassin's Creed game series (Ubisoft 2007, 2009, 2010, 2011, 2012, 2013a, 2013b, 2014, 2015, 2017) revolves around an alternative interpretation of human history as an ongoing battle between two rival factions: the Assassin Brotherhood (modelled on the historical Nizar Isma'ilis) and the Templar Order (inspired by the historical Order of the Knights Templar). Both factions compete over the possession of mythical artefacts, called the 'Apples of Eden', which once belonged to a now extinct proto-human race. The possession of these artefacts gives the owner incredible knowledge and the ability to manipulate large numbers of people. The Templars strive for world domination, while the Assassins want to prevent this; their aim is to develop human consciousness and individual freedom. Considering games as 'playable texts', I make an inventory of three in-game rituals, two of the Assassin Brotherhood and one of the Templar Order. Both initiation and assassination rituals are quite elaborate given the context of the games in which they are displayed. Progression and regression can be observed in terms of ritual practices within the primary series of the game series, which stretches from ancient Egypt to modernity. This article describes the three ritual practices mentioned within the Assassin's Creed series, and links them to the larger metanarrative of the series.

Keywords: ritual; rituality; ritualism; digital games; assassination; initiation; nizarism; Templar Order

---

> One upon a time, we had a ceremony on such occasions. But I don't think either of us are really the type for that. You have your tools and training, your targets and goals. And now you have your title. Welcome to the Brotherhood, Connor. (AC3)

The event described is rather minimalistic, at least materially, but for the young Native American Connor (birth name Ratonhnhaké:ton) it constitutes his formal initiation into the Assassin Brotherhood, a secret organization dedicated since the dawn of time to the protection of human freedom. After being trained by an Assassin mentor called Achilles Davenport, Connor is given the task to find and slay seven targets, all members of the American Rite of the Templar Order, while simultaneously conducting his own personal quest to find those responsible for the destruction of his native village. To mark his readiness for such a severe task, his mentor gives him the traditional clothing of the Assassins, strikes him on the shoulder, and utters the strange little speech quoted above.

It is only one of several scenes with ritual overtones in the *Assassin's Creed* series (2007–2017) produced by Ubisoft. Ubisoft re-images world history as an ongoing confrontation between the Assassin Brotherhood and the Templar Order over the possession and use of certain powerful artefacts, the 'Apples of Eden', left behind by a now extinct superhuman race. Both secret organizations are responsible for many historical revolutions, discoveries, and disasters, and they have their own initiation rituals, while the Brotherhood also has its own assassination ritual.

In this article, I will investigate the various forms in which the three fictional rituals (two initiation rituals and one assassination ritual) are depicted by Ubisoft in its *Assassin's Creed* series, including the changes that they undergo during the series. I take 'initiation' to mean a particular rite of passage (Van Gennep 1909), defined by Eliade (1975, p. X) as 'a body of rites and oral teachings, whose purpose is to produce a decisive alteration in the religious and social status' of the initiate. The initiate's 'existential condition' changes; once he has undergone the ritual 'he has become another'. In the *Assassin's Creed* series, both Templar and Assassin 'pupils' are ritually initiated into their respective fraternities.

The assassination ritual of the Brotherhood will be discussed in terms of human sacrifice, 'a practice that once was near universal, but nowadays increasingly abandoned' (Bremmer 2007, p. 1). It has returned to our present collective consciousness in the context of Islamic inspired terrorism, paradoxically applied to (or claimed for) both perpetrators and victims alike. Sacrifice, both human and animal, is community-oriented, ritual in performance, and constitutive of a collective or individual identity (Duyndam et al. 2017, p. 5). In the *Assassin's Creed* series, ritual assassination is re-imagined in a context that is both political and religious.

As we will discover, not all instances of the in-game rituals can be characterized as the elaborate, stylized, more or less 'classical' rituals we know from institutionalized religion; the minimalistic and/or abbreviated forms of the two rituals are also very informative about the nature of the rituals. 'The possibility of making mistakes and of failure is a constitutive feature of rituals,' as Hüsken (2007) has already observed. And precisely the possibility of failure adds to the importance of the ritual: if nothing is at stake, why bother at all? This is also the reason why I will construct an 'ideal form' of both rituals, not to correct or differentiate between 'successful' and 'failed' forms of the rituals through the series, but to show what is at stake in both cases.

In order to be able to carry out my investigation properly, I will start with a description of the metanarrative of the *Assassin's Creed* universe (Section 1), including a short overview of the Assassin Brotherhood and the Templar Order, their historical inspiration (the Nizari Isma'ilis and the Templar Knights) and a short characterization of the way in which Ubisoft has—rather critically—incorporated the concept of religion into its series. Before turning to the actual rituals itself, I will briefly describe the complex narratological structure of the game series to enable me to make my subsequent claim that the player of the series is her- or himself also initiated into the Brotherhood or the Order (Section 2).

In Section 3, I will describe four different forms in which Ubisoft presents initiation into the Brotherhood, and then the forms of initiation into the Order (Section 4). After some initial reflections on both initiation rituals, I will discuss the assassination ritual that is performed by almost all playable Assassins within the series (Section 5). After some short reflections on the assassination ritual, I will argue that the gamer her- or himself is—virtually—initiated into the Brotherhood (or the Order) by using the complex narratological structure of the series described earlier (Section 6). I will end with my conclusions (Section 7).

A word on methodology: I consider games to be 'digital (interactive), playable (narrative) texts' (Bosman 2016a). As a text, a video game can be an object of interpretation. As a narrative, it can be conceived as communicating meaning. As a game, it is playable. And as a digital medium, it is interactive. Treating these video games as playable texts and using a gamer-immanent approach in this article, I will use close reading of the primary sources of my research, the actual video games themselves, as well as secondary sources, i.e., material provided by critics and scholars discussing the game in question (Heidbrink et al. 2015). Close reading of the video game series is performed by playing the games themselves (multiple times), including all possible (side) missions.

While the *Assassin's Creed* franchise consists of primary and secondary games for multiple devices, together with novels, comics, and (animated) films, I will concentrate exclusively on the main video games (see Table 1). All games were played in their PC versions.

Table 1. Primary games. Overview of primary games within the *Assassin's Creed* franchise, including in-game time frame, dramatic period, main protagonists, and release dates. The games are listed in the order of the game-internal time frame.

GAMES (Main)	Ab.	Period	Title	Protagonist	Release
Ptolemaic Egypt	ACO	49–43 BC	Assassin's Creed: Origins	Bayek & Aya	2017
Third Crusade	AC1	1191	Assassin's Creed I	Altaïr ibn La'Ahad	2007
	AC2	1476–1499	Assassin's Creed II	Ezio Auditore da Firenze	2009
Renaissance	ACB	1499–1507	Assassin's Creed: Brotherhood	Ezio Auditore da Firenze	2010
	ACRe	1511–1512	Assassin's Creed: Revelations	Ezio/Altaïr	2011
	AC3	1754–1783	Assassin's Creed 3	Haytham Kenway/Connor	2012
Colonial Era	AC4	1715–1722	Assassin's Creed 4: Black Flag	Edward Kenway	2013
	ACRo	1752–1776	Assassin's Creed: Rogue	Shay Cormac	2014
French Revolution	ACU	1776–1808	Assassin's Creed: Unity	Arno Dorian	2014
Victorian Age	ACS	1868	Assassin's Creed: Syndicate	Evie & Jacob Frye	2015

1. Those Who Came Before. The Metanarrative of the Assassin's Creed Series

The metanarrative of the *Assassin's Creed* series is a multi-leveled allohistorical complex, ranging up to four narratological levels.

1.1. On the First Level

Assassin's Creed draws inspiration from the pseudoscientific 'Ancient Astronauts Hypothesis' (Feder 2002), popularized for instance in Von Däniken (1969) bestseller *Chariots of the Gods?*. Some 100,000 years ago, humankind was genetically engineered by a super-advanced, Earth-born race, known in-game as the Isu, 'Those Who Came Before' or 'the Precursors'. Originally designed as a cheap and docile labor force for and by the Isu, humankind eventually rebelled against its creators, at the instigation of two human-Isu hybrids Adam and Eve, who were unaffected by the Isu's mind-controlling apparatus, called 'Apples of Eden' or 'Pieces of Eden' in the game. The Isu-human war ended with the victory of the far more primitive, but more resilient *homo sapiens* when a cosmic disaster changed the Earth's magnetic fields, known in-game as the 'Toba Catastrophe'. Humankind thrived, but the few remaining Isu could not hold out. They vanished into history, gradually 'remembered' as the gods and godheads of human civilization.

1.2. On the Second Level

Ubisoft re-imagines human history as a struggle between two secret factions, the Assassin Brotherhood and the Templar Order, over the possession of the artefacts left by the Isu after their extinction. Both factions, which have existed from the time of the Isu-human hybrids Adam and Eve, have the same ideal: the ending of all conflict, the undisturbed development of humankind, and everlasting world peace. The means they use are different, however: the Order wants to use the Apples of Eden to force humankind into obedience, order, and discipline, while the Assassins want to guard human freedom by keeping these artefacts out of their adversaries' hands. All major conflicts in world history are orchestrated by, or are a consequence of, the manipulations of one of these two factions, including—for example—the rise and fall of Julius Caesar, the French Revolution, and the moon landing.

The in-game Assassin Brotherhood is inspired by the historical Shi'ite sect of the Nizari Isma'ilis (Bosman 2016b; Daftary 1998, 1994; Bartlett 2011; Mirza 1997). Before and after the Third Crusade, the Nizaris occupied numerous mountain fortresses in Syria and Persia, of which Alamut and Masyaf were the most famous. Political assassination was one of their main military tactics, used to preserve their precariously independent position between a Sunni majority and the Christian crusaders. The Assassin leader of Masyaf in AC1, Al-Mualim (Arabic for 'mentor') is a reference to the historical Nizari leader Rashid ad-Din Sinan (1162–1192/3).

The Templar Order is based on the historical *Poor Fellow-Soldiers of Christ and of the Temple of Solomon*, also known as the 'Order of Solomon's Temple', the 'Knights Templar' or simply as 'Templars' (Haag 2009). Founded by Huguess de Payens (1070–1136) and King Baldwin II of Jerusalem (reign 1118–1131) the Templar Order developed from a military group dedicated to the protection of pilgrims in occupied Jerusalem and the surrounding area into a powerful international organization with branches across Europe that possessed vast amounts of property and gold.

The sudden and spectacular end of this influential Order in 1307 has kindled several enduring conspiracy theories and inspired many novels and films, the best known of which are the pseudoscientific *The Holy Blood and the Holy Grail* (Baigent et al. 1982) and the fictional *The Da Vinci Code* (Brown 2003).

While both the Assassin Brotherhood and the Templar Order are thus inspired by historical organizations with very clear religious identities, Muslim and Christian respectively, the *Assassin's Creed* series addresses the topic of religion very critically (Bosman 2016c). The miracle stories from Old and New Testament are re-interpreted as tricks by the (possessors of the) Apples of Eden: Cain and Abel, Joseph, Moses and ultimately Jesus of Nazareth.

The initiation and assassination rituals of the Brotherhood and the Order therefore have little or nothing to do with the historical rituals of the Nizaris and the Templar Knights. The Assassin's Creed—'Nothing is true, everything is permitted'—is not religious nor ideological, but represents a radical, phenomenological approach to reality: all human knowledge is relative and contextual (Bosman 2018). And the Templar's ritual uttering—'May the Father of Understanding guide us'—is vaguely connected with the French deism of Maximilien de Robespierre (1758–1794), a Templar in the *Assassin's Creed* universe (Scurr 2014). I am not suggesting, however, that the in-game rituals are not religious in nature, but only that they cannot be attributed to the two historical religious organizations.

1.3. On the Third Level

Every instalment tells the story of one (sometimes two) historical Assassins (and in two cases a Templar), ranging from Ptolemaic Egypt to Victorian London.

1.4. On the Fourth Level

Every instalment also features a modern-day Assassin (in one case a Templar), who interacts with her or his historical counterpart, in a rather complex narratological structure that I will discuss in Section 4.

2. Playing the Animus. The Narratological Structure of the Assassin's Creed Series

The vast metanarrative of the *Assassin's Creed* universe gives scope to rather complex naratological structures. In modern times, Abstergo Industries, the above-ground 'face' of the Templar Order, has discovered the existence of 'genetic memory' within human DNA: the collection of memories of one's ancestors that are passed down to subsequent generations embedded in their DNA. With the help of the Animus (Latin for 'life'), a machine used to decode this genetic memory, it has become possible for people to actively relive the memories of their genetic forefathers.

The Animus presents these memories in a kind of virtual environment in which the subject who uses the Animus is able to control the movements of her or his ancestors. When the subject who uses the Animus fails to 'imitate' the movements and other acts of her or his ancestors sufficiently closely, the subject will be regarded as 'out of synchronization' and will be pulled out of the specific memory, enabling them to try another time.

While this idea of 'controlling an ancestor' is a bit odd from a narratological perspective (reliving memories suggests a passive spectator), ludologically it produces a very sound game mechanic (activating the player to take action). Later on in the game series, the Assassins have developed their own version of the Animus, which achieves precisely the same function as the Templar device. In the second part of the series (from AC4 onwards), access to the memories of a specific historical figure is also available to people who do not share their DNA.

Both the Order and the Brotherhood try to access the parental DNA of historical Templars and Assassins to discover clues to the hidden locations of the Apples of Eden. Some Isu artefacts have not yet been found, others were lost by accident or were hidden on purpose by men and women (predominantly Assassins) to prevent misuse.

Three types of narratological structure can be found in the *Assassin's Creed* game series: triple layered, double layered, and merged layers (see Table 2).

Table 2. Narratological structures. Overview of the different narratological layers in the primary games of the *Assassin's Creed* series. They are listed in the order of narratological complexity (primary) and game-internal time frame (secondary).

Ab.	Actual Situation		In-Game Situation				
	Actual player	*Actual device*	*Contemporary Assassin*	*Primary in-game device*	*Primary historical Assassin*	*Secondary in-game device*	*Secondary historical Assassin*
A. Triple layered (PC, Animus, Masyaf Keys)							
ACRe	Player	(PC)	Desmond	(Animus)	Ezio	(Masyaf Keys)	Altaïr
B. Double layered (PC, Animus)							
AC1	Player	(PC)	Desmond	(Animus)	Altaïr		
AC2	Player	(PC)	Desmond	(Animus)	Ezio		
ACB	Player	(PC)	Desmond	(Animus)	Ezio		
AC3	Player	(PC)	Desmond	(Animus)	Connor/Haytham		
AC4	Player	(PC)	Employee 1	(Animus Omega)	Edward		
ACRo	Player	(PC)	Employee 2	(Animus Omega)	Shay		
ACO	Player	(PC)	Layla	(Animus HR-8)	Bayek/Aya		
C. Merged layers (PC = Helix/Animus)							
ACU	Player	(PC)	=	(Helix/Animus)	Arno		
ACS	Player	(PC)	=	(Helix/Animus)	Evie/Jacob/Lydia		

2.1. *Double Layered*

In AC1, AC2, ACB, and AC3, the story revolves around a present-day Assassin, Desmond Miles, who is controlled by the player. Desmond is sent into the Animus (in AC1 of Templar origin) to relive the memories of his genetic ancestors Altaïr ibn La'Ahad during the Third Crusade (AC1), Ezio Auditore da Firenze in Renaissance Italy (AC2 and ACB), and Connor and Hatham Kenway (a Templar) in colonial North America (AC3). Thus the player controls Desmond through his gaming console; Desmond (and through him the player) controls his (mainly) Assassin and Templar forefathers through the Animus. This is the double layered narrative structure.

When Abstergo manages to improve the Animus technology so that it is no longer necessary for the present-day user and the historical figure to share the same DNA, the games follow other modern-day persons who use the Animus Omega, and who unwittingly assist either the Assassins or Templars. In most cases the persons in question are two nameless Abstergo employees (AC4, ACRo), and on one occasion an obstinate Abstergo scientist called Layla Hassan (ACO). The double layered narrative structure is maintained, however: the player controls Abstergo employees through his gaming console; the employees (and through them the player) controls historical Assassins/Templars through the Animus Omega.

2.2. *Triple Layered*

In ACRe, Ezio—an old man by then—acquires a certain object called 'Masyaf Keys', which allows him to relive particular memories of his ancestor Altaïr, who used these 'keys' to send messages to his unknown Assassin successors. The player, however, can control Desmond, Ezio, and Altaïr, and desynchronization can occur even when he controls Altaïr. Thus the player controls Desmond through his gaming console; Desmond (and through him the player) controls his forefather Ezio through the Animus; Ezio relives Altaïr's life, and the player and Desmond control Altaïr's life through Ezio). This is the triple layered narrative structure.

2.3. Merged Layers

When genetic memory technology no longer requires that users be descendants of historical Assassins/Templars, Abstergo commercializes the Animus, producing a gaming console (still called 'Animus') that uses a cloud service (known as 'Helix' after the DNA structure with the same name). In ACU, and ACS the suggestion is that the player is actually playing on the Animus/Helix instead of their own gaming device. The player directly controls the historical Assassins Arno Dorian (ACU), and Jacob, Evie, and Lydia Frye (ACS), thus merging the layers of the real-world and in-game gaming devices. This is the merged layers narrative structure.

This suggestion of merging and emerging is enhanced by 'hacks' into the game carried out by a mysterious group known as Erudito, which is allied with the Assassins, and which invites the player (addressed as 'Initiate') to join the Brotherhood's efforts to locate the Isu artefacts.

3. Nothing Is True. The Brotherhood's Initiation Ritual

The Assassins' initiation ritual does not appear in all instalments, but only in AC2, ACB, AC3, and ACU, and then in rather varied forms and variations. I will differentiate between a 'typical form', found twice (AC2 and ACB), a 'minimalistic form' (only found in AC3), and the 'new form' of the French branch (ACU). I will conclude with the construction of a hypothetical full-fledged ritual.

3.1. Typical Form: Ezio and Claudia

In 1488, Ezio Auditore, the protagonist in AC2, ACB, and ACRe, is formally initiated into the Brotherhood during a nocturnal ceremony at the top of a tower somewhere in Venice (AC2). In attendance are seven of the highest-ranking Assassins of the Italian branch: Paola (leader of the Florentine courtesans), Teodora Contanto (leader of the Venetian courtesans), Antonio de Magianis (leader of Florence's guild of thieves), Bartolomeo d'Alviano, Nicollo Machiavelli, Mario Auditore, and Gilberto (known as *La Volpe*, 'the fox' in Italian).

All attendees are standing in a classical position of reverence: holding their folded hands before the lower abdomen. All stand in a circle, while Ezio stands inside the circle, his hands beside his body. Mario Auditore, Ezio's Assassin mentor and uncle, presides over the ceremony, making the sacerdotal *orans* gesture with his hands as he faces a big fire lit in one of the corners of the tower. He says:

> Laa shay'a waqi'un moutlaq bale kouloun. These are the words spoken by our ancestors that lay at the heart of our creed.

Mario is referring to the master Assassin Altaïr ibn La- Ahad (AC1), and the Arabic text of the Assassin's Creed: 'Nothing is true, everything is permitted'. The Italian branch of the Brotherhood was founded in 1269, by the famous Venetian travelers Niccolo and Maffeo Polo (the explorer Marco Polo's father and uncle, respectively) who had been initiated into the Brotherhood by the same Altaïr (ACRe).

The creed is broken down into a simple exchange of questions and answers between the initiate and Niccolo Machiavelli (1469–1627), the famous Italian diplomat and author. At the end, all attendees repeat the creed collectively.

> **Machiavelli:** Where other men blindly follow the truth, remember …
>
> **Altaïr:** Nothing is true.
>
> **Maciavelli:** Where other men are limited, by morality or law, remember …
>
> **Altaïr:** Everything is permitted.
>
> **Machiavelli:** We work in the dark, to serve the light. We are Assassins.
>
> **All:** Nothing is true, everything is permitted.

After this exchange, Ezio is branded with a mark on his left ring finger by Antonio. Mario refers to the older form of the same ritual in which the finger was entirely amputated, both as a token of dedication to the Brotherhood's cause and as a practical measure, to be able to handle the typical Assassin hidden blade. But this form was discarded by Altaïr as 'a false promise of paradise' (AC2), a reference to the Christian legends about the Nizaris that included stories about young men being enticed into obedience to their leader by being drugged and brought into paradise-like gardens (Bosman 2016c; Daftary 1994).

> **Machiavelli:** It is time, Ezio.
>
> **Mario:** In this modern age, we are not so literal as our ancestors. But our seal is no less permanent. Are you ready to join us?
>
> **Altaïr:** I am.

Antonio takes two long iron pincers and burns the mark onto Ezio's finger. Although the older form of amputation became obsolete after Altaïr's takeover of the Order, Ubisoft traces its origin to the proto-Assassin Bayek, who accidentally cut off his finger with his own hidden blade, and then cauterized his mutilated finger on purpose to stop the bleeding, leaving him without his left ring finger (ACO). Back to Ezio's initiation, where Machiavelli continues:

> **Machiavelli:** Welcome, Ezio. You are one of us now. Come! We have much to do!

All attendees, including Ezio, preform a 'leap of faith', a characteristic feature of the Assassins in the *Assassin's Creed* series. It enables the Assassin to jump from very tall buildings onto a haystack that is frequently and helpfully found under such buildings. This leap is a further reference to a Christian myth about the Nizaris: the death-defying obedience of the Nizaris to their leader was such that they would fling themselves from the palisade of their mountain fortress into the depths below on his command, just to impress the advancing armies. While the jump was more or less trickery, both historically and in-game, the effect on the Nizaris' enemies was understandably great (Bosman 2016c; Daftary 1994).

Another initiation ceremony is found in ACB, the direct sequel to AC2. In 1503, Ezio is appointed 'mentor' (effective ruler) of the Italian branch of the Brotherhood during the initiation ceremony of Claudia Auditore, Ezio's sister, in their Roman hideout. The ceremony is attended by Bartolomeo d'Alviano, Niccolo Machiavelli, Gilberto, Claudia, Ezio, and seven nameless assassins, whom Ezio has inducted into the Brotherhood earlier in the game. Claudia, Ezio, and Machiavelli are standing on a little platform like those found in Christian churches, all facing the rest of the room where the other attendees are gathered, themselves facing the platform. All attendees have their arms beside their body, except Machiavelli who speaks the first words *in orans* as he takes over Mario's job after his assassination by the Templar Order. Ezio takes over Machiavelli's place in the ritual.

> **Machiavelli:** Laa shay'a waqi'un moutlaq bale kouloun moumkine. The wisdom of our Creed is revealed through these words. We work in the dark, to serve the light. We are Assassins.
>
> **Ezio:** Claudia. We here dedicate our lives to protecting the freedom of humanity. Mario, our father and our brother, once stood around this fire, fighting off the darkness. Now, I offer the choice to you. Join us.

Claudia does not speak, as Ezio certainly did at his own initiation ceremony. Her left ring finger is branded by Machiavelli. The question and answer sequence does occur, but this time in the context of Ezio's elevation to the rank of mentor, which takes places directly after Claudia's branding.

> **Machiavelli:** Ezio Auditore da Firenze. You will now be known as il Mentore, the guardian of our order and our secrets.
>
> **Ezio:** Where other men blindly follow the truth, remember ...
>
> **All:** Nothing is true.
>
> **Ezio:** Where other men are limited, by morality or law, remember ...
>
> **All:** Everything is permitted.

Again, a leap of faith is performed, but this time we only see Claudia jump off a high building. Machiavelli and Ezio witness Claudia, but only Ezio follows her after a short discussion with Machiavelli.

3.2. Minimalistic Form: Connor

It AC3, another initiation ritual finally appears in an *Assassin's Creed* series. In an unknown year after 1770, Ratonhnhaké:ton (also known as Connor) is initiated into the Brotherhood by mentor Achilles Davenport. Connor is the illicit child of Kaniehtí:io, a Native American woman, and the English Templar Haytham Kenway. Intriguingly enough (and it is illustrative of the high narratological complexity of the *Assassin's Creed* series), it was this same Kenway who crippled Davenport in 1760 (ACRo).

Together with an Assassin-turned-Templar, Shay Cormac, Haytham succeeds in eliminating the Brotherhood presence in the New World, with the exception of Achilles, who is left to live with the knowledge of his ultimate failure. Achilles becomes depressed and cynical after his crippling, until Connor more or less forces him to train him as an Assassin. Connor's initiation heralds the rise of a new generation of Assassins.

After Connor has finished his training, and has returned from a naval expedition, Achilles takes his apprentice to the basement of his Davenport Manor, near Rockport (Massachusetts). There, he simply hands over the classical Assassin outfit to Connor, asking him to put it on. When Connor does this, Achilles speaks a few simple words to him.

> Once upon a time, we had a ceremony on such occasions. But I don't think either of us are really the type for that. You have your tools and training. Your targets and goals. And now you have your title. Welcome to the Brotherhood, Connor.

After this somewhat minimalistic initiation, Achilles pats Connor on the shoulder in encouragement, leaving the new brother to his own thoughts.

3.3. New Form: Arno

At the end of ACRo, in 1776, the rogue Assassin Shay Cormac performs a last assassination, of the French Assassin Charles Dorian. Charles's son, Arno, is left an orphan and, in a bizarre twist of plot, he is raised by François de la Serre, the Grand Master of the Parisian Rite of the Templar Order. When De la Serre is murdered by another Templar, Arno is framed for the deed and is sent to the Bastille in Paris. In 1789, he escapes during the historical storming of the Bastille that marked the beginning of the French Revolution. Arno reports to the Assassin Council in the Sainte-Chapelle, where he is formally initiated into the Brotherhood.

This initiation is the most formal one. The Assassin Council stands on a balcony, towering over Arno who stands in the large space between two staircases leading up. An unknown number of silent and masked Assassins lurk in the shadows, ready to obey the council's every word. Arno is still wearing his simple prison clothes, while the council members are dressed in beautiful uniforms and large, gray, hooded cloaks. The Council consists of Honoré Gabriel Riqueti (Comte de Mirabeau), Pierre Bellec, Sophie Trenet, Hervé Quemar, and Guillaume Beylier.

Mentor Gabriel starts the inquiry, and Arno answers sarcastically.

> **Gabriel:** Very well. Out of the dark, you have come to the light. From the light, you will return to the dark. Are you prepared to travel the eagle's path?
>
> **Arno:** If that is a fancy way of asking 'do I want your help', yes.
>
> **Gabriel:** Then drink.

Arno drinks from a golden chalice, engraved with the Latin word for 'brotherhood', *Fraternitas*. The potion instantly induces psychedelic effects, and fractured dreams of Arno's own past, including the death of his biological and adoptive fathers. While this liquid in ACU primarily seems to produce an introspective state of mind in which the initiate is forced to 'face' the demons of his past, the potion is also another reference to the Nizari drug legend from medieval times (Bosman 2016c; Daftary 1994).

After the effects of the potion have worn off, Gabriel continues with the ceremony, now starting a variation of the question and answer sequence.

> **Gabriel:** These are the words spoken by our ancestors. The words that lay at the heart of our creed.
>
> **Guillaume:** Stay your blade from the flesh of the innocent.
>
> **Sophie:** Hide in plain sight.
>
> **Hervé:** Never compromise the Brotherhood.
>
> **Gabriel:** Let these tenets be branded upon your mind. Let these be branded upon your mind. Follow them, and be uplifted. Break them at your peril. Rise, Assassin.

Gabriel obliquely refers to the ritual of the branding of the left ring finger—absent here—by using the phrase 'let these tenets be *branded* upon your mind'. It is also the first time that the so-called 'three tenets' of the Brotherhood are used in the initiation ritual. While the tenets were already discussed in AC1, they were never part of the initiation ceremony before. Afterwards, Arno is greeted by the council members and his assassin's clo thes are presented to him. Although the leap of faith is still an integral mechanic throughout the game in ACU (especially for Arno), it is not part of the initiation itself.

3.4. Theoretical Structure

After the description of four of the Assassin Brotherhood's initiation rituals, it is possible to construct an 'idealized' form and identify its main constitutive elements as they appear in all instalments of the series that have been mentioned.

(1) The initiate is presented to a 'council' of elder, experienced Assassin masters, in the presence of other assassins of lower rank (if these are available). The atmosphere is solemn, resembling a traditional religious (Christian) ceremony. Sometimes the attendees have their hands folded in reverence, while the 'minister' recites the creed 'Nothing is true, everything is permitted' *in orans*. Sometimes another ritual utterance is used, evoking the three tenets of the Assassin's Creed. The minister, usually the highest-ranking Assassin, the initiate, and the attendees perform a simple question and answer ritual, which is also based on the creed or its tenets.

(2) The recitation of the creed is followed by a branding ceremony, which is physical and mental in nature. The ring finger of the initiate's left hand is branded by another high-ranking Assassin as a symbol of their commitment to the Brotherhood and its creed. In later times, the branding of the finger is replaced by a ceremonial draught from a chalice which induces visions that are 'branded' onto the initiate's mind.

(3) After the recitation and the branding (in either form), there seem to be two possibilities. If the initiate is already working with the Brotherhood (like Ezio and Claudia), they already wear their distinct uniforms. In this case the initiate and/or the other attendees perform a leap of faith, as a visible token of their acceptance and—again—of their dedication to the Brotherhood. (It takes nerves of steel to 'trust' that the fall will not be deadly.) If the initiate is not already working for the Brotherhood (like Arno), the leap of faith is replaced by the handing over of the Assassin's uniform. In Connor's case, the handing over is the only part of the ritual that Achilles uses.

4. The Father of Understanding. The Order's Initiation Ritual

The Templar Order's initiation ritual is simpler and receives much less attention in the game series, both qualitatively and quantitatively, mainly because the Brotherhood perspective is dominant in the franchise (with the exception of ACRo and the first part of AC3). The Templar Order's initiation ritual comprises three elements: (1) the swearing of an oath, not unlike the ritual question and answer sequence of the Brotherhood initiation; (2) the handing over of a ring; and (3) the ritual utterance.

4.1. Typical Form

In AC3 and ACRo, we find two initiation ceremonies which are quite similar in structure and phrasing. In AC3, Charles Lee (1732–1782) is sworn into the Order by Grand Master Haytham Kenway (the father of the Assassin Connor, discussed above) in 1755. In ACRo, the Assassin-turned-Templar Shay Cormac (1731–?) is sworn in by, again, Grand Master Haytham, in 1757. Both initiations are witnessed by numerous Templars, and in the case of Shay also by Lee. In both cases the Templars are gathered at a large table, lit by candles. The grand master presides over the meeting at the head of the table. All Templars have folded their hands in reference to the severity of the situation, just like the Assassins in their ceremony. All the Templars have their eyes fixed on the initiate. In both scenarios the questioning is as follows:

> **Kenway:** Do you [Lee or Cormac] swear to uphold the principle of our order and all that for which we stand?
>
> **Lee/Cormac:** I do.
>
> **Kenway:** And never to share our secrets nor divulge the true nature of our work?
>
> **Lee/Cormac:** I do.
>
> **Kenway:** And to do so from now until death, whatever the cost?
>
> **Lee/Cormac:** I do.
>
> **Kenway:** Then we welcome you into our fold, brother.
>
> In AC3, Kenway adds to Lee:
>
> Together we will usher in the dawn of a New World. One defined by purpose and order. Give me your hand. Give me your hand. You are a Templar.
>
> In ACRo, Kenway adds to Cormac:
>
> You are a Templar now, a harbinger of the New World.

In both AC3 and ACRo, Kenway presents the initiate with the ceremonial Templar ring, to be worn on the ring finger of the right hand (unlike the branding of the *left* ring finger performed by the Assassins). The initiate puts the ring on his finger, and then Kenway utters the traditional formula 'May the Father of Understanding guide us', and all attendees respond with the same phrase.

The ring presented to the initiates is from a deceased Templar, thus suggesting a kind of spiritual-hereditary succession between different Templar generations. The ring presented to Lee, by Kenway (AC3), had been taken by the same Kenway from his rogue fellow Templar Edward Braddock (1695–1755) in 1755 (without killing him). The ring presented to Cormac, also by Kenway (ACRo), had been given to Cormac by the Templar George Monro (1700–1757), after Cormac rescued him from a burning house (in vain though, because Monro died directly after the rescue).

4.2. Atypical Forms

There are two further references to the ceremonial rings of the Templar Order: in AC4 and in ACRo. In AC4, the grand master of the Caribbean Rite of the Templars, Laureano de Torres y Ayala (1645–1722), calls together a meeting of several important Templars to plot their next operations. In attendance are, in addition to Laureano, Julien du Casse (1682–1715), Woodes Rogers (1679–1732), and Edward Kenway (posing as the Templar Robert Walpole, whom Kenway had killed earlier). Before the meeting starts, Laureano presents the attendees with a Templar ring. The presentation lacks any other aspect of the initiation rite as described above. Laureano speaks:

> Please, hold out your hands. Mark and remember our purpose. To guide all wayward souls 'till they reach a quiet road. To guide all wayward desire until impassioned hearts are cooled. To guide all wayward minds to safe and sober thought. By the Father of understanding's light, let our work now begin.

The last 'ring ceremony' can be found in ACRo, at the end of the game, when the nameless Abstergo employee (with whom the player has relived Cormac's past) receives the offer to join the Order. Abstergo officials Melanie Lemay, Violet da Costa, and Juhani Otso Berg stand before the player/the nameless employee, when Melanie offers him/her the ring, saying:

> Join us, and a bright future will be all yours. Refuse ...

The consequences of refusal are not spelled out, but no leaps of imagination are required to know what it would be: death. The choice which the nameless Abstergo employee makes is not shown in the game, thus also relieving the player of responsibility to choose. I will return to this situation in Section 6 when discussing the initiation of the player.

The ritual utterance 'May the Father of Understanding guide us' sounds rather religious, but its true meaning remains vague during the series. It is normally used in the Order's initiation ritual described, but also as a secret password (AC3), as a ritual saying for the opening of a secret meeting (AC2), or more casually in letters and conversations (ACRo, ACU, and ACS). In ACU, which is set in revolutionary France, the Assassin Elise Dorian comments on Robbespierre's historical cult of the Supreme Being as 'a popularized version' of the Order's true doctrine (Bosman 2018).

The cult of the Supreme Being was a historical cult established by Robespierre during the French Revolution, a form of classic deism intended to replace Roman Catholicism (and its competitor, the Cult of Reason) as the state religion. Robespierre's religion included belief in a Supreme Being, an eternal human soul, and a life dedicated to 'civil virtues' (Scurr 2014). It lost its momentum with the execution of Robespierre in 1794, and was abolished by Napoleon Bonaparte, an ally to the Brotherhood according to Ubisoft, in 1802.

4.3. Theoretical Structure

After examining these four examples of the Order's initiation ritual (two in its typical, and two in its atypical form), we can distinguish three constitutive elements: (a) the swearing of an oath in which the initiate is asked to uphold the Order's principles and to guard its secrets until death; (b) the handing over of the Templar's ring, often one that previously belonged to a now deceased Templar, to be worn on the initiate's right ring finger; and (c) the ritual utterance of the words about the Father of Understanding, to be repeated by all present.

5. Requiescat In Pace. The Brotherhood's Assassination Ritual

The second ritual frequently shown in the *Assassin's Creed* series is the assassination ritual. Although the presentation does cloud the ritual form somewhat, when all the primary games of the series are examined, a definite ritual pattern can be distinguished, with diverse forms and constitutive elements (see Table A1: Assassinations, in the Appendix A). I will start with the theoretical structure and then differentiate between the different instalments and scenes (instead of the other way around, as I did with the initiation rituals).

In every instalment of the *Assassin's Creed* series, the protagonist is given the task of assassinating certain high-profile targets, usually high-ranking Templars or their accomplices. When the protagonist is about to attack (by striking with a hidden blade or sword, by firing a pistol, or by some other means), the assassin and his target enter the so-called 'memory corridor'. The memory corridor is a special feature of the Animus (which the modern-day Assassin, and through him the player, uses to control the historical protagonist) which slows time and intensifies contact between the assassin and his target. The corridor shows blue and white lights and patterns in the background, leaving only the assassin and the target in the scene.

Sometimes a high-profile target does not trigger the memory corridor, but certain ritual traits similar to those which do trigger the corridor still occur. They have been included in this study. For all other exceptions and anomalies, see Table A1: Assassinations (Appendix A).

5.1. Theoretical Structure

In all instalments, assassinations include certain ritual characteristics, all with their in-game origin and purpose: (1) the Assassin holds the head of his target in his arms, as the target lies on the ground; (2) the Assassin and his target exchange last words, usually in the form of a confession by the latter; (3) the Assassin closes the eyes of the dead person; (4) the Assassin collects a sample of the victim's blood; and (5) the Assassin ritually utters a final short prayer, usually 'rest in peace' or a variation thereof.

The entire ritual evinces piety and respect for the victim, making the act less about personal motives or vendettas and more about 'something that has to be done' for the greater good of the Brotherhood's long-term goals. This is shown particularly well in AC2, when the young (but uninitiated) Ezio kills Vieri de'Pazzi, one of the murderers of his brothers and father. Ezio burns with the desire to avenge their deaths, and he not only kills Vieri, but also shakes his dead body while shouting angrily:

> [In Italian] Piece of shit! I only wish you'd suffered more! You met the fate you deserved! I hope you ...

Then his uncle Mario intervenes, asking his nephew to show some 'respect' for the dead. When Ezio responds that Vieri would not have shown either of them 'such kindness', Mario replies:

> [to Ezio in English] You are not Vieri. Do not become him. [to Vieri in Italian] May death provide the peace you sought. Requiescat in pace [Rest in peace].

Like all mentors, Mario teaches Ezio that their victims should not be killed out of emotion alone, but through minuscule planning and deliberation.

5.2. Holding the Target

Approximately half of the assassination victims that trigger the memory corridor are first held in their Assassin's arms. Altaïr (AC), the younger Ezio (AC2, ACB), and Jacob Frye (ACS) often provide some comfort to their victims in the last seconds of their lives by doing this, while the older Ezio (ACRe), Connor (AC3), Edward (AC4), Shay (ACRo), Arno (ACU), and Bayek (ACO) do not hold their victims, or only on rare occasions. There seems to be a connection between the emotional involvement of the Assassin and his willingness to hold his victims. Altaïr, Ezio, and Jacob are rather calculated in their manner, while Ezio very quickly learns to overcome his hunger for vengeance. Connor, Edward, Shay, and Bayek are very much involved personally in the deaths of their targets, as they hold them responsible for the deaths of loved ones (tribe, friends, or family), with the exception of Shay (the Assassin-turned-Templar) who wants to prevent his former brothers from possessing the Apples of Eden.

5.3. Confession

In the majority of the assassinations that trigger the memory corridor, a discussion between the Assassin and his target takes place, and/or a confession in which the victim either pleads innocence, ignorance, or steadfast belief in the Templar's goals. In the cases of Altaïr (AC), Ezio (AC2, ACB, ACRe), and the Frye twins (ACU), the discussion/confession is calm and 'reasonable': the Assassin and his target exchange motives for their own choices and behavior, sometimes causing the Assassin to doubt his own actions (AC1) or the victim to come to terms with his.

In the cases of Connor (AC4), Edward (AC4), Shay (ACRo), and Bayek (ACO), the exchanges are often far more violent: the Assassin and his target(s) argue bitterly, shouting to each other, disagree with each other, and constantly belittle each other. In the case of ACU, the memory corridor set-up is slightly different than in the other instalments. When Arno assassinates a target, flashbacks from the target's life are shown, which allow both Arno and the player to understand the target's motives, and to obtain insight into the true nature of past events.

5.4. Closing the Eyes

The closing of a dead person's eyes is an old ritual known in many parts of the world as part of wider ceremonies of death and dying. It is also used in the *Assassin's Creed* series, especially as a token of respect to the deceased (as Mario explains to Ezio). In a minority of the assassinations, the killer does not close the eyes of his victims. Even Ezio hesitates, even though Mario explicitly instructs him to do so. There are eight victims whose eyes are closed by their assassins throughout the primary instalments of the series: Vieri (by Mario, AC2); four out of seven assassinations in ACB (by Ezio); Leandros (by Ezio, ACRe); John Pitcairn (by Connor, AC3); and El Tiburón (by Edward, AC4). In three instances, the protagonist is seen closing the eyes of fallen comrades: Bartolomeo's mercenary (by Ezio, AC2); Yusuf Tazim (by Ezio, ACRe); and George Monroe (by Shay, ACRo).

5.5. Collecting of Blood

The collecting of blood occurs in AC (9 out of 10 assassinations), ACS (11 out of 12 assassinations) and—partially—in ACO (7 out of 12 assassinations). Altaïr (AC1) collects the blood of his fallen victim by sweeping a white feather over their cut throat, and then putting it into his pocket. The same act does not occur again until the penultimate instalment of the series, ACS. Evie and Jacob Frye take the blood of their slain victims by wiping a white handkerchief over the victim's open throat, and putting this into their suits too.

Before the release of ACO in 2017, the use of a feather (AC1) is a reference to the name of the main fortress of the Nizaris in Persia, called Alamut, which possibly means 'eagle's nest'. Other in-game references are 'eagle vision', the ability of certain Assassins to 'scan' the environment, and 'eagle points', the tops of tall buildings, mountains, and trees where the Assassins scout the perimeters of designated areas.

In ACO, it becomes clear that the feather 'originally' stems from the Egyptian idea of the weighing of the soul before entering the afterlife. The feather of the Egyptian god Ma'at is used as a counterweight to determine the moral value of the individual soul (Allen 2004, pp. 115–16). The Assassin touches his or her own head before touching the body of the target, which dissolves into a cloud of black dots. The rationale behind this ritual is probably that the Assassin asks Ma'at not to 'weigh' the soul of his victims against him when it is his own turn to enter the underworld.

5.6. The Ritual Prayer

The closing part of the assassination ritual is the utterance of a short religious phrase. In the case of Altaïr, three victims are said to 'be at peace (now)' or to 'rest now'. In Ezio's case, he mostly uses the Latin phrase *Requiescat in pace*, 'Rest in peace', although Ezio is not as consistent in using this phrase later in his life (ACRe). Arno uses 'Rest in peace' once (ACU), while Evie Frye jokingly says 'Rest in peace' as she throws her unwanted ball gown into the water (ACS).

In ACO, *Requiescat in pace* is heard again only after the last assassination (by Aya), of Julius Caesar himself. Other 'prayers' also appear in ACO, all connected to Egyptian mythology. Bayek uses 'May the Hidden One Greet you; the Lord of the Duat awaits' twice, and 'Apap, devour your fetid heart' once. The 'Hidden One' and 'the Lord of the Duat' are both references to Osiris, the lord of the underworld in Egyptian mythology. Again, as was the case with the feather, the Assassin pleads to the gods to judge his victim for his crimes, but not his executioner.

Sometimes, especially in AC1, AC2, ACB, and AC3, the short prayer is preceded by a longer quote, in Ezio's case in Italian, the content of which is usually closely connected to the victim's life, and to the reasons why he had to die. For example: 'Your schemes are at an end' (Altaïr, AC1); 'Meglio essere felici in questa vita che aspirare a esserlo nella prossima [Better to be content in this life, than aspire to it in the next]' (Ezio, AC2); 'Che tu sia pari nella morte. [May you be equal in death]' (Ezio, ACB) and 'Your words may have been sincere, but that does not make them true' (Connor, AC3).

6. Welcome, Initiate. The Gamer as Initiate

Usually, it is the game's protagonist, an Assassin (sometimes a Templar), who is initiated into the Brotherhood (or the Order). In two cases however, the initiation is transferred from an in-game ritual to a ritual on the level of the player himself. Once, the player is given the opportunity to join the Order (ACRo), and on another occasion to join the Brotherhood (ACU/ACS). This is made possible by the complex narratological structures Ubisoft uses in the series (see: Table 2).

In ACRo, the narratological structure provides the following sequence: the player, through his game device, controls a nameless Abstergo employee, who—in turn—controls the historical Assassin Shay Cormac through the in-game Helix Animus. (The same structure can also be found in AC4). At the end of ACRo, the nameless employee is asked to join the Order Melanie offers him the ring, asking:

> Join us, and a bright future will be all yours. Refuse ...

While the outcome of the choice is not shown (the end credits are screened), acceptance is the most likely outcome, since a refusal would probably result in the employee's swift death. But because of the complex narratological structure of ACRo, it is not only 'numbskull' who is asked to join the Order, but the player, too, is offered this choice. Since it is the player who makes the actual choices in the game, it is the gamer who ultimately has to decide whether or not to 'join' the Order.

This 'capacity' of the player of *Assassin's Creed* is also played out in ACU and ACS, but then with regard to the Brotherhood. The initial double narratological structure is broken by both ACU and ACS in this sense that the player's real-life gaming device and the in-game Helix Animus narratologically merge into a single device. When the player of ACU and ACS starts the game, the Abstergo logo is shown, as well as that of the Helix cloud service. The screen reads: 'Developed by Abstergo; powered by the Animus'. No contemporary Assassin of Templar is shown or used: the player directly controls the historical protagonist. The player is directly using the Helix Animus.

At the beginning of ACU, the player is confronted with a brief narrative about the arrest and death (at the stake) of Jacques de Molay (1244–1314), the historical last grand master of the Templar Order. After the player has finished this little section of the game, which is clearly told from a Templar point of view, an electronic interference appears across the screen of the gaming device (the Helix Animus).

An unknown woman is shown sitting behind a large computer desk communicating with other unseen characters (although these can be identified by hardcore fans of the series as Desmond's fellow Assassins Shaun Hastings and Rebecca Crane). The woman identifies herself by the codename 'Bishop', asking the player to 'join' the Brotherhood by pressing the designated key on the game device/Helix Animus.

> Hey there ... This is probably disorienting, so I'll be brief. I'm Bishop, not my real name obviously, but that's as much as you'll get today. (...) These guys [Templars] (...) have their fingers in countless corporations, governments, and media outlets, and NGOs, but now they want control over history itself. If that doesn't frighten you, it should. But we're here to stop them. And I need your help. (...) This is where you come in. We are confident that you are up to the task. (...) Are you willing to take up the fight and join us? (...) By pressing "play" you'll be joining the Assassins. If you want to fight the Templar menace, or if you're willing to save civilization from Abstergo's clutches, press "play". [When the "play" button is pressed] Sit back and ready yourself for the truth.

The game does not proceed if the player does not press the 'play' button, and Bishop will wait indefinitely for the player to answer her question. By pressing 'play', the player indicates (at least in the reality of the game) that he is willing to join the Brotherhood in its fight against the Templars. Bishop shows the 'Initiate', as she subsequently calls the player, the truth behind the Abstergo façade. In the rest of the game, the player/Initiate 'works' for the Brotherhood by uncovering the life of the historical Assassin of the French Revolution, Arno.

This narratological frame in which the real-life gamer is 'initiated' into the in-game Brotherhood, is maintained in ACU (but not in ACO, where the old 'double' frame is re-installed). At the start of ACU, the player is welcomed once more by the screen text 'developed by Abstergo; powered by the Animus', again suggesting the merging of the in-game device (Helix Animus) and the real-life game device the player is actually using to play the game. The screen is then blurred by static interference and the logo of the Assassin Brotherhood is shown, with the text 'welcome, Initiate'.

Bishop is seen again talking to the player, and her first words are, 'Hello, Initiate'. The player is then sent to Victorian London, but without being asked by Bishop to pledge his or her alliance (as was the case in ACU), to re-live the lives of the historical Assassins Jacob and Evie Frye. The player does not have to choose, as if Bishop (and the Brotherhood) already know what to think of her or him, narratologically connecting ACU and ACS to each other.

Ultimately, of course it is the player who decides in the game. The assassinations are carried out by means of the player's direct input (pushing the 'assassinate' button), while the (historical) initiations are indirectly triggered by the player (by reaching a certain point within the game's narrative).

7. Conclusions

In this article, I have inventoried the occurrences of three fictional rituals in the *Assassin's Creed* series: the initiation rituals of the Assassin Brotherhood and the Templar Order, and the Brotherhood's assassination rituals. I have constructed a hypothetical and theoretical 'ideal' or 'full-fledged' ritual for each of these three cases, based on the numerous and often varied occurrences within the different instalments of the game series.

The initiation ritual of the Brotherhood proceeds as follows: (1) the initiate is ritually questioned about his knowledge of and loyalty to the Assassin's Creed; (2) the initiate's left ring finger is branded by fire; and (3) the initiate performs a leap of faith. The ceremony is presided over by the branch's mentor in the presence of other high-ranking Assassins and other initiates.

The Templar equivalent proceeds as follows: (1) the initiate is ritually questioned about his knowledge of and loyalty to the Templars' goals; (2) the initiate is offered a Templar ring, which has to be worn on the right ring finger; (3) the 'Father of Understanding' phrase is uttered. The Templar ritual is presided over by the grand master of the rite and witnessed by other high-ranking Templars, but not by other initiates.

The assassinations carried out by the Brotherhood are accompanied by rituals too: (1) the assassin holds his victim; (2) last words are exchanged; (3) the victim's eyes are closed; (4) a sample of the victim's blood is collected; and (5) a short prayer is said, usually a variation of 'rest in peace'.

Whereas the initiation rituals clearly mark the initiate's transition from the outside world to the confined group of the Brotherhood, the Assassins' assassination rituals are more or less safeguards to make sure that the killings are not due to personal dislike or vengeance, but to cold and calculated long-term political plans. It is interesting to note that the Order does not have a comparable ritual, although it carries out almost as many assassinations as the Assassins.

Ubisoft, it appears, uses the three rituals in its *Assassin's Creed* series for four purposes, (1) creatively, to add a sense of suspense and mysticism to both groups, but especially to the Assassins; (2) morally, to imply that the Templars are more prone to assassinating people for personal motives than the Assassins are; (3) socially, to mark the distance between the members of the Brotherhood/Order and the rest of the world, and (4) epistemologically, to mark the difference between those how know the true nature of human existence and evolution (the initiated), and the rest of the 'people', who do not have this knowledge.

Ubisoft makes this even more compelling to the player by merging the narratological layers of the real-life gaming device and the in-game device (Animus), thus successfully involving *and initiating* the player of the series in initiation into Brotherhood or Order. In a certain way, playing the games becomes a ritual practice in itself.

Conflicts of Interest: The author declares no conflict of interest.

Appendix A

Table A1. Assassinations. Overview of all assassinations performed in the p rimary games of the *Assassin's Creed* series. The list includes (1) all assassinations that triggered the Animus' memory corridor; (2) high profile assassinations that did not trigger the memory corridor; and (3) allies to whom the same rites are applied.

	Holding of Target	Closing of Eyes	Collecting of Blood	Memory Corridor	Ritual Utterance
AC1 (performed by Altair)					
Tamir	y	n	y	y	Be at peace. (a)
Garnier	y	n	y	y	...
Talal	y	n	y	y	...
Abu'l Nuqoud	y	n	y	y	Be at peace now.
William of Montferrat	y	n	y	y	Rest now.
Majd Addin	y	n	y	y	...
Jubair	y	n	y	y	...
Sibrand	y	n	y	y	...
Robert de Sable	y	n	y	y	...
Al Mualim	y	n	n	y	...
(a) The collecting of blood is always done with afeather.					
AC2 (performed by Ezio)					
Uberto Alberti	y	n	n	y	
Vieri de' Pazzi	n	y	n	y	Requiescat in pace. (a)
Francesco de' Pazzi	y	n	n	y	Requiescat in pace.
Bernardo Baroncelli	y	n	n	y	Requiescat in pace.
Antonio Maffei	y	n	n	y	Requiescat in pace.
Francesco Salviati	y	n	n	y	Requiescat in pace.
Stefano da Bagnone	y	n	n	y	Requiescat in pace.
Jacopo de' Pazzi	y	n	n	y	Requiescat in pace. (b)
Emilio Barbarigo	y	n	n	y	Requiescat in pace.
Carlo Grimaldi	y	n	n	y	Requiescat in pace.
Marco Barbarigo	y	n	n	y	Requiescat in pace.
Silvio Barbarigo; Dante Moro	n	n	n	y	Requiescat in pace.
Ludovico Orsi	y	n	n	y	Requiescat in pace.
Checco Orsi	y	n	n	y	Requiescat in pace.
The nobleman	y	n	n	y	Requiescat in pace.
The preacher	y	n	n	y	Requiescat in pace.
The priest	y	n	n	y	Requiescat in pace.
The painter	y	n	n	y	Requiescat in pace.
The merchant	y	n	n	y	Requiescat in pace.
The farmer	y	n	n	y	Requiescat in pace.
The condottiero	y	n	n	y	Requiescat in pace.
The guard captain	y	n	n	y	Requiescat in pace.
The doctor	y	n	n	y	Requiescat in pace.
Girolamo Savonarola	y	n	n	y	Requiescat in pace.
Rodrigo Borgia (1st attempt)	y	n	n	y	Requiescat in pace, you bastard. (c)
Rodrigo Borgia (2nd attempt)	y	n	n	y	Requiescat in pace. (d)
(allies)					
Bartolomeo's mercenary	n	y	n	n	Requiescat in pace.
(a) Closing of eyes and prayer performed by Mario.					
(b) Jacopo does not speak during the memory corridor.					
(c) Assassination is interrupted.					
(d) Ezio lets Rodrigo live.					
ACB (performed by Ezio)					
Il Carnefice	y	y	n	y	Requiescat in pace. (a)
Malfatto (by apprentice)	y	n	n	y	Requiescat in pace. (a)(b)
Silvestro Sabbatini (by apprentice)	y	y	n	y	Requiescat in pace.
Juan Borgia the Elder	y	y	n	y	Requiescat in pace.
Octavian de Valois	y	y	n	y	Requiescat in pace.
Micheletto Corella	y	n	n	y	... (c)
Cesare Borgia	y	n	n	y	Requiescat in pace. (d)
(a) Il Carnefice and Malfatto do not speak during the memory corridor.					
(b) Closing of eyes prevented by doctor's mask.					
(c) Micheletto is spared by Ezio.					
(d) Cesare is thrown from wall by Ezio.					

Table A1. *Cont.*

	Holding of Target	Closing of Eyes	Collecting of Blood	Memory Corridor	Ritual Utterance
ACRe (performed by Altaïr)					
Haras	n	n	n	y	...
Abbas	n	n	n	y	...
(performed by Ezio)					
Leandros	n	y	n	y	Requiescat in pace, bastardo. (a)
Vali cel Tradat (by apprentice)	y	n	n	y	Peace be with you. (b)
Tarik Barleti	y	n	n	y	... (c)
Shahkulu	n	n	n	y/n	... (d)
Manuel Palaiologos	n	n	n	y	...
(allies)					
Yusuf Tazim	n	y	n	n	Requiescat in pace.
Altaïr	n	n	n	n	Requiescat in pace.
(a) Leandros is thrown back in anger by Ezio.					
(b) All rituals are performed by the apprentice.					
(c) Holding only commences after Ezio's insight.					
(d) Shahkulu's assassination is interrupted.					
AC3 (performed by Haytham)					
Miko	n	n	n	n	...
Louis Mills	n	n	n	n	...
Cutter	n	n	n	n	...
Edward Braddock	n	n	n	y	...
(performed by Connor)					
William Johnson	n	n	n	y	...
John Pitcairn	y	y	n	y	...
Thomas Hickey	n	n	n	y	...
Benjamin Church	n	n	n	y	...
Kanen'tó:kon	n	n	n	y	...
Haytham Kenway	n	n	n	y	...
Charles Lee	n	n	n	n	...
(performed by Desmond)					
Daniel Cross	n	n	n	n	... (a)
Warren Vidic	n	n	n	n	... (a) (b)
(a) No memory corridor can be formed because target is not generated by the Animus.					
(b) Desmond kills Warren by mind-controlling a guard through the Apple.					
AC4 (performed Edward)					
Duncan Walpole	n	n	n	n	...
Julien du Casse	n	n	n	y	...
Laurens Prins	n	n	n	y	...
Peter Chamberlain	n	n	n	y	...
Charles Vane	n	n	n	y	... (a)
Josiah Burgess; John Cockram	n	n	n	y	...
Benjamin Hornigold	n	n	n	y	...
Woodes Rogers	n	n	n	y	... (b)
Bartholomew Roberts	n	n	n	y	... (c)
El Tiburón	n	y	n	y	... (d)
Laureano de Torres y Ayala	n	n	n	y	...
(a) Charles is spared by Edward.					
(b) Woodes is spared by Edward.					
(c) Bartholomew's corpse is taken away by Edward.					
(d) El Tiburón's eyes are closed by Edward out of respect.					
ACRo (performed by Shay as an Assassin)					
Lawrence Washington	n	n	n	y	...
Samuel Smith	n	n	n	y	...
James Wardrop	n	n	n	y	...
(performed by Shay as a Templar)					
Le Chasseur	n	n	n	y	...
Kesegowaase	n	n	n	y	...
Adéwalé	n	n	n	y	... (a)
Hope Jensen	n	n	n	y	...
Louis-Joseph Gaultier	n	n	n	y	... (b)
Liam O'Brien	n	n	n	y	... (c)
Charles Dorian	n	n	n	y	...
(allies)					
George Monroe	y	y	n	n	...
(a) Haytham joins Shay in the memory corridor.					
(b) Shay throws Louis overboard in the memory corridor.					
(c) Shay puts Liam's hood in place after he dies.					

Table A1. *Cont.*

	Holding of Target	Closing of Eyes	Collecting of Blood	Memory Corridor	Ritual Utterance
ACU (performed by Arno)					
Charles Gabriel Sivert	n	n	n	y	... (a)
Roi des Thunes	n	n	n	y	... (a)
Chrétien Lafrenière	n	n	n	y	... (a)
Pierre Bellec	n	y	n	y	Rest in peace.
Frédéric Rouille	n	n	n	y	... (a)
Marie Lévesque	n	n	n	y	...
Louis-Michel le Peletier	n	n	n	y	...
Aloys la Touche	n	n	n	y	...
François-Thomas Germain	y	n	n	y	... (b)
(a) The assassinations trigger relived memories from targets within memory corridor instead of a conversation.					
(b) François is the only target with whom Arno has a conversation in the memory corridor.					
ACS (performed by Evie)					
David Brewster	y	n	y	y	... (a)
Lucy Thorne	y	n	y	y	...
(the dress)	n	n	n	n	Requescat in pace. (b)
(performed by Jacob)					
Rupert Ferris	y	n	y	y	...
John Elliotson	y	n	y	y	...
Malcolm Millner	y	n	n	y	...
Pearl Attaway	y	n	y	y	...
Philip Twopenny	n	n	y	y	...
James Brudenell	n	n	y	y	...
Maxwell Roth	y	n	y	y	... (c)
(performed by Jacob and Evie)	n	n	y	y	.
Crawford Starrick	n	n	y	y	... (d)
(a) The collecting of the with ablood is done by handkerchief.					
(b) Evie repeats old phrase from Ezio after throwing her dress away.					
(c) Maxwell kisses Arno in the memory corridor.					
(d) After Crawford's assassination, both Evie and Jacob collect his blood.					
ACO (performed by Bayek)					
Rudjek	n	n	n	n	...
Medunamun	n	n	n	y	May the Hidden One greet you. The lord of the Duat awaits.
Gennadios	n	n	y/n	y	Ditto. (a)
Eudoros	n	n	y/n	y	Son of Apep, The lord of the Duat awaits.
Taharqa	n	n	y/n	y	...
Khaliset	n	n	n	y	...
Hetepi	n	n	y/n	y	I have my gods, now face yours.
Berenike	n	n	n	y	...
Pothinus	n	n	y/n	y	...
Flavius	n	n	y/n	y	... (b)
(performed by Aya)					
Septimius	n	n	y	y	May Apep devour your fetid heart. (c)
Julius Caesar	y	n	n	y	Requiescat in pace, Caesar. (d)
(a) The target is touched by an eagle's feather (no blood).					
(b) Khemu handles the feather.					
(c) Aya is the first to collect the blood of her target using a feather.					
(d) The feather is used to open Caesar's eyes in the memory corridor.					

References

Digital Games

Ubisoft Montreal. 2007. *Assassin's Creed*. Rennes: Ubisoft Montreal.

Ubisoft Montreal. 2009. *Assassin's Creed II*. Rennes: Ubisoft Montreal.

Ubisoft Montreal. 2010. *Assassin's Creed: Brotherhood*. Rennes: Ubisoft Montreal.

Ubisoft Montreal. 2011. *Assassin's Creed: Revelations*. Rennes: Ubisoft Montreal.

Ubisoft Montreal. 2012. *Assassin's Creed III*. Rennes: Ubisoft Montreal.

Ubisoft Montreal. 2013a. *Assassin's Creed IV: Black Flag*. Rennes: Ubisoft Montreal.

Ubisoft Montreal. 2013b. *Assassin's Creed Rogue*. Rennes: Ubisoft Sopfia.

Ubisoft Montreal. 2014. *Assassin's Creed Unity*. Rennes: Ubisoft Montreal.

Ubisoft Montreal. 2015. *Assassin's Creed Syndicate*. Rennes: Ubisoft Quebec.

Ubisoft Montreal. 2017. *Assassin's Creed Origins*. Rennes: Ubisoft Montreal.

Secondary Sources

Allen, James P. 2004. *Middle Egyptian. An Introduction to the Language and Culture of Hieroglyphs*. Cambridge: Cambridge University Press.

Baigent, Michael, Richard Leigh, and Henry Lincoln. 1982. *The Holy Blood and the Holy Grail*. London: Jonathan Cape.

Bartlett, Wayne B. 2011. *The Assassins. The Story of Islam's Medieval Secret Sect*. Sutton: Stroud.

Bosman, Frank. 2016a. The Word Has Become Game: Researching Religion in Digital Games. *Online-Heidelberg Journal of Religions on the Internet* 11: 28–45.

Bosman, Frank. 2016b. Nothing is true, everything is permitted. The portrayal of the Nizari Isma'ilis in the Assassin's Creed game series. *Online-Heidelberg Journal of Religions on the Internet* 10: 6–26.

Bosman, Frank. 2016c. The poor carpenter. Reinterpreting Christian Mythology in the Assassin's Creed Game Series. *Gamenvironments* 4: 61–87.

Bosman, Frank. 2018. Never compromise the brotherhood. Contrasting religious brotherhoods and orders. The case of the Assassin's Creed series. *E.T. Studies*. forthcoming.

Bremmer, Jan, ed. 2007. Human sacrifice. A brief introduction. In *The Strange World of Human Sacrifice*. Leuven: Peeters, pp. 1–8.

Brown, Dan. 2003. *The Da Vinci Code*. New York: Doubleday.

Daftary, Farhad. 1994. *The Assassin Legends. Myths of the Isma'ilis*. New York: I. B. Tauris.

Daftary, Farhad. 1998. *A Short History of the Ismailis. Traditions of a Muslim Community*. Princeton: M. Wiener.

Duyndam, Joachim, Anne-Marie Korte, and Marcel Poorthuis, eds. 2017. Sacrifice in modernity. Community, ritual, identity. In *Sacrifice in Modernity: Community, Ritual, Identity. From Nationalism and Nonviolence to Health Care and Harry Potter*. Leiden: Brill, pp. 3–16.

Eliade, Mircea. 1975. *Rites and Symbols of Initiation*. New York: Harper & Row.

Feder, Kenneth. 2002. Ancient Astronauts. In *The Skeptic Encyclopedia of Pseudoscience*. Edited by Michael Schemer. Santa Barbara: ABC-CLIO, vol. 1, pp. 17–22.

Haag, Michael. 2009. *The Templars. History & Myths*. London: Profile.

Heidbrink, Simone, Tobias Knoll, and Jan Wysocki. 2015. Venturing into the Unknown (?) Method(olog)ical Reflections on Religion and Digital Games, Gamers and Gaming. *Online-Heidelberg Journal of Religions on the Internet* 7: 68–71.

Hüsken, Ute, ed. 2007. Ritual dynamics and ritual failure. In *When Rituals Go Wrong. Mistakes, Failures and the Dynamics of Ritual*. Leiden: Brill, pp. 337–65.

Mirza, Nasseh Ahmad. 1997. *Syrian Ismailism. The Ever Living Line of the Imamate, AD 1100–1260*. Richmond: Curzon.

Scurr, Ruth. 2014. *Fatal Purity. Robespierre and the French Revolution*. New York: Henry Holt.

Van Gennep, Arnold. 1909. *Les Rites de Passage*. Paris: Nourry.

Von Däniken, Erich. 1969. *Chariots of the Gods? Unsolved Mysteries of the Past*. New York: Putnam.

religions

Article

Lamòling Bèaka: Immanence, Rituals, and Sacred Objects in an Unwritten Legend in Alor

Francesco Perono Cacciafoco and **Francesco Cavallaro** *

Linguistics and Multilingual Studies, School of Humanities, Nanyang Technological University, Singapore 637332, Singapore; fcacciafoco@ntu.edu.sg
* Correspondence: cfcavallaro@ntu.edu.sg; Tel.: +65-65921710

Received: 8 June 2018; Accepted: 4 July 2018; Published: 7 July 2018

Abstract: This paper recounts a parallel story of the *Lamòling* myth. The original analysis of the legend addressed the relationship between two gods, *Lamòling* and *Lahatàla*, from the Abui traditional religion. The myth evolved from ancestral times to the arrival of Christianity in Alor, with the resultant association of the 'bad' god as a demon and, finally, as the devil. This paper completes the myth as handed down from traditional 'owners' of the narrative and storytellers by telling a parallel version centered around an Abui 'prophet', Fanny, who was the only person able to travel to *Lamòling Bèaka*, 'the land of the *Lamòling* gods/servants'. We also focus on a number of sacred objects and rituals associated with this religious myth and on their symbolic meaning for the Abui. This account tells a different version of the killing and eating of an Abui child by these gods/supernatural entities and of how Fanny came upon the gruesome feast. The paradoxical absence of *Lamòling* in this version of the myth depicts him as an immanent being, pervading and sustaining all that is real and created in nature, existing anywhere and nowhere at the same time.

Keywords: Abui; Alor; Lamòling; Alor-Pantar Archipelago; oral legends and myths; traditional religions

1. Introduction

This paper presents a parallel version and, therefore, a completion of an Abui oral legend, the *Lamòling* founding myth. The original version was analysed (Perono Cacciafoco and Cavallaro 2017) in the context of it being the origin and explanation for a number of toponyms and micro-toponyms still existing in the Abui territory on the island of Alor (South-East Indonesia, Alor-Pantar Archipelago) shown in Figure 1. Right up to today, the Abui believe that the tale of *Lamòling* is true and they claim that it is a historical episode dating to before the arrival of the Portuguese and Dutch colonizers and, therefore, concurrent with the arrival of Christianity. In this article, besides the reconstruction of a parallel (still unpublished) version of the legend, we focus on a number of sacred objects and rituals associated with this religious myth and on their symbolic meaning for the Abui.

Abui (ISO 639-3: abz; Glottolog: abui1241) is a Papuan language (Trans-New Guinea family, Alor-Pantar sub-family) spoken by around 17,000 speakers in the central part of Alor, South-East Indonesia, Timor area (Kratochvil 2007; Klamer 2014, pp. 5–53). The local name for the language is *Abui tangà*, which literally means 'language of the mountain'. The Alor-Pantar languages are a set of related Papuan languages spoken on a number of islands in the Alor Archipelago (Figure 2).

Figure 1. Location of Alor (Source: CartoGIS Services, College of Asia and the Pacific, The Australian National University).

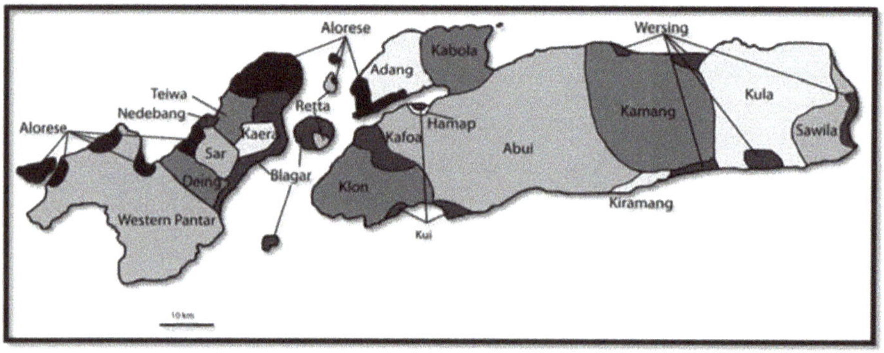

Figure 2. A linguistic map of the island of Alor and its neighbour Pantar (Source: Robinson 2015, p. 20).

2. Oral Traditions among the Abui

The legend of *Lamòling* was recorded and reconstructed during a period of language documentation fieldwork conducted in Alor by one of the authors (1 June 2015–10 June 2015). The main Abui villages involved in this linguistic investigation are *Takalelàng* and *Takpàla*, located in the Northern coastal area of Alor. Six other places, villages and areas of those villages, are involved in the story (Perono Cacciafoco and Cavallaro 2017, p. 59). The tale was told by a number of local storytellers. The story, in all its versions, was recounted in Abui and translated with the help of local informants. Traditionally, among the Abui, only the 'owner' of a story knows the full version and is authorized to tell it in its entirety, both to the local 'audience' and to individuals not belonging to the community. Other people who have heard the story from the 'owner' are allowed to recount it, but are only authorized to tell an abridged version of it and not the full story or specific details. The story and the plot of the story are not taboo in themselves.

This custom is akin to the anthropological concept of the 'Big Man' (Sahlins 1963). The similarities between the 'Big Man' and the Abui story owner lie in the fact that, for the Abui, the owner of the story is also the 'moral owner' of all the land and villages that are part of the story. So, for example, if a man wants to marry a woman from another village, and both the villages are included in a story, they need to ask permission to wed from the owner of the story. Or, if some people want to build a house in one of the villages in the story, then they have to ask permission to do so from the owner of the story. A notable example of this notion of the 'ownership' of oral traditional stories can be seen in the Abui history of the recounting of the giant snake, *Mon Mot*, another founding myth belonging to the Abui people. Researchers carrying out language documentation fieldwork in Alor in 2003 first reported the story of *Mon Mot* as it was narrated by Anderias Padafani, and thought it was the complete version. However, over time, they came to be aware of the practice of the 'ownership' of the oral stories (or the 'Big Man' tradition) among the Abui and realized that the story they had was not the full version of the original legend. It took researchers 11 years to finally track down the true owner of the story, Mansur Maata (Kratochvíl and Delpada 2008, pp. 68–77).

We do not know who the original owner of any Abui story was. These stories are ancient. We assume that the original, first owner may be the one who first told or 'invented' the story. It may also have been someone involved in the 'real events' of the story, since, generally, a legend is not a completely invented tale, but derives from possibly real and very ancient events (Tangherlini 1990, pp. 371–90). The next owner of a story is chosen by the previous owner. The transmission is not necessarily within the family of the owner. The owner is chosen because of her/his moral qualities and because of her/his potential as a moral leader. Of course, the owner can be also a child of the previous owner, but there may not be a 'family lineage' in the ownership.

The Abui 'owner' of the original *Lamòling* myth (the widespread, complete, version) is Markus Lema, connected with the Delpada family, which shares and passes down that version generation by generation. Moreover, the 'owner' of the parallel version (the 'immanent' one) has always been a member of the Delpada family, with the current owner being Martinus Delpada.

Like for most indigenous oral rituals and cults, there are no written records of Abui traditional religion. Unlike, among others, Christianity and Islam, which have records dating back hundreds of years, the Abui only have songs, sayings, proverbs, and stories passed down as oral traditions generation by generation, over centuries. One of the aims of the present paper is, indeed, to preserve this noteworthy (and threatened) part of the Abui tradition and oral culture.

Due to the complex 'ownership' system among the Abui, that is, the fact that only the true 'owner' of the story can tell it in its entirety, with all the details, and with all the names of characters and places, the legend of *Lamòling* exhibits various inconsistencies and different 'chronological' layers and developments that compose a sort of 'stratigraphy of the myth' (Perono Cacciafoco and Cavallaro 2017, pp. 52–53 and 58). However, these 'anomalies' in the *fabula* of the legend do not detract from the story itself, but authenticate it as a real and coherent oral tradition. Contradictions and inconsistencies (Lord 1938), or variations and embellishments (Finnegan 1992), have been an accepted and often debated characteristic of oral traditions all over the world and in different diachronic contexts, from the Homeric *epos* to the oral myths of Africa and Australian Aboriginal people. Indeed, a 'fixed' story can only be found in written texts and, even then (both in oral traditions 'standardized' by being transcribed at a specific point in time and in stories originally written), examples of contradictions and inconsistencies are not rare (Lord 1938). Foley (1991) takes this one step further and argues that what readers of a text may consider gaps in a story as flaws are not flaws in the context of the orally transmitted stories: "For if we understand that a literary reception of an oral traditional text (whether unambiguously oral or oral-derived) must by its very nature fail to bridge all of the gaps of indeterminacy in anything approaching a way faithful to the aesthetic reality of the work, then we shall see that calling these gaps 'flaws' is itself a mistake" (p. 47).

3. The *Lamòling* Myth

The *Lamòling* legend is a founding myth (Campbell 1976, 1990) centred on the opposition, or dichotomy, between the ancient (originally animistic) primordial god, *Lamòling*, who was also seen as a friend by the Abui people, and the 'new' god *Lahatàla*, who ultimately usurped *Lamòling*'s place at the head of Abui's hierarchy of gods and, eventually, became the personification of the God of the 'new' Abui Christian faith (introduced by Western missionaries from around the XVI century) (Aritonang and Steenbrink 2008; Schröter 2011), the 'only and true God'. Semantically, we can see that the name *Lamòling* has gone through distinct changes, over time, in the Abui language. The name began being associated with the mightiest of local 'gods' (perhaps the 'best' of local gods and the one more connected with humans). Then, it changed slowly to refer to a 'demon'. With the arrival of the rival character in this religious dichotomy, *Lahatàla*, the 'other god' (then become 'the only and true God' of the Christian tradition), *Lamòling* became the personification of the 'devil'.

Some of the intrinsic characteristics of the figure of *Lamòling* contributed in 'making' this change. The *Lamòling* that the Abui identified with was a trickster deity, deeply connected with human beings, but also living in a dimension beyond the understanding of humans (being a god), and becoming, sometimes, a terrible punisher beyond human rationality (Perono Cacciafoco and Cavallaro 2017, pp. 51, 53, 55, 57, and 58). In this, *Lamòling* could be identified with other figures (from other religious contexts) of very important deities who were also tricksters, connected with the humans, but 'located' in a dimension oriented beyond the human understanding (a 'feature' foreshadowing the primordiality of these gods), like Dionysus/Bacchus (in Ancient Greek and Roman traditions), Loki (in Old Norse tradition), and, to some extent, Kokopelli (in Native American traditions) (Perono Cacciafoco and Cavallaro 2017, pp. 52, 55, and 58).

The original or more ancient story (its 'core', coming directly from the mythopoesis process) can be identified, therefore, in the earlier period of the tale, when *Lamòling* was the main god and had a friendly and continuous relationship with the Abui people. *Lahatàla* only makes an appearance later in the story (as a very spiritual god, living in the sky, not assuming anthropomorphous appearance, and entering the body of individuals in order to communicate with the Abui people), if we consider the story itself composed of several diachronic 'layers' (the aforementioned 'stratigraphy of the myth'). Before the arrival of Europeans (and, with them, Christianity), and in the early days of European contact, the two gods coexisted for a while, both worshiped by the Abui people (*Lamòling* as the god 'friend' of Abui people, *Lahatàla* as the transcendent and less 'humanized' god), until *Lahatàla* supplanted *Lamòling* (telling the Abui that he was 'the only and true God'—the 'Christian God'—and that the Abui people had to stop worshiping *Lamòling* and all other deities but Him). The coming of the new god represents the more modern part of the tale, foreshadowing the introduction and, then, the spread of Christianity in Alor and in the Abui community. Historically, as mentioned, this happened with the arrival of the Portuguese and Dutch colonizers and their missionaries, beginning from the XVI century (Aritonang and Steenbrink 2008, especially Chapter 4). To this day, the Abui are still mostly Christian.

The story goes that *Lamòling* and the Abui people lived often together side-by-side. The ancestral god seemed to prefer living among the humans over in the supernatural world. *Lamòling* spent his time with the Abui people and shared their everyday life events. He danced with them. He dined with them and taught them many things, including arts and crafts, introducing technology and music to them. The Abui people had a sacred place for them to meet with *Lamòling*, called *Karilìk*. During the meetings with the god, the Abui people danced a ritual dance, called *lego lego* dance (discussed below). At that time and for a long time, *Lamòling* was seen as a benevolent god. However, something happened to change this relationship. *Lamòling* showed a dark side of his character that the Abui were not aware of (the 'irrational' side proper of atavistic deities like the aforementioned Dionysus and Loki). This happened at the time that *Lahatàla*, the 'alternative' and 'transcendent' god, made his appearance. At that time, *Lahatàla* lived in the sky, being a more metaphysical presence than *Lamòling*. At one point, though, *Lahatàla* started to meet the Abui people more and more often, becoming part of their lives, without ever showing himself, but always entering the bodies of people and speaking to the Abui through them. The two gods lived side-by-side, apparently peacefully. However, the change in relationship between the Abui and *Lahatàla* became a source of jealousy for *Lamòling*.

One characteristic of *Lamòling* was that he could take on animalistic and anthropomorphic shapes. The original animal-appearance of *Lamòling* was that of a python, characterizing him as a primordial chthonic god. Indeed, he could change himself into different animals, especially the snake, a very typical and widespread hypostasis of chthonic deities, or even a human being. He had a number of minor deities as his servants, who could also do the same, although, not being as powerful as he was, they were able to assume only shapes of various animals. *Lahatàla*, instead, was more of a pure spirit, a transcendent god who did not want to show himself and used to enter human bodies of local individuals in order to talk to the Abui only for very important communications. We are not aware of the Abui believing in 'spirit possession' (Laycock 2015). There are no traces of that in other records or tales that we have come across. In this case, *Lahatàla* enters the bodies of people merely to talk, and only on special occasions (he just 'talks' through them and does not 'force' them into any other act). It is difficult, therefore, to see this aspect as a spirit possession in a classical form. It seems merely a way for *Lahatàla* to 'contact' the Abui.

One day, the Abui people organised a party to celebrate both *Lamòling* and *Lahatàla* and their valuable friendship with the humans. The gods and lesser gods were all present, and they all drank and danced together (all but *Lahatàla*, who was attending the party as a transcendent spirit). The story tells how, sometime during this party, *Lahatàla* entered the body of a woman and told the Abui people that *Lamòling* was not a good god and that they would have had to end their relationship with him. No Abui would have to worship *Lamòling* anymore. He instructed them that *Karilìk* would become the sacred place only for him and used for his meetings with the Abui people only, excluding *Lamòling*. He also told them that he would remain with them forever as their 'only and true God' (the Biblical references of this part of the story are evident). The Abui people were very impressed by the power of *Lahatàla* and accepted his 'conditions'. However, *Lamòling* found out or heard of this conversation and he was not happy, even if he pretended that nothing had happened.

As the evening unfolded, something terrible transpired. An Abui child went missing. The reason why is not apparent. The story tells of a very jealous *Lamòling* out for revenge on what he deemed a betrayal by the Abui people. The Abui people, naively, had no reason to think anything sinister had happened because of the party and went looking for the missing child, thinking it was lost on the way to the village. Their search took them from the very steep hill where *Takalelàng* and *Takpàla* are located towards the coast. On the way to the coast, a group of searchers passed through a place normally used by *Lamòling* to rest or meet with the Abui people on some occasions. At that time, that place did not have a name, since it was not properly a 'specific' place, but just an 'intermediate point' on the road between the villages and the coast. Upon reaching the place, the Abui met some of *Lamòling*'s servants who were in animalistic form. These servants invited the Abui to join them for dinner. On sitting down for supper, the Abui were horrified to see that the food offered to them was actually the dismembered body of the missing child, including the head, which was placed in the middle of the table. Being mere mortals and surrounded by minor deities, they could do nothing. They partook of the food offered, but did not eat the meat. When they took their leave, they asked whether they could take the head of the child back to the villages to eat later, cooked with potato leaves, and to share with the other Abui people. They were given the head quite readily, which they took back to the villages. From that day on, that place, where the gruesome dinner took place, was known as *Lamòling Bèaka, 'Lamòling* bad/cruel', and it is from that episode that it got its name.

The enraged Abui immediately began to plan their revenge. They exacted their vengeance by organising another party, to which they invited *Lamòling* and all his servants. From here, we can start to see the downward spiral of *Lamòling* from 'god' to the status of a demon with his servants as minor demons themselves. The party went on for days, with lots of food, dancing, and drinking. The plan worked, as all the demons became tired and fell asleep. The Abui people, then, locked and boarded up the house where the party took place and set it on fire. All the demons burned to death. *Lamòling*, however, was only pretending to sleep and, changing into the semblance of a pregnant woman, managed to escape.

On that day, *Lamòling* completed his descent from the status of god, to demon, to the devil. *Lahatàla*, conversely, became the 'only and true God'. The legend shows a 'vertical' passage of diachronic layers from an animistic context (with *Lamòling* and his servants as the representation of chthonic, primordial entities), to a sort of polytheistic—mainly dichotomous—context (with *Lamòling*, *Lahatàla*, and minor deities), to a monotheistic context where *Lahatàla* is the 'only and true God' (the Christian God) and the other 'original god' (*Lamòling*) has become the devil.

The roles of *Lamòling* and *Lahatàla* can be summarized as the scheme below (from Perono Cacciafoco and Cavallaro 2017, p. 58).

Lamòling

↓

Original, primordial, ancestral, atavistic, and archetypal god, with anthropomorphous appearance, very close to the mortals

↓

Demon

↓

Devil

- -

Lahatàla

↓

Originally a purely spiritual and transcendental god living in the sky, who communicated with humankind and approached humans by entering the bodies of people

↓

Good spiritual god opposed (in dichotomy) to the 'demon' *Lamòling*

↓

The 'only and true' God in Christian tradition

There are a number of slightly different versions of the story, which enrich the 'standard' plot and which are added to the 'official' version 'owned' by the Abui 'Big Man' in a juxtaposition. With the arrival of Christianity in Alor, the story became 'fixed' in the version that depicts *Lamòling* as the 'devil', and the opposition of *Lamòling* and *Lahatàla* became that of the devil versus the 'only and true God' in Christian terms.

The unpublished variant of the story we are recounting in this article is one of the more important and original versions we were able to acquire.

4. The Prophet Fanny's Story and *Lamòling Bèaka*

An Abui man called Fanny, who, according to our informants, really did exist around two generations ago, from *Takalelàng*, was said to have been able to live in two words: the real one and the supernatural one. He was the only Abui to be able to go between the two worlds freely. Fanny was recognized by the Abui people as a 'prophet' not because he was able to predict events, but because he was connected with the story of *Atèng Afèng*. This is the name of the mythically original Abui village from where, according to the Abui tradition, the Abui people first came into being. The story of this village is another sacred Abui founding myth (indeed, the myth about the ancestral origins of Abui people), and no one in the Abui community (apart from the 'owner' of the story, so far not found) is allowed to tell it in its entirety. The little details we were able to get from those that had heard the story are full of Biblical references, and the legend seems to be about a couple who gave birth to seven children (a clear reference to the seven sons of Japheth in the Bible, *Book of Genesis*), who founded the

Abui village, and all Abui are descended from them. There is no precise documentation of this story and, so far, it has been impossible to find the related storyteller/'owner'. Fanny was supposed to be the only one who knew the full story, being, in a way, the 'owner' of that sacred founding myth and a sort of 'proto-storyteller' (or 'principal storyteller') of the community. The specific word 'prophet', if applied to Fanny, could be considered 'improper'. However, the Abui define the character this way and we'll keep this term to describe him.

Fanny, indeed, was not properly a 'prophet', but a man with a pure heart and whose eyes were as innocent as those of a very young child. Most Abui use the name Fanny as a nick-name (or abbreviation) for children called Franciscus. Fanny, indeed, was named after Saint Francis of Assisi (San Francesco d'Assisi, in Italian, Sanctus Franciscus Assisiensis, in Latin, 1181–1226). Fanny is considered, in Abui folklore, as an individual able to live in both the real world and the supernatural world. He is not a 'prophet' and, much less, a shaman. His innocence and purity allow him to travel from the real world and to meet the local gods/entities in the supernatural world. In this version of the story, it is the supernatural world that goes by the name *Lamòling Bèaka*. Before the horrible and gruesome act of killing the child and eating his meat was committed, that place had no name and there were no connotations (good or bad) attached to its location. In the original version of the story, the name was given to the real physical place where the child was killed, after the fact. The place was just a nameless location between the villages of *Takpàla* and *Takalelàng* and the coast, nothing else. In this version, *Lamòling Bèaka* is also the name of the supernatural world, a parallel world accessible only through the 'gate' of pure eyes. *Lamòling Bèaka* is the land—or the 'kingdom'—of the *Lamòlings* (see below) and, at the same time, the 'entrance' of that land. These *Lamòlings* were, according to the variant of the story, supernatural creatures, beyond the human laws and understanding, substantiated by the 'soul' of *Lamòling*, a god so 'transcendent' and 'imperceptible' (but substantiating of himself all things and the creation) to become a purely immanent deity (he is nowhere, but he is in everyone and in everything, anywhere). Fanny lived with the Abui people, in the common physical world, and also in the supernatural metaphysical world, fraternizing with the supernatural beings, the *'Lamòlings'*, entities which were emanation of the *'anima mundi' Lamòling*.

This version follows the original story until the kidnapping and killing of the child. However, this variant does not depict *Lamòling* as a 'single god' (as the *Lamòling* of the widespread version), but takes the *'Lamòlings'*, his servants, as the representation/emanation of *Lamòling* himself. The legend seems more precise in describing the figure of the child, telling of the day when an Abui woman and her young son went down to the beach, from *Takalelàng*, in order to collect shells. That happened at the same time of the 'replacement' of *Lamòling* (as an immanent god, or of the *'Lamòlings'* as his emanation, in this version) with *Lahatàla* in the Abui religion. Coming back to the village, the woman was faster than the child. He lagged behind and was soon out of his mother's sight. The child started crying as he made his way slowly up the mountain path. While he was walking and crying, he arrived at *Lamòling Bèaka* and, his eyes being pure, passed from the real world to the supernatural world of *Lamòling*'s gods/entities. According to the Abui, those *Lamòling* deities could look at normal people, without being seen, interacting with them without people being able to notice their actions (unless they wanted to show themselves). They lived in a parallel world linked to the real world and were able to act in both of them. The child's innocence had allowed him to involuntarily cross between the two worlds and reach *Lamòling Bèaka* and, because of that, his destiny was sealed. The inhabitants of *Lamòling Bèaka* were supernatural entities and their behavior was beyond human laws, understanding, rationality, and beliefs. The beings in *Lamòling Bèaka* were indeed very happy to see the child and said: "Here, our grasshopper has come" (Abui people used to eat grasshoppers as a source of proteins). They killed him and cut his body in small parts in order to cook and eat them.

By this time, the mother had reached the village and reported that her son was missing. The Abui people looked everywhere for him, both on the mountains and at the seashore, village by village. However, they were unable to find him. They consequently asked Fanny to help them. The 'prophet' went out searching for the child, without knowing that the child had already been killed. Looking for him, Fanny, as was his habit, crossed into the supernatural world, *Lamòling Bèaka*, thinking he would be able to get some help from the *'Lamòlings'*. They, as a sign of hospitality, asked him to join them for dinner and offered him meat to eat. The man immediately noticed that it was human meat and he understood that it was the body of the missing child. He did not do anything that would reveal his horror and his pain. He simply told them he was in a hurry at that time and asked them to give him the head of the child in order to bring it back to the villages, to cook it later with potato leaves. "Please give me the head of the meal, so that I can bring it back to the villages and cook it to be eaten with potato leaves", were his words. The *'Lamòlings'* gave him the head, which he was able to bring to the villages, to organize a funeral. This way, the villagers discovered the truth. Since only Fanny was able to travel to the supernatural world, the Abui people were unable to go to *Lamòling Bèaka* to exact their revenge. So, they set their vengeance to take place in a village north of *Takalelàng* and *Takpàla*, *Lù Melàng* ('the village of the river'; in Abui, *lù* is 'river' and *melàng* is 'village'), currently abandoned, a place considered as the original 'house' of the Delpada family of *Takalelàng* and *Takpàla*.

From here, the story continues almost uniformly in both versions, but with the very significant variant and/or inconsistency of the absence of *Lamòling* in the second one. In the second version, the *'Lamòlings'* are burned in the wooden house, and the Abui people are able to get their revenge, but *Lamòling* does not attend the party, never appearing (since he never appears, in this variant of the story, being a purely immanent deity). He does not change himself into a pregnant woman, nor does he need to escape, since he is not there or, better, he is 'also' there, since he is considered the entity substantiating not only the *'Lamòlings'*, but all of creation. Paradoxically, also the Abui people who burn the *'Lamòlings'* are substantiated by *Lamòling*, who appears, as mentioned, a sort of Platonic (Plato, *Timaeus*, VI, 30b–30c) and Neo-Platonic (Plotinus, *Enneads*, IV, 4, 32) *anima mundi* (ψυχή κόσμου), the principle at the origins of all the 'items' in the world, pervading them of its essence. The notion of this 'soul' that makes and keeps stable the world is also common in Hinduism with the concept of 'universal soul', often identified with the *Ātman*, the principle of the individual and inner 'self', inextricably joined with the *Brahman*, the principle of the outer world (Werner 2005, pp. 10 and 58). In the West, the Neo-Platonic tradition of the notion of *anima mundi* was continued, in the Humanism and Renaissance times, by Marsilio Ficino (1433–1499) and Giovanni Pico della Mirandola (1463–1494). The XVI century had in the work of Giordano Bruno (1548–1600) the most important representation of the *anima mundi* intended as pure immanentism, with the identification of God and Nature (the so-called Pantheism, 'All is God'), emblematized by the famous sentence attributed to Baruch Spinoza (1632–1677), *Deus sive Natura* ('God or The Nature') (Picton 1905). The Neo-Platonic idea of an immanent god identified with Nature has also been recovered, in the Romantic age, by Friedrich Schelling (1775–1854) (Grant 2010).

After the burning of the *'Lamòlings'*, the Abui people abandoned the primordial religion of gods and entities, the 'emanation' of the immanent *anima mundi Lamòling*, to exclusively worship the transcendent 'only and true God' (the Christian God), *Lahatàla*.

Both the versions of the story identify *Lamòling* as the one responsible for the taking and killing of the child, even though in the first variant *Lamòling* himself does not appear as the kidnapper and the killer (the action is accomplished by his servants, apparently) and in the second version *Lamòling* is a purely immanent god who does not act directly in the world, since he completely substantiates it.

According to Loisa Delpada (a member of the Delpada family from *Takalelàng* and, originally, from *Lù Melàng*), after Fanny passed away, his burial place rolled inside the river *Kanaài Loohù* because of a flood, as if Nature wanted to take the 'prophet' again within itself (in a sort of cosmic Panism or Naturism). However, people were able to recover his body. Another version tells of his wooden coffin taken away during a flood, but directly returned by the river, which carried it uphill against the flow of the current (the water reversed its course) to his final resting place. The belief of the Abui is that he was dear to the creator and all mighty God, although they do not know if that god was the Christian God, *Lahatàla*. However, since his story is entwined with that of *Lamòling*, it could be possible that he (the forsaken god) saved his body from the flood.

5. Comparing the Two Versions

The main difference between the two accounts is the paradoxical absence of *Lamòling* himself in the second version of the myth. The original story tells us that *Lamòling* is a god who is 'real' in every sense, materially, with his ability and penchant to take on animal or human forms and physically consorting with his followers and believers, and metaphysically, in that he is their god and is worshipped as such. *Lamòling* is a more 'human' (or 'humanized') god than a transcendent god like *Lahatàla*, and spends most of his time with the humans. The second version, conversely, has no mention of him, even if the speakers/storytellers 'know' that *Lamòling* is 'there' and exists, since they interpret him as the 'soul' originating and substantiating the world and also the *'Lamòlings'* and the humans. The place where his 'servant gods' meet bears his name and even these 'servant gods' do not have an individual name, but carry his name all together. The Abui refer to them, indeed, as the *'Lamòlings'*. This version depicts *Lamòling* as an immanent being, pervading and sustaining all that is real and created in nature.

6. Abui Traditional Concept of Religion

The Abui religion and culture was originally characterized by animistic and, then, polytheistic beliefs. Nowadays, the majority of the communities in Alor Island are Christians. They are predominantly Protestant, with some Catholic groups. More recently, significant numbers of Muslims have migrated to coastal areas in Alor from neighbouring islands (Kratochvíl 2007; Rodemeier 2010, pp. 27–42). The legend of *Lamòling* is the mythical description of people's passage to a monotheistic creed, Christianity (characterized by the figure of *Lahatàla*, the Christian God introduced in Alor by Western missionaries) (Perono Cacciafoco and Cavallaro 2017).

Little is known or written about the Abui earlier animistic practices. Their polytheistic beliefs can be discerned, among others, from the legend of *Lamòling*, when we consider the coexistence of *Lamòling* and *Lahatàla*, and the fact that the 'servants' of *Lamòling* are always referred to as some types of deities at first and, later, as demons, although none of these lesser deities have individual names in any version of the legend. In fact, also in the second variant, they are only known through the collective name *'Lamòlings'*, derived from the name of the main god. This points not to a pantheon of gods, as this implies a pluralism that is not apparent in historical data or in the legend, but to a possible polytheistic order, also foreshadowed by other legends where other gods appear, like the aforementioned giant snake *Mon Mot* (even though it is unclear if the snake could be defined 'a god' in the proper sense of the word or if he could rather be a hypostasis of natural violent and catastrophic phenomena). However, this context cannot be considered polytheism in the classic sense, as here the gods are not independent from each other or have in any way equal status and power. This polytheism has, apparently, a strict hierarchy, with *Lamòling* originally at the head. Negedu (2014) says of the Igala in Nigeria: "This understanding of the concept of polytheism justifies the claim of the Igala in monotheism, since what appears to be many is just a hierarchy of supernatural beings." (p. 123). Just like Igala's god, *Lamòling* is not on the same level as all the other deities around him. He is the Supreme Being and is beyond the realm of what is known by the Abui people. *Lahatàla* is a later addition that does not affect the original interpretation of the *Lamòling* figure.

Both stories show how *Lamòling* was regarded as, possibly, the creator of all things. He was connected with the origins of life and the guarantor of man's actions on this world. According to the widespread version, he displayed his anthropomorphic attributes by walking the real world in an animal form (originally the snake, as discussed above, a typical and universal hypostasis of chthonic deities) or human form, as did his entourage of lesser deities (only in animal form). In the second version, he is, instead, above all beings, including his pantheon of lesser deities, and, in his absence, reminds us that his immanence is also, to some extent, transcendent. It is complicated, indeed, to understand, in the second version, if *Lamòling* is a purely immanent god (as he seems to be, in any case) or if, besides generating and substantiating the world (immanence), he also tacitly spreads his action in the creation (transcendence). The two contrasting variants make it difficult to understand to what extent *Lamòling* is involved with the Abui people, what is his 'real' relation to the humans in the widespread version and if he has part in the actions of the second version. When speaking about West African religions, O'Connell (1962) put forth the concept that these religions "[. . .] have a high-god who is also a sky-god. But he is often a withdrawn high god, a *deus otiosus*. There is an apparent contradiction between the supremacy of the high-god and his withdrawal from concern with the world" (p. 67). Is *Lamòling*, in the second version of his legend, purely an *anima mundi* or, rather, a *deus otiosus* ('idle god'), delegating the actions in the world to natural spirits or intermediate entities? An example of *deus otiosus* is given by the notion of "first unmoved mover", the *primum movens* (ὃ οὐ κινούμενον κινεῖ, 'that which moves without being moved') by Aristotle (Metaphysics, XII, 1072a). *Lamòling* could also (and/or better) be identified with the notion of *deus absconditus* ('hidden god'), originally theorized by Saint Thomas Aquinas (1225–1274), but developed, in the context of apophatic theology (or negative theology), by Nicolaus Cusanus (1401–1464) (Belzen and Geels 2003, pp. 84–87). The *deus otiosus*, indeed, could be intended as a god who has created the world, but does not want to be involved in it anymore, and who is often replaced by not original, lesser gods. The *deus absconditus*, conversely, is a god who has consciously left this world, after giving shape to it, to hide elsewhere, closed in his perfection (Eliade 1978).

7. Objects, Places, and Rituals

Lamòling Bèaka became for Abui people a sacred place linked inextricably to this story. In the original telling, the name was given to the (real) place where the horrific dinner occurred after the death of the child. This place was also the venue for the meetings of *Lamòling* with his servants. In the other version, the place had always existed as a sort of 'portal' to the supernatural world (the world of the '*Lamòlings*', entities who were direct emanation of the *anima mundi Lamòling*). Only children with very pure eyes were able to (involuntarily) enter the 'portal'. Fanny, being pure in his heart like a child, was the only adult Abui able to cross over to the other world. The place, being not a 'human' place, but a 'gate' to the supernatural world, did not have a name (since Abui people—apart from Fanny—did not perceive it as a significant place). It was, apparently, just an 'intermediate point' in the route from the villages of *Takpàla* and *Takalelàng* to the coast. After the child was killed, the place itself (the 'real' and 'physical' place) was called *Lamòling Bèaka*, meaning '*Lamòling* the bad/evil'. The toponym, after Fanny (crossing the border between the physical world and the metaphysical world) discovered the terrible action committed by the '*Lamòlings*', referred to the place in both the real and the supernatural worlds. The place became part of the traditional religion of Abui people, inextricably connected with the *Lamòling* myth.

There are a number of other places that are associated with this legend. They appear in both versions. In the *Takpàla* village, two ritual houses, called *Kolwàt* ('the dark house') and *Kanurwàt* ('the bright house'), were (and are still) places of cult for Abui people and symbolize the passage from the 'old' ('dark') religion, the animistic and, then, polytheistic traditional Abui religion, to the 'new' ('bright') one, Christianity. The *Kolwàt* house, in the eastern part of *Takpàla*, is linked to the cult of *Lamòling* and is decorated with a geometric pattern symbolizing the primordial snake (the python), *Lamòling*. *Kanurwàt*, instead, is deeply characterized by a white geometric pattern, representing the ineffable and bright nature of *Lahatàla*

Karilìk, the place in which (according to the widespread version of the story) *Lamòling* and Abui people met periodically (with an offer of food by the Abui to 'trigger' the arrival of the python/primordial god to eat with them at the *Karilìk* altar and with the ritual *lego lego* dance), is located in front of the two ritual houses and is characterized by the presence of an altar with three ritual stones, symbolizing, according to the speakers, the skulls of enemies killed in war when Abui people were head-hunters. The micro-toponym *Karilìk* derives from the cult of *Lamòling* and is traditionally associated with an offer of rice, being the name of the ritual *karilìk hè hàk*, 'offer to the big old stones' (more popularly known by its shortened name, *karilìk*) (Perono Cacciafoco and Cavallaro 2017, p. 53). These three flat stones are the cultic referents of the *karilìk* ceremony. The Abui people would bring cooked rice to the ceremony. They placed the rice on the altar offering it, symbolically, to the gods (in particular, to *Lamòling*) through the three stones. *Lamòling* would have joined the ritual in the shape of a python. The rice was, then, eaten by those attending the ceremony—and, symbolically, also by *Lamòling*—establishing, through this sacred ritual, a connection with the god. In the original cult, the god joining the Abui people was *Lamòling* (probably, sometimes, with his lesser gods). It is difficult to establish if, at the origins, also other gods of the Abui people joined the ceremony. In the current versions of the story, the god joining the ritual with Abui people is *Lamòling*. Later, the Abui symbolically offered the rice also to *Lahatàla*, configured as a 'newer' god, as discussed earlier, who was more transcendental than *Lamòling*. *Karilìk* was, therefore, the sacred name of the meeting venue of the Abui and *Lamòling*. Possibly, *Karilìk* was also the place where the banquet hosted by the Abui set off *Lamòling* in his gruesome path and led to his abandoning by the Abui after *Lahatàla* told Abui people he was the 'only and true God' and they decided to worship only him. The original story says that *Lamòling* was angered by *Lahatàla*'s instructions to the Abui to exclude *Lamòling* from the *karilìk* and from all other rituals, and asking that *Karilìk* be a place exclusively reserved for *Lahatàla*. This led to the anger of *Lamòling* and to the tragedy that followed. Altars with ritual stones are common in the traditional Abui inhabited centres, and they can also be found in currently abandoned Abui villages. As mentioned above, the stones could be, according to the local speakers, the 'representation' of the severed heads of enemies killed in war, when the Abui community was at war against other clans in Alor and when the Abui people were head-hunters. At least from the time of the introduction of Christianity in Alor, but, probably, also earlier, when a sort of 'diplomacy' was established among Papuan communities in Alor, the practice of exposing the heads of enemies killed in war was abandoned and stones were used in order to symbolize that specific past. Possibly, that is the reason of the 'power' of the stones, considered, by the Abui people, to be able to connect, during the *karilìk hè hàk* ritual, the humans with the god *Lamòling*. So far, it has been impossible to document the names of the other altars with ritual stones (and of the related places) in other Abui villages.

The *lego lego* dance is a traditional ritual dance of Abui people, typical of the villages 'touched' by the story of the *Mon Mot* giant snake, including also (because of ties of kinship among Abui families) *Takpàla* and *Takalelàng* (Kratochvil and Delpada 2008, pp. 68–77), and danced at the *Karilìk*, in the *Takpàla* village, during the *karilìk hè hàk* ritual, when Abui people shared their rice with *Lamòling* (and, then, with *Lahatàla*). Once, the *Mon Mot* snake, a primordial (but, paradoxically, mortal) god comparable to *Lamòling*, descended from the Alor mountains, killed almost all of the Abui people, and destroyed their villages. Only a woman was able to escape. She was pregnant and, hiding in a cave, gave birth to twins. When the kids grew up, their mother told them the story of *Mon Mot* and they decided to get their revenge. They prepared traps and weapons, and, then, they went to look for the snake, on the mountains. They found him, and they told him they were the only two survivors of the Abui people he had killed in the past. They challenged him to kill them as well. The snake started to hunt them and, when they reached the place with traps and weapons, the twins started to fight the snake. Nothing seemed able to stop him, but then the twins threw boiling oil in his mouth and the snake started to burn from the inside. He became weak and, despite being a god, he noticed he was dying. As he was dying, he told the twins that his life was in their hands and that he knew beforehand that they would have killed him. Calling them "my children", he added that, after his death, they would have to cut his body in parts of flesh and skin and they would have to distribute those body parts during the night in all the houses throughout all the villages he had destroyed, while killing all the Abui people. Then, they would have to dance the *lego lego* dance all over those places. The twins followed his instructions. After having killed him, they dismembered his body in parts of flesh and skin and they brought all those parts to the destroyed villages, putting them in the ground, house by house. Then, in the night, they started to dance the *lego lego* dance. As they were dancing, from the houses, Abui people killed years before by the snake started to come out, without any memory of having been killed, and joined the dance. All the Abui villages were suddenly populated again; the Abui people were back.

The *Mon Mot* story is locally known as the *Children of Mon Mot Legend*, since the Abui people from the villages 'touched' by this ancestral tale believe to be (re-)born from the flesh and the skin of *Mon Mot* and to be, in a way, his 'descendants'. The *Mon Mot* legend is, indeed, a founding myth and the story shows points in common with other analogous myths in unrelated contexts. The legend of the god snake killing all people is a sort of variant of the flood myths widespread in a number of different cultures (Dundes 1988; Pleins 2010, p. 110). The same character of the snake can be considered as the representation of a natural catastrophe (a big snake descending from the mountains and destroying all the villages, killing all people, could, for example, foreshadow the eruption of a volcano in ancient times). The 'operation' to bring back to life the Abui people through the spreading of the body parts of the snake and the dance can be associated with the Ancient Greek founding myth of Deucalion and Pyrrha (Ovid, *Metamorphoses*, I, 327; Pseudo-Apollodorus, *Library*, I, 7, 2), who, being the only two survivors of the flood called upon by the gods to punish the corrupted humans (the myth of the flood is widespread among cultures, be it enough to think of the Biblical story from the *Book of Genesis*—Noah—and the flood myth—Utnapishtim—in the *Epic of Gilgamesh*), in order to populate again the world had to throw stones (the 'bones' of the Mother Earth, Gaia) over their shoulders. The stones gave birth to new people, with Pyrrha's stones becoming women and Deucalion's stones becoming men. The Abui legend adds the element of the sacred dance, the *lego lego* dance, which could be considered original. The dance, accompanied by chants with the value of spells, is the 'catalyst' of the (re-)generation of the Abui people from the parts of the body of the *Mon Mot* snake. The myth, as well as the story of *Lamòling*, is deeply connected with Abui genealogies and is used often by the Abui in order to establish kinship relationships among people and hierarchies in the 'antiquity' of family units among Abui clans.

The *lego lego* dance appears also in the *Lamòling* myth, danced at the site of the two Abui ritual and ceremonial houses, *Kolwàt*, 'the dark house', and *Kanurwàt*, 'the bright house', in the center of the *Takpàla* village, discussed above. The *lego lego* dance is usually performed not only during the *karilìk* ritual, but also on the occasion of other religious and cultic ceremonies (Perono Cacciafoco and Cavallaro 2017, pp. 53–55).

8. Transcendence and Immanence in the *Lamòling* Myth

As mentioned above, the notion of immanentism in the *Lamòling* myth seems to be a product of the 'stratigraphy' of the Abui legend, residing in one of the 'sides' of the representation of this god. From animistic and, then, polytheistic origins, to a 'Christian interpretation', to a version where the god is possibly cause (origin) and principle (substance) of the world. The transcendence of *Lamòling* is different from *Lahatàla*'s transcendence. However, in the widespread version of his myth, *Lamòling* is transcendent to the extent of being a god who belongs to both worlds, the 'real' one and the supernatural one, since it is he who decides to enter the 'real' world and to spend his time, often in anthropomorphic shape, among the Abui people. In the 'immanent' variant, *Lamòling* is a sort of *anima mundi*, or *deus absconditus*, probably cause (origin) of the creation and surely principle (substance) of the world. In a way, he is also 'transcendent', through the action of the '*Lamòlings*', his emanation (even though, by definition, all the 'items' of the world should be his emanation), on the world.

This dialectic between transcendence and immanence of the immanent divinity and the intelligible world (the creation) could find an interesting parallel in the second dialogue of *De la causa, principio et uno* (1584) by Giordano Bruno. In that work, Bruno starts his reasoning from the Pythagorean doctrine, describing the world soul (*anima mundi*) and universal intellect (*νοῦς*)—a single entity, indeed—as immanent, position shared by the Neo-Platonic ontology ("The universal intellect is the intimate, most real, peculiar, and powerful part of the soul of the world", *De la causa, principio et uno*, II). This specific definition, in truth, derives, more precisely, from the Stoics, who defined 'immanence' as the 'world soul', while the Neo-Platonists considered it as a 'hypostasis soul', intermediary between the universal intellect and the physical reality (the world) (Knox 2013, pp. 465–77). Bruno, in his dialogue, adopted an originally Neo-Platonic distinction between the notions of 'cause' and 'principle', derived by the concepts outlined by Saint Thomas Aquinas in his *De principiis naturae*. The aim was to explain the simultaneous transcendence and immanence of the intelligible world. This philosophical issue was addressed by Bruno in the second book of *De la causa* (Knox 2013, pp. 477–81), and shows analogies with the representation of the divinity of *Lamòling* in the second variant of its legend in Abui oral culture and tradition.

9. A Possible Etymology of the *Lamòling* Name

The name of *Lamòling* could be connected, in the Abui language, with the word *mòling*, which indicates a specific part of the bride-price negotiation in Abui society, something needed to be paid for 'clearance' from a mother's obligation. That is, the daughter has to pay her mother before marrying to clear her mother's obligation. According to Benny Delpada (one of the consultants of our language documentation team and a member of the Delpada family from the *Takalelàng* and *Takpàla* villages), this 'mother's obligation' can be connected, as far as its mythical and traditional origins, with the mother of the killed child in the *Lamòling* story. It is possible, therefore, that *Lamòling* derives a section of his name from this part of his legend, plausibly the original core of the myth itself. It is also possible, in any case, the opposite option, that the word *mòling* derives from the name of *Lamòling*, since in Abui culture the onomatopoesis of 'common' words (and toponyms) in many cases originates from traditional stories. According to Benny, *Lamòling* could have been the surname of the child's mother. The name of *Lamòling*, therefore, could have been derived from her, starting to be used from this point of the legend. Our consultant does not know of any other name that the god would have had before this passage. As above, it is also possible that the surname *Lamòling* derives directly from the traditional story. Interestingly enough, *Lamòling* is still an attested Abui family name among local people, but not in *Takalelàng*, where it is considered inappropriate and also 'sinister'. Benny remembers a little girl attending middle school with him in *Mebùng* (4 km distant from *Takalelàng*, coming from *Kalabàhi*), whose surname was *Lamòling*. She was from *Forlèng*, located in the central Abui area, in Alor.

10. Conclusions

The impact and relevance of the *Lamòling* story, a founding myth in Abui religion, can be found not only in the consecration (and 'invention') of places (*Karilìk*, *Kolwàt*, *Kanurwàt*, *Lamòling Bèaka*), rituals (*karilìk hè hàk*, *lego lego* dance), and artefacts (the three ritual stones), but also in the close relation between Abui oral traditions and Abui original religion. By combining the two versions of the *Lamòling* story, we can highlight a significant and unexpected passage in the representation of *Lamòling* from a primordial god of animistic origins to a god inserted into a polytheistic context, then resolved in a monotheistic cult by the clash between *Lamòling* and *Lahatàla* in the original story, with the demonizing of the former and the deification of the latter, to an immanent context (in the alternative version), where *Lamòling* is a spirit comparable to the notions of *anima mundi* and *deus absconditus*, substantiating the world and all creation. Throughout the two versions of the story, *Lamòling* appears like a 'god among the humans' (in its anthropomorphic 'shape'), a transcendent god (less transcendent than *Lahatàla*, but transcendent by definition, since, even if he likes to live among the humans, he is a god acting in the world), and an immanent deity. The concept of the connection between transcendent and immanent and the joined representation of transcendence and immanence of gods in aboriginal contexts are not uncommon across the world, even if they appear according to many variants. Research in Africa (Metuh 1973; Ushe 2017), for example, has struggled with the question of whether African religions are purely anthropocentric, and the 'African god' is on the periphery of African world view. Talking about Igbo religion, Metuh concludes that "God in Igbo religion is at once transcendent and immanent. The transcendent God is the creator, the father of the Alusi, the consort of the Earth-Mother. The immanent God is the Supreme Spirit, who sends sparks of himself in the form of *chi* into men, natural phenomena, and things" (p. 9). The *Lamòling* myth, in its different versions, seems to share similarities with the Igbo paradigm.

Our paper is the first record of the so far unpublished (and never documented before) second version on the *Lamòling* legend in Abui traditional religion. Besides highlighting a significant pattern in the development of the figure of the god from animistic origins, to polytheistic contexts, to the 'clash' with the introduction of a monotheistic religion (Christianity) in Abui culture, and to the representation of the god as an immanent entity, the paper analyses specific rituals, places of worship and objects. Moreover, as in our previous work on the widespread version of the *Lamòling* story (Perono Cacciafoco and Cavallaro 2017), this paper shows how, in Abui culture and religion, places are indissolubly connected with local myths, with the very significant link between mythopoesis and onomatopoesis in the coinage of specific place names (and micro-toponyms) after the local legends.

With the *Lamòling* myth having been recorded and collected during language documentation fieldwork, this paper is also a contribution to Field Linguistics and Anthropological Linguistics, with the aim to shed light on Abui traditional religion and culture and to help preserve the Abui language and oral intangible heritage and traditions.

Author Contributions: Conceptualization, Francesco Perono Cacciafoco and Francesco Cavallaro; Writing—original draft, Francesco Perono Cacciafoco and Francesco Cavallaro; Writing—review & editing, Francesco Perono Cacciafoco and Francesco Cavallaro.

Funding: This work was supported by the AcRF Tier 1 Research Project RG56/14, Nanyang Technological University, Singapore.

Acknowledgments: We wish to acknowledge the two Abui native-speakers who recounted the story to us: Markus Lema and Darius Delpada, both from *Takalelàng;* and the Abui native-speaker who operated as an Abui-English translator/interpreter, Anselm Delpada, also from *Takalelàng*.

Conflicts of Interest: The authors declare no conflict of interest.

References

Aritonang, Jan Sihar, and Karel Adriaan Steenbrink, eds. 2008. *A History of Christianity in Indonesia*. Leiden and Boston: Brill.

Belzen, Jacob A., and Antoon Geels. 2003. *Mysticism: A Variety of Psychological Perspectives*. Amsterdam: Rodopi.

Campbell, Joseph. 1976. *The Masks of God: Primitive Mythology*. New York: Penguin.

Campbell, Joseph. 1990. *Transformations of Myth through Time*. New York: Harper Perennial.

Dundes, Alan, ed. 1988. *The Flood Myth*. Berkeley: University of California Press.

Eliade, Mircea. 1978. *A History of Religious Ideas: From the Stone Age to the Eleusinian Mysteries*. Chicago: The University of Chicago Press.

Finnegan, Ruth. 1992. *Oral Poetry: Its Nature, Significance, and Social Context*. Bloomington and Indianapolis: Indiana University Press.

Foley, John Miles. 1991. *Immanent Art: From Structure to Meaning in Traditional Oral Epic*. Bloomington and Indianapolis: Indiana University Press.

Grant, Iain Hamilton. 2010. F.W.J. Schelling, On the World Soul (Translation and Introduction). In *Collapse VI: Geo/Philosophy*. Edited by Mackay Robin. Falmouth: Urbanomic, pp. 58–95.

Klamer, Marian. 2014. The Alor-Pantar Languages: Linguistic Context, History, and Typology. In *The Alor-Pantar Languages: History and Typology*. Edited by Klamer Marian. Studies in Diversity Linguistics. Berlin: Language Science Press, pp. 5–53.

Knox, Dilwyn. 2013. Bruno: Immanence and Transcendence in *De la causa, principio et uno*, Dialogue II. *Bruniana and Campanelliana* 19: 463–82.

Kratochvíl, František. 2007. *A Grammar of Abui: A Papuan Language of Alor*. Utrecht: Landelijke Onderzoekschool Taalwetenschap (LOT).

Kratochvíl, František, and Benidiktus Delpada. 2008. *Netanga neananra dei lohu naha: Abui tanga heateng ananra/Cerita-cerita dalam Bahasa Abui dari Takalelang/Abui Stories from Takalelàng*. Leiden: Leiden University Press.

Laycock, Joseph P. 2015. *Spirit Possession around the World: Possession, Communion, and Demon Expulsion across Cultures*. Santa Barbara: ABC-CLIO.

Lord, Albert B. 1938. Homer and Huso II: Narrative Inconsistencies in Homer and Oral Poetry. *Transactions and Proceedings of the American Philological Association* 69: 439–45. [CrossRef]

Metuh, Emefie E. 1973. The Supreme God in Igbo Life and Worship. *Journal of Religion in Africa* 5: 1–11. [CrossRef]

Negedu, Isaiah Aduojo. 2014. The Igala Traditional Religious Belief System: Between Monotheism and Polytheism. *OGIRISI: A New Journal of African Studies* 10: 116–29. [CrossRef]

O'Connell, James. 1962. The Withdrawal of the High God in West African Religion: An Essay in Interpretation. *Man: The Journal of the Royal Anthropological Institute* 62: 67–69. [CrossRef]

Perono Cacciafoco, Francesco, and Francesco Cavallaro. 2017. The Legend of Lamòling: Unwritten Memories and Diachronic Toponymy through the Lens of an Abui Myth. *Lingua: An International Review of General Linguistics* 193: 51–61. [CrossRef]

Picton, James Allanson. 1905. *Pantheism: Its Story and Significance*. London: Constable.

Pleins, J. David. 2010. *When the Great Abyss Opened: Classic and Contemporary Readings of Noah's Flood*. New York: Oxford University Press.

Robinson, Laura C. 2015. The Alor-Pantar (Papuan) Languages and Austronesian Contact in East Nusantara. In *Language Change in Austronesian Languages: Papers from 12-ICAL*. Edited by Malcom D. Ross and I. Wayan Arka. Canberra: Asia-Pacific Linguistics, vol. 3, pp. 19–33.

Rodemeier, Susanne. 2010. Islam in the Protestant Environment of the Alor and Pantar Islands. *Indonesia and the Malay World* 38: 27–42. [CrossRef]

Sahlins, Marshall. 1963. Poor man, rich man, big man, chief: Political types in Melanesia and Polynesia. *Comparative Studies in Society and History* 5: 285–303. [CrossRef]

Schröter, Susanne, ed. 2011. *Christianity in Indonesia: Perspectives of Power*. Münster: LIT Verlag.

Tangherlini, Timothy R. 1990. "It happened not too far from here ... ": A survey of legend theory and characterization. *Western Folklore* 49: 371–90. [CrossRef]

Ushe, Mike Ushe. 2017. God, divinities, and ancestors in African traditional religious thought. *Igwebuike: An African Journal of Arts and Humanities* 3: 154–79.

Werner, Karel. 2005. *A Popular Dictionary of Hinduism*. New York: Routledge.

religions

MDPI

Article

When Children Participate in the Death Ritual of a Parent: Funerary Photographs as Mnemonic Objects

Laurie M.C. Faro

Postdoc Researcher Department of Culture Studies, Tilburg School of Humanities and Digital Sciences, Tilburg University, 5037 AB Tilburg, The Netherlands; l.m.c.faro@uvt.nl

Received: 26 June 2018; Accepted: 9 July 2018; Published: 11 July 2018

Abstract: When children lose a parent during childhood this offers emotional and life changing moments. It is important for them to be included in the death ritual and to be recognized as grievers alongside adults. Recent research has shown that children themselves consider it relevant to be part of the 'communitas' of grievers and do not like to be set aside because they are considered to be too young to participate. In this case study, I describe how a Dutch mother encouraged her three children, aged 12, 9 and 6, to participate in the death rituals of their father. She asked a funeral photographer to document the rituals. In that way, later on in their life, the children would have a visual report of the time of his death in addition to their childhood memories. The objective of my case study research was first, to explore in detail hów children are able to participate in death rituals in a carefully contemplated manner and in accordance with their age and wishes, and second, to examine the relevance of funeral photographs to them in later years. The funeral photographs will be presented as a visual essay of how and when the children took part in the rituals and which ritual objects, such as the coffin and the grave, but also letters, poems and drawings were important in creating an ongoing bond with their deceased father. The conclusion of this case study presentation is that funeral photographs of death rituals may function as mnemonic objects later on in the life of children who lost a parent in their childhood. These photographs enable children, when necessary, to materialize how they participated in the death ritual of their father or mother. In this respect they can be seen as functional means of continuing bonds in funeral culture, linking the past with the present, in particular when young children are involved.

Keywords: children; objects; funerary photography; death ritual; continuing bonds

---

1. Introduction

Remember me

Though I have to say goodbye[1]

Remembering deceased family members by means of photographs is the leading theme in the 2017 Disney Pixar movie, *Coco*. Traditional Mexican death rituals, especially related to Día de los Muertos (Day of the Dead), are presented in the movie. On this day, relatives come together and share stories about family members who have passed away. Ofrendas (homemade altars created in honor of dead family members) are decorated with valued photographs, favored foods and other objects symbolizing the life of the family members (Dakin 2017, p. 12; Disney PIXAR 2017, p. 35). The entire family, including young children, are involved in these traditional and culturally embedded rituals.

---

1 https://www.disneyclips.com/lyrics/coco-remember-me.html; Lyrics from 'Coco', written by Kristen Anderson-Lopez and Robert Lopez, performed by Miguel, featuring Natalia Lafourcade.

The principal message of the movie, and the message that the main character, Miguel finally understands is that your family is at the center of your life, it offers security and a basis for development. Deceased ancestors still belong to the family and it is important to stay connected, to reach out to them: not having a photograph on the ofrenda means you are forgetting the particular family member. To Miguel, these photographs function as mnemonic objects as they help him in keeping the memory of his ancestors alive. Zerubavel describes these type of photographs as "physical mnemonic bridges", as objects which create "tangible links between past and present." (Zerubavel 2003, pp. 43–44) Obviously, *Coco* is fiction, and an animation movie for children, but it is interesting to see how Miguel seems to be at ease and comfortable with all matters related to death, particularly, when nowadays in many western countries with less traditional and culturally embedded death rituals, death is often a taboo subject when children are involved. Participation of children in the death ritual has diminished as Western attitudes towards death have changed (Ariès 1994; Søfting et al. 2016).

In the Netherlands in the twenty-first century, death has become a more publicly discussed subject in a variety of media, including scientific publications, but also media targeted towards the general public, for instance, in television programs or in glossy periodicals.[2] However, it still remains difficult to discuss the subject with children even though educational materials have been developed and are distributed, for example by funeral directors. The Dutch Funeral Museum, 'So Long' has developed educational material for children, including an educational program for pupils at elementary schools. The objective is to lift the taboo and to offer tools to facilitate discussions with children about death.[3]

The focus of my qualitative and explorative research is on the position of Dutch children, aged six to twelve years, during the death ritual. Ethnographic methods were used to collect data. The initial fieldwork comprised of interviews with funeral directors, ritual coaches and families with young children about issues related to death in the family context.

At the time of my fieldwork, in September 2017, I met Astrid Barten and her eighteen-year old daughter Bente Stam.[4] In 2009, the Astrid's husband, and the father of Brechtje, Bente and Wytze, Jan Leen Stam, died unexpectedly while they were on holiday in Austria. Notwithstanding the immense grief, Astrid had no doubts about including their three young children in every element of the death ritual.[5] She decided to ask a funeral photographer to participate in the rituals because she considered it important to create material memories for the children. These could help them later on in life to remember what went on at the time of their father's death.[6]

Astrid Barten's actions were very much in line with the conclusions of the research by Søfting et al. They argue that it is important for children to be included in death rituals and to be recognized as grievers alongside adults. Being included meant an improved understanding of what was going on in order to accept the reality of the loss (Søfting et al. 2016). These conclusions affirm the ongoing question of whether young children should attend funerals (Hilpern 2013; Halliwel 2017). Already in 1976, John Schowalter reported on this dilemma: "Although some young children can tolerate funerals well if sensitively supported by their parents, the fact is that such support is more often absent than present. A child no matter how young, who feels secure in attending should usually do so." (Schowalter 1976, p. 139) My field work results indicate that in the Netherlands children and the death ritual is still a much-debated issue. This raises the question of how 'death ritual' is understood. Is it only attending

---

2 For an impression of this glossy see: http://www.later-alsikdoodben.nl/doelgroep/ (consulted on 18 June 2018).

3 http://www.totzover.nl/educatie/ (accessed on 10 June 2018).

4 This semi-structured interview took place on 1 September 2017. The interview was recorded and transcribed for analysis. Informed consent was obtained for publication of the data.

5 Eldest daughter Brechtje Stam was twelve years old, Bente nine years old and Wytze six years old at the time of the death of their father.

6 The photographs were made by Dasha Elfring, a Dutch funeral photographer with her own company *Stilbeeld Uitvaartfotografie*: http://www.stilbeeld.nl/index.html. Permission was obtained to publish the photographs.

the funeral or should children participate in other rituals, for example, saying goodbye or closing the coffin?

This case study on the Barten family contributes to the discussion in a threefold manner. Firstly, it illustrates how a parent was able to support her children so that they felt confident in participating in the death ritual when their father died, and secondly, it shows and describes hów the children participated and which ritual objects and places were relevant to them. Lastly, the relevance of funeral photographs as mnemonic objects later on in the life of children will be discussed.

2. Research Question and Method

Astrid Barten decided that it was important to document as much as possible for her young children at the time of the death of their father. How were they included in the rituals? What happened and what was their contribution in taking leave of their father? The photographs, put together with a day-to-day description by Astrid and by her mother, the grandmother of the children, in a memorial album could function later as a linking object with that time.

In the nineteenth century, in Western countries, death related photographs were socially and publicly accepted and an acknowledged form of photography (Van der Zee et al. 1978; Ruby 1989, 1995; Linkman 2011). Later generations thought this kind of photography to be inappropriate, and upsetting and as late as 2006, Hilliker acknowledged "the rarity of postmortem photography in the twenty-first century", although she appreciated the value of "using postmortem photographs as an historical and cultural grieving ritual". Like Ruby in 1989, she recommended that further research would be appropriate to study the role of death related pictures in bereavement processes (Hilliker 2006, p. 245; Ruby 1989, p. 1).

In this case study I focused on the linking function of photographs, how they served and have become an effective means of memory. Every photo bears the potential of the punctum (Barthes 1981) and "one look, one face, one name can "prick" the casual spectator, trigger a memory [...]." (Tandeciarz 2006, p. 139) However not only photographs, but other objects may also act against obliviousness, as described by Hirsch in the context of the memory of the Second World War:

> Roland Barthes's much discussed notion of the punctum has inspired us to look at images, objects, and memorabilia inherited from the past [...] "points of memory"—points of intersection between past and present, memory and post-memory, personal remembrance and cultural recall. The term "point" is both spatial—such as a point on a map—and temporal—a moment in time—and it thus highlights the intersection of spatiality and temporality in the workings of personal and cultural memory. The sharpness of a point pierces or punctures: like Barthes's punctum, points of memory puncture through the layer of oblivion, interpellating those who seek to know about the past. (Hirsch 2012, p. 61)

In this case study presentation, based on the funeral photographs of the death ritual of Jan Leen Stam, in combination with the interview with both Astrid Barten and her daughter Bente, I considered the meaning of the photographs of the death ritual, in particular when children lose one of their parents at a young age. A description of the rituals and how the children participated, the places and objects which were created and used during the rituals is given. The photographs, in combination with the story told by Astrid and Bente thus present a visual essay, a "combination of spoken words and visual images" which will, according to Sarah Pink, help me imagine how the events were at the time of death and burial of Jan Leen (Pink 2008, p. 125). Also, the photographs would help me to understand the participation of the children in the death ritual of their father which I was not able to observe personally.

In cultural studies, analysis of the visual has always been integrated. Pink takes a three-fold stand in situating the visual in her research method. The first is that "[...] both researcher and research subjects' uses of visual methods and visual media are always embedded in social relationships and cultural practices and meanings." (Pink 2008, p. 131). In this respect, I needed to reflect on the situation when children lose a parent in their childhood, which offers, according to Worden, a very fundamental experience: "The death of a parent is one of the most fundamental losses a child can face." (Worden 1996, p. 9).

Secondly, Pink argues that "[...] no experience is ever purely visual, and to comprehend 'visual culture' we need to understand both what vision itself is, and what its relationship is to other sensory modalities." (Pink 2008, p. 131). While I did not personally attend the death ritual and was unable to grasp the emotions at the time, I needed the oral story to comprehend the situation when children lose a parent. This is confirmed by the third argument of Pink in upholding the analysis of visual objects:

> [...] we are usually actually dealing with audio-visual (for example, film) representations or texts that combine visual and written texts. Thus, the relationship between images and words is always central to our practice as academics. (Pink 2008, p. 131; 2007)

In compliance with these arguments, I audiotaped the interview and made a full transcript of the recordings which I used for analysis.

Thus, I was able to reconstruct the social context of the death of Jan Leen Stam and consequently, gain insight into the function and leitmotif of his death ritual.

3. Function and Theme of Jan Leen's Death Ritual

3.1. Function

Both Astrid and Bente say that the death ritual was very important to them at the time of Jan Leen's death in 2009. Astrid explained that when he was Austria in a coma and the family understood he was going to die, they initiated the first ritual acts. Together they had all very intensely said goodbye to him. They sat down at his side and spoke to him. Astrid counselled the children to, "Touch him once more, and have a good look at him" and so they did. They also cut a piece of his hair. These were very intimate and private moments, and for that reason they decided not to take pictures at that time. However, both the written diaries of Astrid and her mother on what happened in Austria, and the stories told later on, allow for an embodied recall of the intimate events in the absence of visual material.

During the interview both Astrid and Bente frequently used the term 'ritual' when they referred to actions taken around the death of Jan Leen.

The rituals we discussed during the interview belong to a repertoire which Davies refers to as the "mortuary ritual" or death ritual. In his view, this type of ritual should be considered as a form of human response to death: "the human adaptive response to death with ritual language and its ritual practice singled out as its crucial form of response" (Davies 2017, p. 4). At the time, Astrid considered that rituals would help the family in coping with the death of Jan Leen. Davies argues that "having encountered and survived bereavement through funerary rites and associated behavior, human beings are transformed in ways which make them better adapted for their own and for their society's survival in the world." (Davies 2017, p. 4). Having spoken extensively with both Astrid and Bente, I would argue that this was the intention of Astrid in organizing, together with the children and closest of kin, a comprehensive death ritual with the objective and focus on the children.

Astrid referred to the mourning process that she realized they all had to go through, a process of adaptation to a life without the physical presence of Jan Leen. Worden defines mourning in terms of the process of adaptation to loss (Worden 1996, p. 11). In order to adapt to the death of a near one he developed what he called "a mourning task model" in which he builds on the concept of Freud's grief work: "The task model is more consonant with Freud's concept of "grief work" and implies that the mourner needs to take action and can do something [...]" (Worden 2009, p. 38). Astrid indicated that she firmly believed that if the children could take action and participate, just like adults, in the rituals, this would help them in their mourning process.

Worden discerns four tasks of mourning which should be executed during the mourning process. The first task concerns the acceptance of the reality of the loss (Worden 2009, pp. 39–43). As a family they had been there when Jan Leen died and this has helped the children in the recognition of his death and the finality of it. Worden's second task relates to the charge of experiencing the pain resulting from the loss and to facing the emotions (Worden 2009, pp. 43–46). Bente reflected on her mourning process and said that there has always been room to grieve but also acceptance of how it was, there was nothing they could do to change the situation:" We have been able to let him go, to accept his death but at that time, being a young child, it was logical that we were standing beside him and saying: don't die, don't die ... ".

The third task concerns the process of adjusting to an environment in which the deceased is (physically) missing (Worden 2009, pp. 46–49). The fourth task is the process of emotionally relocating the deceased within one's life and finding ways to memorialize the person and consequently to move on with life (Worden 2009, pp. 50–53).

Worden initially developed his model for adults. Other researchers in bereavement studies have developed models with specific mourning tasks for children (Baker and Sedney 1992; Cook and Oltjenbruns 1998). Worden, accordingly commented as follows:

> Researchers who apply my "tasks of mourning" concept to children have suggested various numbers of mourning tasks [...] Although their conceptualizations are interesting, I do not believe we need to include additional tasks. The issues concerning bereaved children can be subsumed under the four tasks of mourning described in my earlier work, but I have modified them here to take into account the age and the developmental level of the child.
>
> (Worden 1996, p. 12; 2009, pp. 230–36)

According to Worden, mourning tasks apply to children, but they should be understood in terms of the cognitive, emotional and social development of the child (Worden 2009, p. 235). For example, a child who has not developed the cognitive abstractions of irreversibility and finality will have difficulty with the first task of accepting and realizing that death is final and irreversible.

Worden specifically mentions family rituals as "important mediators influencing the course and outcome of bereavement." (Worden 1996, p. 21) They can help children in a three-fold manner: as a means of acknowledging the death, as a way to honor the life of the deceased and as a means of comfort and support. However, Worden concludes that children should be given a choice as to whether they want to attend, and for example, whether they want to view the body. In all cases they should be clearly informed of what they are about to experience (Worden 1996, p. 21).

Astrid was very much in charge of organizing the rituals. She said that she knew what and how she wanted it. She thought it was important that the children should decide for themselves whether they wanted to participate: "The funny thing was that they wanted to participate in everything that took place. They were not one moment scared of death." She remembers one particular time when in fact the children took the lead: "At the moment we were about to close the coffin, you (Bente) were the first one to give dad a kiss to say goodbye. The others followed."

3.2. Theme

Astrid explained that in Austria, when Jan Leen was in a coma, she had told him that it was okay to go. It had been the 'ultimate letting go'. This letting go of his physical presence became a recurring element in his death ritual. Although the family believes him to be somewhere else, he still remains a part of their life, and they treasure him within their hearts. They refer to his transfer from being a physical presence to a presence elsewhere. This transfer turned into the leitmotif of his death ritual and may be explained by applying the framework of so called 'rites de passage' (rites of passage). In 1908, Arnold van Gennep described the way people passed from one social status to another (Van Gennep 1960, pp. 10–11, 21). He recognized three stages in this process of transfer: separation, transition and reincorporation. Using the Latin word limen (threshold) to describe these phases, he spoke of pre–liminal (separation), liminal (transition), and post–liminal (reincorporation) phases in rites of passage.

These phases can be applied both to the transfer of the deceased but also to the position of the family left behind who also have to adapt to the transfer from physical presence to another presence.

Herz, in his seminal essay on death and the collective representation of death, presented just before Van Gennep, discussed the death ritual in a similar way too (Hertz 1960). In a commentary on his work, Davies reflects on the change of status emphasized by Hertz:

> Writing just before Van Gennep published his now familiar thesis of rites of passage in 1909, Hertz speaks of funerary rites in a very similar way. These rites resemble initiation in that the dead, like the youth who is withdrawn from the society of women and children to be integrated into that of adult males, also change status. Poignantly, then, death resembles birth in transferring an individual from one domain to another. (Davies 2000, p. 99)

Turner elaborates on the different phases identified by Van Gennep. The first phase of separation comprises "symbolic behavior signifying the detachment". During the dominant, second, liminal period, the characteristics of the ritual subjects, which are the "passengers through this phase'", both the deceased and bereaved are ambiguous and in the third phase, the phase of reincorporation, the passage has been completed and the ritual subjects should be in a sort of stable state, while the deceased has made the transfer to the other world (Turner 1969, pp. 94–95).

Turner emphasized the liminal period and explored the dynamics of what happens to people when thrown together in periods of stress and the change of identity caused by the death of a near one. He developed the concept of communitas to describe this shared fellow-feeling, a feeling of connectedness (Turner 1969, p. 96), and this was interpreted by Davies as "[...] a sense of unity and empathy between people undergoing ritual events together" (Davies 2017, pp. 26–27, 94).

Although discerning the exact phases in the death ritual of Jan Leen is arbitrary, applying the discussed concepts in a case where children participate may be useful in interpreting the process and accompanying rituals. Bente commented that you might think that when you are nine years old, you will remember everything but when she looks back on these days it seems like everything happened in just two days: one day they got to know in Austria that Jan Leen was braindead and to her it seemed as if the funeral was held the day after. In her view they really were in a sort of 'liminal' period where there was no comprehension of time.

In the next paragraph I will discuss six photographs of Jan Leen Stam's death ritual. These photographs were chosen in consultation with both Astrid, Bente and myself. The funeral photographer advised on the quality of the pictures. In particular, these six photographs were chosen because they create a comprehensive visual narrative and materialize the events that took place at the time. The photographs have a two-fold function: the first is to illustrate how the Stam children participated in the death ritual of their father and secondly, these photographs function as mnemonic objects to memorialize the events at the time of the death of their father.

The first photograph (Photograph 1) was taken after Jan Leen had returned home from Austria. At that time, they created a special place for him in order to welcome him back home.[7] Astrid said: "All together we organized the room where he would stay. I put up photographs of Jan Leen and the children, there were flowers". Other symbolic acts at this time included the objects they placed in his coffin for him on his way to the other world.

[7] Out of respect to Jan Leen, and because, obviously, he was not able to give his consent, Astrid decided not to include any photographs of Jan Leen himself in the visual essay.

Photograph 1. Saying goodbye—personalizing the coffin. © Stilbeeld Uitvaartfotografie.

Astrid asked the children: "What would you like to put in the coffin, when you think of dad, what comes up, which things would you like to place with him?".

Bente wrote a letter and put it in the coffin. Her older sister Brechtje made a drawing about how she thought it would be up there in his future home in the clouds. There was also discussion and they put things in the coffin which would remove again later, for example, a pickax that was his and symbolized him as a mining engineer. Astrid thought the children were better off keeping the ax as an object of memory, and instead they placed a stone in the coffin. They also took care that he had his glasses with him as they very much belonged to him as the person he was.

In the photograph we see the children painting the coffin. They left their hand prints on top as a personal sign of bonding with their father.

The objects they put into the coffin functioned as so called "transitional objects". Winnicott was the first to describe this term 'as an object that becomes crucially important to the child in the process of separation from the mother (Winnicott 1997, pp. 1–34). These objects seem to be invested with a certain magical quality and offer comfort and security to the child (Gibson 2004, p. 288). In this case there were two type of transitional objects: first, the objects belonging to Jan Leen himself that they thought characterized him and that had to go with him, like his glasses, and second, the objects the children especially created for him as memory objects. These objects connect the world their father was leaving with the world he was about to enter and may be helpful in the transition process of separation and acceptance of the fact that the parent has actually died (Winnicott 1997; Worden 1996, 2009). Margaret Gibson argues that, "In grieving, as in childhood, transitional objects are both a means of holding on and letting go" (Gibson 2004, p. 288).

These two aspects of a transitional object are illustrated by the pick ax which they first decided to 'let go' with him but consequently decided to 'hold on' to.

According to Turner, these are all ritualistic acts of "symbolic behavior signifying the detachment" from Jan Leen which is part of the phase of separation from his physical presence (Turner 1969, pp. 94–95).

The male family members, including six-year-old Wytze, closed the coffin (Photograph 2). Astrid remembered: "This was a very emotional moment because I knew "I am never going to see you again", the funny thing is that I sort of thought it was okay that the body would leave, but there was also the understanding that this was really the end." She did not think that the children had a proper understanding of the finality of that moment. Bente confirms: "When I look back, I now realize much more than I did at the time that that moment was really the last time that you actually see someone. I think it is a very intense moment. But at the time I was just watching, fascinated how they were putting the screws on." Thus, the photograph functions as a reminder, a mnemonic object, of the finality of the death of her father.

Photograph 2. Wytze closing the coffin. © Stilbeeld Uitvaartfotografie.

Astrid decided at the time that the actual burial should be focused on the family, a small intimate group of close family members, so that the children could be with her, without having to worry about other people. As Van Gennep points out, "[...] during mourning, the living mourners and the deceased constitute a special group, situated between the world of the living and the world of the dead" (Van Gennep 1960, p. 147).

They acted together as a communitas of dear ones, the next of kin of Jan Leen, to feel a sense of unity and empathy in sharing their emotions and grief (Turner 1969, p. 96; Davies 2017, pp. 26, 94). Astrid explained: "There was so much sorrow, I strongly felt the need to do the burial with the children without a leaking of energy to other people who mattered less at that moment." Hence, she held the actual burial of Jan Leen separately, with a public service held in his honor a couple of weeks later.

Astrid decided that at all times during the burial ritual, they would be together in the communitas of the family. That is why she decided to hire a coach used especially for funeral processions: "I did not want him to be somewhere else than we were." All together in the coach, they made a good-bye tour through their village including the important places in the life of Jan Leen, for instance, they passed the house where he was born and raised.

The day of the burial, they all dressed in white. Astrid explains: "Jan Leen was very much a bon vivant, he lived so to say, as a "light life". During his life, he did not spend one minute on the wrong energy, and that went hand in hand with a sort of lightness. I did not hesitate for a second; everything would be in white."

Before going to the graveyard, Astrid wanted to have lunch with the family but Jan Leen had to be there as well. It was his day. The funeral director found a restaurant where they could take him in his coffin with them. They had lunch as one family, and there was time for the children to play (Photograph 3).

Photograph 3. Having lunch altogether, the children playing. © Stilbeeld Uitvaartfotografie.

The design, places and enactment of the burial rituals appear to be out of the ordinary. In this respect, they seem to refer to the liminal zone in which they were positioned at that time. In the words of Turner, "Liminal entities are neither here or there; they are betwixt and between the positions assigned and arrayed by law, custom and convention, and ceremonial" (Turner 1969, p. 95). That is why, maybe not unexpectedly, we observe children playing as if they are having a good time at the day of their father's burial, "betwixt and between". Here, the rituals were designed and performed taking into account the young age of the children. In Bente's opinion they were celebrating his life. That is how they experienced the ritual: "We have been celebrating, and we have not, well . . . of course we were sad, but we did not despair so to say." There are no tears, not in any photograph. However, Astrid said: "Sometimes the photographs still frighten me because we all look so very much fatigued."

Astrid explained that she and the children chose the actual place of burial (Photograph 4): "What would be a nice place for dad?" They chose a place which would be easy for the children to visit later on and so that they would not have to cross the whole graveyard on the way to their dad.

Photograph 4. At the graveyard. © Stilbeeld Uitvaartfotografie.

A couple of months before his death, Astrid had discussed with her husband whether he wanted to be cremated or buried. He had to have surgery and Astrid wanted to know, just in case. He preferred to be cremated, but Astrid felt that at such a young age it would be important for their children to have a place to go to: "When you have young children, I think that burial enables rituals, to experience their father, also after his death." Jan Leen had agreed.

Maddrell argues that maintaining bonds with the deceased may be experienced in different forms, for example, through ritual but these bonds can also be sustained through material objects such as graves, memorials or photographs (Maddrell 2013, p. 508). Hallam and Hockey argue that a "material focus" facilitates relations between the living and the dead. As they state: "Past presence and present absence are condensed into a spatially located object", like the grave or photographs (Hallam and Hockey 2001, p. 85).

At the moment of burial, they lit candles and put rose petals on the coffin. They sent up balloons as a symbolic act of letting him go.

According to Astrid, the actual burial was essentially about seeing Jan Leen off to his last resting place. In terms of Van Gennep and Turner, the phases of separation and transition had been achieved by this time. There were no speeches at the graveyard. Jan Leen had a large social network and Astrid also felt the need to show the children who their father was. Therefore, she asked all his friends, colleagues and family to document his life on behalf of his children. At the public service they celebrated his life and the children fully participated by lighting candles but also by presenting (Photograph 5). Bente recited a poem written by herself, Brechtje recited an English poem and Wytze read his self-written text, which was also in the death notice. The service turned out to be extremely long; around 2.5 h. Astrid had bought pencils and coloring books and candy for the children who were partly listening and partly playing, but they were present at all times.

Photograph 5. The public service with family and friends. © Stilbeeld Uitvaartfotografie.

Grimes comments on the elements of a good funeral: "If deaths can be good or bad, so can funerals. A good funeral is one that celebrates life, comforts the bereaved, and facilitates working through grief" (Grimes 2000, p. 230). However, from Astrid's perspective, the celebration of Jan Leen's life could not be done at his burial. That moment was in fact the closing of the period in which they were separating themselves from his physical presence, a very sorrowful time. Celebration of his life would be the start of incorporation into the new world without the physical presence of Jan Leen and the ending of the liminal period defined by Van Gennep and Turner (Van Gennep 1960; Turner 1969). Altogether, the rituals comprised a 'good funeral' in their eyes (Grimes 2000, p. 230).

Jan Leen's grave is an important place to the family. When there are memorable moments, such as passing exams, the family visit his grave and tell him. In the beginning, they would go every week on their way to school, a genuine ritual, but now they go less. Yearly, on his birthday in January, the family gather around his grave at 5 p.m (Photograph 6). Sparklers are lit, and there is room for informal speeches. There may even be cheerful moments: one time a little nephew said that he wanted to sing a Dutch birthday song, Lang zal hij leven (Long shall he live) for his uncle. They thought that this was probably not a very good idea!

Photograph 6. Celebrating dad's 53d birthday, 12 January 2018. © Stilbeeld Uitvaartfotografie.

Astrid said: "On the day of his death, the children think it is important to do the same thing every year." They visit the grave and afterwards they all go and have Chinese food. This year, it is going to be different because Brechtje, the oldest daughter, will be abroad studying in Vienna.

Davies reflects on the words of Herz and how the mourning process takes some time: "Still, he speaks of the "painful psychological process" of separating the dead from the consciousness of the living. Ties with the dead are not "severed in one day", memories and images continue through a series of "internal partings"" (Hertz 1960, p. 81; Davies 2000, pp. 99–100).

The rituals that the family performs on relevant days also relate to the mourning tasks described by Worden and which are concerned with the process of emotionally relocating the deceased, in this case Jan Leen as father of the children, within one's life and finding ways to memorialize the person and consequently, to move on with life (Worden 1996, pp. 10–17). Discussion on the issue of how to maintain a relationship with the deceased without being too troubled in daily life, is topical in bereavement studies. In 2018, more than twenty years after the term "continuing bonds" was introduced, Klass and Steffen conclude that retaining bonds with the deceased is an accepted option in bereavement processes (Klass and Steffen 2018). The Stam children cherish the bond they still have with their father. At the time of the interview Bente was wearing one of his old fleece jackets.

Up until the 1990s, based on the philosophy and ideas of Freud, the "breaking bonds" approach was dominant, that is, the bereaved should be freed from all ties with the deceased in order to create energy for new relationships (Freud 1917). Now, in 2018 the continuing bonds paradigm is supported by a reasonable amount of research and described practices (Stroebe et al. 1992; Shuchter and Zisook 1993; Klass et al. 1996; Goss and Klass 2005). The bereaved may "retain the deceased" (Walter 1996, p. 23) and the relationship does not have to be severed but may be transformed and achieve a different character (Shuchter and Zisook 1993, p. 34). As Astrid says: "Jan Leen is always with us. There is not a day when his name is not mentioned. The children have always had the possibility to reach out to their father and to continue in bonding with him." (Silverman and Worden 1992a, 1992b; Silverman and Nickman 1996; Worden 1996).

Up until today, the leading research in this area is the Child Bereavement Study, which investigated the impact of a parent's death on children from ages six to seventeen (Silverman and Worden 1992a, 1993; Silverman and Nickman 1996; Worden 1996) Interestingly, in this study the children themselves were interviewed and invited to express their opinion. Analysis of the data focused on how children talked about the deceased near one. It appeared that relationships with deceased parents were maintained rather than broken. The children kept all kinds of objects belonging to their parents and created a continuing link. In time, when there was less grief and when the children grew older, the relationship appeared to change and there was less need for such objects. A continuing relationship appeared to be part of a normal bereavement process. At that time, such a conclusion was contrary to what the researchers called traditional bereavement theory, that is, the breaking bonds paradigm. It was observed that the construction of a continuing bond with the dead parent provided comfort to the children and seemed to facilitate coping with their grief (Silverman and Nickman 1996, p. 73). The advice was that children should learn to remember and to find ways to maintain a way of reaching out to the deceased. This way should be coherent with the child's cognitive development, how death is understood, and the dynamics of the family in order to allow the child to continue living despite the loss of the parent (Nagy 1948; Silverman and Worden 1992a; Worden 1996; Silverman 2000).

One of Astrid's mantras when Jan Leen died was "to get back to a normal life as soon as possible and do the things that the children used to do", like going out and having dinner at the beach. She also realized this would be very emotional because it would be the four of them instead of five, and their life had been completely turned upside down. However, at the time of the interview she reflected that for them the mourning process seems to have finished in the sense that they have all regained "an interest in life, feel more hopeful, experience gratification again, and adapt to new roles. (Worden 2009, p. 77). Worden describes the completion of the mourning process:

> One benchmark of mourning moving to completion is when a person is able to think of the deceased without pain. There is always a sense of sadness when you think of someone you have loved and lost, but it is a different kind of sadness—it lacks the wrenching quality it previously had. One can think of the deceased without physical manifestations such as intense crying or feeling tightness in the chest. Also, mourning is finished when a person can reinvest his or her emotions into life and in the living. (Worden 2009, pp. 76–77)

According to Astrid, when a parent dies at a young age you should see it as a life that was accomplished, you should not live on with the thought of what could have been but instead try to be thankful for what has been. Sometimes this is difficult, particularly for her youngest son, Wytze. Wytze was only six years old when his father died. He does not have many of memories of him. Astrid tell him he should try to remember the feeling of loving him and they have photographs and movies which they watch.

3.3. Function and Meaning of the Photographs

During the interview Astrid Barten, her daughter Bente and I looked at the photographs of the death ritual of Jan Leen. Bente had not seen them for a long time. As her mother recalled the time of her father's death, the photographs brought back lost memories and not only provided a bridge between past and present, but also (re)constructed this past, particularly for Bente. In this way, the photographs seemed to construct a bond between emotional and important moments at a time when she was young, and the present. In the context of this article, I would argue that not only objects belonging to the deceased parents, but also objects, like photographs showing relevant moments of the death ritual may serve as transitional or in the words of Gibson, "melancholy objects", recalling the memory of early grief and the grief of time passing" (Gibson 2004, p. 289). These may be helpful in the construction of a new relationship with the deceased parent. In her book, *Objects of the Dead*, Gibson discusses photographs in the context of transitional objects: "As children and parents look at photographs together, a bridge between the past and the present is created, through stories, conversations, questions and answers" (Gibson 2008, pp. 88–89).

A memorial book was made with written stories about Jan Leen's life and the death ritual photographs were put together in an album with descriptions of what happened at the time of his death.

However, the children do not seem to need these material objects at this time of their life. Astrid explained, "I have made a wonderful memorial photo album, the children have never looked at it, but that's okay, it is there, so if they need it, it is there, but apparently they never felt they needed it. They all have a book in their own room and they can take it with them when they are going to live on their own."

In line with Sontag and Gibson, the photographs may be considered as melancholy objects as they create" the image of time, and the time of the image" (Gibson 2004, p. 286; Sontag 1977). At this time of their life there is no need to reflect on the time of the death of their father. They have found other ways, like visiting his grave and daily talking about him, to create a presence of what could be an absence because of their young age at the time he died (Maddrell 2013).

Although the photographs do not seem to have an apparent function for them at this moment, they have potential agency (Meyer and Woodthorpe 2008): intrinsically, they have the power to recall emotional and difficult times in the past and they are right at hand, in the children's rooms whenever they need them.

They construct a visual narrative that displays traces of the family life through significant events (Gibson 2004). In general, funerary photography may have this function (Ruby 1989, 1995; Hilliker 2006; Linkman 2011). For example, the value of having photographs of stillborn babies has been expressed by bereaved parents and family (Meredith 2000). For children who lose a parent at a young age, there might also be value in these photographs because they enable the children to construct the history of the time of the death of their parent.

The photographs showed how the Stam children consciously participated in the death ritual of their father and how they were recognized as grievers alongside adults, in particular, by their mother. The importance of taking part in the ritual is shown by the study of Søfting et al. Their mother's open attitude and focus on involving them the whole time, contributed to their accepting and coping with the death of their father (Søfting et al. 2016). This case study presentation helps to answer the question of whether young children should attend funerals in the affirmative (Hilpern 2013; Halliwel 2017).

4. Conclusions

Dear daddy,

Make a nice tiny house on your little cloud. Go to your new life. We will pull through, daddy.

O daddy, daddy, we will miss you for ever and always.

You are the sweetest daddy of the whole world.

Wytze[8]

The sorrowful words of six-year-old Wytze also carry a powerful statement: we will manage daddy . . . .

And they did.

Jan Leen Stam died when the children were still at a young age and Astrid Barten will always regret that the children lost their father: "I regret so very much that the children lost a wonderful father. It is horrible that he has not been able to educate them with his esteemed spirit, with his "being". But I

8

Lieve papa. Maak maar lekker een huisje op je wolkje. Ga maar naar je nieuwe leven. Wij redden onszelf wel, papa. O pappa, pappa, wat zullen wij je voor eeuwig en altijd missen. Je bent de allerliefste pappa van de hele wereld.

Wytze

Text written by Wytze Stam to appear on the death announcement of his father.

know, as a family we went through a lot of good things together. I am very proud how the children went on with their lives".

The funeral photographs showed how they participated as a family in the death ritual of their father. Presently, the funeral photographs of Jan Leen Stam do not seem to have a specific function. However, these photographs may become effective media for remembering and learning about a decisive moment in their life whenever the children feel the need to do so.

The conclusion of this case study presentation is that funeral photographs of death rituals can function as mnemonic objects when children lose a parent during childhood. In this respect, they can be seen as meaningful objects in funeral culture, particularly when young children are involved.

Funding: This research received no external funding.

Acknowledgments: The author wishes to thank the Stam–Barten family and Dasha Elfring (Stilbeeld Uitvaartfotografie) for their kind cooperation in this project.

Conflicts of Interest: The author declares no conflicts of interest. The author declares that all privacy and copyrights issues have been cleared.

References

Ariès, Philippe. 1994. *Western Attitudes toward Death: From the Middle Ages to the Present*. Translated by Patricia M. Ranum. London: Marion Boyars Publishers Ltd. First published 1974.

Baker, John E., and Mary A. Sedney. 1992. Psychological tasks for bereaved children. Theory and review. *American Journal of Orthopsychiatry* 62: 105–16. [CrossRef] [PubMed]

Barthes, Roland. 1981. *Camera Lucida: Reflections on Photography*. Translated by Richard Howard. France: Farrar, Straus and Giroux, Inc., Available online: https://monoskop.org/images/c/c5/Barthes_Roland_Camera_Lucida_Reflections_on_Photography.pdf (accessed on 10 June 2018).

Cook, Alicia S., and Kevin A. Oltjenbruns. 1998. *Dying and Grieving: Lifespan and Family Perspectives*. Forth Worth: Harcourt & Brace.

Dakin, Glenn. 2017. *Coco The Essential Guide*. New York: DK Publishing.

Davies, Douglas. 2000. Robert Hertz: the social triumph over death. *Mortality* 5: 97–102. [CrossRef]

Davies, Douglas. 2017. *Death, Ritual and Belief. The Rhetoric of Funerary Rites*, 3rd ed. London: Bloomsbury Academic.

Disney PIXAR. 2017. *The Art of Coco*. San Francisco: Chronicle Books.

Freud, Sigmund. 1917. Trauer und Melancholie [Grief and melancholy]. *Internationale Zeitschrift für Artztliche Psychoanalyse* 4: 288–301.

Gibson, Margaret. 2004. Melancholy objects. *Mortality* 9: 285–99. [CrossRef]

Gibson, Margaret. 2008. *Objects of the Dead. Mourning and Memory in Everyday Life*. Victoria: Melbourne University Press.

Goss, Robert E., and Dennis Klass. 2005. *Dead but Not Lost: Grief Narratives in Religious Traditions*. Oxford: Alta Mira.

Grimes, Ronald L. 2000. *Deeply into the Bone. Re-Inventing Rites of Passage*. Berkeley: University of California Press.

Hallam, Elizabeth, and Jenny Hockey. 2001. *Death, Memory and Material Culture*. Oxford: Berg.

Halliwel, Rachel. 2017. Is It OK to Take a Young Child to a Funeral? *The Telegraph*. October 7. Available online: http://www.telegraph.co.uk/women/family/ok-take-young-child-funeral/ (accessed on 28 November 2017).

Hertz, Robert. 1960. *Death and the Right Hand*. Translated by Rodney, and Claudia Needham. London: Cohen and West.

Hilliker, Laurel. 2006. Letting go while holding on: Postmortem photography as an aid in the grieving process. *Illness, Crisis & Loss* 14: 245–69.

Hilpern, Kate. 2013. Should Young Children Go to Funerals? *The Guardian*. July 12. Available online: https://www.theguardian.com/lifeandstyle/2013/jul/12/should-young-children-go-to-funerals (accessed on 29 November 2017).

Hirsch, Marianne. 2012. *The Generation of Postmemory. Writing and Visual Culture after the Holocaust*. New York: Columbia University Press.

Klass, Dennis, and Edith M. Steffen, eds. 2018. *Continuing Bonds in Bereavement: New Directions for Research and Practice*. New York: Routledge.

Klass, Dennis, Phyllis Silverman, and Steven L. Nickman, eds. 1996. *Continuing Bonds: New Understandings of Grief.* London: Taylor and Francis.

Linkman, Audrey. 2011. *Photography and Death.* London: Reaktion Books.

Maddrell, Avril. 2013. Living with the deceased: absence, presence and absence-presence. *Cultural Geographies* 20: 501–22. [CrossRef]

Meredith, Rachel. 2000. The photography of neonatal bereavement at Wythenshawe Hospital. *Journal of Audiovisual Media in Medicine* 23: 161–64. [CrossRef] [PubMed]

Meyer, Morgan, and Kate Woodthorpe. 2008. The material presence of absence: A dialogue between museums and cemeteries. *Sociological Research Online* 13: 1–9. [CrossRef]

Nagy, Maria. 1948. The child's theories concerning death. *The Pedagogical Seminary and Journal of Genetic Psychology* 73: 3–27. [CrossRef]

Pink, Sarah. 2007. *Doing Visual Ethnography.* London: Sage.

Pink, Sarah. 2008. Analysing visual experience. In *Research Methods for Cultural Studies.* Edited by Michael Pickering. Edinburgh: Edinburgh University Press, pp. 125–49.

Ruby, Jay. 1989. Portraying the dead. *Omega: Journal of Death and Dying* 19: 1–20. [CrossRef]

Ruby, Jay. 1995. *Secure the Shadow. Death and Photography in America.* Cambridge: The MIT Press.

Schowalter, John E. 1976. How do children and funerals mix? *The Journal of Pediatrics* 89: 139–42. [CrossRef]

Shuchter, Stephen R., and Sidney Zisook. 1993. The course of normal grief. In *Handbook of Bereavement.* Edited by Margaret Stroebe, Wolfgang Stroebe and Robert O. Hansson. New York: Cambridge Univesrity Press, pp. 22–43.

Silverman, Phyllis R. 2000. *Never too Young to Know. Death in Children's Lives.* New York: Oxford Univesrity Press.

Silverman, Phyllis R., and Stephen L. Nickman. 1996. Children's construction of their dead parents. In *Continuing Bonds. New Understandings of Grief.* Edited by Dennis Klass, Phyllis R. Silverman and Steven L. Nickman. New York: Routledge, pp. 73–86.

Silverman, Phyllis R., and William Worden. 1992a. Children's reactions to the death of a parent in the early months after the death. *American Journal of Orthopsychiatry* 62: 93–104. [CrossRef]

Silverman, Phyllis R., and William Worden. 1992b. Children's understanding of funeral ritual. *Omega: Journal od Death and Dying* 25: 319–31. [CrossRef]

Silverman, Phyllis R., and William Worden. 1993. Children's reactions to the death of a parent. In *Handbook of Bereavement.* Edited by Margaret Stroebe, Wolfgang Stroebe and Robert O. Hansson. New York: Cambridge University Press, pp. 300–16.

Søfting, Gunn Helen, Atle Dyregrov, and Jari Dyregrov. 2016. Because I'm also part of the family. Children's participation in rituals after the death of a parent: A qualitative study from the children's perspective. *Omega-Journal of Death and Dying* 73: 141–58. [CrossRef]

Sontag, Susan. 1977. *On Photography.* London: Penguin Books.

Stroebe, Margaret, Mary Gergen, Kenneth J. Gergen, and Wolfgang Stroebe. 1992. Broken hearts or broken bonds. Love and death in historical perspective. *American Psychologist* 47: 1205–12. [CrossRef] [PubMed]

Tandeciarz, Silvia R. 2006. Mnemonic hauntings: Photography as art of the missing. *Social Justice* 33: 135–52.

Turner, Victor. 1969. *The Ritual Process. Structure and Anti-Structure.* New Brunswick: Aldine Transactions.

Van der Zee, James, Owen Dodson, and Camille Billops. 1978. *The Harlem Book of the Dead.* New York: Morgan & Morgan.

Van Gennep, Arnold. 1960. *The Rites of Passage.* Translated by Monika B. Vizedom, and Gabrielle L. Caffee. Chicago: The University of Chicago Press.

Walter, Tony. 1996. A new model of grief: bereavement and biography. *Mortality* 1: 7–25. [CrossRef]

Winnicott, David. 1997. *Playing and Reality.* Kent: Tavistock/Routledge. First published 1971.

Worden, William. 1996. *Children and Grief. When a Parent Dies.* New York: The Guilford Press.

Worden, William. 2009. *Grief Counseling and Grief Therapy: A Handbook for the Mental Health Practitioner*, 4th ed. New York: Springer.
Zerubavel, Eviatar. 2003. *Time Maps. Collective Memory and the Social Shape of the Past*. Chicago and London: The University of Chicago Press.

religions

MDPI

Article

The Ritualizing of the Martial and Benevolent Side of Ravana in Two Annual Rituals at the Sri Devram Maha Viharaya in Pannipitiya, Sri Lanka

Deborah de Koning

Department of Culture Studies, Tilburg School of Humanities and Digital Sciences, Tilburg University, 5037 AB Tilburg, The Netherlands; d.d.c.dekoning@uvt.nl

Received: 29 June 2018; Accepted: 19 August 2018; Published: 21 August 2018

Abstract: Within the context of *Ravanisation*—by which I mean the current revitalisation of Ravana among Sinhalese Buddhists in Sri Lanka—multiple conceptualizations of Ravana are constructed. This article concentrates on two different Ravana conceptualizations: Ravana as a warrior king and Ravana as a healer. At the Sri Devram Maha Viharaya, a recently constructed Buddhist complex in Colombo, Ravana has become the object of devotion. In addition to erecting a Ravana statue in a shrine of his own, two annual rituals for Ravana are organized by this temple. In these rituals we can clearly discern the two previously mentioned conceptualizations: the Ravana *perahera* (procession) mainly concentrates on Ravana's martial side by exalting Ravana as warrior king, and in the *maha Ravana nanumura mangalyaya*, a ritual which focusses on healing, his benevolent side as a healer is stressed. These conceptualizations from the broader Ravana discourse are ritualized in iconography, attributes, and sacred substances. The focus on ritual invention in this article not only directs our attention to the creativity within the rituals but also to the wider context of these developments: the glorification of an ancient civilization as part of increased nationalistic sentiments and an increased assertiveness among the Sinhalese Buddhist majority in post-war Sri Lanka.

Keywords: Ravana; Sri Lanka; Sinhalese Buddhist Majority; ritualizing; procession; healing; ritual creativity

1. Introduction

Every Sunday evening a group of around twenty five people gather together at the *Sri Lankesvara maha Ravana raja mandiraya* for the weekly Ravana *puja*. In Sri Lankan Buddhism, the *puja* has to be considered as 'the formal act of worship carried out before a god or a Buddha image' (Gombrich and Obeyesekere 1988, p. xvi). The Ravana *mandiraya* (palace)—where this particular *puja* for Ravana is conducted—is located at the premises of the Sri Devram Maha Viharaya, a recently constructed massive Buddhist temple complex in one of the suburbs of Colombo (Pannipitiya). After the inauguration of the *mandiraya* in 2013, the head monk of the Sri Devram Maha Viharaya (Kolonnave Siri Sumangala Thero, hereinafter referred to as Sumangala Thero), has appointed a lay-custodian to take care of the Ravana *mandiraya*.

The weekly Ravana *puja* is one of the public rituals performed for Ravana under the responsibility of this lay-custodian. Although—compared to the annual rituals for Ravana organized by the Sri Devram Maha Viharaya—the number of attendants is relatively small, the ritual itself is rather extensive: it has to be conducted exactly in the way it has been prescribed by Sumangala Thero, even if there is no public at all. Thus, every Sunday around five o'clock a group of volunteers starts with the preparation of different types of semi-fluid herbal substances (which are stored in between nine up to eleven different cups)[1], and prepares two plates with pieces of nine different types of fruits and nine different types of traditional Sri Lankan sweets. The herbal substances prepared on Sunday evenings for the Ravana *puja* are used by the main lay-custodian or his assistants to anoint (two of) the statues of Ravana in the inner sanctuary of the *mandiraya*. This part of the ritual is called the *nanumura*: the anointing or bathing of the statue (the verb *nanava* means to bathe). The *nanumura* is regarded as the most important part of the ritual: according to the lay-custodian the weekly ritual for Ravana would be incomplete without the performance of the *nanumura* (Lay-Custodian Ravana *Mandiraya* 2017c).

After the statues have been anointed and dressed behind a closed door, the plates with oil lamps containing three different types of oil (mustard oil, sesame oil, and ghee), the plates with fruits and sweets, a bowl with *murethen* (sweetened rice), and baskets with flowers are brought in a small procession from the kitchen to the entrance of the *mandiraya*. The offerings are handed over by the volunteers (and by the sponsor of the *puja*) at the entrance of the *mandiraya* to the lay-custodian and/or his assistants, who place the offerings inside the inner sanctuary. The people outside the *mandiraya* join the next element of the ritual: the chanting of some well-known Buddhist *gathas* (a *gatha* is a stanza, to be recited or sung) followed by special songs and invocations for Ravana. After the chanting session the plates with fruits and sweets, three bowls filled with different types of substances and the bowl with *murethen*, are taken out of the *mandiraya*. The fruits, sweets, substances, and *murethen* are served to the attendants of the *puja* after they have bowed in reverence to the freshly anointed and newly dressed statue(s) of Ravana.

The liturgy for the Ravana *puja* includes 12 different elements such as poems, songs, and mantras. These poems, songs, and mantras for Ravana are composed by Sumangala Thero. Without discussing the layered imagery in detail, I would like to present here four out of the nine stanzas of the following invocation for Ravana: *Maha Ravana pujave di gayana kavi*:

දඬු මොනරෙන් වඩිනා දෙවියෝ
මහා ඇතුපිට වඩිනා දෙවියෝ
සිවු රඟ සේනා ඇති දෙවියෝ
වඩිනු මැනිවි රාවණ දෙවියෝ

1 The god who arrives on the *dandu monara*
The god who arrives on the great tusker
The god who owns the fourfold armies
May god Ravana arrive

හිස් දහයක් ඇති මහ දෙවියෝ
අත් විස්සක් ඇති මහ දෙවියෝ
දය බලයක් ඇති මහ දෙවියෝ
වඩිනු මැනිවි රාවණ දෙවියෝ

2 The great god with ten heads
The great god with twenty arms
The great god with ten powers
May god Ravana arrive

---

[1] The number of substances used to anoint the statues on Sunday evenings seemed to vary between nine and eleven. I assisted several times in the kitchen to prepare the necessities for the Ravana *puja* and I often counted nine big cups filled with porridges made out of herbal substances (such as turmeric and sandalwood) and two small ones filled with milk and king coconut. That for the latter two no 'preparation' is needed might explain the difference in the number of substances mentioned to me.The number and ingredients used for different rituals for Ravana are also prescribed by Sumangala Thero in for instance his book *Sri Lankesvara Maha Ravana* (Sumangala Thero 2014, pp. 45–47).

වෙද දුරු මහ රජ මහ දෙවියෝ
කෙත් වතු සරු කළ මහ දෙවියෝ
හිරු එළියෙන් වෙඩගත් දෙවියෝ
වඩිනු මැනිව් රාවණ දෙවියෝ

3 The great god who's a doctor and a great king
The great god who brought prosperity to paddy fields
The great god who received favors from the light of the sun
May god Ravana arrive

මුළු ලොව ජයගත් මහ දෙවියෝ
හෙළයට පණ දුන් මහ දෙවියෝ
තුන් ලොව පුජිත මහ දෙවියෝ
වඩිනු මැනිව් රාවණ දෙවියෝ

6 The great god who won the whole world
The great god who gave life to the land of *Hela*
The great god worshipped by the threefold worlds
May god Ravana arrive

The invocation for Ravana unveils some of the multi-layered conceptualizations directed at the figure of Ravana within the current Ravana discourse in Sri Lanka: its imagery and ideas can be traced back to the *Hela* movement, to rural lore, and to Hindu mythology.[2] The *Hela* concept—which is mentioned in the sixth stanza—became extensively employed in the early-twentieth century *Havula* or *Hela* movement in Sri Lanka, a movement focused on the re-establishing of an indigenous language (*Hela*). Cumaratunga, the leading representative of this linguistic movement, considered the *Hela diva* (country) *Hela daya* (nation) and *Hela basa* (language) as the three constitutive elements of the nation (Cumaratunga 1941, p. 394).[3] The *Hela* concept is in the current Ravana discourse primarily employed to denote the earliest inhabitants of Lanka who are divided in four different *Hela* tribes (*siv Hela*).[4] Among these tribes the *yaksha* and *naga* tribes stand out. To underscore the presence of these tribes in ancient Lanka references are made to the sixth century chronicle the *Mahavamsa*.[5] These references to the *Mahavamasa*, which became the foundational myth for the Sinhalese in the twentieth century (Wickramasinghe 2014, p. 94), unveil the attempt to suture the current Ravana myth into well-known Sri Lankan myths and chronicles.

In the first and second stanzas ideas which have been present in the ancient Hindu epic the *Ramayana* are touched upon. Ravana is introduced as arriving on the *dandu monara*, which can be loosely translated as 'peacock made out of wooden bars'. In the *Ramayana* a flying machine (the *puspaka*) used by Ravana is also mentioned (Dutt 1894, p. 1604). The idea of aircraft technology as mastered by Ravana is one of the main focus points in the current Ravana discourse.

When it comes to his physical appearance, Ravana as believed to have ten heads and twenty arms (second stanza) is also known already from the *Ramayana*. In the seventh book of Valmiki's

---

2 The reference to Ravana in the third stanza as the one who brings prosperity to paddy fields also occurs in popular publications in the Ravana discourse, for instance in one of the publications from the most famous writer in the Ravana discourse Mirando Obeyesekere. Obeyesekere has elaborated upon an irrigation system which allegedly was extant in Ravana's time in the surroundings of Lakegala (Obeyesekere 2016, p. 79). According to him people in that area believe that this irrigation system dates back to Ravana's time. The interactions between Ravana imaginations from rural lore (and Lakegala in particular) and imaginations from the Ravana discourse will be discussed in detail in my upcoming dissertation.

3 The role of one particular *Hela* representative for the current Ravana discourse with a special focus on the iconographic representation of Ravana within the Ravana discourse will be discussed in more detail in the third section of this article.

4 The *Hela* concept also appears in Sinhalese perception prior to the *Hela* movement (Dharmadasa 1995, pp. 20–21).

5 The first parts of the *Mahavamsa* have been written in the sixth century and after that it was updated three times: in the twelfth century, the fourteenth century, and the eighteenth century (Dharmadasa 1995, p. 4).

Ramayana (considered to be a latter addition) Ravana is referred to as born with '[...] having ten necks, furnished with large teeth, and resembling a heap of collyrium, with coppery lips, twenty arms, huge faces, and flaming hair' (Dutt 1894, p. 1583). Ravana with ten heads and twenty arms became a popular iconographic representation in temple iconography and is also employed in Hindu temples in Sri Lanka.[6]

The terrifying representation of Ravana with ten heads and twenty arms is—as also becomes evident in the poem—in the current Ravana discourse interpreted in a symbolic way: the ten heads symbolize the ten powers or capabilities which Ravana allegedly mastered. Examples of these skills are aircraft technology and medicine. In general, in the current Ravana myth under construction (story), fragments and ideas from different sources are integrated as far as they contribute to the glorification of Lanka's ancient and indigenous civilization or can be re-interpreted as such. The current Ravana myth under construction is drifting away from the well-known Rama Sita Ravana myth. In its focus to exalt Ravana and Lanka and by suturing Ravana and the ancient tribes into well-known Sri Lankan chronicles and myths, the current Ravana myth from the Ravana discourse cannot even be considered as an anti-*Ramayana*.[7] As I will show in this article by discussing fieldwork observations and conversations,[8] the display of positive Ravana conceptualizations in the two rituals helps to construct this myth of Sinhalese-Buddhist national pride.

Most of the rituals, statues, and objects related to Ravana in the Sinhalese-Buddhist context are recently invented and tend to promote positive Ravana ideas. To underscore the recent development of these rituals I use Grimes' concept of ritualizing: 'the act of cultivating or inventing rites' (Grimes 2014, p. 193). As I will discuss, in the two annual rituals two positive Ravana conceptualizations are ritualized. The conceptualizations of Ravana as a warrior king and as a healer become visible and tangible in objects, attributes, and sacred substances used in those rituals.

After a brief introduction of the Sri Devram Maha Viharaya in the next section, I will concentrate in the third section on the iconographic elements of the sword and the scripture. The discussion of the sword and the scripture, as part of the main statue of Ravana at the Sri Devram Maha Viharaya, serves as a starting point to further discuss the ritualizing of Ravana's martial side (as warrior king) and benevolent side (as healer) in the two rituals.

In the fourth and fifth sections I will analyze how the conceptualizations of Ravana as warrior king and as healer are displayed in the two annual rituals: the *maha Ravana perahera* (*perahera* means procession) and the *maha Ravana nanumura mangalyaya* (*mangalyaya* means festival—together with *nanumura* it can be translated as 'festival of anointing'). By the use of certain attributes, objects, and herbal substances conceptualizations of Ravana are constructed in these rituals. In the final section I will evaluate how these rituals have to be understood in the current process of *Ravanisation* in Sri Lanka's post-war context.

2. The Sri Devram Maha Viharaya

The Sri Devram Maha Viharaya is a Buddhist complex located in Pannipitiya, one of the suburbs of Colombo. The first part of the complex's name (*devram*) refers to a monastery mentioned in for

[6] Examples of Hindu temples in Sri Lanka where this particular iconographic representation of Ravana is employed are the temples of Munnesvaram (visited 4 May 2016), Konesvaram (visited 23 March 2016), and the Nagapoosani Amman Kovil located on the island Nagadipa (visited 2 February 2016).

[7] As discussed by Velcheru Narayana Rao the common core in the anti-*Ramayana* discourse in India is its anti-Brahmanism. The criticizing of pro-Brahmanic biases in Valmiki's *Ramayana* appears for instance in retellings or rewritings of the *Ramayana* in Telegu and Tamil (Rao 1991, p. 162). As pointed out by Paula Richman for instance E.V. Ramasami, who is sometimes referred to as the founder of the Dravidian Movement, was more occupied with criticizing North Indians and the *Ramayana* than by defining a South Indian identity (Richman 1991, p. 197). In contrast to this anti-*Ramayana* discourse in the Indian context the Ravana myth under construction in Sri Lanka is not a retelling or rewriting of the *Ramayana* and the main focus within the current Ravana discourse is to construct a myth of Sinhalese-Buddhist national pride.

[8] I have participated in the annual and weekly rituals for Ravana from 2016 onwards and conducted extensive fieldwork research at this Buddhist temple complex in 2017 and 2018.

instance the seventeenth century *Rajavaliya*. According to the *Rajavaliya*, the Buddha is believed to have returned to the monastery of Devram (*devuram vehera*) after his second visit to Lanka (Suraweera 2014, p. 168). *Vihara* is used in Sinhala to denote a temple, or the complex of monastic buildings (Gombrich and Obeyesekere 1988, p. vx).

Sumangala Thero is the monk who initiated the construction of the Sri Devram Maha Viharaya. He is well-known in Sri Lanka, especially because he was involved in politics. In 2004 he was one of the three leading election candidates of the JHU (Jathika Hela Urumaya, National Sinhala Heritage Party). The JHU—the first political party in Sri Lanka which was exclusively ran by monks—won nine out of 225 seats in the parliament (Rahula 1974, 2011, pp. 380–82; Deegalle 2004, 2011, pp. 383–94).[9] Despite the success of the JHU, Sumangala Thero had already resigned from the party in the very first year (Sumangala Thero 2017b).

Sumangala Thero is highly venerated by most of the people who visit the Sri Devram Maha Viharaya. Because he is believed to possess special powers, people come to the temple to ask Sumangala Thero to bless and heal them and their relatives. Also, because of his experience in meditation he is believed to have developed special mind reading skills. Therefore, he is also wanted for advice in family and business related issues. These days it is, however, increasingly hard to get an appointment with Sumangala Thero, since he is believed to have withdrawn himself from worldly matters.

The Sri Devram Maha Viharaya only came into existence around twenty years ago. With new buildings regularly constructed and older ones restored, enlarged, or replaced by newer ones, the complex is continuously in a process of transformation. On *poya* days (the full moon days) and festival days the complex is visited by people coming from far and wide. They walk around at the extensive site, pay a visit to the different shrines, the stupa, and Buddha statues for offering lotus flowers and incense, do a *baraya* (place an intention) by tying a coin with a piece of cloth to the branch of a tree or a fence (*panduru*), walk around the Bodhi tree, visit one of the informative buildings pertaining to the temple, the role of Thai monks in the revival of Buddhism in Sri Lanka, and the 'hell' (these educational buildings are called museums) located on the site, wait to participate in a special *puja* and to receive the blessing of the monk, participate in the chanting, listen to teachings in the *dhamma* hall, watch the spectacles and rituals, enjoy the natural surroundings and luxurious decorations, read the texts on the hundreds of stone slabs (including the hundreds of black marble stone slabs on which the *Tripitaka* is inscribed), and enjoy the food which is on most *poya* days offered for free.

In addition to a Bodhi tree, stupa, and shrines and statues constructed for devotional activities for Buddha, there is also a section with shrines for the gods at the Sri Devram Maha Viharaya. Shrines for gods—for instance for Visnu, who is considered to be one of the four guardian gods in Sri

---

[9] In the manifesto of the JHU—which contains twelve points for constructing a righteous state—it is formulated that it is regarded as the duty of the government to protect Buddhism. Also, it states that the "*[…] national heritage of a country belongs to the ethnic group who made the country into a habitable civilization*" (Deegalle 2004, 2011, p. 391). Around the time of the opening of the Ravana *mandiraya* at the Sri Devram Maha Viharaya in 2013, also twelve goals of the temple complex were formulated by Sumangala Thero. These goals are put on display at one of the offices located at the Sri Devram Maha Viharaya. Roughly translated these goals are: (1) the protection/maintaining of the Sinhalese race/nation (to) protect/maintain the rights of other races/nations, (2) to make the ancient history/pedigree known to the young generation, (3) to give new life to agriculture, (4) to get the population used to the everyday living of *Hela* people, (5) to upkeep Ayurveda, (6) to take care of language, (7) to take care of music, dance, and rituals, (8) to give aid to/support new developments, (9) to create a young generation of *bodhisattas* (he who is going to become a Buddha), (10) to give aid/help to good intelligent children for education, (11) to take care of the older generation who gave power to our race/nation and, (12) to give to the youth a sense of 'ourness'. Social activities organized by the Sri Devram Maha Viharaya such as housebuilding projects for poor people and the organization of blood donation campaigns, bear witness to the social engagement of Sumangala Thero and this temple complex.

Lankan Buddhism (Holt 2008, p. 145)—are present at most Buddhist temple complexes in Sri Lanka.[10] These shrines for gods are taken care of by lay-custodians.[11]

On weekdays there is almost no ritual activity taking place around the shrines at the Sri Devram Maha Viharaya. All the doors of the inner sanctuaries of the shrines are closed and no lay-custodians—probably since most of the lay-custodians responsible for different shrines have regular jobs—are around on weekdays. In the weekends there is, however, a lot of ritual activity at the compound where the shrines are located. On Saturday evenings an extensive *puja* for Mahamaya (the mother of Gautama Buddha) is conducted. This *puja* of around 1.5 h takes place in the *mandiraya* for Mahamaya, the largest building at this part of the site which has been constructed in 2010. Sunday evenings are reserved for the Ravana *puja*. As I was told by the secretary of Sumangala Thero, unlike other Buddhist temples where the central place—after Buddha—is given to one god, at the Sri Devram Maha Viharaya prominence is given to both Mahamaya and Ravana (Secretary Sumangala Thero 2018a).

The Ravana *mandiraya* constructed at the Sri Devram Maha Viharaya (see Figure 1) is the second largest building at this section. According to the stone slab which is immured in the front wall, it has been formally inaugurated on the 19 September 2013 by Mahinda Rajapaksa, the president of the previous government of Sri Lanka (2005–2015).

Figure 1. The *Sri Lankesvara maha Ravana raja mandiraya* (left side). This building is located at the premises of the Sri Devram Maha Viharaya. On the right side: one of the chariots for Ravana. This chariot is taken around in the annual *perahera* organized by this Buddhist temple. Picture taken by author, 6 June 2017.

In contrast to most of the paintings of Ravana in Hindu temples in Sri Lanka (such as the Sita Amman temple in Nuwara Eliya) in which the Ravana depictions are presented in the context of the *Ramayana*, the paintings in the *mandiraya* concentrate on the extraordinary character of Ravana and his

[10] In addition to shrines for gods located on the premises of a Buddhist temple complex there are also shrines in Sri Lanka not located on Buddhist sites (Gombrich and Obeyesekere 1988, p. xvi).

[11] Gombrich and Obeyesekere refer to the officiant at a Sinhala shrine as a *kapuva* or *kapurala* (Gombrich and Obeyesekere 1988, p. xvi). At the Sri Devram Maha Viharaya the lay-custodian who is responsible for the Ravana *mandiraya* considered himself not a *kapurala* or *kapuva* but a care-taker. That the words *kapurala* or *kapuva* are less used at the Sri Devram Maha Viharaya is probably because the job is not inherited and it is not the custodians' full-time occupation.

advanced civilization: multiple paintings show for instance the ten capabilities of Ravana and one side of the *mandiraya* contains a painting in which the Ravana civilization is equated with the Maya and Inca civilizations (see Figure 2). In addition to that, the ability of space travelling and the development of aircraft technology is a topic on its own in the wall paintings. Only two depictions of the war-scene (including Rama and his monkey army) show similarities with Hindu-temple paintings. Paintings of the well-known couple Sita and Rama or devotional depictions of Hanuman (the famous monkey devotee of Rama) as known from Hindu temple iconography are absent in the *mandiraya*.

Figure 2. Wall painting in the Ravana *mandiraya*. This painting shows (from left to right) depictions of the Maya, Inca, and Ravana civilization. The latter is represented by a depiction of the famous Sigirya rock. The painting between the two windows depicts books on medicine. Picture taken by author, 6 June 2017.

This shrine for Ravana constructed at the Sri Devram Maha Viharaya is the most extensive shrine for Ravana that I have encountered in Sri Lanka.[12] Also, regular ritual activities for Ravana take place at the shrine and these ritual activities attract people with an interest in Ravana from all over the country. It is also the only shrine for Ravana in Colombo. The construction of the Ravana shrine and the ritual activities for Ravana are not the only striking element at the Sri Devram Maha Viharaya: the devotional activities for Mahamaya and the outstanding role of the specially gifted monk are noteworthy as well. Although the Sri Devram Maha Viharaya is exclusive in the veneration for Mahamaya and Ravana, the autonomous positions of (political engaged) monks and idiosyncratic developments at urban Buddhist temple sites in post-war Sri Lanka are not limited to this particular temple.[13]

During my fieldwork research I have encountered several Buddhist monks in Sri Lanka who show an interest in Ravana. They consider him to be an outstanding king of ancient Lanka and some of them

[12] Other shrines for Ravana at Buddhist temple sites are for instance constructed at Boltumbe Saman *devalaya* (visited May 6, 2016) and Rambadagalla Viharaya in Kurunegalla (visited 2 March 2016). Also in Katuwana, there is a Ravana image enshrined in a cave and this is the only site where annually a small *perahera* for Ravana is organized. This *perahera* concentrates on the performances of *Angampora* and there are no elephants or chariots included. The statue taken around in the *perahera* is the Ravana statue from the shrine (Angampora Teacher 2018).

[13] See for some recent examples of politically engaged Buddhist monks in Sri Lanka and the exceptional status of impunity they enjoy—even if they use violence—Gunatilleke 2018, pp. 77–82.

openly talk and publish about Ravana.[14] The imagination of Ravana as believed to be the inventor of medicine—whether Ayurveda or 'traditional Sinhalese medicine'—is also widespread in the current Ravana discourse: his knowledge of medicine is believed to be one of his ten outstanding capabilities.

The imaginations of Ravana as king of Lanka and Ravana as believed to have healing powers are present in the broader Ravana discourse—and beyond. In general, positive Ravana imaginations and ideas of an ancient and advanced civilization in Sri Lanka are primarily mediated through (social) media. Newspaper articles, especially the ones written by Mirando Obeyesekere, are of central importance.[15] Also, in the past ten years, plenty of popular books on Ravana have been published and several private research groups started to promote their Ravana ideas on Facebook and other webpages. In addition to that, songs are written in praise for Ravana and special radio and TV-programs dealing with Ravana occur.[16]

Sumangala Thero has written some popular books on Ravana as well. But it is the construction of a shrine for Ravana and the inventing of Ravana rituals that makes the Sri Devram Maha Viharaya outstanding in the way positive Ravana imaginations are actively promoted. The *mandiraya* is believed to contain four Ravana statues (Lay-Custodian Ravana *Mandiraya* 2017b).[17] Only two out of the four statues are the object of ritual activities: the main black statue standing in front of the inner sanctuary and a small black one behind it (hidden from public view). When the door of the inner sanctuary is open, also a statue of Ravana seated on a platform at the back of the sanctuary can be witnessed (see Figure 3). Since the black statue in front of the *mandiraya* is the object of the weekly and annual ritual activities and (instead of the small one) can be witnessed by the audience, I will discuss this statue in detail in the next section.

---

[14] Examples are a monk from Vidurupola (Nuwara Eliya district) who delivered a speech on the day a movie about Rama and Ravana was released in Sri Lanka (around 2014) and a monk from Galgamuwa area who is publishing about the ancient *yaksha* language. Both monks consider Ravana the ancient king of Lanka. They did not conduct devotional activities for him. The latter monk explicated that Ravana has not be considered a god (Monk Vidurupola 2016; Monk Galgamuwa 2017).

[15] In several informal conversations with visitors of the Sri Devram Maha Viharaya conducted in 2018 I asked them how and when their interest in Ravana started. They frequently answered that they learned about Ravana through newspaper articles, especially the ones written by Mirando Obeyesekere.

[16] In addition to interviews with so called Ravana experts in TV- and radio programs, it is archaeological sites, caves and mountains which are discussed in length. These geographical spots allegedly proof the presence of Ravana and Lanka's highly advanced civilization. Although there is some overlap with sites developed for *Ramayana* tourism in post-war Sri Lanka, in documentaries produced within the Ravana discourse mainly sites which are not storied within the *Ramayana* are discussed. See for some details of the development of *Ramayana* tourism Spencer (2014).

[17] At one of the upper levels of the 'sanctuary tower' there is allegedly another Ravana statue kept.

Figure 3. Statue of Ravana in the *Sri Lankesvara maha Ravana raja mandiraya*. The statue is richly decorated after the annual *maha Ravana nanumura mangalyaya*. Picture taken by author, 25 March 2018.

3. The Sword and Scripture of Ravana

The black stone statue of Ravana in the *mandiraya* differs from the popular iconographic representation of Ravana with ten heads and twenty arms.[18] The statue depicts Ravana with one head and two hands, holding two attributes: the sword and the scripture (see Figure 3). A similar depiction of Ravana was designed in Sri Lanka in the eighties according to the ideas of the famous writer and scholar Arisen Ahubudu.[19] At the start of his career Ahubudu (1920–2011) joined the *Hela* movement. As Coperahewa suggests, there was also a nationalistic motivation within this linguistic movement to construct an

[18] Also in Sri Lanka some of the recently erected statues for Ravana at Buddhist complexes, for example the statue at Boltumbe Saman *devalaya*, depict Ravana with ten heads and twenty arms, This particular iconographic representation of Ravana is called *dasis* Ravana in Sinhalese, a contraction of *dasa* (ten) and *hisa* (head).

[19] This information was gained through Ahubudu's daughter (Ahubudu 2018).

indigenous (*Hela*) identity (Coperahewa 2012, pp. 860, 879). In this context, Ravana was exalted as king of an ancient indigenous civilization (Dharmadasa 1995, p. 264).

In the current context of *Ravanisation* some of the later publications of the *Hela* representative Arisen Ahubudu are translated and reprinted to promote the story of Ravana.[20] Also, the text of a song in praise of Ravana originally written by Ahubudu in the eighties for the theatre play *Sakwithi Ravana* (loosely translated as *Ravana as world ruler*) is now for instance duplicated in a popular song for Ravana (*Sakwithi Ravana*) by the *Ravana Soruyo* (*Ravana Brothers*), an association conducting research on the history of Sri Lanka with a focus on Ravana.[21]

At the time of the theatre performance (1987), Ahubudu also wanted to create a proper depiction of Ravana (Ahubudu 2018). According to the president of one of the popular research groups on Ravana (the *Ravana Shakti*) who discussed the particular depiction of Ravana with Ahubudu when he was still alive, Ahubudu had appointed a young man who transferred his ideas into an actual depiction of Ravana on a banner and also molded a Ravana statue (President of *Ravana Shakti* 2018). Ravana in this depiction (see Figure 4) has only one head and two hands and holds two attributes in his hands: a sword and a book.[22] The banner is now duplicated in a moderate size on plastic by the popular research group the *Ravana Shakti*. This research group gives the banners for free to people who have a special interest in Ravana (President of *Ravana Shakti* 2018).

The statue of Ravana that has the most prominent position in the Ravana *mandiraya* at the Sri Devram Maha Viharaya also holds these two attributes: the sword and the *ola* leaf book. According to Sumangala Thero, the design of the black stone statue of Ravana was based on a statue of a *bodhisatta* he has noticed at a place in Sri Lanka called Maligavila. This statue is by some people considered to be the *bodhisatta* Avalokitesvara (Sumangala Thero 2018). Although the Ravana statue shows similarities with this particular statue at Maligavila—especially the standing position and the adornments around waist, hips, and neck—the two attributes of the sword and book are not part of the statue at Maligavila.[23] That is why I asked Sumangala Thero explicitly about these particular objects.

> [...] It is the *ola* leaf book and the sword. The sword signifies his power and bravery and that there is nothing he cannot do. The *ola* leaf book signifies his wisdom or intelligence. [...] In the present day why we have given the statue a sword is because there is a lot of injustice, crime and lack of peace around the world. We believe that these problems should be solved and that king Ravana has the power to solve them. *[The book symbolizes]* knowledge about peace, justice and ruling, as well as universal knowledge about war and medication. Since the brain cannot be given to the hand, we have signified his great wisdom using this book (Sumangala Thero 2018).

Most of the visitors of the Ravana *mandiraya* did not notice these two attributes and I only got answers with regard to the meaning of these attributes by showing them pictures of the statue. Like the monk, they gave different interpretations—or had no idea. With regard to the book, people frequently mentioned Ravana's knowledge on medicine or medical spells when I asked them to specify what

---

20 An example of this is his book *Hela Derana Vaga* which has been translated into English and published in 2012 under the title *The Story of the land of the Sinhalese (Helese)*.

21 http://ravanabrothers.com/open/ (accessed on 6 August 2018).

22 This is also the way the Ravana statue is molded in one of the earliest shrines for Ravana at the famous site of Kataragama. This shrine at Kataragama has been constructed under president Premadasa in 1987 (Lay-Custodian Ravana Shrine Kataragama 2018). At that time Ahubudu was appointed as consultant for president Premadasa (Coperahewa 2018).

23 I have not seen this statue at Maligavila myself and my observations of the statue are based on pictures published on the internet. Interestingly, a few more people from the Ravana discourse I talked with considered Ravana to be the same as Avalokitesvara. The particular objects (sword and scripture) are in Mahayana Buddhist iconography associated with another *bodhisatta:* Manjusri. With Manjusri both objects are connected to wisdom: the sword symbolizes the awareness of this *bodhisatta* which cuts through all delusion and the text indicates his mastery of all knowledge (Beer 2003, pp. 123–24; Robinson and Johnson 1997, pp. 106–7). In my fieldwork research (conducted in Sri Lanka which is primarily but not exclusively a Theravada Buddhist country) this *bodhisatta* was never referred to.

knowledge the book represented.[24] The sword is also open to multiple interpretations like justice, power, bravery, fighting, and kingship.[25] Though these objects are multi-interpretable they direct our attention to two sides of Ravana: his martial side as warrior king and his benevolent side as healer.

Figure 4. Picture originally taken in the eighties of Arisen Ahubudu with the Ravana banner and statue. This picture has been retrieved from the Official website of A. Ahubudu (n.d.).

4. The Ritualizing of Ravana as a Warrior King in the Annual *Maha Ravana Perahera*

The Sri Devram Maha Viharaya organizes two major festival 'weeks' each year: one in September and one in March. September is regarded a special month at the Sri Devram Maha Viharaya because the head monk was born on the 24 September 1969, and the foundation stone of the complex was laid on his 30th birthday (Most Ven. Kolonnawe Sri Sumanagala Thero n.d.; The History n.d.). It was

24 The word *vedakama* was used by the monk to denote this medicinal knowledge (Sumangala Thero 2018).

25 These interpretations are examples of answers given by people who were closely involved in the rituals performed for Ravana at the Sri Devram Maha Viharaya. Their answers show that a variety of interpretations even exists among the people who are closely involved in the rituals for Ravana.

also in September that the Ravana *mandiraya* has been inaugurated and in that particular year (2013) the first *perahera* for Ravana took place in the month of September (Secretary Sumangala Thero 2017; Lay-Custodian Ravana *Mandiraya* 2017a). From 2014 onwards, the Ravana *perahera* was organized together with the Suddhodana Mahamaya *perahera*, a *perahera* devoted to the parents of Buddha, which in previous years had already been organized in March (Lay-Custodian Ravana *Mandiraya* 2017a).[26]

The *Medin maha perahera* consists of three parts: the first part is the *theruwan puja maha perahera*. This procession is held in reverence to the triple gem: the Buddha, the *dhamma* (teachings), and the *sangha* (the monastic order).[27] The Suddhodana Mahamaya *perahera* is dedicated to Buddha's parents. With between 60 and 70 different elements, the Ravana *perahera* constitutes the biggest part of the *Medin maha perahera*. According to the website of the temple it is organized to '[...] felicitate Father of the nation King shree Lankeshwara Rawana' (Madin Maha Perahera (Procession)). In the *Budumaga* (the monthly magazine published by the Sri Devram Maha Viharaya), an explanation for organizing the Ravana *perahera* is given as well:

> [The Ravana *perahera*] is dedicated towards all the kings of ancient Sri Lanka who sacrificed not just their time, but also their lives towards protecting and bringing prosperity to the nation and its people. The statue of king Ravana is taken as a representation of all the kings of the country due to the great wisdom and holiness with which king Ravana ruled not just Sri Lanka but the entire universe. He is considered the greatest among the kings in the country [...] (N.A. 2018, vol. 4, pp. 18–19).

In one of the interviews with Sumangala Thero he explained that the Ravana *perahera* is organized out of respect for the great talents Ravana had (Sumangala Thero 2017b). As mentioned before, the talents or skills of Ravana are in the current Ravana discourse frequently connected to the iconographic representation of Ravana with ten heads and twenty arms. The ten skills as formulated by Sumangala Thero in one of his popular books on Ravana can roughly be translated as: (1) languages, (2) law, (3) philosophy, (4) ruling, (5) technical wisdom/physical sciences, (6) spiritual wisdom, (7) astrology, (8) medicinal science, (9) war skills, and (10) aesthetics (Sumangala Thero 2013, pp. 15–16).[28]

When it comes to the display of Ravana's talents in the *perahera*, a prominent position is given to war skills and fighting. This talent seamlessly fits the conceptualization of Ravana as warrior king. In the remaining part of this section I will discuss how the imagination of Ravana as warrior king is ritualized in this *perahera* by paying attention to some of the main objects in this particular *perahera*.

In addition to groups of drummers/dancers in one of the three Sri Lankan traditional dance styles, the Ravana *perahera* includes some remarkable instruments: two enormous shields (*maha pali*) placed on red-color decorated hand carts. These shields are used as gongs—creating a heavy noise which carries across the streets. Also remarkable are the giant drums. These *rana bera* and *yuda bera* (war drums) are believed to have been used to announce important happenings, especially in a war context. As was explained by a volunteer of the Ravana *perahera*:

> It [the *rana bera*] was used in fight and battle and it symbolized strength. When going to war, the *rana bera* announced the arrival of the armies. It is also used as music in *Angampora* [martial arts]. (Volunteers *Perahera* 2018).

[26] The month March has been selected because the wedding of Buddha's parents allegedly took place in that particular month (Madin Maha Perahera Meritorious Activity n.d.).

[27] The first approximately 45 elements of the *perahera* are part of the *theruwan puja maha perahera*. This part shows similarities with the Kandy Esala *perahera*, the most famous *perahera* of Sri Lanka annually held in Kandy in honor of the sacred tooth relic of the Buddha. The tooth relic of the Buddha in Kandy is believed to be connected with rainfall (Wickremeratne 2006, p. 108). The tooth relic at the Sri Devram Maha Viharaya also allegedly belongs to Buddha. During the *Medin maha perahera* the relic is kept inside because taking it out is believed to cause extreme rainfall (Secretary Sumangala Thero 2018b).

[28] An alternative symbolic interpretation of the ten heads is that Ravana is believed to have ruled ten countries. This interpretation is in the contemporary Ravana discourse less widespread than the opinion that his heads symbolizes skills.

The poundings of the drums and the shields—together with the exclamations of performers in the *perahera*—creates a powerful soundscape resembling the sound of impending doom and war. In addition to creating a particular soundscape these instruments—known as 'war instruments'—also contribute to the war-like scene by their visual outlook: the shield is generally known as a tool for self-defense in a fighting context. Moreover, the massive size of these instruments—they have to be taken around on hand carts because they are too heavy to carry—add to the impressive scenery of the Ravana *perahera*.

In addition to this, in 2018, a sound system was taken around in one of the chariots. This sound system continuously played songs in praise for Ravana, composed by the *Ravana Brothers*. Their music compositions includes up-beating drum rhythms and their songs include loud exclamations. The chorus of one of the songs repeats over and over again *vira* Ravana which means brave or powerful Ravana (https://www.youtube.com/watch?v=cp_EhLcHSzc).

The most omnipresent objects in the Ravana *perahera* are weapons. Weaponry is displayed in a variety of ways. In addition to an active use of weaponry in performances, there is also the display of multiple types of weapons, and the weaponry as part of the royal ornaments.

The Ravana *perahera* includes performances which are not directly related to Ravana such as fire ball dancers and performances related to specific village (exorcism or healing) rituals. The performances exclusively related to Ravana are the *Angampora* performances. In the broader Ravana discourse *Angampora* is believed to be one of the ten skills of Ravana (Sumangala Thero had used war skills in his book instead) and some people say it has been invented by Ravana (Volunteer Perahera 2018). *Angampora* is increasing in popularity in post-war Sri Lanka as the 'traditional martial art of Sri Lanka', and has been promoted by the government of Sri Lanka as such as well. Although there are different types of *Angampora* (Angampora Teacher 2018)—also a type of self-defense in which no tools are used—the *Angampora* performances in the Ravana *perahera* mainly display the type of *Angampora* in which weapons or tools are used. One of these *Angampora* groups closely related to the Sri Devram Maha Viharaya consists of young men led by a charismatic leader who perform *Angampora* in the *perahera* with different types of weapons. He and his students are all dressed in a red skirt and carry with a bare torso weapons and/or shields around (see Figure 5).

The display of weaponry is closely related but not limited to *Angampora* performances in the Ravana *perahera*. In 2017, another group of *Angampora* performers brought an enormous variety of 'tools' to the Ravana *mandiraya*, including swords, sticks, a walking stick, a knife which is used to cut the paddy, and mace. These *Angampora* students just carried around these tools in the *perahera*.

Weaponry is also of central importance at one of the two chariots for Ravana which are taken around in the Ravana *perahera*. In addition to a replica of the *dandu monara*, a bird shaped chariot made out of wood resembling Ravana's flying machine (an example of his talent of physical science and technology), there is a rather tall chariot taken around. This chariot closely resembles a Hindu procession chariot used for taking around the statue of a god.[29] The objects taken around on this chariot are referred to as *abarana*, which translates as ornaments or jewelry. These *abarana* include Ravana's royal ornaments but also symbols of the ten weapons that Ravana allegedly used. Some of these weapons are believed to be from Ravana's time and some of them are believed to be replicas (Secretary Sumangala Thero 2018a). This combination of royal ornaments including jewelry and swords contributes to the construction of the conceptualization of Ravana, not just as king, but as warrior king.

[29] I encountered a similar chariot with a depiction of the ten-headed Ravana on the front panel (knelt on one leg) and with similar hand gestures in the Munnesvaram (Hindu) Kovil (visited 4 May 2016). The chariot used in the Ravana *perahera* bears on the front panel also a wood carved image of the ten-headed Ravana who poses with various hand gestures and holds various objects in his numerous hands (of which some are broken).

Figure 5. A group of *Angampora* students and their master performing in the *Medin maha Perahera* organized by the Sri Devram Maha Viharaya in Pannpipitiya on 24 March 2018. The picture was published on the Facebook Webpage Sri Devram Maha Viharaya (2018a).

The culmination of the Ravana *perahera* is the tenth and final elephant who carries on his back a Ravana *piliruva* (image or statue), as it was called by one of the monks involved in the organization of the *Medin maha perahera*. As he explained in the live broadcasting of the *perahera* on ITN TV in 2017, all kings in the past had royal elephants—and consequently Ravana's statue has to be placed on an elephant as well (see Figure 6). The audience also rose to its feet to pay respect to this statue of Ravana at the time it passed by. This 'responding to representations as if they embody the things they represent' is according to Ronald Grimes one of the clearest signs of ritualization (Grimes 2014, p. 92). This representation of Ravana who is dressed as a king, adorned with royal ornaments and a crown on his head, seated on the back of the elephant is an outstanding example of the ritualization of the imagination of Ravana as king: the statue is treated with respect as if king Ravana himself passes by.

The cloths used to dress the statue and also the decoration of the elephant on which the Ravana statue is seated are red colored (see Figure 6). Most of the people in the Ravana *perahera* are dressed in red as well (see Figure 5). Also, red is the dominant color for the decorations in this *perahera*. The dominance of the red color for the Ravana *perahera* is related to power, blood, and war. In the broadcasting of the *Medin maha perahera* in 2017 the monk involved in the organization of the *perahera* elaborated in the commentary upon the use of red colors. According to him the red color is a color of pride, symbolizing strength. It represents the strength, pride, and power of the nation, the power of the Sinhalese (ITN Live Broadcasting of Perahera 2017).

In an informal conversation with the same monk he further explained that the red color used in the *perahera* functions as a spiritual invitation for Ravana. It symbolizes Ravana's braveness as a warrior (Organizing Monk *Medin Maha Perahera* 2017). Like the objects in the *perahera* such as the swords and the war instruments, the use of red contributes to the display of Ravana as a powerful (warrior) king. It reinforces the war-like scenery of the *perahera* while the connection with blood—a life-giving substance—connects the past to the present: red symbolizes the power of the Sinhalese both back in Ravana's days and in the present and it symbolizes the descendancy—or bloodline—of the Sinhalese from Ravana.

In 2018, even the crowning statue of Ravana was dressed in red fabric. High above the masses, and wearing a crown and jewelry, the Ravana statue was richly adorned. Sumangala Thero explained on the *perahera* day in 2017 that Ravana should better be dressed in a subtle and refined manner in the *perahera*, to underscore his extremely peaceful character, instead of wearing all kinds of ornaments (Sumangala Thero 2017a). The benevolent side of Ravana becomes increasingly prominent at the Sri Devram Maha Viharaya or at least for the head monk. It is exactly this benevolent side of Ravana which dominates the ritual that follows in the night after the *perahera:* the *maha Ravana nanumura mangalyaya*.

Figure 6. The statue of Ravana taken around in the *Medin maha Perahera* organized by the Sri Devram Maha Viharaya in Pannpipitiya on 24 March 2018. The picture was published on the Facebook Webpage Sri Devram Maha Viharaya (2018b).

5. The Ritualizing of Ravana as Healer in the Annual *Maha Ravana Nanumura Mangalyaya*

In the night following the *Medin maha perahera*, preparations are made for a second annual ritual for Ravana: the *maha Ravana nanumura mangalyaya*. Compared to the weekly *nanumura* on Sunday evenings not only a larger number of substances is used to anoint the statues; the substances are also handed over to the audience in a different way. As I will discuss in this section these substances play a major role in the ritualizing of the conceptualization of Ravana as healer in this ritual.

According to Sumangala Thero, there are multiple reasons for him to organize the annual *maha Ravana nanumura mangalyaya*. As explained by him, similar to the *maha Ravana perahera*, it is a kind of 'counter ritual' to oppose the negativity allegedly brought upon Ravana by the ritual of *dasara*. Ravana is regarded as the ultimate representation of evil in the festival of *dasara* which is celebrated among Hindus in India. The summit of *dasara* is the burning of massive effigies of the ten headed Ravana.[30] In the *maha Ravana nanumura mangalyaya*, the negativity as allegedly brought upon Ravana

[30] The annual ritual of *dasara* is according to Anita Shukla one of the most popular symbols of the victory of good over evil in Indian culture (Shukla 2011, p. 175). However, as she also points to, the persona of Ravana is open to multiple interpretations.Also in India Ravana was seen as a good person from time to time. In for instance the nineteenth-century poem *Meghanadavadha kavya* (the slaying of Meghanada) composed by the Bengali poet Michael

through the ritual of *dasara* is literally washed away by using different substances to anoint the statue(s). As Sumangala Thero explained, the rituals for Ravana at the Sri Devram Maha Viharaya are performed to counterbalance the annual ritual of *dasara*:

> This is done to pay tribute to all the talents and skills Ravana had. When 100 million people consider Ravana a villain and curse and burn his image every year, it is our responsibility to show the world his actual image and communicate the truth about him. We respect Ravana greatly because he is not a person destroying the world, Ravana keeps the world alive, Ravana is a person the world needs. If Ravana is allowed to come back to this world and work among the people he will be able to find solutions for the problems that prevail in the world. Ravana should be respected and loved more than this [...] (Sumangala Thero 2017b).

The *nanumura mangalyaya* is rarely described in literature except by for instance Richard Gombrich who defines this ritual as the 'ceremony of bathing and anointing a Buddha image' (Gombrich 2009, p. 400).[31] As I observed in Narangamuwa (one of the rural villages in Sri Lanka, visited 17 May 2017) the *nanumura mangalyaya* is not limited to the anointing of (Buddha) images. In this *nanumura mangalyaya*—as part of the annual village ritual (*yakkama*)—attributes allegedly belonging to different gods (mainly weapons and a shield for Kanda *deviyo* in this particular village) were the objects taken out of the village shrine to be anointed (Fieldwork Visit Narangamuwa Village 2017).

The *nanumura mangalyaya* is also annually performed at famous religious sites in Sri Lanka such as Kataragama, the Temple of the Tooth in Kandy and Bellanvila Raja Maha Viharaya in Colombo.[32] In addition to an annual *nanumura mangalyaya* in Kandy a weekly *nanumura mangalyaya* is performed for the tooth relic on Wednesday mornings by monks and by the lay-custodian. After they finish the ritual in the inner sanctuary a custodian takes out one massive bowl which contains a warm red coloured substance. When I was there observing the ritual (28 March 2018), the people who were waiting in the queue for more than one hour were served this substance in the small cups or bottles that they brought for this occasion. They applied the substance to their heads because they believe that it will bring healing and protect them from illnesses.

The application of the substance to the head for the sake of healing after it has been used to bathe a sacred object or statue is exactly what happens during the annual *maha Ravana nanumura mangalyaya*. But as a newly invented ritual for Ravana this ritual also has its own specific characteristics. In the remaining part of this section I will therefore primarily focus on how the imagination of Ravana as healer is ritualized in the *maha Ravana nanumura mangalyaya*.

On regular Sunday evenings approximately eleven substances are used to bathe two of the Ravana statues. For the annual *maha Ravana nanumura mangalyaya*, more than twenty types of substances are

---

Madhusudan Datta both the characters Rama and Ravana are subject to transformation (Dutt 2005, p. 3). Ravana becomes in this poem the hero and his son Meghanada the symbol of the oppressed Hindus under the British rule (Doniger 2010, p. 667). Also, in the context of early twentieth century Dravidian nationalism (mainly 1930–1950) in India, E.V. Ramasami praised Ravana in his work as the true hero of the *Ramayana* and as a monarch of the ancient Dravidians (Richman 1991, pp. 175–201). A positive appropriation of Ravana can also be found among Tamils in Sri Lanka for instance in the temple literature of the famous Konesvaram temple (Henry 2017, p. 172). As Henry points to, influenced by the presence of Tamils in Sri Lanka, Ravana became accepted as a historical ruler in Sinhalese literature from the 14th century onwards, for instance in *Kadayim* (boundary books) and the *Rajavaliya* (Henry 2017, pp. 60–61, 148).

31 As he described in the ritual which he observed no laymen were allowed to witness the ritual and an exception was made for him as a researcher. As I also encountered, the information of the ritual is often not shared with outsiders. At several shrines for gods at Kataragama (visited 17 April 2018) and Kandy (visited 27–29 March 2018) I tried to gather information on the *nanumura mangalyaya*, but most of the lay-custodians were reluctant to give out information on this particular ritual. The ones who did, stressed that they normally do not share the details of the ritual with outsiders.

32 At Bellanvila Raja Maha Viharaya they perform a *nanumura mangalyaya* for all the statues of the gods in the shrines thrice a year: in January, around the time they have the annual *perahera* and with Sinhala New Year. (Lay-Custodian of One of the Shrines of *Bellanvila Raja Maha Viharaya* 2018).

used to bathe the statues.[33] Also, a larger amount of each of the substances is prepared: instead of the regular bowls used on Sundays, for this annual ritual, tubs in the size of rain barrels are used. For this special occasion the lay-custodian is assisted by the main secretary of Sumangala Thero.

In the context of the *maha Ravana nanumura mangalyaya* some of the volunteers used the term *Abhishekha* to refer to the ritual: a ritual of anointing as part of the crowning ceremony for Indian kings in the past. *Abhishekha* is also used to denote the ritual anointing of images in Hindu temples, for instance the Shiva lingam. One of the volunteers explained why this *maha Ravana nanumura mangalyaya* is special to her:

> It is held just once a year [*it is special*] because it is the *Abhishekha*, like a crowning ceremony. That makes it very special (Volunteer *Sri Devram Maha Viharaya* 2018).

Although the imagination of Ravana as king is touched upon in the *maha Ravana nanumura mangalyaya*, it mainly ritualizes Ravana as healer. This becomes primarily evident in the substances used within the ritual and the way the people interpret and employ these substances. The substances are believed to get blessed during the ritual because the *nanumura mangalyaya* is done to show respect to Ravana. This general explanation was, for instance, given by an attendant of the *maha Ravana nanumura mangalyaya*:

> [...] after the *nanumura mangalyaya* is completed, we believe that the gods are pleased and that they are present. Bathing with the water and substances that were used will also do some good for us because of this reason (Attendant A of the *Nanumura Mangalyaya* 2018).

In addition to a general reason the secretary of Sumangala mentioned another reason:

> Firstly, Ravana is believed to be the founder of medicine. Therefore, when the statue is washed it would evoke powers of healing; and generally when we show respect to any god he will send blessings to the people (Secretary Sumangala Thero and Caretaker of Temple Site 2018).

The first reason is related to the *persona* of Ravana in particular. As explained earlier, in the current Ravana discourse Ravana is praised for his knowledge of medicine, whether Ayurveda or 'traditional Sinhalese medicine'. In this ritual the imagination of Ravana as someone who mastered extensive knowledge of medicine in the past, is made vivid in the present. According to Sumangala Thero, Ravana does not even want people to die in our contemporary world. In one of his lectures preceding the *Medin maha perahera* in 2017 Sumangala Thero has set out his ideas on Ravana:

> Have people found cures for certain diseases? Why do we let people die of sicknesses? Ravana has constantly kept saying, "people in this world cannot die because of sickness, they need to be cured." Reasons behind why people get sick has to be looked into. Though Ravana challenges the world: if a person is terribly sick in bed and drawing their last breathes, we cannot let them die like that, that patient has to recover and then die. We are a pride nation born of Ravana's blood (Sumangala Thero 2017c).

The *mandiraya* for Ravana at the Sri Devram Maha Viharaya is built with a special drainage system: at the backside of the 'tower' of the *mandiraya* in which the sanctuary is located, there is a small space where the 'waste' of the substances used for the bathing of the statues is collected during the annual ritual (see Figure 7). Because a large amount of substances is used in this annual ritual some people

---

[33] On a list I received from one of the main caretakers of the site in 2017, after the *maha Ravana nanumura mangalyaya*, 23 ingredients were mentioned: sesame oil, rice flour, turmeric powder, raw turmeric, *vada* turmeric, *sandanam*, cows' milk/buffalo milk, king coconut water, fruit sap, herbal leaves sap, lime juice, river water, lake water, sea water, rain water, *vibuthi*, *kunkuma*, red sandalwood, white sandalwood, scented water (rose water), jasmine water, pure water, and honey.

anoint their heads with the substances instead of drinking just a small sip like the people do on a regular Sunday evening. On a regular Sunday evening the substances also drain to this small space, but it is only during the annual ritual that people collect the substances from the back side.

Figure 7. People queuing up at the back side of the Ravana *mandiriya* to 'bathe' themselves with the substances used for the annual *maha Ravana nanumura mangalyaya*. Picture taken by author, 26 March 2017.

One of the reasons why these substances are believed to contain healing powers is related to the imagination of Ravana as an expert in medicines. As one of the attendants of the ritual explained, all of the medicines in the world have been founded by Ravana. Although people referred to medicines as one of the ten skills of *dasis* Ravana that he invented and/or mastered approximately 6000 years ago, this imagination becomes tangible in the present through the substances used in this particular ritual:

> Ravana was the first king in Sri Lanka and he had skills including medicine and dance [. . .]. When you look at his personality and power even the substances connected to him should have some power (Attendant B of the *Nanumura Mangalyaya* 2018).

The ritual anointing performed with the substances in the inner sanctuary of the Ravana *mandiraya* is believed to transfer the healing power (of Ravana) into the substances. The statue of Ravana (most often only 'one' statue was mentioned by people, although two statues are actually anointed) plays a significant role in transferring the healing power into the substances. That the substances have touched the Ravana statue make these substances believed to contain healing powers. As one of the assistants of the lay-custodian explained:

> The substances are believed to contain healing powers because they are used to bathe the Ravana statues. After these substances are used for the ritual, the substances are no longer ordinary: they gather some sort of power (Assistant of Lay-Custodian Ravana *Mandiraya* 2018).

And as one of the attendants of the *nanumura mangalyaya* explained:

> After they bathe the statue, the water and the substances collect a power that heals us when we bathe with it. The statue is first bathed. The power the statue gives, is used to heal us (Attendant B of the *Nanumura Mangalyaya* 2018).

The stories and the beliefs of the around one hundred fifty people who queue up once a year in the early morning to collect the substances enforce the ritualizing of the conceptualization of Ravana as healer. Most of the people who come for the *maha Ravana nanumura mangalyaya* actually suffer from a 'disease': from cancer to childlessness. They come with the belief that Ravana will cure them. Others attend the ritual to be protected from illnesses and/or were cured in one of the previous years.

Compared to the *Maha Ravana perahera* which took place only half a day before, another side of Ravana is stressed in the annual *nanumura mangalyaya*: instead of his martial side as a warrior king, this ritual shows Ravana's benevolent side: a god who cares about his devotees and provides them with healing.

The *Maha Ravana perahera* attracts a larger audience than the *nanumura mangalyaya*. A reason for this is that the *Maha Ravana perahera* goes across the streets and the *nanumura mangalyaya* takes place at the temple site itself. Also, the *nanumura mangalyaya* aims at a specific audience—those who suffer from illnesses—whereas the *perahera*—like the famous Kandy *Esala perahera*—can be considered as a pageant which celebrates the national identity.[34]

Also, the imagination of Ravana as king of Lanka is commonly accepted in the Ravana discourse and beyond and can be found in recently published books on history and children's books as well. Although the imagination of Ravana as inventor of medicines—as one of his ten different skills—is broadly agreed upon within the Ravana discourse too, Ravana is in the *nanumura mangalyaya* (a lesser known ritual) treated like a god. The deification of Ravana is less widespread and considered by some people as an excess.

6. Reflection

The Ravana imaginations constructed in the current Ravana discourse can be traced back to various sources. From the fourteenth century onwards, an acceptance of Ravana as historical ruler of Sri Lanka in Sinhalese literature can be noticed. These references, influenced by the positive rendering of Ravana by the Tamil minority in Sri Lanka, are for instance present in *Kadayim* (boundary books) and the Sinhalese chronicle the *Rajavaliya* (Henry 2017, p. 157).[35] Although the South Indian version of the *Ramayana* was known in early Sri Lanka it is not referred to in the earliest Sri Lankan chronicles such as the *Dipavamsa* and *Mahavamsa* (Henry 2017, pp. 145–46). It is these chronicles which are well-known in contemporary Sri Lanka.

In the early twentieth century, the imagination of Ravana as famous king of Lanka became part of the nationalistic agenda of the *Hela* movement. This imagination of Ravana as the famous king of Lanka did not find support among a wider public: the linguistic movement—with a focus on language purification—never appealed to a broader audience. Also, as Nira Wickramasinghe points to 'the Rama Sita Ravana myth which saw the king of Lanka ultimately defeated by Rama did not give Ravana a persona Sinhala people could easily identify with' (Wickramasinghe 2014, pp. 96–97).

In addition to references of Ravana as historical ruler of Lanka in literature and in the *Hela* movement, traces of the *Ramayana* story can be found in Sinhala folklore. The references to a Rama and Sita story in, for instance, the folk ritual of the *Kohomba yakkama* are however unknown to a wider

[34] The role of kings and the legitimization of political power in the history of the Kandy *Esala perahera* is discussed in detail by Paul Younger. As he points to the Kandy *Esala perahera* aims to express loyalty to kingship and celebrates national identity (Younger 2002, pp. 69–79).

[35] In the seventeenth century *Rajavaliya* it is said that there were 1844 years between the end of Ravana's war and the enlightenment of Buddha (Suraweera 2014, p. 16).

public.[36] References to Rama, Ravana, and Sita in literature and folk rituals in the past were rather marginal, integrated as a side note within elaborated cosmological ideas, or special rituals, and their story never became a fully-fledged myth: there is, for instance, no Sinhala *Ramayana*.

The large scale appropriation of Ravana as ancient king of Lanka among the Sinhalese-Buddhist majority in Sri Lanka is quite recent. In post-war Sri Lanka, we see a process which I have coined as *Ravanisation*: the current revitalization of Ravana among Sinhalese Buddhists in Sri Lanka. One of the core conceptualizations of Ravana within the current Ravana discourse is that he is believed to be the most famous king, not just of Lanka, but of an ancient and indigenous (*Hela*) civilization. The Ravana discourse aims at the exaltation of Ravana and Lanka's ancient and indigenous civilization. The imagination of a glorious past and, more specifically, the revitalization of Ravana finds its expression in multiple ways among Sinhalese Buddhists such as the publication of popular books and articles, the production of TV and radio programs, songs and Ravana statues, and the promotion of *Angampora*.

The newly invented rituals for Ravana at the Sri Devram Maha Viharaya are another creative expression of Ravana imaginations and the imagination of an ancient highly advanced civilization. In addition to Ravana ideas as expressed in (social) media, these rituals appeal multiple senses: in the annual *maha Ravana nanumura mangalyaya*—a small size ritual conducted at the temple site itself—the substances used to anoint the statue(s) become visible and tangible expressions of Ravana's benevolent side as healer. The display of weaponry in the *maha Ravana perahera*, the use of the red color, and the position of the Ravana statue on the back of the elephant help to construct the conceptualization of Ravana as a warrior king.

As described in this article existing formats of rituals are used at the Sri Devram Maha Viharaya, though they are completely adapted to Ravana. The *perahera* is a famous ritual in Sri Lanka and the *nanumura mangalyaya*—although not studied in detail—is also conducted at famous religious sites in Sri Lanka and as part of rural rituals.

I have employed the concept of ritualizing as it is defined by Grimes to denote this phenomenon: 'the act of cultivating or inventing rites'. As he further explains:

> The "-izing" ending is a deliberate attempt to suggest a process, a quality of nascence or emergence. Ritualizing is not often socially supported. Rather, it happens in the margins, on the thresholds; therefore it is alternately stigmatized and eulogized (Grimes 2014, p. 193).

Though both rituals (still) happen in the margins as an experiment by the Sri Devram Maha Viharaya (a recently constructed Buddhist temple site) these rituals unveil key characteristics and processes which are present in the broader context of *Ravanisation* in Sri Lanka.

First of all, the production of shrines and statues, and the performances of rituals for Ravana, show that Ravana is appealing to a broader audience. As I have pointed to, Sumangala Thero is not the only monk with an interest in Ravana, and people from different layers of the society show an interest in Ravana. The latter becomes for instance evident in the fact that the *perahera* organized by the Sri Devram Maha Viharaya attracts thousands of people. The ritualizing of Ravana also shows that in the current Ravana discourse, Ravana is not an idea which only exists in the minds of the people: it is a myth complex with multiple material expressions such as statues, shrines, and rituals.

Secondly, as these rituals show, multiple conceptualizations of Ravana are constructed in the Ravana discourse. In addition to the imagination of Ravana as king of Lanka—which is also known from earlier sources—plenty of efforts are undertaken to construct positive Ravana imaginations.

[36] A village ritual from the Kandyan district, the *Kohomba yakkama*, contains a different and complex story of Rama, Sita and Ravana from a Sinhalese perspective. This story is embedded into a particular Kuveni-Vijaya myth and, according to Godakumbura, known by a limited number of people only (Godakumbura 1993, p. xcv). Although, it was through state intervention by the end of the twentieth century turned into a kind of a heritage ritual (Reed 2010) it was never referred to by people in my fieldwork conversations.

With reference to the iconographic representation of Ravana with ten heads and twenty arms, Ravana is believed to have exceeded in ten different skills. One of them, as discussed in more length in this article, is the conceptualization of Ravana as healer which is related to his allegedly outstanding knowledge of medicine.

Thirdly, although not discussed in detail in this article either, in addition to the multiple positive Ravana imaginations, the construction of an extensive myth of an ancient, indigenous, and highly advanced civilization is also of central importance in the context of *Ravanisation*. Ravana is in the Ravana discourse disassociated from the *Ramayana* context and embedded within the Sri Lankan chronicle tradition. An example of this are for instance the extensive references in the Ravana discourse to the *yakshas* and *nagas*—mythical beings which are, with reference to the famous chronicle the *Mahavamsa*, turned into highly advances tribes. With reference to the *Mahavamsa*, it is also frequently stressed in the Ravana discourse that these tribes were present in Sri Lanka long before the arrival of the Indian prince Vijaya. It thus unveils an anti-India sentiment by stressing that these tribes are indigenous tribes.

That the Ravana myth should not be considered a version of the *Ramayana* becomes for instance clear in the wall paintings of the Ravana *mandiraya*: These wall paintings concentrate on Ravana's skills and the ancient Ravana civilization (also referred to as *Hela* civilization in the broader Ravana discourse). References to the *Ramayana* are also absent in the rituals for Ravana. Instead of a defeated Ravana as known from the *Ramayana*, the pride of the nation and the national identity (of the SinhaleseBuddhists)—which allegedly can be traced back to Ravana—is celebrated in the *maha Ravana perahera*.

This glorification of Ravana—who is turned into a legendary national hero of the Sinhalese-Buddhist majority—and his ancient civilization has to be understood in the context of increased assertiveness and nationalistic sentiments among the Sinhalese Buddhist majority in post-war Sri Lanka. Although not studied in detail, in the aftermath of the civil war (2009 onwards) a tendency similar to the post-independence period can be noticed among the Sinhalese-Buddhist majority: fostered by feelings of triumphalism there is an increase of feelings of majoritarianism, instead of the inclusion of minorities.[37]

The glorification of an (imagined) ancient indigenous civilization in Sri Lanka is a way to express feelings of triumphalism and superiority over minorities. Lanka belongs to the *Hela* and the *Hela* are considered the ancestors of the Sinhalese. The recently invented rituals performed for Ravana at the Sri Devram Maha Viharaya and the broader efforts undertaken in the Ravana discourse have to be understood in this context: to help create an image of a glorious past. As also pointed to in this article, in the rituals a connection with the present is made. In the contexts of both rituals, references are made to power—not just of Ravana—but also of the nation (of the *Hela* or Sinhalese). In speeches and comments the audience is addressed to as born from Ravana's blood. Both the rituals and the speeches are thus stimulating the audience to awaken a sense of the strong (imagined) heritage of Sri Lanka and a pride of being Sinhalese.

Funding: This research is funded by The Netherlands Organisation for Scientific Research (NWO). Additional funding for fieldwork research in 2017 and 2018 was provided by J. Gonda Fund Foundation (KNAW).

Conflicts of Interest: The author declares no conflict of interest. The funders had no role in the design of the study; in the collection, analyses, or interpretation of data; in the writing of the manuscript, and in the decision to publish the results.

[37] As formulated in a policy rapport on *Dynamics of Sinhala Buddhist Ethno-Nationalism in Post-War Sri Lanka* (Zuhair 2016) the government under Rajapaksa nurtured a majoritarian mind-set among the Sinhalese majority which comprises between 70% and 75% of Sri Lanka's population. Also, as pointed out by Gunatilleke, although Sirisena—who won the elections in 2015—expressed in his election manifesto a commitment to end ethno-religious violence, this promise has not been fulfilled (Gunatilleke 2018, pp. 1, 11; Zuhair 2016). Communal violence is for instance still commonplace in Sri Lanka.

References and Notes

Ahubudu, Samanthi. 2018. Relative of Arisen Ahubudu, Dehiwala, Sri Lanka. Group conversation with author, May 7.

Angampora Teacher. 2018. Katuwana, Sri Lanka. Interview with author, May 14.

Assistant of Lay-Custodian Ravana *Mandiraya*. 2018. Pannipitiya, Sri Lanka. Informal conversation with author, March 18.

Attendant A of the *Nanumura Mangalyaya*. 2018. Pannipitiya, Sri Lanka. Informal conversation with author, March 25.

Attendant B of the *Nanumura Mangalyaya*. 2018. Pannipitiya, Sri Lanka. Informal conversation with author, March 25.

Beer, Robert. 2003. *The Handbook of Tibetan Buddhist Symbols*. Boston: Shambhala, ISBN 9780834824232.

Coperahewa, Sandagomi. 2012. Purifying the Sinhala Language: The *Hela* movement of Munidasa Cumaratunga (1930s–1940s). *Modern Asian Studies* 46: 857–91. [CrossRef]

Coperahewa, Sandagomi. 2018. Senior Lecturer Department of Sinhala, University of Colombo, Colombo, Sri Lanka. Interview with author, April 18.

Cumaratunga, Munidasa. 1941. Hela nama. *Subasa* 2: 392–95.

Deegalle, Mahinda. 2004. Politics of the *Jathika Hela Urumaya* Monks: Buddhism and Ethnicity in Contemporary Sri Lanka. *Contemporary Buddhism* 5: 83–103. [CrossRef]

Deegalle, Mahinda. 2011. Politics of the *Jathika Hela Urumaya*: Buddhism and Ethnicity. In *The Sri Lanka Reader: History, Culture, Politics*. Edited by Jonathan Holt. Durham: Duke University Press, pp. 383–94. ISBN 9780822349822.

Dharmadasa, Karuna N. O. 1995. *Language, Religion, and Ethnic Assertiveness: The Growth of Sinhalese Nationalism in Sri Lanka*. Ann Arbor: University of Michigan Press, ISBN 9780472102884.

Doniger, Wendy. 2010. *The Hindus: An Alternative History*. Oxford: Oxford University Press, ISBN 9780199593347.

Dutt, Manmatha Nath. 1894. *Valmiki's—The Rāmāyaṇa: Book 7 Uttara Kandam*. Calcutta: Chackravarti, ISBN 9785872432791.

Dutt, Michael Madhusudan. 2005. *The Slaying of Meghanada: A Ramayana from Colonial Bengal*. Translated by Clinton B. Seely. Oxford: Oxford University Press, ISBN 9780195167993.

Facebook Webpage Sri Devram Maha Viharaya. 2018a. Available online: https://scontent-ams3-1.xx.fbcdn.net/v/t1.0-9/29683804_202516050522807_913063297766908626 6_n.jpg?_nc_cat=0&oh=35cd4fe4e63d645f67f1b18247ddedd5&oe=5BB15CC3 (accessed on 29 June 2018).

Facebook Webpage Sri Devram Maha Viharaya. 2018b. Available online: https://scontent-ams3-1.xx.fbcdn.net/v/t1.0-9/29570557_202516587189420_4982647518222686437_n.jpg?_nc_cat=0&oh=0a68c858777df26c4755cb4561860853&oe=5BE1C050 (accessed on 29 June 2018).

Godakumbura, Charles E. 1993. Rāmāyaṇa in Śrī Laṅkā and Laṅkā of the Rāmāyaṇa. In *A Critical Inventory of Rāmāyaṇa Studies in the World: 2*. New Delhi: Sahitya Akademi, ISBN 8172015070.

Gombrich, Richard. 2009. *Buddhist Precept and Practice: Traditional Buddhism in the Rural Highlands of Ceylon*, rev. ed. London: Routledge, ISBN 9780710304445.

Gombrich, Richard F., and Gananath Obeyesekere. 1988. *Buddhism Transformed: Religious Change in Sri Lanka*. Princeton: Princeton University Press, ISBN 0691019010.

Grimes, Ronald L. 2014. *The Craft of Ritual Studies*. Oxford: Oxford University Press, ISBN 9780195301434.

Gunatilleke, Gehan. 2018. *The Chronic and the Entrenched: Ethno-Religious Violence in Sri Lanka*. Pannipitiya: Horizon Printing, ISBN 9789555802154. Available online: https://equitas.org/wp-content/uploads/2018/05/The-Chronic-and-the-Entrenched-FINAL-WEB-PDF.pdf (accessed on 10 August 2018).

Henry, Justin. 2017. Distant Shores of Dharma: Historical Imagination in Sri Lanka from the Late Medieval Period. Ph.D. Thesis, University of Chicago, Chicago, IL, USA.

Holt, John. 2008. *The Buddhist Viṣṇu: Religious Transformation, Politics, and Culture*. New Delhi: Motilal Banarsidass Publishers, ISBN 9788120832695.

ITN Live Broadcasting of *Perahera*. 2017. March 25.

Lay-Custodian of One of the Shrines of *Bellanvila Raja Maha Viharaya*. 2018. Bellanvila, Colombo, Sri Lanka. Informal conversation with author, March 16.

Lay-Custodian Ravana *Mandiraya*. 2017a. Pannipitiya, Sri Lanka. Informal conversation with author, March 15.

Lay-Custodian Ravana *Mandiraya*. 2017b. Pannipitiya, Sri Lanka. Informal conversation with author, April 2.

Lay-Custodian Ravana *Mandiraya*. 2017c. Pannipitiya, Sri Lanka. Informal conversation with author, April 23.

Lay-Custodian Ravana Shrine Kataragama. 2018. Kataragama, Sri Lanka. Interview with author, April 17.

Madin Maha Perahera (Procession) 2016. n.d. Available online: http://www.sridevramvehera.org/index.php?option=com_content&view=article&id=148&Itemid=185 (accessed on 23 January 2018).

Madin Maha Perahera Meritorious Activity. n.d. Available online: http://www.sridevramvehera.org/index.php?option=com_content&view=article&id=152&Itemid=187 (accessed on 21 January 2018).

Monk Galgamuwa. 2017. Galgamuwa, Sri Lanka. Interview with author, April 4.

Monk Vidurupola. 2016. Vidurupola, Sri Lanka. Interview with author, March 11.

Most Ven. Kolonnawe Sri Sumanagala Thero. n.d. Available online: http://sridevramvehera.org/index.php?option=com_content&view=article&id=57 (accessed on 9 January 2018).

N.A. 2018. Devram Maha Vehere Medin Maha Perahera. *Budumaga* 4: 18–19.

Obeyesekere, Mirando. 2016. *Ravana Amaraniyayi*. Hettigama: Samanthi Printers, ISBN 9789550841547.

Official website of Arisen Ahubudu. n.d. Available online: https://www.ahubudu.lk/images/gallery/018.jpg (accessed on 29 June 2018).

Organizing Monk *Medin Maha Perahera*. 2017. Pannipitiya, Sri Lanka. Informal conversation with author, April 4.

President of *Ravana Shakti*. 2018. Nawinna, Sri Lanka. Interview with author, May 12.

Rahula, Walpola. 1974. *The Heritage of the Bhikku: A Short History of the Bhikku in Educational, Cultural, Social, and Political Life*. Translated by K. P. G. Wijayasurendra and revised by Walpola Rahula. New York: Grove Press, ISBN 9780394178233.

Rahula, Walpola. 2011. Politically Engaged Militant Monks. In *The Sri Lanka Reader: History, Culture, Politics*. Edited by Jonathan Holt. Durham: Duke University Press, pp. 380–82. ISBN 9780822349822.

Rao, Velcheru N. 1991. The Politics of Telegu Ramayanas: Colonialism, Print Culture, and Literary Movements. In *Questioning Ramayanas: A South Asian Tradition*. Edited by Paula Richman. Berkeley: University of California Press, pp. 159–86. ISBN 0520220730.

Reed, Susan A. 2010. *Dance and the Nation: Performance, Ritual, and Politics in Sri Lanka*. Madison: University of Wisconsin Press, ISBN 9780299231644.

Richman, Paula. 1991. E.V. Ramasami's Reading of the Ramayana. In *Many Ramayanas: The Diversity of a Narrative Tradition in South Asia*. Edited by Paula Richman. Berkeley: University of California Press, pp. 175–201. ISBN 9780520072817.

Robinson, Richard H., and Willard L. Johnson. 1997. *The Buddhist Religion: A Historical Introduction*, 4th ed. Belmont: Wadsworth Publishing Group, ISBN 0534207189.

Secretary Sumangala Thero. 2017. Pannipitiya, Sri Lanka. Informal conversation with author, March 14.

Secretary Sumangala Thero. 2018a. Pannipitiya, Sri Lanka. Group conversation together with caretaker of the site, group conversation with author, March 11.

Secretary Sumangala Thero. 2018b. Pannipitiya, Sri Lanka. Informal conversation with author, February 25.

Secretary Sumangala Thero and Caretaker of Temple Site. 2018. Pannipitiya, Sri Lanka. Group conversation with author, March 11.

Shukla, Anita. 2011. From Evil to Evil: Revisiting Ravana as a Tool for Community Building. In *Villains and Villainy: Embodiments of Evil in Literature, Popular Culture and Media*. Edited by Anna Fahraeus and Yakali-Çamoğlu Dikmen. Amsterdam: Rodopi, pp. 175–91. ISBN 9789401206808.

Spencer, Jonathan. 2014. Anthropology, Politics, and Place in Sri Lanka: South Asian Reflections from an Island Adrift. *South Asia Multidisciplinary Academic Journal* 10: 1–14. [CrossRef]

Sumangala Thero. 2013. *Vishwadipati Maha Ravana*. Pannipitiya: Divya Ramya Jaya Maluva.

Sumangala Thero. 2014. *Sri Lankesvara Maha Ravana*. Pannipitiya: Divya Ramya Jaya Maluva.

Sumangala Thero. 2017a. Head Monk Sri Devram Maha Viharaya, Pannipitiya, Sri Lanka. Informal conversation with author, March 25.

Sumangala Thero. 2017b. Head Monk Sri Devram Maha Viharaya, Pannipitiya, Sri Lanka. Interview with author, June 5.

Sumangala Thero. 2017c. Head Monk Sri Devram Maha Viharaya, Pannipitiya, Sri Lanka. Lecture, March 22.

Sumangala Thero. 2018. Head Monk Sri Devram Maha Viharaya, Pannipitiya, Sri Lanka. Interview with author, May 11.

Suraweera, Alankarag V. 2014. *Rājāvaliya: A Critical Edition with an Introduction*. Nugegoda: Nanila Publications, ISBN 9789556652345. First published 2000.

The History. n.d. Available online: http://sridevramvehera.org/index.php?option=com_content&view=article&id=61 (accessed on 19 January 2018).

Volunteer *Perahera*. 2018. Pannipitiya, Sri Lanka. Informal conversation with author, March 24.

Volunteer *Sri Devram Maha Viharaya*. 2018. Pannipitiya, Sri Lanka. Informal conversation with author, March 24.

Volunteers *Perahera*. 2018. Nawinna, Sri Lanka. Group conversation with author, March 9.

Wickramasinghe, Nira. 2014. *Sri Lanka in the Modern Age: A History*. Oxford: Oxford University Press, ISBN 9780190257552.

Wickremeratne, Swarna. 2006. *Buddha in Sri Lanka: Remembered Yesterdays*. Albany: State University of New York Press, ISBN 079146881-X.

Younger, Paul. 2002. *Playing Host to Deity: Festival Religion in the South Indian Tradition*. Oxford: Oxford University Press, ISBN 0195140443.

Zuhair, Ayesha. 2016. *Dynamics of Sinhala Buddhist Ethno-Nationalism in Post-War Sri Lanka*. Colombo: Centre for Policy Alternatives, Available online: http://sangam.org/wp-content/uploads/2016/11/CPA-Dynamics-of-Sinhala-Buddhist-Ethno-Nationalism-in-Post-War-Sri-Lanka.pdf (accessed on 4 May 2018).

religions

MDPI

Article

On the Xiapu Ritual Manual *Mani the Buddha of Light*

Xiaohe Ma [1,*] and Chuan Wang [2]

1 Harvard-Yenching Library, 2 Dvinity Ave., Cambridge, MA 02138, USA
2 Department of Applied Chinese, Ming Chuan University, 5 De Ming Rd., Gui Shan District, Taoyuan City 333, Taiwan; cwang@mail.mcu.edu.tw
* Correspondence: xhma@fas.harvard.edu; Tel.: +1-781-643-4263

Received: 30 May 2018; Accepted: 29 June 2018; Published: 9 July 2018

Abstract: This paper first introduces *Mani the Buddha of Light*—a collection of ritual manuals of the Religion of Light from Xiapu county, Fujian Province, China and *Diagram of the Universe*—a Manichaean painting produced in South China in the late 14th to early 15th century. It then gives a detailed description of *Mani the Buddha of Light* with some illustrations of *Diagram of the Universe*. This paper further compares *Mani the Buddha of Light* and Buddhist worship and repentance ritual to demonstrate that the former utilized the form of the latter. It also analyzes the similarities and differences between the pantheons of *Mani the Buddha of Light* and other Manichaean materials. Ultimately it discusses the hypothesis that many pieces of the original texts in *Mani the Buddha of Light* should have come into being during the 9th–11th centuries and have been handed down generation after generation because of the strong vitality of its rituals.

Keywords: Manichaeism; ritual manual; Xiapu manuscripts; Buddhist worship and repentance ritual; *Diagram of the Universe*

Mani the Buddha of Light, a manuscript from Xiapu County, Fujian Province, China, is undoubtedly the most important collection of ritual manuals of the Religion of Light (i.e., Manichaeism in China). First, we considered that the painting *Diagram of the Universe* in a private collection in Japan is perhaps the important ritual object of the Religion of Light. Then we realized that we do not have enough evidence. Many texts in *Mani the Buddha of Light* can be compared with the upper half of the *Diagram of the Universe*. But almost no texts mention the lower half of the painting. So, we decided that the main ritual object of our research should be the manuscript *Mani the Buddha of Light* and the *Diagram of the Universe* is some kind of "illustration" to help us to understand the manuscript. When we bring artistic and literary artefacts into dialogue with one another, we gradually realize that both pictorial and written forms of evidence—especially the *Diagram of the Universe*—can be apprehended as texts. The manual also can help us to understand the painting. This article will provide a detailed analysis of the text of *Mani the Buddha of Light* in comparison to earlier Chinese Manichaean texts, some of their Middle Iranian antecedents, external Chinese sources about the Manicheans and Chinese Manichaean art, especially the *Diagram of the Universe* painting discovered a decade ago and fully reconstructed and understood only recently (i.e., 2015). It demonstrates the strong continuity between Tang-period Manichaeism and later forms of the Religion of Light, the latter's continued assimilation of Buddhist terminology and themes and the lasting vitality of Manichaean practice in later Chinese history. It introduces Buddhist worship and repentance rituals (Kuo 1994) and shows how the authors and compilers of *Mani the Buddha of Light* fit the Manichaean content into the Buddhist rituals.

1. Introduction of Xiapu Ritual Manual *Mani the Buddha of Light*

Ma Xiaohe did not know *Mani the Buddha of Light* when he reported the discovery of the Chinese Manichaean materials from Xiapu in 2009 (Ma 2015a). In 2011, Yang Fuxue and Fan Lisha introduced *Mani the Buddha of Light* and pointed out that some excerpts are from Dunhuang Chinese Manichaean texts (Fan and Yang 2011). Yuan Wenqi revealed some important pieces of *Mani the Buddha of Light* and carried out preliminary research (Yuan 2011). Gábor Kósa gave a list of important names of Manichaean pantheon in Xiapu texts and translated some texts about Mani and his forerunners in *Mani the Buddha of Light* into English (Kósa 2013, 2014a, 2014b). Ma Xiaohe collected his articles of research on the texts of *Mani the Buddha of Light* revealed by Yuan Wenqi in a book (Ma 2014a).

Lin Wushu published the entire *Mani the Buddha of Light* in traditional Chinese with a postscript in his books published in 2014 (Lin 2014, pp. 457–92). Yang Fuxue and Bao Lang published the entire *Mani the Buddha of Light* in simplified Chinese with emendations and annotation in 2015 (Yang and Bao 2015). The number of column of *Mani the Buddha of Light* in this article follows the simplifed Chinese version. We published an edited text of *Mani the Buddha of Light* in 2016 (Wang and Ma 2016).

83 pages (the 83rd page is blank, 673 columns (abbr. c. or cc.), about 10,000 characters) of *Mani the Buddha of Light* are extant and the last part is missing. *Mani the Buddha of Light* with clear Buddhist color is different from later Xiapu documents both in style and content and it should be considered an early Xiapu document under the strong influence of the Manichaean documents of the Tang dynasty (618–907) (Yang and Bao 2014). The content of the whole manuscript comprises ritual acts like invoking the presence of Manichaean deities at the ritual service, praising these deities and confession of hearers (lay followers). Its format is similar to the Buddhist worship and repentance rituals. Sometimes there are specific instructions related to the rituals themselves, however, its main content is Manichaean. This is a collection of ritual manuals for congregational cults and the basic goal of collective worship is cooperative advancement in piety by means of the ritual. Such congregational cults followed the established practice of group worship in Manichaeism in Central Asia.

The original front cover of this Xiapu manuscript is missing and a new cover page with the title *Moni guangfo* 摩尼光佛 *Mani the Buddha of Light* was written by the owner—master Chen Peisheng 陳培生 (Figure 1) (Yang and Bao 2015, pp. 74–75).

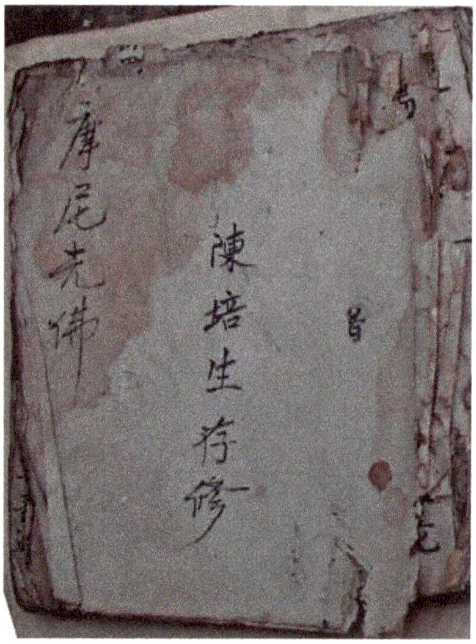

Figure 1. The front cover of *Mani the Buddha of Light* (Yang and Bao 2015, p. 74).

In 2016, Ma Xiaohe published an article comparing the text of *Mani the Buddha of Light* with the painting entitled *Diagram of the Universe*, kept in a private collection in Japan (Ma 2016). Before we give a thick description of *Mani the Buddha of Light* with the illustrations of the *Diagram of the Universe*, we shall briefly introduce this painting in Japan.

2. Introduction of the *Diagram of the Universe* in Japan

The *Diagram of the Universe*, kept in an anonymous private collection of Japan, should, in our view, be considered the most important, extant painting of the Religion of Light.

Yutaka Yoshida published a Japanese article with photographs of five Manichaean color paintings on silk in 2010. These paintings contain no inscription. Yoshida names the five as (a) *Cosmogony Painting* (Japanese 宇宙図, 137.1 × 56.6 cm); (b) *Realm of Light Painting* (天界図) (A) (17.0 × 37.4 cm); (c) *Realm of Light Painting* (B) (17.2 × 22.5 cm); (d) *Hagiography Painting* (1) and (e) *Hagiography Painting* (2). Among them (a) *Cosmogony Painting* is the most intriguing in that it obviously depicts the Manichaean cosmos as described in the Manichaean texts and as well as recorded by non-Manichaean authors. Scholars of Manichaeism can recognize the ten firmaments supported by forty angels, the Sun and the Moon and the eighth earth with Mr. Sumeru (須彌山). In his article, Yoshida argued that the painting should be identified as the South Chinese version of Mani's *ārdhang*. The *Realm of Light Paintings* (A) and (B) are two fragments dismembered from a larger painting and depict the Father of Greatness and his five attendant worlds or dwellings (Yoshida 2010).

Shōichi Furukawa also published a Japanese article in the same issue of *Yamato bunka* that explored these Manichaean paintings. He compared the five Manichaean paintings with dated Buddhist paintings and hypothesized that they had been painted during the late Yuan to early Ming Dynasty, that is, late 14th to early 15th century by painters belonging to ateliers based in the area around Ningbo 寧波, China (Furukawa 2010).

Gábor Kósa published several English articles: he gave a general overview of the *Cosmology Painting* (Kósa 2011), explored the figures of Atlas and the Keeper of Splendor in it (Kósa 2012) (offering a new identification of the latter one), analyzed its upper section (Kósa 2015a), its judgment scene (Kósa 2014b), as well as devoting an article to the motif of ships in the *Cosmology Painting* (Kósa 2015b). He reconsidered the relation of the *Cosmology Painting* to Mani's Eikōn (Kósa 2014a).

Yoshida and Furukawa published a Japanese volume entitled Studies of the Chinese Manichaean paintings of South Chinese origin preserved in Japan in 2015 and did comprehensive research on the Cosmology Painting and the Realm of Light Paintings. This book also includes Japanese translations of Kósa's research on the figures of Atlas, the Keeper of Splendor and the judgment scene in the Cosmology Painting (Yoshida and Furukawa 2015, Plates 4–13, pp. 99–127, 261–302).

In 2015, Zsuzsanna Gulácsi, partly with Jason BeDuhn, published English articles in which she matched what turned out to be three fragments—the *Cosmology Painting* and the two *Realm of Light Paintings* together as the *Diagram of the Universe* and did more research on it (Gulácsi 2015; Gulácsi and BeDuhn 2015). This reconstruction permitted Gulacsi & BeDuhn to correctly identify the New Paradise/New Aeon in the painting for the first time, which before had been mistakenly identified as the Realm of Light. In the following year, she published an English book about Mani's Picture-book, which includes the *Diagram of the Universe* (Gulácsi 2016).

Based on this reconstruction, in 2016 Gábor Kósa published an article to research the upper part of the *Diagram of Universe* and to analyze the Manichaean "New Paradise" in text and image (Kósa 2016a).

The *Diagram of Universe* is about 158 × 60 cm (Figure 2) and can be divided into seven major registers:

1. The uppermost part depicts the Realm of Light (49 figures).
2. The New Aeon (38 figures).
3. Liberation of light, that is, triad of the Sun, Moon and a third divine figure between them (93 figures).
4. Ten Firmaments (ca. 195 figures).
5. Atmosphere: the "snake-cage" in the middle, the scene of the Virgin of Light on the left and the judgment scene on the right (85 figures).
6. The Sumeru mountain surrounded by the four continents (59 figures).

7. The eight earths (ca. 70 figures).

Figure 2. The *Diagram of Universe*. (Gulácsi 2016, Figure 5/14 [p. 248]).

There are totally more than 500 figures in the *Diagram of Universe*. The figures include divine figures, monsters and animals but not the objects (Kósa 2011, pp. 21–22; Gulácsi 2016, Figures 6/36–39, 41–45 [pp. 439, 446, 448, 453, 460–61, 465, 470–71]).

The *Diagram of Universe* has so many figures and gives us vivid visual materials that help us understand the manuscript *Mani the Buddha of Light*.

3. The Ritual Manual *Mani the Buddha of Light* with the Illustrations from the *Diagram of the Universe*

This extant manuscript *Mani the Buddha of Light* is divided into two parts. The title of the first part (cc. 1–292) is "*qing fu ke* 請福科 (rituals for good fortune)". The second part (cc. 292–695) is without title and perhaps is a collection of rituals for the deceased.

3.1. [Rituals for Good Fortune] (cc. 1–292)

This part is divided into four *shi* 時 (periods) and an independent section.

3.1.1. [First Period] (cc. 1–148)

The content for the first period can be divided into six sections.

[Inviting Buddhas (*qingfo* 請佛) (Five Buddhas and Triratna)] (cc. 1–48)

First the priest recites the gatha (verse) of worship [for gods] and the hearers join in the chanting. Then the priest invites Five Buddhas–Nārāyaṇa, Zoroaster, Śākyamuni, Jesus and Mani and the hearers sing. Then the priest recites two mantras (incantations) of Chinese transcription of Middle Iranian (the second one is for *Jingkou* 淨口 "Purification of Speech") and gatha of confession.

Inviting Triratna (*sanbao* 三寶) means inviting the Buddha, the Dharma and the Saṅgha. The Buddha should be Mani because he is described as "eight forms of fearlessness and displaying supernatural power" and "auspices nine-fold and surpassing the secular matters"[1] which are similar with the descriptions of Mani in the *Compendium of the Doctrines and Styles of the Teaching of Mani, the Buddha of Light* (abb. *Compendium*) (Haloun and Henning 1952, p. 191).

The Dharma should be the Manichaean *Living Gospel*, because the priest invites "*yinglun* 應輪 [Pth./MP. *'wnglywn*]) treasure—secret wonderful mysterious text which is the substitute of Mani".[2]

"Pure Saṅgha Jewel—the saintly Masses in the light"[3] should be Manichaean community of the elect (i.e., monks).

[Venerating the Triratna (*san guiyi* 三皈依)] (cc. 49–66)

"Venerating buddhas, [the buddhas of] the past, present and future. [They are with] Unequalled marks and busy with [human] souls. The one who smiles and sits on the lotus seat enters the realm of Mani [and enjoys] ultimate bliss".[4]

"Venerating the Dharma—*yinglun* 應輪 treasure excellent truth. The merits are inconceivable. Indic writings as golden flowers are given extensively and write down all the two great principles—the idea of the founder [of Manichaeism]".[5]

"Venerating Saṅgha, clearly distinguishing two principles as usual. [They] think to save all sentient beings from suffering. [Great] sages are willing to teach trillion students whose number is as the number of grains [of sand] in the Ganges river and you can't imagine".[6] The two principles (of light and darkness) are the core doctrine of Manichaeism.

[Incense Offering Praise (*xiangzan* 香讚)] (cc. 67–85)

First the priest recites a gatha: "Fragrance, spreading as vapor, pervades the whole world, being the pure, unalloyed sea of life; developing and fully extending without hindrance; and the wonder

---

1 八無畏而表威神 and 九靈祥而超世俗.
2 應輪寶藏，秘妙玄文，是忙（示）[尔]之替身.
3 清僧寶，光中聖眾.
4 皈依佛，過去現在未來。無等相，營靈台。蓮花座上笑咍咍，便是摩尼境界，極樂最.
5 皈依法，應輪寶藏妙諦。功與德，不思儀（議）。金華梵字廣弘施，載盡二大義理，祖師意.
6 皈依僧，分明二宗如故。思得度，眾生苦。[大]聖願意教生徒，萬億恆河[沙]數，弗爾思.

of perfume gains perfection when the saintly Masses walk about". (*H.* 301).[7] Then the priest burns incense and recites gathas to make offerings to the gods and the hearers join in the chanting. Then the priest recites another gatha: "In those realms mountains of treasures amount to a billion and a thousand varieties and scented vapors gush out in a million shapes: Bright within and without, clean and pure are the substances, filled with the sweet dew overflowing with no limit". (*H.* 303).[8]

This section ends with *huixiang* 回向 "to transfer one's merit to another" including three *fayuan* 發願—making a vow to save all beings.

[Inviting Buddhas (Buddhas of Five Directions)] (cc. 86–97)

The priest first uses *H.* 140 to invite gods: "I also petition all the persons in the complete Vacuity, the herculean, respectful and trusted venerable Spirits and the sons of Heaven in many celestial realms, The protectors and upholders of the clean and pure Right Teaching".[9]

Then the priest recites a mantra with six names of Buddhas of Five Directions. Then the priest invites the Buddhas of Five Directions and the hearers to join in the chanting. In Buddhism, the Five Wisdom Buddhas are as follows: Vairocana in the center, Amoghasiddhi related to north, Amitābha—west, Ratnasambhava—south and Akshobhya—east. Here the Buddhas of Five Directions are Manichaean angels and related to four entities of calmness (Ma 2012, 2013a):

Four entities of calmness	Direction	Chinese Angel name[10]	Middle Iranian Angel name	English angel name
Purity	North	嚧縛逸 (*luo-b'i̯wak-i̯ět)天王 (heavenly king)	rwp'yl	Raphael
Light	East	彌訶逸 (mjie̯-xâ-i̯ět)天王 (heavenly king)	mys'yl	Michael
Power	South	業囉逸 (ngi̯ɐp-lâ-i̯ět)天王 (heavenly king)	gbr'yl	Gabriel
Wisdom	West	娑囉逸 (sâ-lâ-i̯ět)天王 (heavenly king)	sr'yl	Səra'el
Majestic virtue	Center	耶具孚 (jia-g'i̯u-fjyə)大將 (Great General) 末秦皎 (muɑt dz'i̯ěn kieu) 明使 (envoy of light)	y'kwb ?	Jacob ?

Praising the King of [Ten] Heavens (*Zan Tianwang* 讚天王) (cc. 98–116)

As for the King of the Ten Heavens, his foreign (Iranian) name is 阿薩漫沙 (*ʔa-sat-muɑn ṣa* < Pth **'sm'n š'h* = King of Heaven). This is why the Taoists call him the Jade August Great Emperor of the Bright Heavens. He dwells in the seventh firmament, resides in a great palace and controls the good and bad events of the ten firmaments. In this firmament, there is a jeweled mirror with twelve faces: the upper face observes the *nirvāṇa*[-land], the lower face reflects the netherworld and the ten (remaining) faces inspect the rebellions of the various demons and similar events of change in the ten firmaments. The four heavenly kings control the four worlds (continents): the heavenly king Raphael governs the northern Uttarakuru, the heavenly king Michael rules [the eastern Pūrvavideha, the heavenly king Gabriel rules] the southern Jambudvīpa, the heavenly king Sariel controls the western Aparagodānīya. If the four heavenly, great, luminous spirits notice that the evil demons of the various firmaments launch(ed) evil plans to stir the saints of the celestial and earthly spheres, they immediately exhibit(ed) their great majestic powers to restrain them (the demons) and make them surrender; they quickly pacify them, swiftly make them surrender.[11]

---

7 The different characters of *Hymnscroll* are in parentheses: 香氣氤氳周世界，純一無雜性命海，迷（彌）綸充遍無障礙，圣眾游中香最妙。Cf. (Tsui 1943, p. 203).

8 彼界寶山億萬眾（種），香煙湧出百萬般。內外光明體清淨，甘露充盈無邊畔。(Tsui 1943, p. 203).

9 復告冥（寘）空一切眾，大力敬信尊神輩，及諸天界諸天子，護持清淨正法者。(Tsui 1943, p. 188).

10 In this article Middle Chinese forms are cited from Karlgren's reconstruction, Cf. *Hanzi ziyin da zidian* 漢字字音演變大字典 *Dictionary of Phonetic Evolution of Chinese Characters*, Jiangxi jiaoyu chubanshe, 2012.

11 十天王者，梵名阿薩漫沙也。是故道教稱為昊天玉皇大帝，住在第七天中，處在大殿，管於十天善惡之事。此天內有十二面寶鏡，上面觀於涅槃[國土]，下面照於陰司地府，十面鑒於十天諸庅（=魔）背叛等事化。四天王管四天下：嚧縛逸天王管北鬱壇界，彌訶逸天王[統御東弗婆提，業縛囉逸天王管]南閻浮提，娑囉逸天王掌握西瞿耶尼。四天大神明，若見諸天惡庅起奸計，搔擾天空地界諸聖，應時展大威神，折挫調伏，速令安定，急使調伏. (Ma 2010) I first put forward that 阿薩

Here, Manichaean King of the Ten Heavens—second son of the Living Spirit—is identified with the Taoist Jade Emperor and the Buddhist four continents are ruled by four Manichaean angels.

Praise to Land's Gods (*Tudi zan* 土地讚) (cc. 117–148)

This section is divided into six pieces. The first, third and fifth are mantras in a transcription of Middle Iranian, the sixth is a transcription of Middle Iranian mixed with Chinese and the second and fourth are in Chinese. From the Chinese text, we know that these hymns are used to praise land's gods. From the transcription of Middle Iranian, we can recognized the names of Buddhas of Five Directions: 嚧縛逸囉 (**luo-b'i̯wak-i̯ět-lâ* = Raphael), 彌阿（訶）逸囉 (*mji̯e-xâ-i̯ět-lâ* = Michael), 業縛囉逸囉(*ngi̯ɐp-b'i̯wak-lâ-i̯ět-lâ* = Gabriel), 娑囉逸囉(*sâ-lâ-i̯ět-lâ* = Sariel), 耶貝孚 (*jia-g'i̯u-fjyǝ̆* = Jacob), 味秦皎(**muɑt dz'i̯ěn kieu*)明使(envoy of light) and two angles: Narses 能遏蘇思 (**nəŋ-ʔɑt- suo-si* <MP *nrsws* [*narsus*]) and Nastikus 能 咥啾啕<蘇>思 (**nəŋ-si̯ět-t̯i-kə̯u-<suo> si*<MP *nstykws* [*nastikūs*]) (Durkin-Meisterernst 2004, pp. 244–45).

3.1.2. Second Period (*dier shi* 第二時) (cc. 148–238)

The contents for the second period can be divided into three sections.

[Inviting Buddhas] (cc. 149–207)

The priest first invites all gods with fragrant flowers. Then he "invites with wholehearted reverence (一心奉請)" Manichaean and Buddhist gods with fragrant flowers one by one and the hearers join the chanting.

[Inviting *Moluo* 默羅] (cc. 159–163)

The priest invites "*Moluo* Purple Emperor Peerless Venerable Buddha whose Five Greatnesses show immense benevolence".[12] *Moluo* 默羅 (*mək lâ*) should be an abbreviation of *Sahuanmoluo* 薩緩默羅 (*sat ɣuan mək lâ*) (c. 427). We cannot decipher the Middle Iranian name of this god but we are sure that this is the highest god of Manichaeism—the Father of Greatness. When he reviewed this paper, Yoshida pointed out that 薩緩 representing such pronunciation as [sarwan] must be the transcription of *zurwan*.

The uppermost unit of the *Diagram of the Universe* is the Realm of Light (Figure 3). The central motif of the Realm of Light is the Father of Greatness and his assembly that includes the Twelve Aeons and two additional attendants (Yoshida and Furukawa 2015, Plates 11–13, pp. 120–21). Gulácsi thinks that most likely, the two figures flanking God represent the Mother of Life and Living Spirit (Gulácsi 2016, Figure 6/37, pp. 444–47). The Five Greatnesses are (1) the Father of Greatness himself; (2) The Twelve Aeons are called *shi'er guangwang*[13] (Twelve Light Kings) (c. 641); (3) The Aeons of the Aeons are called *weichen zhu guotu*[14] (Various lands as fine dust) (c. 393); (4) The Living Air; (5) the Land of Light (the diamond floor).

After the priest invites the highest god, he continues to invite the holy triad: Jesus, Virgin of Light and Mani.

漫沙 < Sogdian *sm'n xšyδ*, Yoshida Yutaka suggested that it should be a Chinese transcription of the hitherto unattested Parthian form *'sm'n š'h*. English translation is based on (Kósa 2016b, pp. 151–52).

12 五大示洪慈之念，默羅紫帝無上尊佛.

13 十二光王.

14 微塵諸國土.

Figure 3. The Realm of Light (Gulácsi 2016, Figure 6/37 [p. 446]).

[Inviting *Yishu* 夷數] (cc. 164–168)

The priest invites "great mercy true wisdom *Yishu* the Buddha of Harmony and wishes that the white dove descends".[15] *Yishu* 夷數 (*i-ṣiu*) < Pth./MP. *yyšw', yyšw, yšw [jišō]* "Jesus". As soon as Jesus was baptized, he saw the Spirit of God descending like a dove and alighting on him.[16]

The New Aeon is depicted beneath the Realm of Light in the *Diagram of the Universe* (Figure 4). The highest-ranking deity is shown enclosed in a *mandorla* (not only a halo) and accompanied by a retinue of twelve attendants. The central seated figure is possibly Jesus and the twelve standing figures are the twelve wisdoms which are Jesus' light hours (Kósa 2016a, pp. 87–90).[17]

Figure 4. The New Aeon and Liberation of light, that is, triad of the Sun, Moon and a third divine figure between them (Yoshida and Furukawa 2015, Plate 5).

15 大慈正智夷數和佛。惟願現乘白鴿下騰空。It maybe 夷數和 belongs to the transcribed name (according to Yutaka Yoshida and S. N. C. Lieu) and should not be translated.

16 Matthew, 3:16; Mark, 1:10; Luke, 3:22.

17 Gulácsi thinks that the central seated god is Third Messenger who is surrounded by 12 Virgins of Light. (Gulácsi 2016, Figure 6/38, pp. 447–50).

[Inviting *Jinni lushen* 謹你嚧詵] (cc. 168–173)

The priest invites "Jinni lushen … great heaven true dominator Lightning Royal Buddha".[18] Jinni lushen 謹你嚧詵 kịən:-ni **luo-ṣiæn* is Chinese transcription of Pth./MP. qnygrwšn, which is not seen in Dunhuang Chinese Manichaean texts and it means "Virgin of Light".

The Virgin of Light is depicted in the atmosphere between the surface of the earth and the firmaments as the Goddess of Lightning in the *Diagram of the Universe*. She is standing on and has six arms. Her lower pair arms points toward the dark cloud. Her middle pair of arms grasps symbols of light (souls of deceased Manichaean priests). Her upper pair of arms holds a red ribbon (Figure 5).[19]

Figure 5. Virgin of Light and Mani (Yoshida and Furukawa 2015, Plate 9).

[Inviting *Moni* 摩尼] (cc. 174–177)

The priest invites "true calm wonderful body *Moni* the Buddha of Light".[20] *Moni*摩尼 (*muɑ-ni*) <Pth./MP. *m'ny* [*mānī*] "Mani".

Mani, clad in a white robe with a red stripe[21], appears a total of 17 times in the *Diagram of the Universe*. He is depicted at least four times in the Paradise, ten times in the New Aeon and Ten Heavens part of the painting and three times in the middle register (i.e., Atmosphere). In the New Aeon, the five beings on the left side of the central assembly include Mani, who is shown receiving a book from the Father of Greatness delivered by the middle of the three angels (Figure 6)[22].

[Inviting Sun and Moon Buddhas of Light] (cc. 178–181)

The priest invites "wonderful wisdom Sun and Moon Buddhas of Light which are great light-ships".[23]

18 謹你嚧詵 … … 大天真宰電光王佛.

19 Yoshida and Furukawa, *Studies of the Chinese Manichaean paintings of South Chinese origin preserved in Japan*, Plates 9, p. 114. Gulácsi, *Mani's Pictures*, Figure 6/43, p. 468. Gábor Kósa, "The Virgin of Light in the New Chinese Manichaean Xiapu Material and the Female Figure beside Mount Sumeru in the Cosmology Painting" (Les femmes dans le manichéisme occidental et oriental, 27–28 June 2014, organized by Madeleine Scopello).

20 真寂妙體摩尼光佛.

21 The red stripe is similar to the Roman *clavus*, a reddish-purple stripe on garments that distinguished members of the senatorial and equestrian orders.

22 Gulácsi, Mani's Pictures, Figure 6/38, p. 450.

23 运大明船於彼岸; 妙智妙恵日月光佛.

Figure 6. Mani the Buddha of Light (Yoshida and Furukawa 2015, Plate 5).

The white and red discs between the New Aeon and the Ten Heavens (i.e., the Liberation of Light) represent the Moon on the left with a white background and the Sun on the right with a red background (Figure 4) (Yoshida and Furukawa 2015, Plates 5, pp. 104–6; Gulácsi 2016, Figure 6/39, pp. 450–57).

[Inviting *Lushena* 盧舍那] (cc. 182–186)

The priest invites the "Diamond Column of Glory *Lushena* Buddha whose body is beyond Eight Earths and Ten Heavens".[24] *Lushena* 盧舍那 (*luo-ça̭ia-na*) is Chinese transcription of Sanskrit (abb. Sk.) *Vairocana* in Buddhist text and means Column of Glory in Manichaean text.

Between the Sun and the Moon, there is a gigantic, mustached and bearded head with a huge green halo and a crown (damaged). Below this head, there is a kind of upper body consisting of red, blue and green streams of light. This is the Column of Glory (Figure 7) (Kósa 2015a, pp. 186–87; Yoshida and Furukawa 2015, Plates 5, pp. 121–23; Gulácsi 2016, Figure 6/40, pp. 454–56).

[Inviting Venerable Buddha Who Upholds the World] (cc. 187–190)

The priest invites "the Venerable Buddha Who Upholds the World and carries the universe. His body lives beyond the sahā world of the six conjunctions (the zenith, nadir and the four directions—in other words, the whole world)".[25] The Venerable Buddha Who Upholds the World (持世尊佛) should be identified with the Envoy of Light who upholds the world (持世明使)/Lord who upholds the world (持世主) in Dunhuang documents, that is, the first son of the Living Spirit—Keeper of Splendor (Lat. *splenditenens*).

Below *Lushena*, the Keeper of Splendor embraces the light-beams with his right arm (Figure 8) (Kósa 2012, pp. 53–57; Gulácsi 2016, Figure 6/40, pp. 450–57).

---

24 金剛相柱盧舍那佛. 唯願身超八地及十天.
25 荷載乾坤持世尊佛。唯願身居六合娑婆外.

Figure 7. The Keeper of Splendor embraces light streams that merge with the Column of Glory (Gulácsi 2016, Figure 6/40 [p. 455]).

[Inviting Four Great Venerable Buddhas] (cc. 191–194)

The priest invites "the Four Great Venerable Buddhas who establish religions and liberate people".[26] The Four Great Venerable Buddhas should be Mani's four forerunners: Nārāyaṇa, Zoroaster, Shakyamuni and Jesus according to the other parts of *Mani the Buddha of Light*.

In the New Aeon, the four on the right side of the central assembly represent the four Prophets: Nārāyaṇa, Zoroaster, Shakyamuni and Jesus (Figure 4).[27]

[Inviting the Jade Emperor] (cc. 195–198)

The priest invites "the precious radiant heavenly lord–Jade Emperor Venerable Buddha. His jeweled mirror with twelve faces is bright and the Jade Emperor in hiddenness lives in the seventh firmament".[28]

This Jade Emperor can be definitively identified with King of the Ten Heavens—second son of the Living Spirit, that is, the King of Honor (Lat. *Rex honoris*) as in "In Praise of the King of [Ten] Heavens" (cc. 98–116).

26 設教度人四大尊佛.

27 Gulácsi believes that they should be Zoroaster, historical Buddha, Jesus and Mani. (Gulácsi 2016, Figure 6/38, p. 450; Figure 6/17, pp. 367–68). Kósa believes that they should be Viṣṇu (Naluoyan), Zarathuštra, Śākyamuni and Jesus. (Kósa 2016a, pp. 90–94). Yoshida once proposed that they are the four kinds of calmness of the Great Father: God (Divinity), Light, Power and Wisdom. (Yoshida and Furukawa 2015, Figures 2–23, p. 119–120).

28 寶光天主玉皇尊佛. 唯願寶鏡明明十二面, 玉皇隱隱七重天.

In the seventh firmament, to the left, the King of Honor sits on a throne and flanked by his eight soldiers, all facing toward the center, while Mani and his attendants face the deity. The right side contains the King of Honor seated cross-legged on a lotus throne and his magic mirror with twelve lenses, observed by Mani, who once again faces the deity (Figure 8) (Yoshida and Furukawa 2015, Plates 6–8, pp. 101–4; Gulácsi 2016, Figure 6/41, pp. 457–64; Kósa 2017).

Figure 8. Ten Firmaments of the Sky (Yoshida and Furukawa 2015, Plate 6).

Then the priest invits various great Bodhisattvas (cc. 199–202) and all past and future Buddhas (cc. 203–206). At last the priest recites a gatha to finish the invitation of the Buddhas.

[Worshipping Buddhas (*lifo* 禮佛) (Three Great Saints)] (cc. 209–229)

First, the priest worships the Lightning King and the hearers join the chanting. The Lightning King (電光王) should be an abbreviation of the Lightning Royal Buddha (電光王佛)—Virgin of Light.

Then the priest worships "true wisdom *Yishu* [the Buddha of] Harmony who from Brahma's realm wipes out demons and descends from the heaves as a dove".[29] Then the priest worships *Moshihe* by bowing his head to his feet and the hearers join the chanting. *Moshihe* 末尸訶 (*muɑt-ɕi-xa*) is the Chinese transcription of Pth./MP. *mšyh'* [*mašīhā*], *mšyh'h̲*, *mšyh"* [*mšīhā*], *mšyh* [*mšīh*], which is not seen in Dunhuang Chinese Manichaean texts and means "Messiah, Christ", the title of Jesus.

At last the priest worships "Long Life Nectar King who from the region of truth descended to *Badi*'s *Sulin* country in the West and showed the spiritual verifications nine-fold. [He was born] from the chest of *Moyan* and was unmatched in the world. [He] achieved perfect enlightenment at the age of thirteen".[30] *Badi* 跋帝 (*b'uɑt-tiei*) is the Chinese transcription of Pth./MP. *ptyg [*pattēg]*, "Pattēg, Pattīg"—the name of Mani's father. *Sulin* 蘇隣 (*suo-li̯ĕn*) means "Suristān"—a region of Seleucid and Ctesiphon. *Moyan* 末艷 (*muɑt-i̯ɛm*) is Chinese transcription of Pth./MP. *mrym [maryam]*, which is

29 正智夷數和，從梵天界，殄妖魔，騰空如鴿下.
30 長生甘露王，從真實境下西方跋帝蘇隣國，九種現靈祥。末艷氏，胷前誕，世無雙。十三登正覺.

written as 滿艷 (*muɑn-i̯ɛm*) in Dunhuang texts and means "Maryam"—the name of Mani's mother. So, this "Long Life Nectar King" definitely is Mani.

Then the priest recites a gatha from *H.* 42: "The Great Saint is no other than the auspicious hour, Shining universally upon our many envoys of light, thy wonderful color finds no compare in the world, thy divine power of transfiguration is just the same".[31]

Reading the Scriptures (*kangjing* 看經) and Reading Goddess Incantation (*nian tiannü zhou* 念《天女咒》) (cc. 230–238)

We cannot decipher the whole incantation, only individual words: *Nalisuohe yizai* 那哩娑和夷口在 *nɑ-lji-sɑ-ɣuɑi-*dz'ɑi̯* < MP. *nrysh̲ yzd* [*narisah yazad*], Narisah-yazd, borrowed from Zoroastrianism (Aw. *Nairyōsaŋha-*); *Yishu jinghe* 夷數精和 *i-s̑i̯u tsi̯ɛŋ-ɣuɑ* <Pa. *yyšw' zyw'* [*yišō' zīwā*] "Jesus the Splendor"; *Jinni lushen* 謹你嚧詵 Virgin of Light; *Humin huse* 護泯護瑟 *ɣwo-mi̯n ɣwo-s̑i̯æt* < MP. *whmn wzrg* [*wahman wuzurg*] "great Wahman", name of the Light-Nous; *Mile pusa* 彌勒菩薩 Maitreya Bodhisattva; *qiedushi* 伽度師 *g'ĭɑ-d'ɑk-ṣi* which was written as *qielushi* 伽路師 *g'ĭɑ-luo-ṣi* in Dunhuang texts and means "holy" (Lin 2017; Ma 2016b).

3.1.3. Third and Fourth Periods (*disan shi* 第三時, *disi shi* 第四時) (cc. 238–247)

Both third and fourth periods include Purification of Speech, Reading the *Scripture of Light* (*kan Guangming jing* 看《光明經》) and Praise of the Four Entities of Calmness (*Siji zan* 四寂讚) (cc. 239–247)

After reconstructing the original of this Chinese hymn *Shiji zan*, Yoshida found the fragments M 1367 and M 361 that only has few words that are different from the phonetically transcribed version in the *Mani the Buddha of Light* (Yoshida 2014). We make emendations of the Chinese text according to M 1367. The first line is Chinese text, second line is Middle Chinese according to Karlgren, the third line is the transliteration of the Middle Iranian and the fourth line is the transcription of Middle Iranian. The fifth line is the English translation.

奥和	匐賀	盧詵	嗟（嵯）鶻囉	哂哩咈哆
ʔaɑ-ɣuɑ	b'i̯uk-ɣɑ	luo-s̑i̯æn	(dz'ɑ)-ɣwat-lɑ	*ȵźi-lji-*pi̯uət-tɑ
'w'	bg'	rwšn'	z'wr'	jyryft'
ō-w-ā	baɣ-ā	rōšn-ā	zāwar-ā	žīrīft-ā
To	God,	Light,	Power, (and)	Wisdom,

嗟（嵯）哩	能河淡	渾淡摩和	夷数	訖（謹）你
(dz'ɑ)-lji	nəŋ-ɣɑ-d'ɑm	ɣuən-d'ɑm-muɑ	ɣuɑ	i-s̑i̯u (ki̯ən:)-ni
z'ry	*ng'y'm'	wynd'm'	'w'	yyšw knyg
zārī	niɣāyām-ā	wendām-ā	ō-w-ā	yišō kanī (g)
We pray humbly.	We give praise	to	Jesus	Maiden, (and)
門乎弥特	味囉	摩尼	阿特	弗里咗德健
muən-ɣuo-mjie̯-d'ək	*muɑt-lɑ	muɑ-ni	ʔɑ-d'ək	pi̯uət-lji-*dz'ăi-tək-g'i̯ɐn
mnwhmyd	mr'	m'ny	'wd	frystg'n
manōhmēd	mār-ā	mānī	ud	frēstagān
Light-Nous,	Mar	Mani	and	the apostles.

代醯渾（潭）麻	阿呼特伽	稽囉縛居
d'ăi-xiei-(d'ăm)-ma	ʔɑ-xuo-d'ək-g'i̯ɑ	kiei-lɑ-b'i̯wk-ki̯wo
dhydwm'	'g'dg'	kyrbg
dahēdum-ā	āɣādag-ā	kirbag
Grant me (my)	pious	wish.

[31] 大聖自是吉祥時，普曜我等諸明使（性）；妙色世間無有比，神通變化（現）復如此.

陣那南	波[耶特]	[羅]緩	步唎
ȡ'i̯ĕn-nɑ-năm	puɑ[-i̯a-d'ək]	[lɑ-]γuɑn	b'uo-*ȵʑi
*tnwm'	p'yd	rw'n	bwjyd
tanum-ā	pāyēd	ruwān	bōžēd
Guard	my body	(and)	save (my) soul.

阿弗哩特	菩和	味囉	摩尼	你耶你耶咗
ʔɑ-pi̯uət-lji-d'ək	b'uo-γuɑ	*muɑt-lɑ	muɑ-ni	ni-i̯a-ni-i̯a-*dz'ăi
''frydg	bw'	mr'	m'ny	?
āfrīdag	bawā	mār-ā	mānī	?
Blessed	be	Mar	Mani,	?

阿弗哩特	[菩和]	味啰	摩尼	你曳你曳咗
ʔɑ-pi̯uət-lji-d'ək	[b'uo-γuɑ]	*muɑt-lɑ	muɑ-ni	ni-i̯ɛi-ni-i̯ɛi-*dz'ăi
''frydg	[bw']	mr'	m'ny	?
āfrīdag	[bawā]	mār-ā	mānī	?
Blessed	[be]	Mar	Mani,	?

[勿那]	阿哆(羅)緩哆(那)	[菩]和	娑[地]
[mi̯uət-nɑ]	ʔɑ-(lɑ)-γuɑn-(nɑ)	[b'uo-]γuɑ	sa-[d'i]
[mn']	rw'n'	*bw'	š'd(yḥ) (?)
[man-ā]	ruwān-ā	*bawā	šād(īḥ)
May my	soul	be	joyful!

遮伊但	伽度師
tɕi̯a-ʔji-d'an	g'i̯a-d'ɑk-ʂi
j'yd'n	k'dwš
ǰāydān	kādūš
(Be) holy eternally!	

3.1.4. [Worship and Repentance]

The last part is an independent one.

First Purification of the Altar (*shou jingtan* 首净壇) (cc. 248–255)

The priest recites three times a mantra mixed with Chinese and Chinese transcriptions of Middle Persian:

清淨	光明	大力	智慧
咦咗	嚧詵	蘇路	和醯
xji-*dz'ăI	luo-ʂi̯æn	suo-luo	γuɑ-xiei
yzd	rwšn	zwr	why<u>h</u>
yazad	rōšn	zōr	wehīh
Purity (God)	Light	Power	Wisdom

Then the priest recites, "North Purity, East Light, South Power, West Wisdom and Center Immeasurable" and recites three times "*yizai, lushen, sulu, hexi*". At last the priest circumambulates the altar and recites *H.* 30: "Pray give me the fragrant water of emancipation, the twelve precious crowns, the clothes, the fringes. Cleanse the altar from dust and dirt, strictly purify my speech and make it graceful".[32]

---

32 願施戒香解脱水，十二寶冠衣瓔珞。洒除壇界（洗我妙性）離塵埃，嚴潔（餝）净口（躰）令端正. Cf. (Tsui 1943, p. 178).

[Inviting Buddhas (North Heavenly King)] (cc. 256–264)

The priest invites North Purity, the heavenly king Raphael. The hearers join to chant a short mantra.

Penitential Mysterious Prayer (*Chanhui xuanwen* 懺悔玄文) (cc. 265–271)

I now repent whatever were my physical, verbal and mental activities; my craving, aversion and ignorance; and had I encouraged the 'robbers' to poison my heart, or not restrained my sense organs; or had I doubted the eternal-living three Treasures and the Two Great Lights; or had I injured the body of *Lushena* and well as the five Light-sons; had I begot a feeling of slight and neglect against the Priest-teachers, our fathers and mothers and against the wise intimates and had I accused and blamed them; or had I imperfectly observed the seven kinds of almsgivings, the ten Commandments and the three Seals: Gates of Teaching—I wish my sins may disappear! (*H*. 410–414).[33]

Reading Prayer, Praise to the Envoys of Light (*xuanshu, mingshi zan* 宣疏、明使讚) (cc. 271–282)

The priest recites a mantra of Chinese transcription of Middle Iranian.

Farewell Ritual for the Buddhas (*songfo* 送佛) (cc. 282–292)

This is the dismissal part of the Rituals for Good Fortune. The priest bids farewell to the Buddhas with fragrant flowers and bows down to the Buddhas again. After *huixiang* "transfer", the priest recites a short mantra.

"The end of the Rituals for Good Fortune (*qingfu ke zhong* 請福科終)".

3.2. [Rituals for Funeral (Jianwang ke 薦亡科)] (cc. 292–659)

The main content of the second part can be divided into ninteen sections.

3.2.1. Praise of the Descent (*Xiasheng zan* 下生讚) (cc. 292–312)

When Mani Buddha descended, he was incarnated in *Sulin* (Suristān). Pomegranates' branches brought auspiciousness. The garden manager ascended the vermilion steps leading up to the palace hall and reported the unusual phenomenon to the throne. *A-shi-jian* ordered the garden manager to pick them, put them on a plate and politely offer them up. *Moyan* 末艷 (Maryam) liked to eat and her lovely face expressed great pleasure. The sage admonished her to rest in another palace. By the time ten full months had transpired, the flower was born; the lovely *baby emerged from her chest. Golden lotus flowers sprang up from the earth and nectar fell from the sky. Buddhas of the ten directions were all pleased. The demon king of three poisons was grieving from afflictions. The lofty precious manifestation was incomparable with this mortal world and looked up to by the court ladies. All entreated the Crown Prince to come back the palace. He [the Crown Prince] renounced the secular life at the age of four and entered enlightenment at the age of thirteen, then inflicted a defeat on the [doctrine of the] Water-washing [Baptists]. The holy *yanmo* (<Pth. *ymg [yamag]* twin) subsequently guided [him] to observe Three Epochs—past, present and future. All things were understood and various phenomena were unobstructed. [He] gradually advanced to *Bosi* (Persia), *Bolu* and other countries. Nāgas and the eight groups all respected his virtue. Everyone praised: "This is a unique moment!" [His] prestige influenced Persia and [he] persuaded the *Persian King to comprehend the *principles. The whole world followed him. The new monks and teachers followed [Mani] Buddha's travels and first transformed to long eyebrows. My Buddha (Mani) preached and completely retained the teachings in the assembly of all human beings and celestials. [People] retained the Buddha's

[33] 我今懺悔所，是身口意業，及貪嗔痴[行]，或乃至從（縱）賊毒心，諸根放逸；或宜（疑）常住三宝并二大光明；或損盧舍那身及（兼）五明子；於僧師（師僧）父母、諸善知識起輕慢心，更相毀謗；於七世（施）十戒、三印法門，若不具修，願罪消滅。Cf. (Tsui 1943, p. 215).

teaching about the fundamentals of the Two Principles and erased old sins through the Three Epochs. Of years, five [times] nine (i.e., 450 years) had passed, the Teaching spread to the eastern land. Long live the present emperor. Peaceful kingdoms of the earth were all converted. Everyone looks for and obtains good fortune and everyone maintains safety and security. May almsgivers of the ten directions live long and prosper![34]

The *Compendium* written in 731 only tells us that Mani was born in the country of *Sulin* at the royal palace of Emperor *Badi* by his wife *Manyan* 滿艷 (*Maryam*). Having sprung into existence from His mother's chest, He surpassed His age and excelled everyone (Haloun and Henning 1952, p. 190–91). Based on this core scene, "Praise of the Descent" added a dozen scenes to the story of Mani's birth under the influence of the story of Sākyamuni's birth. At the same time, Manichaeans composed the *Painting of the Birth of Mani* which now is in Kyūshū National Museum, Japan (Yoshida and Furukawa 2015, Plates 14, pp. 128–37; Gulácsi 2016, Figure 6/13, 6/20, pp. 386–93). It depicts approximately nine scenes described in "Praise of the Descent" (Ma 2016c, 2016d).

3.2.2. Incantation of St. George (*Jisi zhou* 吉思咒) (cc. 312–331)

[We] wholeheartedly and respectfully praise Great Saint George (*Yihuojisi* 移活吉思). Because Roman Empire (*Folin* 佛林 *b'i̯uət-li̯əm*< Sogdian (Sogd.) *βr'wm*) Caesar (*Jisa*計薩 *kiei-sat* < Sogd. *kysr*) issued an imperial edict to destroy Christianity (*Yishu fo jiao* 夷數佛教), [George] faced the Two Great Lights, made vows to practice the orthodox religion and exterminate false gods. A ladder of knives and iron matte, iron boots, caltrops and so forth, a wheel of swords, [all] the instruments of torture, [he] endured willingly and was ready for any suffering. [He] recited [the name of] Jesus Buddha and although he had died, he revived again. [He] recited Jesus Buddha and let dead wood luxuriate. [He] recited Jesus Buddha and let all the fallen ones be liberated; recited Jesus Buddha and let the decaying bones be resurrected. This body was imprisoned and [he] let the pillar in the house become a big tree. The sick child prayed: "Please relieve my various pains". [He] recited Jesus Buddha again and the dumb and blind, deaf [child] could speak and hear, see. [He] broke that false god temple, by shouting, [he] detained various demons, overthrew the clay idol in the niche; and the evil spirits and ghosts were all exterminated. The Caesar angered again, as four poisons [snakes] wanted to torture and execute [him]. What [he] did was all done and as soon as the fight against the army of demons was finished, [he] wanted to return to calmness and extinction (nirvāṇa). [He] supplicated Jesus Buddha to make infinite vows together: "Whoever shall have a nightmare, or be jailed in a lawsuit, or have severe drought all over the land, or live in misery and recite [the name of] St. George, [I] shall search [their] voice and never fail to answer any call". [George] finished arousing vows and returned to true quiescence. Many people all confessed and begged to correct their mistakes: sought after to eliminate various evils and all attained the supreme way.[35]

---

34 《下生讚》：摩尼佛，下生时，托蔭於蘇隣。石榴樹，枝呈瑞，園官詣丹墀，表奏希奇。阿师健氏，命宫官，摘捧盘，殷懃奉献。末艶氏喜食，花顔喜歡，神人誡责"别宫安"。 十月满，将花誕出；詣嬌培，湧化智間。地湧金蓮，{捧}天洒甘露。十方諸佛盡歡忻，三毒庅(魔）王悲煩惱。巍巍宝相，九間难比。嬪妃仰止，咸迎太 子歸裏。年四出家，十三成道，便破水洗。於今闇默聖，引觀三際初、中、後，事皆通知，般般无凝(礙)。漸次前行，薄(波）斯、波魯諸國，龍天八部咸仰徳，人人讚："曹(遭)想"。威感波斯，說勃(波）王悟里(理)，四維上中下，皆從皈依。沙密(彌）、闍黎随佛遊，先化眉。我佛說法，人天會裏總持。持佛二宗大義，三際消舊罪。五九数，法流東土。上祝當今皇帝千秋萬萬，海清萬國盡皈依。各求福利，各保平安。惟願十方施主，崇福壽永綿綿！Yoshida's comment: "波斯說勃：While I cannot explain 說, this is likely to transcribe Shabuhr. 說 is to be emended to 沙?" Kósa believes that "長眉 Long Eyebrowed" refers to one of the Arhats—Pindola.

35 志心敬稱讚：移活吉思大聖。為佛林計薩照（詔）滅夷數佛教，對二大光明，誓願行正教，殄滅諸妖神。刀梯及铁鏣，铁靴、減（蒺）藜等，劍輪刑害具，甘心不辞苦。称念夷數佛，曁（既）死而復甦。稱念夷數佛，枯木令茲（滋）茂。稱念夷數佛，沉輪（淪）俱解脫；稱念夷數佛，朽骨再甦<還>活。是身在囚擊，令彼所居舍，柱化為大樹。病兒請乞願："救我諸疾苦。"再念夷數<尊>佛，瘖瘂及盲聾，能言復聞見。破彼妖神厝，喝禁諸庅（魔）鬼；摧倒坭龕像，邪祟殄滅。計薩復祚恕（作怒），四毒加刑害。所作皆已，戰敵庅軍<已>畢<日>，即欲歸疾（寂）滅。仰啟夷數佛，同弘無盡願："若人有惡夢，或被官司囚<擊>，及一天亢旱，苦難逼身者，稱念吉思聖，尋聲皆如應。"發願已竟還真寂，眾皆懺悔求捨過：願求斷[諸]惡，盡成如（無）上道.

Yihuojisi 移活吉思 (*ie̯-kuat-kiĕt-si*) is the Chinese transcription of Sogdian *yw'rks* "George". *Jisi* is an abbreviation of *Yihuojisi*. The Incantation of *Jisi* (George) may be a Chinese summary of the Nestorian Sogdian *The Martyrdom of St. George* (Ma 2017).

3.2.3. [Worshipping Buddhas] (cc. 331–365)

The priest recites "The Praise to heavenly king", which is the Chinese transcription of a Middle Iranian original. Yoshida found that it is the Chinese transcription of a Middle Persian text found in M 19 when he reviewed this paper. It is our honor to get his permission to publish his research as Appendix A of this paper.

Then the priest recites gathas in which there are several lines from the *Hymnscroll* (abbr. *H.*) with a few different characters, for example: "I also petition the universal Light of Lord Mani, *yanmo* (twin), Light-Nous and Sun of enlightenment, who came from that great Light-realm into this world, distributed and exalted the correct teaching, rescuing the good Sons". (*H.* 135)[36]. "I also petition the Sun and Moon buddhas of light, the safely-settled place of all the Buddhas of the three Generations, the seven (and) the twelve great (Ship)-masters and all the Masses of Light". (*H.* 127)[37] "May all of the souls go on to the right road and quickly gain Nirvāṇa, the land of the Pure Kingdom. There seven distresses and four hardships are naturally absent and it is therefore called the lace of eternal happiness". (*H.* 119)[38] "I therefore, purifying my heart, worship, laud and praise, and, removing all confused thoughts, speak truly: in the immediate past, I had unknowingly committed may iniquities, tonight I repent beseechingly so that my sins shall disappear". (*H.* 11)[39] "I only wish now that they will listen to my petitions, grant great invincible might and protect us, letting us have skillful means to cover and defend ourselves, so that we shall gain peace and security and be away from the hateful enemy". (*H.* 206)[40].

The priest recites a gatha of *huixiang* "transfer" as the end of this section.

3.2.4. [Inviting Buddhas (Five Buddhas)] (cc. 366–373)

The priest invites Five Buddhas—Nārāyaṇn, Zoroaster, Śākyamuni, Jesus and Mani and the hearers join the chanting.

3.2.5. [Worshipping Buddhas] (cc. 374–388)

The priest worships the Five Buddhas: Nārāyaṇa, Zoroaster, Śākyamuni, Jesus and Mani and the hearers join the chanting.

Then the priest recites: "The first one, the unsurpassed Buddha of Light, the second, wisdom—Good Mother Buddha, the third, constant victory—First Thought Buddha, the fourth, happiness—Five Light (i.e., Ether, Wind, Light, Water and Fire) Buddhas, the fifth, zeal—Enjoyer of the Lights Buddha, the sixth, truth—Creator of forms Buddha, the seventh, faith—Pure Wind Buddha, the eighth, patience—Sun-radiance Buddha, the ninth, honest thought—*She'na* (Vairocana) Buddha, the tenth, gratitude—Jesus Buddha, the eleventh, unanimous mind—Lightning Buddha, the twelfth, splendid—Wise-Light Buddha. Who is the King of Teaching of the three Generations, who opens and exalts all the secret things; of the Two Principles, the Three Periods and the meaning of the natures and forms, he can reveal all clearly without doubt or hesitation" (*H.* 169–72).[41]

---

36 又啟普遍摩尼光（尊），閻默惠明警覺日，從彼大明至此界，敷揚正教（法）救善子。Cf. (Tsui 1943, p. 186).

37 又啟日月光明佛（宮），三世諸佛安置處。七級（及）十二大般（船）主，并諸（餘）一切光明眾。Cf. (Tsui 1943, p. 187).

38 普願靈魂（齊心）登正路，速脫（獲）涅槃淨國土。七厄四苦彼元無，是故名為常樂處。Cf. (Tsui 1943, p. 186).

39 是故澄心礼称讃，除諸乱意真言。承前不覺造諸愆，今夜（時）懇懺罪消（銷）滅。Cf. (Tsui 1943, p. 176).

40 惟願今時听我，降大神威（慈悲）護我等。任巧方便自遮防，務得安寧離冤（怨）敵。Cf. (Tsui 1943, p. 193).

41 一者無上光明佛（王），二者智惠善母佛，三者常勝先意佛，四者懽（歡）喜五明佛，五者勤修樂明佛，六者真實造相佛，七者信心淨風佛，八者忍辱日光佛，九者直意舍那佛（盧舍那），十者知恩夷数佛，十一者齊心電光佛，十二者莊嚴惠明佛（惠明莊嚴佛）。自是三世法中王，開揚（楊）一切秘密事。二宗二際性相儀（義），悉能顯現無疑滯。Cf. (Tsui 1943, p. 191).

3.2.6. [Purification of Speech] (cc. 388–394)

The priest recites a mantra transcribed from a Middle Iranian original as a small purification of speech and a gatha as a great purification of speech.

3.2.7. [Inviting Buddhas (Heavenly Kings and Envoys of Light)] (cc. 394–403)

The priest invites the Four Heavenly Kings–Raphael, Michael, Gabriel, Sariel and other envoys of light.

Mt. Sumeru is the center of the surface of the eighth earth of the *Diagram of Universe*. There is a plateau on the top of Mt. Sumeru. The plateau contains an unidentified central figure, with four supplicants kneeling before him, amid thirty-two gates that symbolize the thirty-two cities (Figure 9).

Figure 9. The Top of Sumeru mountain (Kósa 2016b, plate 2 [p. 182]).

In Buddhism, Śakra (*Dishitian* 帝釋天) is located on the top of Mt. Sumeru. In China, Śakra is sometimes identified with the Taoist Jade Emperor. The Four Heavenly Kings serve Śakra and dwell each on a side of Mt. Sumeru and who ward off the attacks of malicious spirits from the world.

According to *Mani the Buddha of Light*, the unidentified central figure on the top of Mt. Sumeru of the *Diagram of Universe* can be understood as the Jade Emperor—King of the Ten Heavens and the four supplicants kneeling before him perhaps should be understood as Raphael, Michael, Gabriel and Sariel.

3.2.8. Praise of Preparing the Altar (*kaitan zan* 開壇讚) (cc. 403–419)

The priest worships and praises the Light-Nous with several different names: Great Nous (*Guangda zhi* 廣大智), Good King of the Mind (*Shanxin wang* 善心王), Great Wise Light (*Da huiming* 大惠明) (Ma 2015b).

3.2.9. Honoring Universal Permanent Triratna (*gongjing shifang changzhu sanbao* 恭敬十方常住三寶) (cc. 420–425)

The priest worships two Bodhisattvas: *Guanyin* 觀音 (i.e., Call, deity of the second emanation; *Avalokiteśvara*) and Shizhi 勢至 (i.e., Answer, deity of the second emanation, *Mahāsthāmaprāpta*); *yanmo* 閻默 (i.e., twin)—Light Treasure; Jesus—Sacred Treasure; Lightning (i.e., Virgin of Light)—Pure Treasure; two Bodhisattvas: *huiming* 惠明 Wise Light and *faxiang* 法相 Glory of the Teaching (i.e., the Light-Nous).

3.2.10. Venerating the Triratna (cc. 425–444)

"Venerating Buddha: *Sahuanmoluo* Holy Lord (i.e., the Father of Greatness). [He] lives out of this world and is always secure. [His] Lofty spiritual marks are like precious jewels. The true essence of all phenomena always exists and lacks any marks of arising or cessation. Trillion sages always look up at [him]. Looking up at [him], wishing [him] to send down authoritative power to give divine protection. The light is with a single determinable nature and with nothing to do with sunrise and sunset. This is the place of peace and happiness for the true essence. Universally whishing that the light-souls of the three realms (earth, atmosphere and heaven) become enlightened quickly and come back to the great light together".[42] Its content is similar to that of "A Gāthā in Praise of the Unsurpassed Venerable Lord of Light" in *Hymnscroll* (*H.* 222–34).

"Venerating the Teaching: Jesus first established the natural wonderful Truth which is most valuable and a ferry (i.e., religion) for myriad worlds as numerous as the sands of Ganges. Two principles and three times—subtle connotation is extensively and publicly stated. The enlightened light-soul escape from the mundane world. Escaping from the mundane world, [the light-souls] come back to the holy body of the absolute reality which continue in the future to turn the wheel of the Dharma. Ten kinds of extraordinary are always refreshing ... ".[43]

"Venerating Saṅgha: *arhats*, true men, sages. The returned light-souls descended from the Ten Firmaments. [They] drive light-ship to wander extensively in the sea of tortures, seek priceless treasures to the Dharma assembly, save countless true good persons who are responsive to the Light. Good persons who are responsive to the Light perfectly observe the five commandments and three Seals. Marvelous teaching is most profound and extensively preached among the multitude of light. Seven prayers daily are performed with most zealous inclination. The true teaching transmits and continues in ten thousand years".[44]

3.2.11. [Incense Offering Praise] (cc. 445–459)

The priest burns incenses of Love (*lianmin* 憐憫 lit. compassion), Faith (*chengxin* 誠信), Wisdom (*zhihui* 智慧), Perfection (*juzu* 具足) and Patience (*renru* 忍辱) (five gifts of New Man, or five cardinal virtues) and make offerings to Nārāyaṇa, Zoroaster, Śākyamuni, Jesus and Mani respectively.

3.2.12. Great Praising Incense Offering (*da zangxiang* 大讚香) (cc. 460–481)

The priest burns various incenses and makes offerings to Buddha of Light, Wonderful Dharma, Pure Saṅgha and an ocean-assembly of venerable saints.

Then the priest praises to Land's Gods, reads the *Scripture of Chaste Light* (*kan Zhenming jing* 看《貞明經》) and does the transfer (*huixiang*) (c. 482).

---

[42] 皈依佛：薩緩默羅聖主。居方外，永安固。巍巍靈相若寶珠。無生無滅、法體真常住。萬億聖賢，常仰瞻慕。仰瞻慕，願降威神加護。一定光，無曉暮。真實元本安樂處。普願三界、明性早覺悟。盡向大明，相將皈去.

[43] 皈依法：夷數始立天真義，最可珍。遍周沙界作通津。二宗三際、妙義廣開陳。覺悟明性，脫離凡塵。離凡塵，復本真如聖身。續來世，轉法輪。十般殊勝永清新.

[44] 皈依僧：羅漢真人上佺。回光性，降十天。廣遊苦海駕明船。撈（撈）漉無價珍寶至法筵。救拔無數真善明緣。善明緣，五戒三印全。微妙義，最幽玄。光明眾廣宣傳。七時禮懺，志意倍精專。流傳正法，相繼萬年。(Ma 2014b, pp. 254 67).

3.2.13. [Inviting Five Buddhas] (cc. 483–515)

The priest invites the five prophets: Nārāyaṇa, Zoroaster, Śākyamuni, Jesus and Mani and hearers join the chanting.

Then the priest sings "The Five Sons of Thunder" and hearers join the chanting "We wish ... ":

> The first buddha was Nārāyaṇa (*Naluoyan* 那羅延 *nɑ-la-i̯ɛn*), who descended into the country of the brahmins in the sahā world (=this world), made generations of people pure and honest; saved the light-nature and liberated it from the sufferings of the birth and death (saṃsāra). We wish that the deceased spirit would ride the buddhas' majestic brilliance and bear witness to the community of bodhisattvas!
>
> The second buddha was Zoroaster (*Suluzhi* 蘇路支 *suo-luo-tɕi̯e* < Pth. *zrhwšt [zarhušt]*), due to the great chain of causation, he preached the teachings (dharma) in Persia, liberated innumerable people. On all the six ways (of rebirths) he stopped the torments and on all the three unfortunate forms of rebirth he ceased the sufferings. We wish ....
>
> The third buddha was Śākyamuni (*Shijiawen* 釋迦文 *ɕi̯ɛk-ki̯a-mi̯uən* < Pth. *š'qmn [šāqman]*), the great merciful father of the four kinds of beings, who attained enlightenment in the Lumbinī park [of Kapilavastu], liberated people from the sufferings of birth and death, he preached holy words from the golden mouth, all the beings became enlightened. We wish ....
>
> The fourth buddha was Jesus [the buddha of] Harmony, the son of the Highest Light Worthy (the Father of Greatness), [he] descended to *Fulin* 拂林 (*p'i̯uət-li̯əm* < frwm, Roman Empire), became a loving father, revealed his true self for an instant in order to show the way to the heaven. We wish ....
>
> The fifth buddha was Mani [the buddha of] Light, the last envoy of light. After his incarnation in a palace, [he] appeared as a crown prince. Preaching the teaching (dharma), he turned the gold wheel and those who were responsive were rescued. We wish ....
>
> [Let us] make obeisance towards our World-Honored Ones, who, due to the great chain of causation by responsive manifestation, were born among us, who became the fathers of the four kinds of beings and who, with merciful hearts, saved the sentient beings, so they would forever be free from the sufferings of birth and death. We would like them to welcome and lead the deceased souls with mercy, so that the souls would be reborn in the Pure Land.[45]

The priest recites a mantra with the name of the five prophets.

Gulácsi demonstrates that the four gods on the right side of the central assembly in the New Aeon of the *Diagram of Universe* represent the Primary Prophets. Zoroaster can be identified by holding a green *barsom* branch at the upper left and Śākyamuni can be identified by his *ushnisha* at the upper right (Figures 4 and 10). She believes that Jesus at the lower right and Mani at the lower left (Gulácsi 2016, Figure 6/17, pp. 367–68, Figure 6/38, p. 450; Kósa 2013, pp. 90–94). According to Xiapu manuscripts, the god at the lower left can be identified as Nārāyaṇa and the god at the lower right can be identified as Jesus.

---

45 隨案唱五雷子：一佛那羅延，降神娑婆界；國應波羅門，當淳人代。開度諸明性，出離生死苦。願亡靈、乘佛威光，證菩薩會。二佛蘇路支，以大因故；說法在波斯，度人無數。六道悉停酸，三途皆息苦。願亡靈、……三佛釋迦文，四生大慈父；得道毘藍苑，度生死苦。金口演真言，咸生皆覺悟。願亡靈……四佛夷數和，無上明尊子；降神下拂林，作慈悲父。刹刹露真身，為指通宵路。願亡靈……五佛摩尼光，最後光明使；托化在王宮，示為太子。說法轉金輪，有緣蒙濟度。願亡靈……稽首我世尊，以大因故，應化下生來，作四生父；悲心度眾生，永離生死苦。願慈悲、接引亡靈，往生淨土。(Ma 2014a, pp. 196–319; Kósa 2013, pp. 20–21). "The Five Sons of Thunder" is the title of a Buddhist music melody.

Figure 10. Four Great Venerable Buddhas (Gulácsi 2016, Figure 6/17 [p. 368]).

3.2.14. Rest (*xieshi* 歇時), Performing Worshipping (*zuo xinli* 做信禮) (cc. 516–540)

The priest worships the four prophets: Nārāyaṇa, Zoroaster, Śākyamuni and Jesus. He praises that the second [buddha], that is, Zoroaster, descended to Persia to save the Pure Wind nature, edified idolaters (*Yuduoxi* 鬱多習 *ʔi̯uət-ta-zi̯əp* < Sogd. *yzt'ys* "idol"). Because there were images of celestials, demons went to Babylon (*Bopi* 波毘 *puɑ-b'ji* < Pth./MP *b'byl*) and ruined under the irradiation of divine light.[46]

3.2.15. Singing "Lotus Stand" (*chang liantai* 唱蓮臺) (cc. 540–565)

The priest worships the first great Tathagata of good aeon (*bhadra-kalpa*) (i.e., Nārāyaṇa), the second Tathagata of good aeon (i.e., Zoroaster), the third Tathagata of good aeon (i.e., Śākyamuni) and the fourth Tathagata of good aeon (i.e., Jesus).[47] The hearers join the chanting.

The priest praises the five buddhas who saved Ether, Wind, Light, Water and Fire.[48]

In the Liberation of Light, flanking the Column of Glory's "neck" are two divine figures who can be identified as the Call and the Answer. They hold five elements—Ether, Wind, Light, Water and Fire on a scarf (Figures 7 and 8) (Yoshida and Furukawa 2015, Plates 5, pp. 121–23; Gulácsi 2016, pp. 450–57).

3.2.16. [Leading the Deceased Souls to the Right Path (*deng zhenglu* 登正路)] (cc. 565–596)

The priest prays that the deceased souls should ascend through four palaces to the New Aeon and World of Eternal Light. The hearers join the chanting.

---

46 第二蘇路支，救淨風性下波斯，開化鬱多習，……為有天神像，妖幻往波毘，放神光照盡崩隳。Ma 2016 "Tracing the sources of Suluzhi 'kaihua Yuduoxi'—Xiapu wenshu *Moni guangfo* kece yanjiu 蘇路支'開化鬱多習'溯源 The Roots of 'Converting Idolaters' by Zoroaster: Study on Xiapu manuscript *Mani the Buddha of Light*", *Tianlu luncong* 天祿論叢 *Journal of Society for Chinese Studies Librarians* 6: 1–15. Yoshida's comment: "鬱多習 may be compared with 烏瑟多習 of the 酉陽雜俎, which stands for (king) Wishtasp, the first supporter of Zoroaster".

47 賢劫一座大如來……賢劫二座大如來……賢劫三座大如來……賢劫四座大如來。"Lotus Stand" is the title of a Buddhist music melody.

48 收救氣、風、明、水、火.

[Ascending the Precious Palace] (cc. 566–572)

The deceased souls first "ascend to the Precious Palace, the path to refuge, First Thought meet with Yama (*Yanluo* 閻羅) in the atmosphere".[49]

A judgment after death appears on the right side of the Atmosphere of the *Diagram of Universe* (Figures 2 and 11). The motif of the judge and his office occupies the upper half of this composition. The judge seated behind his desk. He can be identified as Yama in Buddhism. In Manichaeism, this judge can be identified as Impartial King (*Pingdeng wang* 平等王, Pth. *d'dbr r'štygr* "Just Judge"). A motif of the judgment scene is a small, seated figure traveling on a white-red cloud on the Judge's right side. The cloud seems to leave the Judge. This small figure possibly represents the soul of a deceased hearer. In the sixth king's court of *Ten Kings sūtra* P.2003 of Buddhism, the King of Transformations (*Biancheng wang* 變成王) has two small figures on two clouds leaving him, which represents the deceased soul ascending to the paradise (Ma 2016, p. 390).[50]

Figure 11. The judgment scene (Yoshida and Furukawa 2015, Plate 6).

[Ascending the Glory Palace] (cc. 573–577)

The deceased souls then "ascend to the Glory Palace, are exposed to *Shena* and go through all the twenty-eight halls".[51] *Shena* is abbreviation for *Lushena*—Column of Glory (Figure 8).

---

49 登寶宮，皈命道，先意太空見閻羅.

50 Gábor Kósa believes that the cloud might represent the verdict of the judge as the cloud leaving the mouth of *Wudao zhuanlun wang* 五道轉輪王 "the King Who Turns the Wheel of Rebirth in the Five Paths" in P. 2003. (Kósa 2014b, pp. 102–3). Gulácsi believes that the judge is shown issuing the verdict (personified as a small figure on a cloud issuing from his mouth). (Gulácsi 2016, Figure 6/43, p. 466).

51 登相宮，見舍那，二十八殿盡經過.

[Ascending the Moon Palace] (cc. 578–582)

The deceased souls then "ascend to the Moon Palace, [meet with three treasures]: First Thought, Lightning and Jesus [the Buddha of] Harmony".[52]

Inside the moon of the Liberation of Light there are three deities. According to textual references, they should be the First Man (i.e., First Thought), the Virgin of Light (i.e., Lightning) and Jesus. There are seven pilots in it (Figure 12).

Figure 12. The Moon in the Liberation Light (Yoshida and Furukawa 2015, Plate 5).

[Ascending the Sun Palace] (cc. 583–587)

The deceased souls then "ascend to the Sun Palace, [are exposed to Compassionate Mother,] Sun-radiance and Pure Wind on their marvelous seats".[53]

Inside the sun of the Liberation of Light, there are three deities too. According to textual references, they should be the Mother of Life (i.e., Compassionate Mouther), the Third Messenger (i.e., Sun-radiance) and the Living Spirit (i.e., Pure Wind) (Yoshida and Furukawa 2015, Plates 5, pp. 104–6; Gulácsi 2016, Figure 6/39, p. 454). There are twelve pilots in it (Figure 13). Seven pilots in the Moon and twelve pilots in the Sun are called "seven and twelve great Ship-masters" (c. 341).

[Ascending the Three Constancies] (cc. 590–592)

The deceased souls then "ascend to the Three Constancies, meet with nine treasures, in New Light[-world] on lotus seats of nine levels".[54] The Three Constancies are Trinity: the Father—the Father of Greatness, the Son—Jesus and the Holy Spirit—the Light-Nous. The deceased souls should ascend to the New Aeon (Figure 4) first and then ascend to the Realm of Light.

52 登月宮，（見慈母）[會三寶]：先意、電光、夷數和.
53 登日宮，(會三寶) [見慈母]、日光、淨風神妙座.
54 登三常，會九寶，新明九品蓮花座.

Figure 13. The Sun in the Liberation Light (Yoshida and Furukawa 2015, Plate 5).

[Ascending Eternal Light] (cc. 588–589)

The deceased souls then "ascend to [world of] Eternal Light (the Realm of Light) and present themselves before *Moluo* (Father of Greatness). They are collected by the Venerable One and get a lot of blessings"[55] (Figure 3).

3.2.17. [Worshipping the Five Buddhas] (cc. 597–630)

The priest worships the five prophets: Mani, Nārāyaṇa, Zoroaster, Śākyamuni and Jesus.[56]

3.2.18. [Praise to Five Pleasures] (cc. 631–645)

The priest praises five kinds of pleasure:

> "Pleasure of wisdom: Ah, homeward bound we go, ah, homeward bound we go! Who can avoid the transmigration through the six kinds of rebirth? To ask where is the home? The stūpa of hundred flowers in the precious world of light".[57]

> "Pleasure of light: [On] The bridge of seven treasures in the lake of seven treasures, all the noble sons in the fragrant Air are invited. The noble sons held flowers and praise together and sing together in the lake for miraculously-born".[58] *Qibao chi* 七寶池 (the lake of seven treasures) reminds us of *qibao xiangchi* 七寶香池 (the perfumed lake of seven Treasures) in *H*.391 and *xiangkong* 香空 (fragrant Air) reminds us *miao xiangkong* 妙香空 (wonderful and fragrant Air) in H.123 (=*miao shengkong* 妙生空 "wonderful, animating Air" in *H*.389, one of the five kinds of greatness).

---

55 登常明，覲默羅，蒙尊攝取恩具多.
56 Its content is similar to "The Five Sons of Thunder" (cc. 494–515). I will translate it completely into English and publish it in the near future.
57 智慧樂:歸去來兮歸去來，誰能六道免輪迴？借問家鄉何處去？光明寶界百花龕。
58 光明樂:七寶池中七寶橋，香空聖子盡相邀。聖子把花齊讚詠，化生池裏齊唱饒。

"Pleasure of power: The paradise cloud towers, villages of seven treasures, golden towers and silvery watchtower, their number reaches three thousands. The palaces and stūpas of beryl reflect each other, auspicious color is bright which is the light of sun and moon".[59]

"Pleasure of purity (divinity): the twelve Kings of Light always assist and follow; endless noble sons compete to come forward. Holy crowd in fragrant Air always circumambulate, flower garlands and bejeweled crowns rain down".[60]

"Pleasure of obeying the Buddha's teaching: The vast sky is brimming over with the tinkling of celestial music, the enchanting notes with the wind can be heard west and east. This should be that the descended soul is saved recently and introduced to the Venerable Lord of Light when the music is over".[61]

3.2.19. [Gatha of the New Light[-World]] (cc. 648–658)

The priest praises the New Light-world (Figure 4):

"The New Light-world is near finished, [light-souls] should call each and come back. [You] should not be fond of the human world which is not the place to live in peace. The light-souls should be saved from the suffering and quickly leap over sea of eternal happiness. […] In the realm of treasure of the New Light-world there are jade palaces and golden gardens. Should not be fond of the human world … .The *councilor on the throne of seven treasures bestows sons who defeats the host of demons to you. The New Light[-world] already commenced and bestows buddhas of one country to you. Should not be fond of the human world … .One country is equal to thousand cities and one city is equal to a myriad of villages. In the palaces of treasures of the New Light[-world] immeasurable lives are born miraculously. Should not be fond of the human world … .Singing and chanting does not stop all day long. The New Light[-world] is the best place to roam, enlightenment is attained forever on the [lotus-]flower dais. Should not be fond of the human world … .When long life with less pleasure, life is limitless".[62]

The end of manuscript is missing and only left two titles: "Praise of the Four Entities of Calmness" and "The Ceremony Held on the Last Day of the Month of Precept (*Jieyue Jie* 戒月結)" (cc. 659).

4. *Mani the Buddha of Light* and Buddhist Worship and Repentance Rituals

4.1. From Bema Festival to A Book of Prayer and Confession

Mani the Buddha of Light is a collection of ritual manuals for congregational cults. We may trace Manichaean congregational cult back to the Bema festival. The Greek word *bēma* meant "platform". The *bēma* festival was dedicated both to the commemoration of the death of Mani and to the glorification of his personality. During the *bēma* festival, Mani's coming from the world of light was symbolized by the adornment of the *bēma* (throne). So *bēma* became the name of the festival itself.

During the Bema festival, the community of all the elect and the laymen gathered together and the main ceremonies included the confession of the hearers and the elect and a quasi-sacramental meal in which the elect partook. Between or before these rites, the elect and the laymen usually recited

59 大力樂:極樂雲臺七寶莊，金臺銀闕滿三千。琉璃殿塔相交映，瑞色高明日月光。
60 清淨樂：十二光王常翊從，無邊聖子競來前。香空聖眾常圍遶，雨下花鬘及寶冠。
61 皈命樂：玲玲天樂滿長空，風散餘聲西復東。應是下凡新得度，引見明尊曲來終.
62 新明界欲成，相喚須歸去。莫戀此閻浮，不是安居處。救性離災殃，速超常樂海。[······]新明寶剎中，玉殿金園裏。莫戀此閻浮，······七寶座踐蹭，賜汝降魔子。新明今已登，賜汝一國佛。莫戀此閻浮，······一國如千城，一城千萬邑。新明寶宮衢，化生無量壽。莫戀此閻浮，······歌詠齊唱饒，終日無停息。新明最好遊，永證花臺上。莫戀此閻浮，······長生少樂時，壽命無限度.

canonical texts, sang hymns and kept vigil; moreover, there were also sermons, catechism classes and telling of parables.

A Book of Prayer and Confession written in Middle Persian, Parthian and Sogdian was used in divine services in Central Asia. The extant manuscript can be divided into two parts. The first part is *Bema liturgy* which includes: Mani's *Letter of the Seal* as canonical text, hymns for the beginning of the Bema, praises of Narisah-yazd (the Third Messenger), Srōsh-Ahrāy (the Column of Glory), Jesus the Savior, the Messengers, the Bema and hymns of the joyful. The second part is *Confessional text for the elect* which includes: discussion of the five commandments (Truthfulness, Nonviolence, Behavior in accordance with religion, Purity of the mouth and Blessed poverty), the five gifts (nous, thought, mind, intelligence and understanding), the "closing of the five gates (eye, ear, nose, hand and feeling)", prayers and hymns, the four Monday prayers and "the divine table" for the quasi-sacramental meal (Henning 1937; Klimkeit 1993, pp. 133–44). *A Book of Prayer and Confession* might be one of the sources for the Chinese *Mani the Buddha of Light*.

But it is obvious that *Mani the Buddha of Light* is not a translation of a book in Middle Iranian. It is under the cloak of Buddhist worship and repentance ritual.

4.2. Buddhist Worship and Repentance Ritual

Since Buddhism came to China, especially with the spread of the Mahayana tradition, the popularity of virtue thought and the promotion of eminent monks, various ritual activities of worship and repentance flourished. Many "Buddha-name" sutras (*foming jing* 佛名經) were popular and widespread since the Jin dynasty (265–420) and established good foundation for the development of worship and repentance ritual. The more extensive *Foming jing* are confessional texts: they consist of an endless invocation of Buddhas, Bodhisattvas and even sacred scriptures, after each name or group of names there is a confession of sins. For example, *Foming jing* "translated" by Bodhiruci contains 11,093 names (T 440).

From the sixth to tenth centuries, Buddhis rules for confession and pardon (*chanyi* 懺儀) can be divided into four kinds: (1) sutra recitation and penitential offering (*jingchan* 經懺); (2) worship and repentance rituals (*lichan wen* 禮懺文); (3) document of penitence (*chanhui wen* 懺悔文); (4) compilation of rituals (*zongji* 總集), for example, *Compilation of Worship and Repentance Rituals (Contained in) Various Sutras* (*ji zhujing lichan yi* 集諸經禮懺儀) compiled by Zhisheng 智昇 in 730 (T 1982).

The prominent example of *jingchan* is *Confessional for realizing the Lotus Samâdhi* (Fahua sanmei chanyi 法華三昧懺儀, T 1941) compiled by Zhiyi 智顗 (538–598). We can find five stages of the confession ritual in it: (1) *chahui* 懺悔 "repentance"; (2) *quanqing* 勸請 "invocation of the Buddha(s)"; (3) *suixi* 隨喜 "responding with joy" (in observing the good behavior of others); (4) *huixiang* 回向 "transfer" (one's merit to another); (5) *fayuan* 發願 "arousing the vow" (to save all sentient beings).

The worship and repentance rituals were used by both monks and the laity for six periods of worship daily and focused on worship. We only know the authors of a few of them. Most of them are Dunhuang manuscripts without names of the authors. Some are mainly for worshipping Buddha(s), such as *Ceremony of Dharma-body [of Buddha]* (*fashen li* 法身禮), *Ceremony of Descending [of Buddha]* (*jiangsheng li* 降生禮), *Laudatory gāthās for Going to be Reborn in the Śukhāvati* (*wangsheng lizan ji* 往生禮讚偈) by Shan Dao 善導 in 662, *Ceremony of Twelve [Buddhas of] Light* (*shier guang[fo] li* 十二光[佛]禮). Some are mainly for worshipping Buddhist teachings, such as *Five Ceremonies of Diamond (Prajñāpāramitā)* (*jinggang wuli* 金剛五禮) and *Seven Ceremonies of Lotus [Sutra]* (*fahua qi liwen* 法華七禮文). Some are mainly for worshipping saṃgha (community of monks and nuns), such as *Ceremony of [Maitreya's] Ascent* (*[Mile] Shangsheng li* [彌勒] 上生禮) and *Ceremony of Avalokiteśvara* (*Guanyin li* 觀音禮) (Wang 1998, pp. 33, 75–114, 201–88; 2008, pp. 6, 21–60, 139–224, 259–304; Giles 1957, pp. 195–96; Kuo 1994, pp. 229–32; Zürcher 1997).

Ennin (793–864), one of the famous Japanese monks visiting Imperial China, gave us a description of the activities of worship and repentance. *Ennin's Diary: The Record of a Pilgrimage to China in Search of the Dharma* records the rituals of Koreans in Dengzhou, Shandong, in 839: "Men and women, monks and laymen, are gathered together in the cloister listening to lectures in the daytime and worshiping and repenting and listening to scriptures and the order [of worship] at night. The monks and others number about forty. The lecturing, worshiping and repentances are all done in accordance with the customs of Korea. The worship and repentance at dusk and before dawn are in the Chinese manner but all the rest are in the Korean language" (Ennin 1955, p. 151; 1992, p. 190).

4.3. Manichaeism under the Cloak of Buddhism

As early as the 8th century, Manichaean congregational cult might already be in the garb of Buddhist worship and repentance ritual. The *Compendium* written in 731 informs us that one of the five halls of Manichaean monastery buildings is a hall for worship and repentance (*lichen tang* 礼懺堂) (Chavannes and Pelliot 1913, pp. 106, 109). This means that Manichaeans already used Buddhist "worship and repentance" to name the hall for their congregational cult.

The original title of Xiapu manuscript *Mani the Buddha of Light* may have been *[Ceremony of] Mani the Buddha of Light* (*Moni guangfo [li]* 摩尼光佛[禮]). We may take *Mani the Buddha of Light* as a compilation of worship and repentance rituals of Manichaeism because homogeneous ritual stages appear again and again.

We can find some traces of the relationship between Manichaeism and Buddhist repentance rituals in a memorial submitted to the throne on 26 November 1120 which was called the "Wenzhou Memorial" by Western scholars. The scriptures and the pictures and images of the followers of the Religion of Light have titles recorded in this memorial includes *The Grand Confessional* (*Guangda chan* 廣大懺) (Xu 2014, v.14, p. 8325; Mou 1938, p. 134; Forte 1973, pp. 238, 243–44; Lieu 1992, pp. 276–77). This may be a Manichaean ritual manual under the cloak of Buddhis confessional ritual.

4.4. Comparison between Mani the Buddha of Light and Buddhist Worship and Repentance Ritual

Most Buddhis worship and repentance rituals are made up of some of the twelve stages. Three stages have nothing to do with *Mani the Buddha of Light*: remembrance of the Buddha['s name] (*nianfo* 念佛), purity while abiding in the world (*chu shijie fan* 處世界梵) and verse of impermanence (*wuchang ji* 無常偈. Therefore, we will not discuss them in detail. We will discuss the other nine stages (Wang 1998, pp. 313–53).

4.4.1. *qingfo* 請佛 Inviting Buddha(s)

A ritual can become of significance only when the Buddhas accept the invitation and descend to the altar. So, inviting Buddhas appears in all rituals. The priest and the laity should kneel and worship, hold flowers in hand and sing gathas.

In a few cases *Mani the Buddha of Light* just follows the Buddhist ritual to invite "various great bodhisattvas" and "all past and future buddhas", and so forth (cc. 199–206). Almost all the "Buddhas" invited in it are Manichaean deities.

4.4.2. *zanfo* 讚佛Praising Buddha(s)

Praising Buddha(s) (also *tanfo* 嘆佛) means the priest and the laity recite gathas/proses to praise the various merits of the Tathāgata.

In *Mani the Buddha of Light*, there is a long prose part to praise the birth of Mani ("Praise of the Descent" cc. 292–312). Praise to five pleasures (cc. 631–645) actually admires the four Entities of Calmness: wisdom, light, power and purity (divinity).

4.4.3. *lifo* 禮佛 Worshipping Buddha(s)

Worshipping Buddha(s) is the most important part of the ritual. It usually takes three steps: first, the priest bows to Buddhas and invokes their names. Before the names, there are usually such words as "namaḥ (*nanmo* 南無)", "to pay homage to (*jingli* 敬禮)", and "whole-hearted taking of refuge in the

Buddha (*zhixin guiming li* 至心歸命禮)". Then the priest recites gatha to praise Buddhas. At last the laity join in the singing or chanting.

Worshipping Buddhas in *Mani the Buddha of Light* follows the same procedure. Of course, most of "Buddhas" are Manichaean deities, prophets, saints and so forth. "Ascending [of the deceased soul] through the Right Path" (cc. 565–596) are special. The text describes that the souls ascend through Precious, Glory, Sun and Moon Palaces to the New Aeon and World of Eternal Light where many deities reside.

4.4.4. *wuhui* 五悔 Five Kinds of Repentance

Buddhist five kinds of repentance are five steps in a penitential service: (1) confession of past sins and forbidding them for the future (*chanhui* 懺悔); (2) appeal to the universal buddhas to keep the law-wheel rolling (*quanqing* 勸請); (3) rejoicing over the good in self and others (*suixi* 隨喜); (4) offering all one's goodness to all the living and to the Buddha-way (*huixiang* 迴向, Sk. *parīṇāma*); (5) resolve or vows (*fayuan* 發願).

In *Mani the Buddha of Light*, the confession is much simpler. In lieu of the hearers, the priest pronounces a confession text which does not mention any specific misdeed but includes every "sin" committed by human beings in the past, the present and the future. This confession text (cc. 265–271) actually is a copy of "This Gāthā is a Penitential Prayer of *Niyusha* 你逾沙 (i.e., MP. *niyōšāg*: hearers)" in *Hymnscroll* (*H*. 410–414). Such sins as doubting the two great Lights (Sun and Moon); injuring the body of *Lushena* (Column of Glory) and as well as the five Light-sons (Ether, Wind, Light, Water and Fire); imperfectly observing the seven kinds of almsgivings, the ten Commandments (the moral code of hearers) and the three Seals (Seals of the mouth, hands and bosom) only can be understood from a Manichaean point view.

In *Mani the Buddha of Light*, *huixiang* is similar to the Buddhist one. Some sections end with *huixiang*. In *huixiang*, only few words betray the Manichaean content, such as new light(-world) (*xin ming(jie)* 新明(界)) (cc. 648, 651, 653, 655, 657).

4.4.5. *san guiyi* 三皈依 Venerating the Triratna

Buddhist venerating the Triratna (also *sangui* 三歸) means the three surrenders to the three treasures (*sanbao* 三寶), that is, to the Buddha (*fo* 佛), to the Dharma (*fa* 法) and to the Saṅgha (*seng* 僧). The obeisance (*henan* 和南) usually follows venerating the Triratna.

Mani the Buddha of Light sometimes takes the Father of Greatness (*Sahuanmoluo* c. 427) as the Buddha, sometimes takes the one who enters the realm of Mani (c. 50) as the Buddha; sometimes takes *The Living Gospel* (*yinglun* c. 55) as Dharma, sometimes takes Jesus (c. 433) as the maker of the Dharma.

4.4.6. *shuoji fayuan* 說偈發願 Explaining in Verse and Making a Vow to Save All Beings

Buddhist *shuoji fayuan* actually has the double functions as *fayuan* and *huixiang*. *fayuan* is giving rise to the intention to save all sentient beings.

In *Mani the Buddha of Light*, *fayuan* is similar to the Buddhist one. Only a few words have Manichaean color, such as "sainthood of great light and eternal happiness" (*daming changle shengguo* 大明常樂聖果) (cc. 83–84).

4.4.7. *liushi jisong* 六時偈頌 Six Periods of Gāthās

Liushi jisong is established to act in concert with the six periods of worshipping and repentance (*liushi lichan* 六時禮懺). The full day is divided into the three daytime periods of dawn (*yinchao* 寅朝), noon (*wushi* 午時), and dusk (*huanghun* 昏), along with the three nighttime periods of the first watch of the night (*chuye* 初夜), midnight (*zhongye* 中夜) and latter part of the evening (*houye* 後夜).

Manichaean elect performed four or seven prayers daily (*qishi lichan* 七時禮懺). *Mani the Buddha of Light* also praises the monks who perform seven periods of worshipping and repentance. (c. 443) There are second period (*dier shi* 第二時) and third and fourth periods (*disan shi* 第三時, *disi shi* 第

四時) in *Mani the Buddha of Light*. There should be a first period (*diyi shi* 第一時) before the second period. The relationship between these four periods and the Buddhist six periods or Manichaean seven prayers daily should be studied in the future.

4.4.8. *fanzhou* 梵咒 Mantra

The mantra, recited, muttered or sung in a ritual as a general name for the verses, formulas or sequence of words in prose, is believed to have religious, magical or spiritual efficiency. In Chinese Buddhism, Sanskrit mantras were transcribed in Chinese characters. Usually the mantra was not translated because the Sanskrit words themselves were thought to incorporate the essence of Buddhism.

There are many transcriptions in *Mani the Buddha of Light*. Besides names, terms and phrases scattered through the manuscript, there are thirteen whole blocks of transcriptions (77 cc. = 936 characters) (Lin 2014, p. 491). While similar to transcriptions from Sanskrit in indigenous Buddhist ritual and penance texts, they are in fact transcriptions from Middle Iranian according to what has already been deciphered. There is more than one Chinese transcription for some Middle Iranian words in the Xiapu documents, even in one hymn of a single manuscript. This phenomenon shows that Middle Iranian prayer and confession texts were recited by foreign Manichaean elect such as master *Hulu* (Uighur: *ulug*) *fashi* 呼祿法師 (great priest, active around middle of 9th century) in congregational cults in South China and recorded in transcriptions by Chinese disciples who were not good at Middle Iranian languages. Or foreign elect brought various Chinese transcriptions of mantra to South China. These Chinese transcriptions of mantra were put into *Mani the Buddha of Light* without emendations made by the elect who were good at both Middle Iranian and Chinese. More and more mistakes were added in the procedure of copying such transcriptions again and again by transcribers who were wholly unfamiliar with Middle Iranian and it becomes extremely difficult for modern scholars to decipher the extant transcriptions.

4.4.9. *(zhong)he* (衆) 和 (Hearers) Joining in the Singing or Chanting

In Buddhist rituals, most verses (poetry) and proses were recited by priests. But the laity joined in singing or chanting some simple but important verses. For example, "(We) wish that we with all sentient beings will come back to the ocean of thusness".[63] (*Ceremony of Dharma-body*) "(We) wish that we with all sentient beings will be born in paradise".[64] (*Ceremony of Twelve [Buddhas of] Light*)

In *Mani the Buddha of Light*, the hearers also join in singing simple verses. For example, they join in singing again and again: "We wish that the deceased spirit would ride the buddhas' majestic brilliance and bear witness to the community of bodhisattvas!" (cc. 497, 500, 503, 505, 509)

Mani the Buddha of Light also has some rituals which are not formal stages of ritual.

4.4.10. *jingtan* 净壇 Purification of the Altar and *kaitan* 開壇 Preparing the Altar (cc. 248–255, 403–419)

Chinese Manichaeans should called *bēma* as 齋壇 "altar" before Manichaeism spread from Louyang to Mongolia around 762. So, in Turkish Manichean texts the equivalent of *bēma* appears to be *čaidan* (Henning 1937, p. 9). This word may be derived from Chinese *zhāitán* 齋壇 (*tṣăi-d'an*) (Müller 1910, p. 93; Asmussen 1965, pp. 226f.). In Sogdian texts, it appears to be *c'yδ'n* and *j'yd'ny* which means "of the Bema" (Henning 1945, p. 155; Sims-Williams 1981, pp. 236–37). But we have no evidence that *tan* 壇 "altar" still related to *bēma* in *Mani the Buddha of Light*.

---

63 願共諸眾生，同歸真如海。
64 願共諸眾生，往生安樂國。

4.4.11. *da zangxiang* 大讚香 Great Praising Incense Offering (cc. 460–481)

There are also other incense offering praises in this collection (cc. 67–85, 445–459). The Manichaeans attached importance to incense offering. The prominent poet and scholar-official Lu You informs us about some details of the Religion of Light of Fujian in his memorial in 1162: "Since they burn frankincense (*ruxiang* 乳香), frankincense has risen in price" (Lu 2011, v.9, p. 125; Chavannes and Pelliot 1913, pp. 351–52).

Other rituals include: *Jingkou* 淨口 "Purification of Speech", *kanjing* 看經 "reading the scriptures", and *songfo* 送佛 "farewell ritual for the Buddhas".

Mani the Buddha of Light shares most of the ritual stages with Buddhist worship and repentance rituals but its content is almost totally different from Buddhist one. Even within Manichaeism, some of its content is also different from that of other Manichaean materials. Here we only take the pantheon as example.

5. Comparison between the Pantheons of *Mani the Buddha of Light* and Other Manichaean Materials

Mani the Buddha of Light not only adopted Buddhist worship and repentance rituals as its form and also changed a lot of Manichaean contents. Its pantheon on the one side is a heritage of the pantheon of Dunhuang version, on the other side is different from Dunhuang version. (see the Table 1) (Sundermann 1979; Bryder 1985, pp. 63–123; Van Lindt 1992; Ma 2013b).

Table 1. Table of Simplified Manichaean Pantheon.

Iranian and other Language Versions	Dunhuang Version	*Mani the Buddha of Light*
1. Father of Greatness (Pth. *pydr wzrgyfṭ*) Zurwān (MP. *by zrw'n*)	Unsurpassed King of Light (無上光明王) Unsurpassed Venerable of Light (無上明尊)	Unsurpassed Buddha of Light (無上光明佛) Unsurpassed Venerable of Light (無上明尊) (c. 125) *Sahuan* 薩緩
1.1. the Four-faced Father of Greatness (ὁ τετραπρόσωπος πατ03AEρ τοῦ μεγέθους)	The Four Entities of Calmness (四寂)	The Four Entities of Calmness (四寂)
1.1.1. Divinity (Pth. *bg'*, MP. yzd)	Purity (夷薩, 清淨)	Purity (阿賀, 咦咗, 清淨)
1.1.2. Light (Pth./MP. *rwšn,*)	Light (烏盧詵, 光明)	Light (嚧詵, 光明)
1.1.3. Power (Pth. *z'wr'*, MP. zwr)	Power (祚路, 大力)	Power (嵯鶻囉,蘇路, 大力)
1.1.4. Wisdom (Pth. *jyryft'*, MP. *whyẖ*)	Wisdom (于咽, 智慧)	Wisdom (哂哩咈哆, 和醯,智慧)
1.2.1–5. The Five Dwellings of the Father of Greatness: nous, thought, mind, intelligence and understanding	Five limbs (五體): nous (相), thought (心), mind (念), intelligence (思) and understanding (意)	
(1) Twelve Aeons (Greek αἱ δυοκαίδεκα αἰῶναι)	Twelve Light-Kings (十二光王)	Twelve Light-Kings (十二光王)
A. The Aeons of the Aeons (Greek αἱ αἰῶναι αἰώνων)	Lands as fine dust (微塵國土)	Various lands as fine dust (微塵諸國土)
2.2. Mother of the Living (MP. *m'dr 'y zyndg'n*)	Good Mother Buddha (善母佛), Compassionate Mother (慈悲母)	Good Mother Buddha (善母佛), Compassionate Mother (慈母)
3.First Man (Pth. *mrd hsyng*), First Enthymesis (MP. *hndyšyšn nxwysṯyn*)	First Thought Buddha (先意佛), First Thought (先意)	First Thought Buddha (先意佛), First Thought (先意)

Table 1. *Cont.*

Iranian and other Language Versions	Dunhuang Version	*Mani the Buddha of Light*
4.1.1. the Five Light Gods (Pth. *pnj rwšn*)	five light buddhas (五明佛), Five light-sons (五明子)	Five Light Buddhas (五明佛), Five light-sons (五明子)
4.1.2. Living Soul (Pth. *gryw jywndg*)	Light-nature (明性)	Light-nature (明性)
4.2.1. Ether (MP. *pr'whr*)	Ether (氣)	Ether (氣)
4.2.2. Wind (Pth./MP. *w'd*)	Wind (風)	Wind (風)
4.2.3. Light (Pth. *rwšn*)	Light (明)	Light (明)
4.2.4. Water (Pth./MP. *'b*)	Water (水)	Water (水)
4.2.5. Fire (Pth./MP. *'dwr*)	Fire (火)	Fire (火)
5. The god of the Answer (Pth. *pdw 'xtg*)	*Mahāsthāmaprāpta* (勢至)	*Mahāsthāmaprāpta* (勢至)
6. Friend of Lights (Pth. *fryhrwšn*)	Enjoyer of the Lights Buddha (樂明佛)	Enjoyer of the Lights Buddha (樂明佛)
7. Great Architect (MP. *r 'z 'y wzrg*)	Creator of forms Buddha (造相佛)	Creator of forms Buddha (造相佛)
8. The Living Spirit (Pth. *w 'd jywndg*)	Pure Wind Buddha (淨風佛), Pure Wind (淨風)	Pure Wind Buddha (淨風佛), Pure Wind (淨風)
9. Five sons of the Living Spirit	Five valiant sons (五等驍健子)	
9.1. the Keeper of Splendor (Sogd. *xšyšpt βyw*)	the Envoy of Light who upholds the world (持世明使), Lord who upholds the world (持世主)	The Venerable Buddha Who Upholds the World (持世尊佛)
9.2.1. King of Honor, King of Heaven (Sogd. *sm'nšyδ*, Pth./MP. **'sm'n š'h*)	Great King of the Ten Heavens (十天大王), King of the Ten Heavens (十天王)	King of the Ten Heavens (十天王) King of Heaven (阿薩漫沙)
		9.2.2. Jade August Great Emperor (玉皇大帝), Jade Emperor Venerable Buddha (玉皇尊佛)
9.3. Adamant of Light, Verethragna (Sogd. *wšγnyy βγyy*)	Victorious envoy who conquers the demons (降魔勝使)	
9.4. King of Glory, the Earth Spenta Armaiti (Sogd. *z'y spnd'rmt*)	Kṣitigarbha Envoy of Light (地藏明使)	
9.5. Atlas (Sogd. *pδf'ry βγyy*)	Envoy of light who urges enlightenment (催光明使)	
10. The god of the Call (Pth. *xrwštg*)	*Avalokiteśvara* (觀音)	*Avalokiteśvara* (觀音)
11.1. The Third Messenger (Pth. *hrdyg fryštg*), Narisah-yazd (MP. *nryshyzd*)	Third Man (三丈夫), Third Envoy of Light (三明使)	Narisah-yazd (那哩娑和夷咗)
11.2. Sun (Pth. *myhr (yzd)*)	Sun-radiance Buddha (日光佛), Sun-radiance (日光)	Sun-radiance Buddha (日光佛), Sun-radiance (日光)
12. The Twelve Virgins (Sogd. *XII βγpwryšt*)	The Twelve Hours (十二時), Twelve Maidens of Transformation (十二化女)	
13.1. The Column of Glory (Pth. *b 'mystwn*) The Perfect Man (Pth. *mrd 'spwryg*) The righteous Sraoša (MP. *srwš'hr'y*)	Diamond Column of Glory (金剛相柱) Perfect Man (具足丈夫) The righteous Sraoša (蘇露沙羅夷, 窣路沙羅夷) Vairocana (盧舍那)	Diamond Column of Glory (金剛相柱) Vairocana (舍那佛, 盧舍那佛, 舍那)
13.2. Final Statue (Pth. *'sṯwmynyzd*)		
D. The Sun and the Moon the Luminaries (MP. *rwšn rhy dw*)	Sun and Moon Buddhas of Light (日月光明佛)	Sun and Moon Buddhas of Light (日月光佛, 日月光明佛)
14.1. Jesus the Splendor (Pth. *yyšw 'zyw'*)	Jesus of Light (光明夷數), Jesus Buddha (夷數佛)	Jesus the Splendor (夷數精和), Jesus Buddha (夷數佛)

Table 1. *Cont.*

Iranian and other Language Versions	Dunhuang Version	*Mani the Buddha of Light*
14.2. Moon (Pth./MP. *m ̓ẖ (yzd)*)		
		14.3. Jesus the Buddha of Harmony (夷數和佛)
E. Jesus the Child	New Jesus (新夷數)	
15. Virgin of Light (Pth./MP. *qnygrwšn*) Sadwēs (Pth. *sdwys*)	Lightning Buddha (電光佛), Lightning (電光)	Virgin of Light (謹你嚧詵) Lightning Buddha (電光佛), Lightning (電光) Lightning Royal Buddha (電光王佛)
16.1. The Light Nous (Parth. *mnwhmyd rwšn*) Great Wahman (MP. *whmn wzrg*)	Great Mind (廣大心), Wise Light (惠明), the Light-Nous (who is) the Glory of the Teaching (惠明法相)	Wise Light Buddha (惠明佛), Great Nous (廣大智), Good King of the Mind (*Shanxin wang* 善心王) Great Wahman (護泯護瑟)
16.2. The Holy Spirit (Pth. *w'd jywndg 'wd wjydg*)	The Living and Chosen Spirit (活時雲喻鬱于而勒)	
17. Just Judge (Pth. *d'dbr r'štygr*)	Impartial King (平等王)	Yama (閻羅)
		(3.1) Five Buddhas (伍佛)
		(3.2.1) Nārāyaṇa (那羅延佛), the first great Tathagatas of good aeon (賢劫一座大如來)
		(3.2.2) Zoroaster (蘇路支佛), the second great Tathagatas of good aeon (賢劫二座大如來)
		(3.2.3) Śākyamuni (釋迦文佛), the third great Tathagatas of good aeon (賢劫三座大如來)
		(3.2.4) Jesus (夷數和佛), the fourth great Tathagatas of good aeon (賢劫四座大如來), Christ (末尸訶)
		(3.2.5) Mani (摩尼光佛), Long Life Nectar King (長生甘露王)
		(4) George (移活吉思,吉思)
		(5) Jacob (耶具孚)
		(6.1) four heavenly kings (四天王)
		(6.2.1–4) Raphael (嚧縛逸囉), Michael (彌訶逸啰), Gabriel (業縛囉逸囉), Səra'el (娑囉逸囉)
		(7) Narses (能遏蘇思)
		(8) Nastikus (能咗嗷响<蘇>思)

It is no doubt that the pantheon of *Mani the Buddha of Light* inherited that of Dunhuang Chinese Manichaean documents. For example, twelve great gods in "A Gāthā, being a list for the 'Collection of Offerings'" of *Hymnscroll*, Twelve Light-Kings, Various lands as fine dust, Ether, Wind, Light, Water, Fire, Avalokiteśvara, Mahāsthāmaprāpta, The Venerable Buddha Who Upholds the World, King of the ten heavens, Sun and Moon Buddhas of Light and Jacob and so forth. Sometimes one or two Chinese character(s) of the names of same gods in Xiapu and Dunhuang versions are different but it is not hard to see the similarity between the two versions.

It is more valuable that *Mani the Buddha of Light* preserved quite a few important names of gods, prophets and saints which are not found in Dunhuang documents. For example, the transcriptions of Zurwān, the Four Entities of Calmness, names of King of Heaven, Narisah-yazd, Jesus the Splendor, Virgin of Light, Great Wahman, Yama, Zoroaster, St. George, four heavenly kings (archangels), angels

Narses and Nastikus and so forth. These terms all can be confirmed by Middle Iranian materials and there is no doubt for their authenticity. We should not deny the fact that the pantheon of *Mani the Buddha of Light* inherited that of Dunhuang documents based on non-Manichaean literature. In contrast, we should judge the authenticity of non-Manichaean literature based on *Mani the Buddha of Light* and other Xiapu documents.

W. Sundermann pointed out: "Manichean hymns and psalms, which are preserved in large numbers in both the Coptic and the Iranian traditions, are mainly directed towards the deities and thus constitute a rich source for the understanding of the role of the gods in the religious practice of the community. In general, one can conclude that those deities to whom complete hymns are dedicated are also the principal ones, while gods of minor rank, receive, at the very most, a mere mention in invocative lists" (Sundermann 2002).

The compiler of *Mani the Buddha of Light* obviously knew the *Hymnscroll* and cited a lot of its verses. He copied "A Gāthā, being a list for the 'Collection of Offerings'" (cc. 380–387) but he changed the status of the twelve gods in other places. Among the twelve great gods, the first one is the highest god and other gods are arranged by three Evocations: First Evocation—Good Mother, First Thought and Five Light Buddhas; Second Evocation—Enjoyer of the Lights, Creator of forms and Pure Wind; and Third Evocation—Sun-radiance, Vairocana, Jesus, Lightning and Wise Light. The highest god is still number one in the list of gods "invited with wholehearted reverence (一心奉請)" (cc. 159–163) but the gods of First and Second Evocations faded. They, with Sun-radiance and Wise Light of Third Evocation, are not in the list of gods "invited with wholehearted reverence". No complete hymns are dedicated to the Enjoyer of the Lights and the Creator of forms. On the other side, the status of Vairocana, Jesus and Lightning of Third Evocation were obviously promoted. The status of Sun and Moon Buddhas of Light, the Venerable Buddha Who Upholds the World and King of the Ten Heavens which were not among the twelve great gods in the *Hymnscroll* were promoted too. They are all in the list of gods "invited with wholehearted reverence" (cc. 159–198).

The most distinct change of the pantheon of *Mani the Buddha of Light* is that prophet Mani was carried to the altar. The well-known triad in Manichaeism was composed of Jesus the Splendor, the Virgin of Light and the Light Nous (Blois 2003, p. 11). Mani replaced the Light Nous and became one member of the triad of the Religion of Light (Mani, Jesus and Lightning). At the same time, Nārāyaṇa, Zoroaster, Śākyamuni and Jesus were collectively called "Four Great Venerable Buddhas" in the list of gods "invited with wholehearted reverence" (cc. 191–194).

Prophet Mani and four of his forerunners—Nārāyaṇa, Zoroaster, Śākyamuni and Jesus were collectively called five buddhas and occupy an important position in *Mani the Buddha of Light* (especially in the second part).

6. The Vitality of Ritual

The extant manuscript of *Mani the Buddha of Light* was copied no earlier than the Qing Dynasty (1644–1911) but it as a collection perhaps was compiled during the same period of the painting of the *Diagram of the Universe*—the late Yuan to early Ming Dynasty, that is, late 14th to early 15th century. Just as the *Diagram of the Universe* was copied Mani's *ārdhang* with some modification, many pieces of the original texts in *Mani the Buddha of Light* should have come into being from Later Tang to early North Song Dynasties (840–1100). Because the original was copied repeatedly and each transcriber might have added something to the text, we cannot deny its antiquity according to some content of later times.

Some scholars believe that the original was compiled during the Qing Dynasty. It is almost impossible, because the local priests already knew little about Manichaeism during the 17–20th centuries. *Mani the Buddha of Light* and Dunhuang Manichaean Chinese texts share a lot in common as well as being very different. *Mani the Buddha of Light* is not a copy of some Manichaean document of the Tang Dynasty (618–907). Its complier used some Manichaean documents and at least two of them (*Hymnscroll* and *Compendium*) are extant as Dunhuang documents, as materials and Buddhist worship and repentance rituals as a form to compile a new collection of rituals of the Religion of Light. We doubt that the local priests still had such materials and such ability to do so during the 17–20th centuries. It is almost impossible for the local priests to have inherited Manichaean Middle Iranian verses and proses orally for about one thousand years and transcribed them into Chinese during the 17–20th centuries.

If we recognize the hypothesis that many pieces of the texts in *Mani the Buddha of Light* were written about the 9th–11th centuries, why was it handed down generation after generation? The answer is the strong vitality of the ritual. Most of the followers of the Religion of Light were illiterate people but they could attend the rituals, look at and watch the paintings, listen to various ritual texts recited by the priests and join in singing and chanting. Various rituals were held annually, monthly, weekly, during some festivals, or even daily.

We have some historical records about the rituals of the Religion of Light. "Wenzhou Memorial" in 1120 describes the followers of the Religion of Light:

> Each year, in the first (lunar) month and on the day of *mi* (密 mi̯ət < Pth. m*y*h*r* 'Sunday') in their calendar, they assemble together the Attendants (*shizhe* 侍者 = male elect), the Hearers (*tingzhe* 聽者 = male auditors), the Paternal Aunts (*gupo*姑婆 = female elect), the Sisters who donate monastic food (*zhaijie* 齋姐 = female auditors) and others who erect the sacred space (*Daochang* 道場) and incite the common folk, both male and female. They assemble at night and disperse at dawn. (Xu 2014, v.14, p. 8325)

Lu You described in his memorial:

> There are even official-scholars and the sons of educated families among their ranks and they will openly say, "Today I am attending the vegetarian feast of the Religion of Light (*Mingjiao zhai* 明教齋)". I have chided them by saying, "These are 'demon [worshippers]'; why should [someone of your standing] keep such company?" They replied: "This is not the case. The 'demon [worshippers]' do not segregate men and women but the followers of the Religion of Light do not permit men and women to come into contact with each other. If a [male] follower of the Religion of Light is presented with food prepared by a woman, he will not eat it". I sometimes manage to procure the scriptures of the Religion of Light for perusal. Their contents are boastful and have nothing of value, precisely what one would expect to find in the works of common and vulgar people who practice magic and sorcery. (Lu 2011, v.11, p. 481; Chavannes and Pelliot 1913, p. 343)

The scriptures of the Religion of Light possibly included ritual manuals, which were used in the vegetarian feast. Congregational cults continued to be held and ritual manuals of the Religion of Light were handed down generation after generation until the Ming and Qing dynasties (1368–1911). So today we fortunately have the chance to do research on a copy of one of the collections of ancient ritual manuals of the Religion of Light—*Mani the Buddha of Light*.

Mani the Buddha of Light is a ritual manual and the physical object of this research. We do not take the *Diagram of Universe* as a physical object of the ritual. But from the very beginning Mani used both scriptures and drawings to preach his doctrines. The Manichaeans of Tang Dynasty (618–907) knew the seven great scriptures and the drawing of the two great principles (Chinese version of *Ārdhang*) of Mani. "Wenzhou Memorial" mentions not only various scriptures but also several drawings, such as *The Sūtra (or Book) of Illustrations* (*Tu jing* 圖經), *The Portrait of the Buddha the Wonderful Water* (*Miaoshui fo zhen* 妙水佛幀), *The Portrait of the Buddha the First Thought* (*Xianyi fo zhen* 先意佛幀), *The Portrait of the Buddha Jesus* (*Yishu fo zhen* 夷數佛幀), *The Portrait of Good and Evil* (*Shan'e zhen* 善惡幀), *The Portrait of the Prince Royal* (*Taizi zhen* 太子幀) and *The Portrait of the Four Heavenly Kings* (*Si tianwang zhen* 四天王幀). The followers of the Religion of Light might use both artistic and literary artefacts in their rituals. The *Diagram of Universe* is to be identified as the South Chinese version of the Mani's Picture Book or *Ārdhang*. Future research may prove that the *Diagram of Universe* is also a physical object of the rituals of the Religion of Light.

Author Contributions: X.M.'s contributions are about Manichaeism and C.W.'s contributions are about Buddhism.

Funding: Ministry of Science and Technology Project Research Grants: "From the Dunhuang Manuscripts to the Xiapu Documents: A study of the Connections between Manichaeism and Buddhism", MOST 105-2410-H-130-045, MOST 106-2410-H-130-045.

Acknowledgments: We are grateful to Yutaka Yoshida, Gábor Kósa and Joanna Wang for comments that helped us to rethink some points. We are satisfied to simply cite Yoshida's comments in this paper and will write another article to introduce and discuss Yoshida's research on Middle Iranian texts and words in Chinese transcription, including these comments.

Conflicts of Interest: The authors declare no conflicts of interest.

Appendix A. By Y. Yoshida

A hymn called *Tianwangzan* "Praise of the Heavenly Lords" (l. 334–39) is to be identified with a Middle Persian text found in M 19. It was published by E. Morano, "Manichaean Middle Iranian incantation texts from Turfan", in: D. Durkin-Meisterernst et al. (eds.), *Turfan revisited: The first century of research into the arts and cultures of the Silk Road.* Berlin, 2003, pp. 221–27, in particular p. 222. The text as edited by Morano's reads as follows:

M 19
1 'w frystg'n °° wyn(d)['m 'w]
2 rwf'yl °° m(y)h'yl ° wzr(g)
3 (g)br'yl sr'yl 'wd (wy)[sp'n]
4 frystg'n °° kwm'n 'rd'[w'n]
5 nywš'g'n h'm'g dyn qwny[nd]
6 r'myš[n] 'wm'n xwd p'ynd (p)[d]
7 š'dyḥ 'w j'yd'n (q)'myš[n]

(i)

奧和	弗裡悉德健那
˙âu γuâ	pi̯uətlji si̯ĕt tək g'i̯ɐn nâ
'w	frystg'n
ō	frēstagān

To the Angels.

(ii)

渾湛	<*奧>嚧縛逸	彌訶逸	罰悉勒去
γuən tậm	luo b'i̯wak i̯ĕt	mjie xâ i̯ĕt	b'i̯wɐt si̯ĕt lək k'i̯wo
wynd'm 'w	rwf'yl	myh'yl	wzrg
wendām ō	rufaēl	mīhaēl	wuzurg

We praise Rufael, Michael the Great

(iii)

喋[縛]囉逸	娑囉逸
ngi̯ɐp [b'i̯wak] lâ i̯ĕt	sâ lâ i̯ĕt
gbr'yl	sr'yl
gabraēl	sraēl
Gabriel	Sarael

(iv)

嗢特	唯悉伴那	弗哩悉德健那
'ut d'ək	i̯wi si̯ĕt b'uân nâ	pi̯uət lji si̯ĕt tək g'i̯ɐn nâ
'wd	wysp'n	frystg'n
ud	wispān	frēstagān

and all the Angels.

(v)

滿	阿囉馱緩	你喻沙健那
ki̯u muân	˙â lâ d'â γuân	ńi i̯u ṣa g'i̯ɐn nâ
kwm'n	'rd'w'n	nywš'g'n
kumān	ardāwān	niyōšāgān

May they give us, Electi and Hearers,

(vi)

訶降庅	陣	滿特	囉彌詵
xâ kång muâ	ďi̯ĕn	ki̯u muân d'ək	lâ mjie ṣi̯ɛn
h'm'g	dyn	qwnynd	r'myšn
hāmāg	dēn	kunēnd	rāmišn

the whole Church, peace

(vii)

烏{思}滿那 {哩}	忽特	波引 特	沙地
˙uo si muân nâ	xuət d'ək	puâ i̯ĕn pi̯əu d'ək	ṣa d'i
'wm'n	xwd	p'ynd pd	š'dyḥ
umān	xwad	pāyēnd pad	šādīh

and protect ourselves with joy

(viii)

阿和	遮伊但
˙â γuâ tśia	˙i d'ân
'w	j'yd'n
ō	ǰāydān

for ever.

Corruptions of the Chinese text:

(a) Loss of *奧 in verse (ii); (b) In verse (vi) 降 and 玄 (=麼) are misplaced. Possibly 降 is an error for some such character as 去, cf. 罰悉勒去 for wzrg; (c) In verse (vi) 滿 is an error for a character like 難 (*nân) or 年 (*nien) influenced by滿 of verse (v); (d) In verse (vii) neither 思 nor哩 is wanted. The reason for this miscopying is hard to see; (e) The last word of M19, q'myšn, is not wanted either.

References

Asmussen, Jes Peter. 1965. *Xuāstvānīft: Studies in Manichaeism*. Translated by Niels Haislund. Copenhagen: Prostant apud Munksgaard.

Blois, de François. 2003. Manes' 'Twin' in Iranian and non-Iranian texts. In *Religious Themes and Texts of Pre-Islamic Iran and Central Asia: Studies in Honour of Professor Gherardo Gnoli on the Occasion of his 65th Birthday on 6th December 2002*. Edited by Carlo G. Cereti, Mauro Maggi and Elio Provasi. Wiesbaden: Reichert, pp. 7–16.

Bryder, Peter. 1985. *The Chinese Transformation of Manichaeism: A Study of Chinese Manichaean Terminology*. Löberöd: Bokförlaget Plus Ultra.

Chavannes, Édouard, and Paul Pelliot. 1913. Un traité manichéen retrouvé en Chine. *Jounal Asiatique* 11: 99–392.

Durkin-Meisterernst, Desmond. 2004. *Dictionary of Manichaean Middle Persian and Parthian*. Turnhout: Brepols.

Ennin. 1955. *Ennin's Diary: The Record of a Pilgrimage to China in Search of the Law*. Translated by the Chinese by Edwin O. Reischauer. New York: Ronald Press, Co.

Ennin. 1992. *Ru Tang qiufa xunli xingji jiaozhu (入唐求法巡禮行記校註 Record of Travel to the Tang in Search of the Dharma with emendation and annotation)*. Shijiazhuang: Huashan Wenyi Chubanshe.

Fan, Lisha, and Fuxue Yang. 2011. Xiapu Monijiao wenxian ji qi zhongyaoxing (霞浦摩尼教文獻及其重要性 The Manichaean documents form Xiapu and their importance). *Shijie zongjiao yanjiu (世界宗教研究 Studies of World Religions)* 6: 177–83.

Forte, Antonino. 1973. Deux études sur le Manichéisme Chinois. *T'oung Pao* 59: 220–53. [CrossRef]

Furukawa, Shōichi. 2010. 新出マニ教絵画試論制作年代をめぐって 'Shinshutsu Manikyō kaiga shiron—Seisaku nendai o megutte' ('Preliminary study of the newly discovered Manichaean paintings concerning their dating'). *Yamato Bunka* 121: 35–54.

Giles, Lionel. 1957. *Descriptive Catalogue of the Chinese Manuscripts from Tunhuang in the British Museum*. London: Trustees of the British Museum.

Gulácsi, Zsuzsanna. 2015. Matching the Three Fragments of the Chinese Manichaean. Diagram of the Universe. *Studies on the Inner Asian Languages, Festschrift for Yutaka Yoshida* 30: 79–93, Plate II, Fig. 1.

Gulácsi, Zsuzsanna. 2016. *Mani's Pictures: The Didactic Images of the Manichaean from Sasanian Mesopotamia to Uygur Central Asia and Tang-Ming China*. Leiden: Brill.

Gulácsi, Zsuzsanna, and Jason BeDuhn. 2015. Picturing Mani's Cosmology: An Analysis Doctrinal Iconography on a Manichaean Hanging Scroll from 13th/14th-century Southern China. *Bulletin of the Asia Institute* 25: 55–105, Plate 4.

Haloun, Gustav, and Walter B. Henning. 1952. The Compendium of the Doctrines and Styles of the Teaching of Mani, the Buddha of Light. *Asia Major* III: 184–212.

Henning, Walter Bruno. 1937. *Ein manichäisches Bet- und Beichtbuch*. Berlin: Akademie der wissenschaften, In kommission bei W. de Gruyter u. co. (*Abhandlungen der Königlich Preussischen Akademie der Wissenschaften [Berlin], Philosophisch-Historische Classe*, 1936, no. 10).

Henning, Walter Bruno. 1945. The Manichaean fasts. *Journal of the Royal Asiatic Society of Great Britain and Ireland* 1945: 146–64. [CrossRef]

Klimkeit, Hans-Joachim. 1993. *Gnosis on the Silk Road: Gnostic Texts from Central Asia*. San Francisco: HarperSanFrancisco.

Kósa, Gábor. 2011. Translating a Vision—Rudimentary Notes on the Chinese Cosmology Painting. *Manichaean Studies Newsletter* 25: 20–32.

Kósa, Gábor. 2012. Atlas and Splenditenens in the Cosmology Painting. In *Gnostica et Manichaica. Festschrift fur Aloïs van Tongerloo anläßlich des 60. Geburtstages überreicht von Kollegen, Freunden und Schülern*. Edited by Michael Knüppel and Luigi Cirillo. Studies in Oriental Religions 65. Wiesbaden: Harrassowitz, pp. 63–88.

Kósa, Gábor. 2013. The Fifth Buddha: An overview of the Chinese Manichaean material from Xiapu (Fujian). *Manichaean Studies Newsletter* 28: 9–30.

Kósa, Gábor. 2014a. Translating the Eikōn. Some considerations on the relation of the Chinese Cosmology painting to the Eikōn. In *Vom Aramäischen zum Alttürkischen. Fragen zur Übersetzung von manichäischen Texten*. Edited by Jens Peter Laut and Klaus Röhrborn. Berlin and New York: De Gruyter, pp. 49–84.

Kósa, Gábor. 2014b. The Iconographical Affiliation and the Religious Message of the Judgment Scene in the Chinese Cosmology Painting. In *Sanyijiao Yanjiu—Lin Wushu Jiaoshou Guxi Jinian Wenji (三夷教研究——林悟殊教授古稀紀念文集 Research on the Three Barbarian Religions)*. Edited by Xiaogui Zhang. Lanzhou: Lanzhou Daxue Chubanshe, pp. 77–161.

Kósa, Gábor. 2015a. The Sun, the Moon and Paradise. An Interpretation of the Upper Section of the Chinese Manichaean Cosmology Painting. *Journal of Inner Asian Art and Archaeology* 6: 171–93. [CrossRef]

Kósa, Gábor. 2015b. *Ships and Ferries in the Manichaean Cosmology Painting. Danfeng Canggui–Zhang Xun Bainian Danchen Jinian Wenji (丹楓蒼檜—章巽百年誕辰紀念文集 Collection of Papers for 100 Anniversary of Zhang Xun's Birthday)*. Guangzhou: Guangdong Remin Chubanshe, pp. 41–67.

Kósa, Gábor. 2016a. The Manichaean 'New Paradise' in Text and Image. *Crossroads* 13: 27–113. Available online: http://www.eacrh.net/ojs/index.php/crossroads/article/view/85 (accessed on 4 July 2018).

Kósa, Gábor. 2016b. The *Book of Giants* Tradition in the Chinese Manichaica. In *Ancient Tales of Giants from Qumran and Turfa*. Edited by Matthew Goff, Loren T. Stuckenbruck and Enrico Morano. Tübingen: Mohr Siebeck, pp. 145–86.

Kósa, Gábor. 2017. Who is the King of Honour and What Does He Do? Gleanings from the new Chinese Manichaean sources. In *Zur Lichten Heimat. Studien zu Manichäismus, Iranistik und Zentralasienkunde im Gedenken an Werner Sundermann*. Edited by Turfanforschung Team. Wiesbaden: Harrassowitz Verlag, pp. 259–72.

Kuo, Li-Ying. 1994. *Confession et Contrition dans le Bouddhisme Chinois du Ve au Xe siècle*. Paris: Publications de l'École française d'Extrême-Orient.

Lieu, Samuel N. C. 1992. *Manichaeism in the Later Roman Empire and Medieval China*. Tübingen: J. C. B. Mohr.

Lin, Wushu. 2014. *Monijiao Huahua Bushuo (摩尼教華化補說 Supplement for the Study on Sinicization of Manichaeism)*. Lanzhou: Lanzhou daxue chubanshe.

Lin, Wushu. 2017. Xiapu chaoben yiji 'Tiannü zhou' 'Tiandi zhou' kaochao (霞浦抄本夷偈《天女咒》《天地咒》考察 On the Middle Iranian Incantations of *Tiannü* (Fairy Maiden) & *Tiandi* (Heaven and Earth) Phonetically Transcribed in Chinese Characters in Xiapu Manuscripts). *Viae Sericae* 5: 109–39.

Lu, You. 2011. *Lu You Quanji (陸遊全集校注 Critical edition of Complete Works of Lu You)*. Edited by Qian Zhonglian. Hangzhou: Zhejiang Jiaoyu Chubanshe.

Ma, Xiaohe. 2010. Monijiao shi tianwang kao—Fujian Xiapu wenshu yanjiu (摩尼教十天王考—福建霞浦文書研究 The King of Ten Heavens in Manicheism—a Study of the Document from Xiapu (Fujian)). *Xiyu Wenshi (西域文史 Literature & History of the Western Regions)* 5: 119–30.

Ma, Xiaohe. 2012. Monijiao Yejufu kao—Fujian Xiapu wenshu yanjiu (摩尼教耶具孚考—福建霞浦文書研究 On Manichaean Jacob: a study of the Xiapu manuscripts). *Zhonhua Wenshi Luncong (中華文史論叢 Collections of Essays on Chinese Literature and History)* 2: 285–308.

Ma, Xiaohe. 2013a. Monijiao si tianwang kao—Fujian Xiapu wenshu yanjiu (摩尼教四天王考—福建霞浦文書研究 The four heavenly kings in Manichaeism—A study based on the documents from Xiapu, Fujian). *Viae Sericae, Si Ci Zhi Lu—Gudai Zhongwai Guanxi Shi Yanjiu (絲瓷之路—古代中外關係史研究 Road of Silk and Porcelain—Research on Ancient Sino-Foreign Relationship)* V: 122–55.

Ma, Xiaohe. 2013b. Monijiao shenmo puxi yu Xiapu wenshu (摩尼教神魔譜系與霞浦文書 Names of gods, demons and humans in Chinese versions of the Manichaean myth and Xiapu documents). *Renwen Zongjiao Yanjiu (人文宗教研究 Journal of Humanistic Religion)* 4: 100–30.

Ma, Xiaohe. 2014a. *Xiapu wenshu yanjiu (霞浦文書研究 Research on Xiapu Documents)*. Lanzhou: Lanzhou Daxue Chubanshe.

Ma, Xiaohe. 2014b. Jingjiao yu Mingjiao de qishi lichan (景教與明教的七時禮懺 Seven Prayers Daily of Nestorianism and the Religion of Light). In *Sanyijiao Yanjiu—Lin Wushu Jiaoshou Guxi Jinian Wenji (三夷教研究——林悟殊教授古稀紀念文集 Research on the Three Barbarian Religions)*. Edited by Xiaogui Zhang. Lanzhou: Lanzhou Daxue Chubanshe, pp. 254–67.

Ma, Xiaohe. 2015a. Remains of the Religion of Light in Xiapu (霞浦) County, Fujian Province. In *Mani in Dublin: Selected Papers from the Seventh International Conference of the International Association of Manichaean Studies in the Chester Beatty Library, Dublin, 8–12 September 2009*. Edited by Siegfried G. Richter, Charles Horton and Klaus Ohlhafer. Leiden and Boston: Brill, pp. 228–58.

Ma, Xiaohe. 2015b. Moni jiao Huiming kao—Fujian Xiapu wen shu yanjiu (摩尼教惠明考—福建霞浦文研究 A Study on the deity 'Hui-ming' of Manichaeism in the Manuscripts from Xiapu). *The Western Regions Studies* 4: 106–14.

Ma, Xiaohe. 2016. Xiapu wenshu Mani guangfo and Ricang Yuzhou quantu (霞浦文書《摩尼光佛》與日藏《宇宙全圖》 Xiapu Manuscript *Mani the Buddha of Light* and the *Diagram of Universe* in Japan). *Yishushi Yanjiu (藝術史研究 The Study of Art History)* XVIII: 387–414.

Ma, Xiaohe. 2016b. *Nalisuohe yizai* (nrysẖ yzd) suyuan 那哩娑和夷口在 (nrysẖ yzd) 溯源 (Tracing to the sources of *Nalisuohe yizai* (nrysẖ yzd)). *Guoji hanxue yanjiu tongxun (國際漢學研究通訊 Newsletter for International China Studies)* 15: 65–88.

Ma, Xiaohe. 2016c. "Ri cang 'Moni dan sheng tu' yu 'Moni guang fo Xia sheng zan'" 日藏《摩尼誕生圖》与《摩尼光佛·下生讚》(*The Painting of the Birth of Mani* in Japan and "Hymn of Descent" in *Mani the Buddha of Light*). *Meishu Xuebao (美術學報 Art Journal)* 3: 5–17.

Ma, Xiaohe. 2016d. "'Moni dan sheng tu' bukao" (摩尼誕生圖補考 A Research on *Mani at Birth* in Japanese Collection). *Xiyu Yanjiu (西域研究 The Western Regions Studies)* 4: 57–69, Plates 1–4.

Ma, Xiaohe. 2017. A Chinese Summary of the Martyrdom of St. George. *Eurasian Studies* 5: 457–89.

Mou, Runsun. 1938. Songdai Monijiao (宋代摩尼教 Manicheism of the Song Dynasty). *Furen xuezhi (輔仁學誌 Fjun Sinological Journal)* 7: 125–46.

Müller, Friedrich Wwilhelm Karl. 1910. Uigurica II. In *Abhandlungen der Königlich Preussischen Akademie der Wissenschaften*. Berlin: Philosophisch-Historische Classe.

Sims-Williams, Nicholas. 1981. The Sogdian fragments of Leningrad. *BSOAS* 44: 236–37. [CrossRef]

Sundermann, Werner. 1979. Namen von Göttern, Dämonen und Menschen in iranischen Versionen des manichäischen Myshos. *Altorientalische Forschungen* VI: 95–133.

Sundermann, Werner. 2002. "Manicheism ii. The Manichean Pantheon" *Encyclopædia Iranica*. Available online: http://www.iranicaonline.org/articles/manicheism-ii-the-manichean-pantheon (accessed on 22 April 2018).

Tsui, Chi. 1943. Mo Ni Chiao Hsia Pu Tsan 'The Lower (Second?) Section of the Manichaean Hymns'. *BSOAS* XI: 174–219.

Van Lindt, Paul. 1992. *The Names of Manichaean Mythological Figures. A Comparative Study on Terminology in the Coptic Sources*. Wiesbaden: Otto Harrassowitz.

Wang, Chuan. 1998. *Dunhuang Lichanwen Yanjiu (敦煌禮懺文研究 Study on Worship and Repentance Rituals from Dunhuang)*. Taipei: Fagu wenhua.

Wang, Chuan. 2008. *Tang Song Guyi Fojiao Chanyi Yanjiu (唐宋古逸佛教懺儀研究 Study on Rediscovered Buddhist Confessional Rituals from Tang and Song Dynasties)*. Taipei: Wenjin chubanshe, pp. 6, 21–60, 139–224, 259–304.

Wang, Chuan, and Xiaohe Ma. 2016. Xiapu wenshu Moni guangfo kece de yiwen fuyuan (霞浦文書《摩尼光佛》科冊的儀文復原 Restored Text of Xiapu Manuscript *Mani the Buddha of Light*). *Dunhuang Xue (敦煌學 = Studies on Dun-Huang)* 32: 1–43.

Xu, Song. 2014. *Song Huiyao Jigao (宋會要輯稿 Compiled Manuscripts of the Important Documents of the Song)*. Shanghai: Shanghai guji chubanshe.

Yang, Fuxue, and Lang Bao. 2014. Cong Xiapu ben 'Moni Guangfo' kan Monijiao dui fojiao de yituo (从霞浦本《摩尼光佛》看摩尼教佛教的依托 Viewing the reliance of Manichaeism on Buddhism in light of *Mani the Buddha of Light* (manuscript)). *Zongjiao Xue Yanjiu (宗教学研究 Study of Religions)* 4: 256–66.

Yang, Fuxue, and Lang Bao. 2015. Xiapu Monijiao xin wenxian *Moni guangfo* jiaozhu (霞浦摩尼教新文獻《摩尼光佛》校注 Xiapu Manichaean new document *Mani the Buddha of Light* with emendation and annotation). *Hanshan Si Foxue (寒山寺佛學 The Buddhism of Hanshan Temple)* 10: 74–115.

Yoshida, Yutaka. 2010. 新出マニ教絵画の形而上 (Shinshutsu Manikyo kaiga no Keijijo 'Cosmogony and church history depicted in the newly discovered Chinese Manichaean paintings'). *大和文華 (Yamato Bunka Biannual Journal of Eastern Arts)* 121: 3–34, Plates 1–9.

Yoshida, Yutaka. 2014. The Xiapu 霞浦 Manichaean text *Sijizan* 四寂讃 'Praise of the Four Entities of Calmness' and Its Parthian Original" (in Chinese translated by Ma Xiaohe). *Newsletter for International China Studies* 95: 103–21.

Yoshida, Yutaka, and Shōichi Furukawa, eds. 2015. *Chūgoku Kōnan Manikyō Kaiga Kenkyū (中国江南マニ教絵画研究 Studies of the Chinese Manichaean Paintings of South Chinese Origin Preserved in Japan)*. Kyōto: Rinsenshoten.

Yuan, Wenqi. 2011. Fujian Xiapu Monijiao keyi dianji zhongda faxian lunzheng (福建霞浦摩尼教科儀典籍重大發現論證 On a significant discovery of Manichaean ritual documents form Xiapu (Fujian)). *Shijie Zongjiao Yanjiu (Studies of World Religions)* 5: 169–80.

Zürcher, Erik. 1997. Book review for Kuo, Li-ying, *Confession et Contrition dans le Bouddhisme Chinois du Ve au Xe siècle*. Paris: Publications de l'École française d'Extrême-Orient, 1994. In *T'oung Pao*. 2nd Series, Fasc. 1/3; Leiden: E. J. Brill, vol. 83, pp. 207–12.

religions

Review

Influences of Egyptian Lotus Symbolism and Ritualistic Practices on Sacral Tree Worship in the Fertile Crescent from 1500 BCE to 200 CE

J. Andrew McDonald

Department of Biology, The University of Texas—Rio Grande Valley, 1201 W. University Dr., Edinburg, TX 78539, USA; andrew.mcdonald@utrgv.edu

Received: 2 August 2018; Accepted: 23 August 2018; Published: 27 August 2018

Abstract: Many conventional features of world tree motifs in the ancient Near East—including stalked palmettes, aureoles of water lily palmettes connected by pliant stems, floral rosettes, winged disks and bud-and-blossom motifs—trace largely from Egyptian practices in lotus symbolism around 2500 BCE, more than a millennium before they appear, migrate and dominate plant symbolism across the Fertile Crescent from 1500 BCE to 200 CE. Several of these motifs were associated singularly or collectively with the Egyptian sema-taui and ankh signs to symbolize the eternal recurrence and everlasting lives of Nilotic lotus deities and deceased pharaohs. The widespread use of lotus imagery in iconographic records on both sides of the Red Sea indicates strong currents of cultural diffusion between Nilotic and Mesopotamian civilizations, as does the use of lotus flowers in religious rituals and the practice of kingship, evidence for which is supported by iconographic, cuneiform and biblical records. This perspective provides new insights into sacral tree symbolism and its role in mythic legacies of Egypt and the Middle East before and during the advent of Christianity. Closer scholarly scrutiny is still needed to fully comprehend the underlying meaning of immortalizing plants in the mythic traditions of Egypt, the Levant and Mesopotamia.

Keywords: Nilotic lotus; sacral tree; ankh; sema-taui; Bible; kingship; libation ritual

1. Introduction

As both a symbol and iconographic prop, sacral tree images on palace and temple reliefs, murals, seals, jewelry and ritualistic implements of the Middle East continue to "provoke more discussion and controversy than almost any other element in Mesopotamian art" (Black et al. 1992, p. 170). Portrayals and historical uses of these motifs remain an enigma to most historians and evoke little agreement with respect to their botanical identity and allegorical significance (Atac 2008; Giovino 2007, pp. 21–30). While most recent commentators identify visual impressions of the motif as a date palm (Albenda 1994; Black et al. 1992, pp. 46, 170–71; Mazar 1961, vol. 4, p. 71; Moldenke and Moldenke 1952, p. 191; Parpola 1993; Porter 1993), this utilitarian plant was in fact a frequent feature in depictions of mundane scenes of palace life and agricultural panoramas. The date palm is occasionally associated with various gods and goddesses, sacrificial rituals and libation scenes in artistic media, but primarily among specimens from the 3rd and 2nd millenia BCE and Achaemedian cylinder seals from the 6–5th c. BCE (Danthine 1937, pls. 3–9, 16). In such examples, the plant exhibits clearly interpretable features of a date palm: i.e., stout, singular trunks with persistent leaf bases, pinnate fronds, several pendent and woody, spathate flowering stalks and date fruits.

On other occasions, historians have also identified a variety of stylized images of a Mesopotamian sacral tree and its exuberant flowers with cedars, firs, oaks, pomegranates, roses, willows or members of the sunflower family (Bonavia 1894, pp. 3–7, 44–45, 58; Danthine 1937; James 1966, pp. 13, 42, 75, 98, 106, 162; Moldenke and Moldenke 1952, pp. 191, 286). These wide-ranging interpretations notwithstanding, a more recent botanical assessment of the issue challenges most of the aforementioned determinations (McDonald 2002), noting that most sacral trees that post-date 1500 BC lack the aforementioned characteristics of a date palm, while manifesting many vegetative and fertile characteristics that are categorically inconsistent with palm tree morphology, such as pliant stems, an aureole of interconnected palmettes with blue-pigmented appendages, the latter often surrounding a golden disk, fruits with prominent calyx segments and close associations with a cone-like object. From a botanical viewpoint, these and other characteristics of the plant suggest a species that once dominated marshes of the Nile, Tigris and Euphrates River systems: the Nilotic lotus (*Nymphaea nouchali* Burm. f.). Blue-pigmented palmettes of these sacred trees appear to represent lateral perspectives of water lily corolla, while trunk-like features signify a stout and succulent water lily stalk. Although this perspective is by no means original (Coomaraswamy 1935; Danthine 1937; Goodyear 1887, 1891; Jones [1856] 1995, pp. 22–23, 28–29), modern historians have inexplicably ignored this interpretation during most of the 20th century.

The use of lotus symbolism throughout the Fertile Crescent and Egypt during the second and first millennia BCE is one of many practices that reveals a long history of cultural contacts between early civilizations of the Nile River and Fertile Crescent. While many of Egypt's earliest written records make direct reference to Middle Eastern peoples (Redford 1992, pp. 19–24, 33), the widespread usage of Egyptian symbols (ankhs, djeds, uraei, lotus flowers, etc.), apparel (robes, sandals, crowns, and staffs) and presentation of zoomorphic gods and chimeras of Egyptian origin (falcons, scarabs, jackals, etc.) throughout the Levant and Mesopotamia during the Middle Bronze Age (2000–1700 BCE; (Keel and Uehlinger 1998, p. 25, Figures 8a,b, 15c, 32c and 34c)), with a secondary peak of popularity during the Middle Iron Age (ca. 1000 BCE; (Keel and Uehlinger 1998, pp. 210–81)), attest to significant and enduring influences of Egyptian culture over peoples throughout the Fertile Crescent. It is well known that Levantine communities in ancient Egypt exercised considerable influence over the Nile delta from the 19–16th centuries BCE (i.e., the Hyksos; (Shaw and Nicholson 1995, p. 136; Keel and Uehlinger 1998, p. 17)), during which period various Canaanite gods and goddesses, such as Qadesh (Qetesh), Anat (Anthat), Ashtoreth (Astarte) and Baal (Bar), joined the ranks of the Egyptian pantheon (Budge [1904] 1969, vol. 2, pp. 278–81; Shaw and Nicholson 1995, pp. 32, 42, 237; Redford 1992, pp. 231–33). Pre- and post-exilic biblical records of Judah reveal in no uncertain terms that Hebrew-speaking tribes of Canaan and their neighbors embraced various pantheons and religious practices of both Egypt and Mesopotamia (Lang 1983, pp. 18–26, 41; Patai 1990; Keel and Uehlinger 1998, pp. 2–3); hence iconographic forms and conventions of ancient Egypt, the Levant, and Mesopotamia intermingle freely with one another in archaeological sites that date from the second and first millennia BCE (Jones [1856] 1995, pp. 23–29; Merhav 1987; Frankfort 1970; Black et al. 1992, p. 84; Cline 1995).

Differing schools of iconology and mythology have yet to reconcile whether or not shared symbolic elements and mythological themes of distant civilizations in Egypt, the Middle East and Europe have arisen coincidentally (independently) or by means of cultural diffusion. While either or both of these explanations might apply to any particular motif, it is incumbent upon historians to argue their specific perspectives on an individual basis and support their views by drawing equally from evidence in archaeological and written records. Ideally, their interpretations should be compatible with ritualistic and religious customs of each historical age. In the present study, botanical considerations on the use of lotus symbolism in Egypt and the Near East focus primarily on iconographic evidence, and then tests hypothetical interpretations of floral and vegetative imagery by matching their visually contextual and mythical presentations with historical and scriptural records.

In the case of lotus symbolism, we are well-informed of the plant's prominent role in Egyptian mythology by a wealth of scriptural and artistic evidence from the distant past. This is not, however, the case for lotus symbolism in the Fertile Crescent, which has yet to be explored and examined comprehensively under these unique geographical and cultural circumstances. This incongruency owes in no small part to the dominant role of linguistic fields of inquiry in the study of Mesopotamian and Near Eastern history, whose ongoing contributions are often at a loss to identify ancient plant names and highly stylized vegetative and floral motifs on a botanical basis (Darby et al. 1977, pp. 36–37; Giovino 2007, pp. 12–16; Moldenke and Moldenke 1952, pp. 2–9). Furthermore, it has long been assumed by art historians that sacral tree imagery relates to the cultivation, pollination, and sanctification of date palms (Black et al. 1992, p. 46), direct botanical confirmation of which has been challenged in many cases by McDonald (2002) and others (Giovino 2007, pp. 77–90; Goodyear 1887, 1891). Since the physical and behavioral attributes of date palms have limited relevance to standard mythical features of the Fertile Crescent's sacred trees, such as aquatic origins, solar attributes or contacts, and close associations with divine serpents and eagles (McDonald 2002), various authorities have concluded that literary references in cuneiform and biblical sources have no direct bearing on sacral tree imagery in the visual arts (James; (Black et al. 1992, p. 171; Parpola 1993)). This perspective seems to be at variance, however, with iconographic records in palaces and temples, which afford ample visual and textual evidence of such a plant, many referring explicitly to an aquatic, resplendent, flowering plant of the immortal gods. References to this plant are encountered frequently in mythic records of the Sumerians, Akkadians, and Canaanites (Pritchard 1969), and often in association with mythical creatures that agree with visual portrayals of sacral trees in archaeological records. They simply defy the logic of suggestions that this ubiquitous and focal symbol of kingship and religious ritual in Akkadia, Assyria, Babylonia and the Levant fails to appear in 3000 years of mythical cuneiform records (Cooper 2000; Parpola 1993, 1997).

If the development of sacral tree symbolism in the Fertile Crescent springs from, converges upon, or parallels the development of sacred lotus symbolism in Egypt (Coomaraswamy 1935; Goodyear 1887, 1891; Jones [1856] 1995, pp. 22–23, 28–29; McDonald 2002), then it only follows that the mythic and symbolic significance of Mesopotamian and Near Eastern sacral trees should share both iconographic and mythic relations with the Nile's ubiquitous water lily motifs. McDonald (2002) explored this subject briefly, primarily by relating mythical attributes of the sacral tree to physical and behavioral characteristics of the Nilotic lotus. But that inquiry hardly scratches the surface of a very complex subject and therefore invites closer examination of the origin and historical developments of sacred tree symbolism in the Middle East. To accomplish this goal, it is useful to consider from the outset the mythic and religious significance of lotus symbolism on the banks of the Nile River.

This investigation approaches a popular and familiar topic from a unique perspective, insofar as the fundamental premises for interpretations of the ubiquitous Nilotic lotus of Egypt and the Middle East are based primarily on the author's botanical background and observations on the distinctive morphic and behavioral characteristics: a plant species that subordinates all other symbolic plants in terms of frequency of use. The diurnal, blue Nilotic lotus, *Nymphaea nouchali* Burm. f. (s.l.), is a member of the aquatic water lily family, and exhibits a natural distribution that ranges across tropical latitudes of Africa and Asia. A related species of this same plant group is also known materially from archeological records and occasionally in iconographic records of Egypt and the Middle East—the nocturnal, white-flowered night lotus, *Nymphaea lotus* L.—but this species plays a relatively minor role in symbolism and religious ritual. The large and blue, resplendent, sun-like flowers of the day-bloomer seem to have captivated the imaginations of Egyptian and Mesopotamian peoples like no other for at least three millennia, and accordingly dominated the use of plant symbolism in mythic and religious traditions of distant human communities. Biological insights provide novel and somewhat heterodoxic viewpoints on ancient iconographic records and, in so doing, highlight details in symbolic expression that are rarely considered while also contesting a number of popular viewpoints of modern historians.

2. The Egyptian Lotus as a Symbol of Immortal Life

Lotus symbolism is a hallmark of religious expression in pharaonic Egypt and permeates most temple complexes and mortuary sites of pre-Christian origin. Some of Egypt's earliest written records make direct reference to the plant, many appearing in early mortuary chambers of Old Kingdom dynasts at Saqqara, particularly those of King Unas (ca. 2375–2345 BCE). A compilation of these hieroglyphic records with English translations in "The Ancient Egyptian Pyramid Texts" (Faulkner 1969) is replete with mythical references to the first living being to emerge from the life-giving waters of ancient Egypt, this being the Nilotic blue lotus. Arising in the sky from a mythical islet of the Nile known as On, not far from the historical city of Heliopolis (modern Cairo) as a solar cum water lily god of creation known as Atum or Nefer-Atum (=Nefertum, or "Beauty Come-to-be"; Figure 1a), this primordial demiurge instigates living creation by breathing his flower's sweet-smelling essence across the face of the earth and shedding his creative seed into the Egyptian sky. Nefertum accomplishes these acts in three symbolically equivalent forms: (1) a water lily shoot (Figure 1a), (2) an aquatic phallus whose life-engendering ejaculum fills the earth and heavens with its procreative "spittle" (Figure 1b), or (3) a scarab beetle (Khepri) with blue-pigmented wings that lifts Egypt's immortal, golden sun-disk (Ra) on a lapis lazuli boat into the heavens (Figure 1c,d). On a symbolic level, the primeval phallus apparently symbolizes an emergent, budding water lily shaft with a swollen apical bud (Figure 2e), while the blue-winged scarab with green calyptras and a golden disk represents a full-blown, blue water lily (i.e., with green calyx, blue corolla and yellow ovarian disk, Figure 2d; (McDonald 2002)).

Figure 1. The cosmogenic Nilotic lotus. (**a**) Although Nefertum leads the Heliopolitan pantheon during the Old Kingdom, personified images of the lotus god occur commonly during the New Kingdom and Ptolemaic periods. Egypt, ca. 3rd c. BCE (Metropolitan Museum). (**b**) The Egyptian obelisk, a phallic symbol of Osiris-Ra, frequently bears at its apex the avian image of his solar offspring, Horus. Here, the pillar surpasses in height the massive papyrus columns of Karnak. Egypt, Karnak, 15th c. BCE. (**c**) Khepri lifts the lapis lazuli boat of Horus's solar eye out of a lotus grove. The divine scarab, a mythic image of the lotus-god, Nefertum, also carries two symbols of immortal life within his talons: shen loops and a cluster of two lotus buds and blossom. Thebes, Valley of the Kings, Tomb of Tutankhamen, 14th c. BCE (Cairo Museum). (**d**) A ram-headed scarab beetle with blue wings emerges from a lotus blossom to push forth the flower's golden disk. A pair of cobras (uraei) dangle from the solar-floral disk, each upholding an ankh. The latter symbols complement the flanking pair of lotus buds to either side of the blossom, as well as paired avian images of Horus (blue falcons) yet to take flight. Egypt, coffin of Pameshen, ca. 10th c. BCE (Cairo Museum).

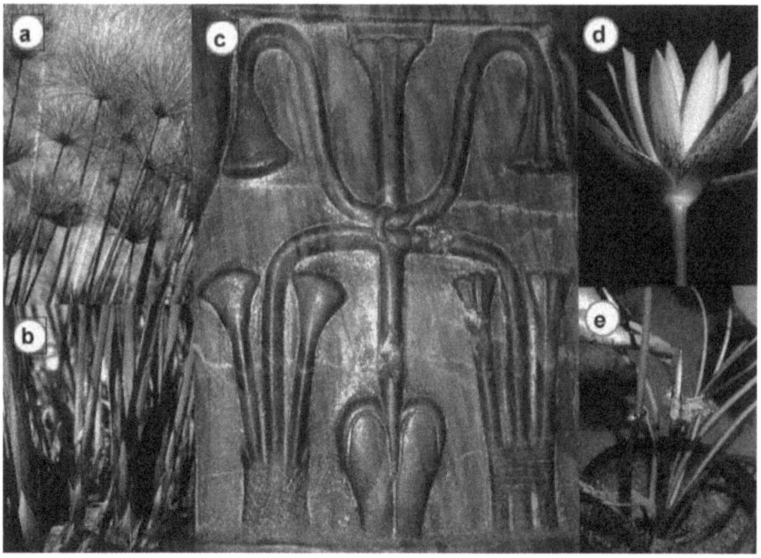

Figure 2. The "Union" Symbol (sema-taui) of ancient Egypt. (**a**) Fertile stalks of the papyrus plant present a cluster of chaffy bracts and a spray of slender shoots. Details of these complex structures are often simplified as a campanulate motif in the visual arts (Figure 2c). (**b**) Papyrus stems are supported at their base by long, chaffy bracts. (**c**) Early renderings of the sema-taui symbol portray a central lotus stalk that is supported by knotted lotus and papyrus stems. Note that the central stalk arises from a testicular base and supports a three-membered palmette (lotus flower) at its apex. Throne of Chephren, Giza, 26th c. BCE (Cairo Museum). (**d**) The profile view of a polypetalous Egyptian water lily exhibits three prominent green sepals and a palmate array of blue-pigmented petals. (**e**) Lotus stalks lack the distinctive basal bracts of a papyrus shoot. Note that a new bud has arisen before a flower stalk has finished its three days of anthesis.

The Heliopolitan perspective on natural creation does not culminate with the cosmogenic activities of a divine flower, but proceeds to describe the subsequent creation of four successive generations of gods and goddesses, the last of which includes two brothers and sisters—namely Osiris, Seth, Isis, and Nephthys—whose conflictive interactions on the banks of the Nile immortalize the natural world's life cycles by establishing the everlasting processes of procreation and death. Nefertum's fourth-generation descendants experience a daily drama of fratricide and necromancy, whereby Seth, the envious brother of the sun god, Osiris-Ra, submerges and drowns his sibling's phallus on the banks of the Nile River at the end of each day (Table 1, l. 1), thereby compelling his divine sisters, Isis and Nephthys, to seek out and guard the virile member of their fallen, solar brother (Table 1, l. 2).

Table 1. Citations from Egyptian Heiroglyphic Inscriptions. PT = Pyramid Texts (Faulkner 1969); CT = Coffin Texts (Faulkner 2004); BD = Book of the Dead (Budge [1899] 1989).

1	PT 24, 615, 972, 1256, 1500
2	PT 616, 1255–56, 2144
3	PT 581–82, 632–633, 1636, 2018–2019
4	PT 766, 1068, 1799–800
5	PT 167–92, 1298, 2098, 2146
6	BD 264, 594
7	PT 198, 238, 976, 1056, 1146–48
8	CT 316, 351, 388–89, 455, 462
9	BD 315–16
10	PT 513–14, 776, 1833–37
11	PT 1624–26, 1824
12	PT 788–92
13	PT 788–92; PT 1180; PT 1227, respectively
14	PT 275, 1247, 1421, 1430
15	PT 1345–46
16	PT 145, 152, 156, 1686; CT 350, 169, 352
17	CT 188
18	PT 1164–67
19	PT 770, 961, 994, 1475
20	PT 632, 956–59, 1061
21	PT 1460–63
22	PT 535
23	PT 946–47
24	PT 792, 1066, 1781
25	PT 770
26	PT 513–14
27	PT 60–61, 264–66
28	PT 391
29	CT 335; 2: 292–300
30	PT 1962–67; CT 223; BD XLII. 10–14, LXXI. 3–8
31	BD XLII
32	PT 22–23, 43, 47, 73, 114, 1682, 1800–802, 2071–73; CT 607; BD CX, CXVI
33	PT 1801, 2071–2073
34	PT 1959
35	PT 1643, 1754, 1802, 2073, 2075, CT 530, 840, 861; PT 1241; PT 332, 1902–903, respectively
36	BD CX, CXVI
37	CT 167

Isis, a fertility goddess, eventually couples with the fallen phallus, conceiving by Osiris her one and only son, Horus, who emerges from the Nile River at the dawning of each day in the image of a golden-crowned, blue-winged falcon (Table 1, l. 3; Figure 4c). Horus, who is often described as the eye of the sun, returns the seed of his father to its original source—an aquatic phallus in the aquatic underworld of the Nile (Table 1, l. 4)—and in so doing revitalizes his own biological/paternal source. In effect, the interactive roles of Horus and Osiris recapitulate the primordial acts of Nefertum's virile member on a daily basis (Table 1, l. 5) by resurrecting a cosmic phallus at the dawning of each day so as to conceive a solar-bodied offspring (Horus) in the form of a blue lotus: or symbolically, a blue-feathered falcon that supports a golden solar disk on his head (i.e., cradled by his blue, outstretched wings).

Egyptians and members of the Heliopolitan pantheon recognized the sun and its animate equivalent, the sun-like blossoms of the Nilotic lotus, as earthly and heavenly aspects of the Nile's first recorded Creator figure, Nefertum. Hence, the lotus flower was deemed as much a creator of life as an incarnate aspect of the everlasting sun itself. The Pyramid Texts are full of refrains that describe the lotus plant as the progenitor (i.e., as Nefertum) of the sun (Ra): not vice versa, as would be our intuitive and modern biological perspective. And judging from historical accounts of the first-century Greek historian, Plutarch, citizens of Greece were equally familiar with this traditional Nilotic perspective on the natural world just prior to the Greco-Roman Periods of Egyptian history (332 BCE—395 CE). In "Moralia: De Iside et Osiride" (V.355.11; (Babbitt 1936, p. 29)), Plutarch acknowledges that Nilotic communities symbolized the sun's aquatic origins by the image of a solar orb arising from a full-blown lotus blossom.

This mythic image endured for thousands of years and appears as though it were transcribed directly from the early dynastic tomb of Unas onto the walls of the famous Denderah temple complex during Egypt's Greco-Roman period:

> The sun which exists since the beginning rises like a falcon out of the center of the lotus blossom. When the doors of the petals open in the shine of sapphire, so He (the sun god, Horus) has separated the night from the day. You are rising like the holy serpent as a living spirit! Creating, you rise and shine in your magnificent body in the boat of the rising sun. The divine master, whose image is kept hidden in the temple of Denderah, is becoming the creator of the world by his work. Coming as the One, he multiplies by millions when the light comes out of him in the form of a child. (translation of (Brugsch 1884, p. 103))

Here the lotus flower is mythically identified with the sun, a divine serpent, blue raptor, and solar barge, all of which motifs echo earlier Heliopolitan themes and ostensibly reflect the solar aspect of water lily blossoms: the serpentoid nature of water lily peduncles, the feathery features of the plant's large petals, and the flower's tendency to float on water like a blue-petalled, sun-like boat (McDonald 2002).

The use of lotus imagery to symbolize eternal life was a standard practice in pharaonic Egypt and successive dynasts were recurrently identified specifically as reincarnations of Horus during their reigns as pharaohs and incarnate spirits of Nefertum, Osiris, and the Nilotic lotus in the afterlife. It was widely believed that upon the death of a pharaoh, each sovereign was bound to arise as a lotus flower "at the nose of Ra" within the paradisal "Fields of Peace" on the Nile (="Fields of Offerings," "Underworld" or "Hidden Place" in the Book of the Dead, Table 1, l. 6; (Budge [1925] 1989, p. 319; Budge [1904] 1969, vol. 1, p. 170)). This optimistic expectation was often represented in the visual arts by the image of an aristocrat, priest or deity upholding a lotus bloom before his or her nose (Lange and Hirmer 1968, Figures 74 and 83, pl. XXIII; El-Mallakh and Bianchi 1980, p. 112; Keel and Uehlinger 1998, Figures 32c and 107), as though the sweet-smelling essence of the Nilotic lotus was a source of his or her eternal life. The same general idea is communicated among the early inscriptions of King Unas at Saqqara, which equate the pharaoh with deified lotus shoots, solar orbs and serpent gods, as noted in the aforementioned translation of Brugsch from Denderah as well as numerous Pyramid Texts (Table 1, l. 7) and funerary papyri known to modern Egyptologists as the Coffin Texts (Table 1, l. 8). Needless to say, Egyptian allusions to an immortalizing plant that bears close relations to the sun and a divine serpent foreshadow mythic themes that relate to various Middle Eastern cuneiform texts and Biblical references to the tree of life (McDonald 2002; Pritchard 1969).

3. The Ankh, Sema-Taui and Lotus Plant

Given the aforementioned mythic roles of the Egyptian lotus, it is not surprising that the plant is often associated with Egyptian hieroglyphs and symbols that relate to eternal life. Foremost among these is the ankh insignia (Figure 3a–c), an enduring motif that eventually served Coptic churches in post-dynastic Egypt as the symbol of the Christian tree of life and sacrificial cross (i.e., the crux ansata; see discussion below and Figure 7; (Lurker 1980, p. 27); Table 1, l. 9) before it disappears from historical records a few centuries after Egypt's adoption of Christianity. The ankh is one of the older and more ubiquitous symbols of ancient Egypt and one that apparently symbolized the lotus flower when it was held to the nose of gods and pharaohs (Figure 7b; (Lange and Hirmer 1968, pl. LI; Schäfer 1974, Figure 20; El-Mallakh and Bianchi 1980, p. 44; Wilkinson 1992, p. 177)). While various anthropomorphic, zoomorphic and chimeric gods and goddesses present the ankh to Osiris and Horus as a means to affect their sanctification, resuscitation, and resurrection (i.e., eternal occurrence), the sign is also employed as a symbol of the Nile's 'waters of life,' usually by portraying a cascading stream of ankh emblems from libation vases (Gillispie and Dewachter 1987, 1: pls. 10.2, 2, 11.A, 13.1; Wilkinson 1994, pp. 159–60) or by fashioning libation vases in the image of an ankh insignia (Schäfer 1974, Figure 30). In either case, the ankh sign symbolized the vitalizing breath and creative seed (i.e., 'waters' or 'efflux') of the sacred phallus and/or solar eye of various Egyptian lotus-gods, whether Nefertum-Ra, Osiris-Ra or Horus-Ra.

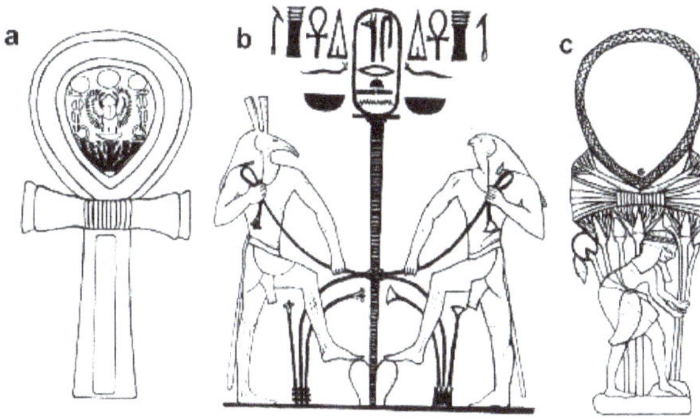

Figure 3. Ankh and lotus. (**a**) Mirrors and mirror cases from Egyptian tombs are often fashioned in the image of an ankh symbol and a flowering lotus stalk. Note that the stalked shen loop (an ankh) contains a lotus blossom and three golden floral disks. The triad of disks presumably symbolizes the natural three-day life span of a lotus flower. Thebes, Valley of the Kings, Tomb of Tutankhamen, 14th c. BCE (Cairo Museum). (**b**) Horus and Seth grasp a lotus and papyrus stalk and sustain the immortal phallus of Osiris-Ra. The phallic symbol takes the form of an ankh symbol and contains a hieroglyphic reference to Seti I. Abydos, 13th c. BCE (Cairo Museum). (**c**) Unguent spoons were often fashioned in the image of an ankh, stalked shen loop, and flowering lotus stalk. Note that the extended arms of the shen loop terminate in lotus blossoms and that a lotus bud and blossom motif—a symbol of immortal life—extends across the spoon. Thebes, Egypt, 13th c. BCE (Louvre Museum).

The origin of the ankh symbol has been debated for more than a century, but with little agreement as to how the symbol was derived. Most dictionaries and encyclopedic works refer to a popular hypothesis of the famous Egyptologist, Alan Gardiner (Gardiner 1928, vol. 8, pp. 19–25; 1950), who envisaged the ankh as a sandal strap. Little support for this proposition can be found, however, in epigraphic and iconographic records, as noted by Gardiner himself. While Budge (Budge [1925] 1989, pp. 315–16) and Chevalier and Gheerbrant (1996, p. 27) speculate that the loop of the ankh sign likely symbolizes the solar eye of the sun-god Ra emerging from an eastern horizon, and others attempt to derive the distinctive emblem from the image of a cow vertebra (Gordon and Schwabe 2004, pp. 102–6) or a penis sheath (Baines 1975), Egyptologists have yet to reach a consensus on the matter.

The ankh symbol is, in fact, a rather simple motif, and one that shares both direct and indirect associations with the Nilotic lotus. Numerous mirrors, mirror cases and 'unguent spoons' discovered in various reaches of the Nile River superimpose a flowering lotus stalk upon the ankh emblem (Figure 3a,c; (Maspero 1913, pp. 190–91; Baines 1975; Wilkinson 1994, p. 161, Figure 127)), identifying the shaft of the emblem with a lotus stalk and the terminal loop with opposing arms (a shen symbol, see below) with a lotus bud or blossom.

In a similar manner, the ankh sign is often associated with the sema-taui hieroglyph (Figures 3b, 4a,b and 7c), or 'union' symbol (*zm3–t3wj* = 'union of the two lands'; (Wilkinson 1994, p. 90; 2003, p. 107)). This motif portrays opposing bouquets of three lotus and papyrus stalks that uphold a centralized, upright, flowering lotus stalk (Figure 2c). The term sema-taui (*zm3 sm'w t3–mhjw*, 'Uniter of the Upper and Lower Egypt') is derived from a royal epithet that traces its origin to the Second Dynasty (Budge [1904] 1969, vol. 2, p. 44) around 2800 BCE and connotes kingship over lands that lie between the mouth and headwaters of the Nile River system. The concept is encountered repeatedly in the Pyramid Texts, where numerous entries celebrate a deceased king's assumption of dominion over lands that lie between Nile delta and the cataracts at Philae (i.e., Upper and Lower Egypt), the natural domains of Osiris (Table 1, l. 10) and Horus (Table 1, l. 11). We also encounter this phrase in association with descriptions of the eternal recurrence of Osiris-Ra (an incarnation of Nefertum's floral phallus) in the aquatic 'Fields' of the sun-god, Ra.

The Nilotic 'Fields of Ra' are described mystically in the Pyramid Texts as an aquatic domain where deceased Kings reincarnate themselves as the underworld phallic sun-god, Osiris-Ra, and return to life upon flooded "serpent mounds" (Table 1, l. 12). The sun-god's aquatic fields are identified in later inscriptions of The Great Litany of Re (Piankoff 1964) as a locality where the King assumes a vegetative aspect in the afterlife: "in the horizon and the Yaro Fields" (Piankoff 1964, pls. 20–21), like Ra himself, who, "resting on his bank" (Piankoff 1964, pl. 3: 5) and "shining in the flood," is manifest as "bodies (pl.) of the Watery Abyss." Or otherwise, the mythic sun, as the eyes (pl.) of Horus (Piankoff 1964, pls. 4: 19–24) and "brilliant bodies (pl.) of the Flaming one from the Netherworld" (Piankoff 1964, pls. 5: 40–42), arises in large numbers on a daily basis. These mythic images call to mind a plurality of golden eyes in an aquatic habitat (i.e., lotus blossoms) rather than a solar orb, for solar disks arise solitarily on dry and stark, eastern terrestrial horizons of Egypt rather than flooded riverbanks.

The Nilotic Fields of Ra are mythically equivalent to Ra's "Fields of Khepri", "Field of Life", and "Field of Strife" (i.e., between Seth and Osiris; Table 1, l. 13), and are just as commonly identified as a Field of Reeds, Field of Felicity, Field of Peace, Field of Offerings, Field of Fire, the Tuat ('Underworld') or Amentet ('Hidden Place'; (Budge [1904] 1969, vol. 1, pp. 170–72)), all of which are conventionally described in terms of, or depicted in images as lotus groves among floating papyrus masses. Thus, Egypt's floral sun-gods are said to bathe in the Lake or Field of Rushes (Table 1, l. 14) and to moor their celestial boats among the Field of Rushes on the "Banks of the Lower Skies" (Table 1, l. 15; (Budge [1904] 1969, vol. 2, p. 120)). Given that the identity of Ra is repeatedly conflated with various lotus-gods known as Nefertum (as Ra-Atum and Nefetum-Ra; Table 1, l. 16), Horus-Ra and Osiris-Ra, and is said to bathe within lotus tanks (Table 1, l. 17), much as deceased Kings in the Field of Rushes on waterways, "like Ra on the banks of the Sky" (Table 1, l. 18), it seems apparent that the sun-god, Ra, in his life-giving 'Fields of Peace,' embodies a dual, cosmic identity that unites the mythic and theological roles of sun-like water lilies with the Egyptian sun.

A classic pictorial representation of the sema-taui symbol is observed on the throne of Sesostris I (1291–1278 BCE), where two central figures in Heliopolitan mythology, Seth and Horus (the nemesis vs. heroic offspring of Osiris, respectively), uphold an upright ankh emblem (=shen loop, symbol of eternal life, subtended by a shaft) by pulling knotted shoots of an Egyptian lotus and papyrus stalk (Figure 3b; (Lange and Hirmer 1968, Figure 88)). This image clearly represents the mythic interactions of Horus and Seth on the Heliopolitan 'mounds' of the Field of Rushes (Table 1, l. 19) who perpetually drown and then resurrect the phallus of Osiris-Ra.

Modern art historians usually interpret the central pillar and bi-lobed mound of this motif (Wilkinson 2003, p. 107) as a lung and windpipe (Gardiner 1950, p. 465; Lurker 1980, p. 125; Wilkinson 1992, p. 81), presumably because the central shaft often exhibits a series of horizontal ringlets. But this interpretation is unconvincing, as Egyptian mythology never associates Horus, Seth, or Osiris with a trachea or lungs. Rather, the focal ankh insignia seems to represent a phallic symbol that supports a terminal cartouche bearing the name of the king: the co-essence of Osiris-Ra or Nefertum-Ra in the Nilotic underworld. Arising from a testicular motif, the ankh appears to embody the phallus of either Nefertum- or Osiris-Ra, as we note its support is governed by the dual efforts of Seth and Horus. The imagery apparently relates to mythic themes in the Pyramid Texts that speak of the daily drowning of Osiris' solar phallus (Table 1, l. 20), the daily loss of Horus' solar eye and dismemberment of Seth's testicles (Table 1, l. 21), followed by the subsequent retrieval of Horus's solar eye, Seth's testicles (Table 1, l. 22), and the rejuvenation of Osiris's solar eye and testicles (Table 1, l. 23), all of which themes relate symbolically to the central ankh or lotus motif (Figures 2c and 3b).

Some of the earliest depictions of the sema-taui during the 5th and 6th Dynasties originally portrayed the central motif as a flowering lotus stalk instead of an interchangeable ankh sign, while the upright stalk sometimes exhibits the same distinctive ringlets that are observed on the ankh shaft of Sesostris I (Figure 3b, compare also Figures 1d and 4a; (Budge [1904] 1969, vol. 2, p. 131)). One of the earliest-known portrayals of the sema-taui symbol appears on the famous marbled throne of an early Old Kingdom pharaoh, Chephren (2558–2532 BCE), which exhibits side panels that emphasize the same testicular element (Figure 2c). By convention, the centralized lotus stalk is supported on one side by a papyrus stem whose campanulate stalks exhibit distinctive lanceolate leaf bracts at their bases (Figure 2b,c), and by a collection of three flowering lotus stalks on the opposite side whose stems are bundled basally by three or four horizontal bars (Figure 2c–e). The central, phalliform shaft of the motif—the axis mundi of Egyptian kingship in the aspect of a flowering lotus stalk—supports the enthroned, living image of Chephren. It is equally noteworthy that the sema-taui motif was employed in the construction of dynastic thrones in a similar manner throughout Egyptian history, ostensibly identifying the central lotus stalk as a phallic axis mundi to represent Egyptian dynasts and kingship.

As regards the symbolic significance of the motif, it is remarkable that the papyrus plant never occurs in the central position of this configuration, as this role is assumed exclusively by a lotus flower, an ankh symbol, or a realistic and/or symbolic image of a king (Gillispie and Dewachter 1987, vol. 1, pls. 45.2, vol. 4, pl. 12), frequently as a cartouche bearing the hieroglyphic inscription of a pharaoh's name (Gillispie and Dewachter 1987, vol. 2, pls. 21.2, 22). Hence, the king was represented iconographically as both an axis mundi and flourishing lotus stalk. Concomitantly, the combination of lotus and papyrus elements symbolizes the blissful Fields of Ra in the upper and lower floodplains of the Nile (Table 1, l. 24).

Since Chephren presided over Heliopolis (On), much as King Unas two centuries later, it is not surprising that the symbolic relationship between the sema-taui symbol and lotus flower on the king's throne relates to verses regarding the interactions of Seth and Horus upon the Nile's 'serpent mounds.' Early inscriptions at Saqqara identify the king's throne as a prominent feature of Nefertum's place of origin on the sacred mounds of On (Table 1, l. 25) while also asserting that the deceased king would cause the lapis lazuli plant (*twn*-plant of Upper Egypt) to sprout up (i.e., lotus) and tie the cords of the *smsmt*-plant (papyrus or lotus?) to unite with the heavens and maintain his power over the southern and northern lands (Table 1, l. 26). In essence, the pharaoh would become Osiris/Nefertum-Ra in the afterlife, at which time he would lift the *zŝzŝ*-flower and place himself "at the nose" of the Great Power (=lotus) while entering the Island of Fire (=Fields of Ra; Table 1, l. 27).

Although the ankh is occasionally employed as a support for the sema-taui motif, as may be observed at Karnak and the Ptolemaic temples of Sobek and Haroeris at Kom Ombo (Baines 1975, Figures 138, 139 and 142), the symbol normally serves as the central and therefore focal element of the motif. Early executions of the sema-taui often place a lotus flower at the summit of the central pillar with Horus and Seth as flanking elements of the central shaft. The symbol varies, however, with respect to the terminal feature of the motif and the twin deities that support the central axis, especially after the turn of the second millennium. In many instances the blossom is replaced with either a pharaoh's cartouche (Figures 3b and 4a; (Baines 1975, Figures 133, 153 and 165)), the realistic image of a king (Figure 4b; (Baines 1975, Figures 128, 146b, 154, 155 and 166)) or and occasionally by Horus (Baines 1975, Figures 140 and 162) or Egypt's divine Ibis, Thoth (Baines 1975, Figures 128, 151 and 155). In later depictions, the sema-taui is sustained by Horus and Thoth or twin Hapy figures (anthropomorphic gods that personify the Nile River's annual inundations; Figures 3b and 4a,b; (Baines 1975, Figures 51, 52, 76, 88, 133, 153 and 154; Gillispie and Dewachter 1987, vol. 3, pl. 60.2)).

A derived and more common rendering of the sema-taui motif during the New Kingdom is observed on the hypostyle at Karnak of Seti I and his famous son, Ramesses II (1279–1212 BCE; Figure 4b), where an anthropomorphized image of Horus (=Khonsu to worshippers of Amen at Karnak) and Thoth, an ibis-headed figure, pull the vegetative ties of the sema-taui's central stalk. Although the lotus blossom of the central axis is now replaced by a kneeling image of Ramesses, we note that the young king's shoulder and chest are decorated with a blue-pigmented, petaloid lotus collar, as was the practice of interring pharaohs during this age (Schweinfurth 1884), ostensibly to identify a deceased king with his immortal lotus aspect in the afterlife. A similar image that decorates the thrones of Ramesses II inside the temple entrance at Luxor presents a sema-taui sign with twin Hapy figures (Figure 4a), these figures suggesting a Pyramid Text passage that identifies the Nile River's annual floodwaters (here personified by Hapy) as the unifier of the two lands of Ra (Table 1, l. 28). This particular inscription identifies the two lands as the heavens and watery netherworld of the Nile instead of Upper and Lower Egypt, suggesting a dual meaning to the sema-taui motif.

Figure 4. Union symbol (sema-taui) and ankh. (**a**) The cartouche of Ramesses II replaces a lotus flower on the central shaft of the sema-taui motif in Thebes. Twin gods (Hapy figures) that personify the floodwaters of the Nile River grasp the lotus and papyrus stems to support the axis mundi. Luxor, 13th c. BCE. (**b**) A kneeling image of Ramesses II replaces the sema-taui's lotus blossom in Thebes. Karnak, 13th c. BCE. (**c**) A winged disk that rises on an aquatic column in the Tomb of Ramesses IX is clearly symbolic of a lotus blossom instead of a solar orb. Twin cartouches of Ramesses IX ascend the lotus stalk and transform themselves into the living image of the solar/floral structure, inside of which is observed the image of the resurrected king as Harpocrates (personified Horus). The floral disk supports two cobras that dangle a triad of ankh symbols. Thebes, Valley of the Kings, Tomb of Ramesses IX, 12th c. BCE. (**d**) Egyptians believed their kings were reborn as lotus blossoms in the afterlife. Thebes, Valley of the Kings, Tomb of Tutankhamen, 14th c. BCE (Cairo Museum).

The ribbed column (Figures 3a and 4a) and platform of the motif supports a collection of heraldic symbols, marking yet another departure from early conventions in lotus symbolism. Among these symbols is observed a stylized childish image of Ramesses as an alternative Egyptian symbol of eternal life: a shen loop (a rope that is tied at its base with two loose ends) flanked by two dangling serpents (uraei), each upholding a shen loop. As various historians have noted, the practice of placing a king's hieroglyphic birth or throne names inside a shen loop (the so-called 'cartouche' when elongated to accommodate the king's written name) identifies the pharaoh as both a god and possessor of eternal life (Wilkinson 1992, pp. 193, 195; Lurker 1980, p. 38), while the supportive shaft ostensibly symbolizes the lotus-god's phallus and stalk.

4. The Shen Sign and King's Cartouche as Symbols of a Lotus Bud and Cosmic Egg

Much like the ankh, the coiled rope that forms a shen loop is conventionally rendered in blue, while the enclosed solar orb is typically rendered in yellow, orange or red. Two shen loops are conventionally held by the talons of either Horus, the blue falcon, or Khepri, the ever-ascendant, blue-winged scarab beetle, and thus conventionally present a triad of golden disks: one exposed disk upon the head of the bird or beetle and two enclosed disks that are held in talons beside the creatures (Figure 1c,d). Since these symbols are often associated with ankh symbols and paired lotus buds and blossom, we are justified in interpreting this motif in terms of a recurrent lotus flower rather than a recurrent sun, for Egyptians often portrayed an open lotus blossom between two buds in order to symbolize the natural three-day blooming cycle of lotus blossoms (Figure 1c,d; (Emboden 1989a, 1989b; McDonald 2002; Wiersema 1988)).

We observe in the tomb of Ramesses IX a pair of uraei (divine cobras) that dangle from a pillared winged disk and support ankh symbols or shen loops (Figure 4c, also Figures 1d and 3a); here, the shen may be envisaged as a bud-like incubus from which Egypt's celebrated sun gods—as a blue-petalled lotus, blue-winged god (note the aforementioned quotation from Denderah) or resurrected king—arise in the Fields of Ra. To confirm this interpretation, we need only refer to coffin inscriptions that speak recurrently of Horus, an earthly manifestation of Ra, hatching out of this cosmic egg within the "Isle of Flame" (i.e., the emergent hillock of On) to take the form of a blue-winged disk (Table 1, l. 29). Other coffin inscriptions associate the egg with Egypt's divine ibis (Thoth) or another avian god, the "Great Cackler" (Geb, a divine goose; Table 1, l. 30), the two birds sharing company with Osiris-Ra in the Nile's divine marshlands. In like manner, Horus is identified as a lord of eternity who "sprouts forth" from the egg in a watery abyss (Table 1, l. 31), implying that the egg and lotus bud are equivalent entities.

The oft-neglected connection between the shen loop and inscribed cartouches (shenu) connote, therefore, a close relationship between the everlasting life of Nefertum's primordial phallus, blossom, and solar/floral "eye of Ra" and the eternal recurrence of Egypt's celebrated dynasts. The emergence of Horus from his cosmic egg (or lotus bud) symbolizes the birth of a new king and dynasty on one level and yet also the passage of a king's soul (ka) to the paradisal Fields of Ra, the former concept applying to a famous rendering of Tutankhamen arising from a lotus corolla as an infant (Figure 4d) and the latter relating to the aforementioned tomb painting of Ramesses IX, on which the king's cartouche ascends the phallus of Osiris-Ra to assume his personified identity as Harpocrates (Horus) within a pillared winged disk (lotus flower; Figure 4c). This interpretation of the cartouche explains why the centralized lotus prop of the sema-taui on Chephren's throne (Figure 2c) is equivalent to the vegetative support of a king's cartouche or the king himself (Figure 4a,b). In both cases, the divinity and everlasting status of the king is symbolized by the eternal recurrence of the lotus. This general concept shares a close parallel in Mesopotamia, where a sacral lotus-tree is similarly identified with kingship, both generally and specifically (Annus 2002, p. 156; Kramer 1974; Parpola 1993).

5. Homologous Features of the Egyptian Lotus and the Fertile Crescent's Sacred Trees

While acknowledging that the ankh emblem derives from, or at least shares a close symbolic association with the sema-taui symbol, in that both images symbolize the lotus plant and immortal life, it is notable that the latter sign shares essentially all the standard features with sacred tree images in the Near East after 1500 BCE. Sacral trees of the Levant and Mesopotamia usually exhibit: (1) a smooth and cylindrical central axis, (2) a terminal palmette, many bearing blue-pigmented appendages, (3) a surrounding configuration of smaller palmettes or campanulate floral motifs, and (4) a series or cluster of supple, lateral stems that tie directly to the plant's central shaft (Figure 5a–d; (Frankfort 1939, pl. 33; Giovino 2007, Figures 1–3, 13–18; Goodyear 1887, pl. 24; Jones [1856] 1995, pl. 15)). Such features constitute classic Neo-Assyrian trees of Ashurnasirpal at Nimrud (Figure 5b) and those that decorate the blue gates of Ishtar's temple in Babylon (Figure 6a,b), where the knotted stalks and terminal palmettes are linked by lotus buds. The resulting bud-and-blossom motif that links the canopies of three sacral trees clearly follows the recurrent pattern of associating lotus palmettes with sacral tree palmettes, as proposed by McDonald (2002, Figure 2a–d). Almost identical iconic trees are encountered on cylinder seals and early Assyrian murals at Kar Tikulti Ninurta that date from 1500–1200 BCE (Frankfort 1970, pp. 135–37).

The use of pigments in the execution of the early Assyrian trees at Kar Tikulti Ninurta as well as ceramics from Ashur (Andrae 1925) follow a similar color formula on Ishtar's gates of Babylon (Figure 6a,b) by presenting the palmette appendages as blue, the sepals as either blue or green, and the central disk as yellow. The use of pigments in the execution of early Assyrian trees at Kar Tikulti Ninurta as well as ceramics from Ashur (Andrae 1925) consistently depict palmette appendages as blue and/or white, the sepals as either blue or green and the central disk as yellow. The intensity of these colors invariably fades over the course of time and almost disappears completely on pieces in museum settings, but the full vitality of these color patterns is preserved on glazed bricks that Nebuchadnezzar II used to construct one of several 'gates' (walled portals) that led to the inner chambers of a principal temple complex in Babylon around 575 BCE. This structure was elaborated during the pinnacle of Neo-Babylonian influences over Mesopotamia and the Levant, during an age in which Nebuchadnezzar held Levantine tribes captive in the city, as is well documented in Hebraic records. The famous king dedicated his bright blue gate to the Babylonian 'Mistress of Heaven,' Ishtar, and covered its façade with an eclectic array of radial and lateral portrayals of the Nilotic blue lotus, a natural and often prominent denizen of marshy enclaves of the Tigris and Euphrates Rivers. Framed within variations on the Egyptian lotus bud-and-blossom motif (Figure 6b), depictions of mythic animals that represented Adad, Marduk and the Goddess established a mythical ambience for the practice of religion and kingship. The largest and most prominent representations of the stalked water lilies (Figure 6a) conserve the basic features of earlier Neo-Assyrian that are observed in the chambers of Ashurnasirpal II at Nimrud during the 9th c. BCE (Figure 5b), but with the unique Babylonian nuance of linking the terminal flowers of each tree with a running bud-and-blossom motif. Nebuchadnezzar's conventional use of pigments clearly follows a precise pattern that reflects the morphology of the Nilotic lotus (Figure 1c,d Figure 4c,d and Figure 7d) and mismatches with the natural coloration of date palm features (cream, green and brown). Interestingly, the aforementioned iconic trees share homologous characteristics with related symbolic trees from Persia and Central Asia during the 1st millennium BCE, as observed on a Scythian pectoral of gold from the same time period at Ziwiye, Iran (Figure 5c), which produces alternating lotus buds, blossoms and fruits.

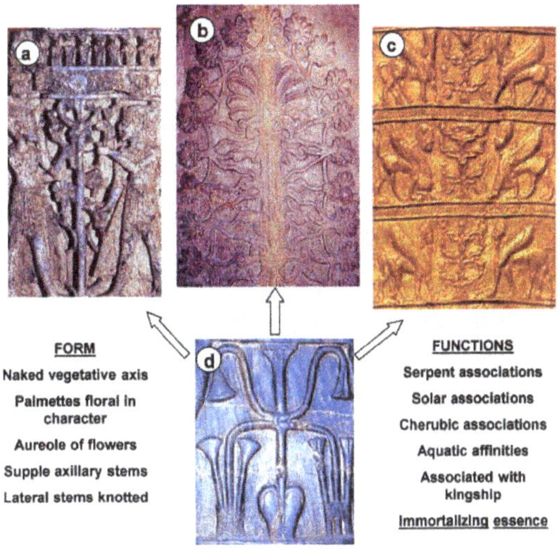

Figure 5. Shared features of the sema-taui symbol and Middle Eastern tree of life. (**a**) A Phoenician tree of life that was excavated from the Mesopotamian temple of Ashurnasirpal exhibits prominent Egyptian features: blue lotus palmettes, a blue-winged solar disk, and sun-bearing cobras. Yet the central stalk displays features of Mesopotamian trees of life: lateral palmettes, trefoil at the apex of the trunk, and corniculate lateral branches. Iraq, Nimrud, 9th c. BCE. (**b**) One of 170 sacral trees uncovered among the ruins of Ashurnasirpal II. Iraq, Nimrud, 9th c. BCE. (**c**) A series of three Perso-Aryan lotus trees of life terminate in a lotus blossom, solar motif, and lotus berry. The lateral branches of each tree support a succession of lotus buds, blossoms, and fruits. Chimeric guardians of the trees exhibit the combined aspects of a bull, lion, human, and eagle, suggesting the biblical features of a cherub. Iran, Ziwiye, 8–7th c. BCE (Metropolitan Museum). (**d**) Early Egyptian sema-taui motifs apparently served as a prototype to sacral tree imagery in the Fertile Crescent since both motifs exhibit a central stalk, terminal palmette, supple lateral stems that tie off to the plant's central column, and surrounding palmettes. Tree of life motifs similarly graced the backs and side panels of Mesopotamia and Levantine thrones and couches, usually as decorative ivory pieces (Barnett 1982, p. 25, pls. 18a,b, 52a,c; Crowfoot and Crowfoot 1938, p. 2; Parrot 1961, p. 155). Throne of Chephren, Giza, 26th c. BCE (Cairo Museum).

The famous blue gates of Ishtar at Babylon portray lotiform trees of life without a hint of ambiguity, but with Egyptian symbolic elements that now reflect the nuances of Mesopotamian iconographic craftsmanship. An interlinking series of water lilies that encompass the interlinking, stout trees conserve the ancient Egyptian bud-and-blossom motif by alternating flowers with opposing bud and blossom elements with flowers comprised of opposing full-blown flowers (Figure 6b). A running 'tendril' of water lily peduncles creates a continuous chain of floral motifs. This stylized composition is then reflected in a series of linked sacral trees at the center of the gates, in what may therefore be deemed the symbol par excellence of the widely celebrated goddess. The stout trunks are surmounted by a vertical configuration of three superimposed lotus tridents, the upper of which displays a bright radiate display of petals (Figure 6a). This common exhibition of three flowers likely represents that standard three-day duration of water lily anthesis. Between each of the stacked flowers is observed a tridentate lotus bud, whose drooping stalks create a standard symbol of everlasting life in Egypt and throughout the Fertile Crescent: recurrent water lily buds and blossoms. The sacral tree trunks emerge from a water line in the lower register and exhibit the familiar collars around the trunks, which conventionally serve as a point of connection between sacral trees and water lily blossom aureoles (Figure 5b,c).

Figure 6. Details of Ishtar's gate. Babylon, ca. 575 BCE. (**a**) A row of lotiformed sacral trees with collared trunks and three terminal corollas are linked by stalked buds, connoting the symbolic theme of eternal recurrence, i.e., immortal life (Right Perspective Images/Alamy Stock Photo). (**b**) The linked trees are framed on four sides by variations on lotus bud and blossom motifs (MuseoPics-Paul Williams/Alamy Stock Photo).

Although various art historians have acknowledged Nilotic water lily imagery shares a common origin with sacral tree imagery (Coomaraswamy 1935; Danthine 1937; Goodyear 1887, 1891; Jones [1856] 1995, pp. 22–23, 28–29; McDonald 2002), modern commentators have yet to recognize an apparent relationship between the tethering of cosmic tree pillars with the use of water lily peduncles and knots to support the Egyptian lotus. Some historians have identified the lateral tethers as 'ribbons' or 'festoons' made of fabric (Garlick 1918; Giovino 2007, pp. 24, 87–88, 118), while others suggest these features represent watery tributaries and irrigation canals (Andrae 1925, p. 5). A less convincing interpretation identifies the knotted ropes as whirlpools (Porada 1945). Since a series of floral palmettes are obviously linked to the central pillared palmette with these supposed 'ribbons,' there is ample reason to ascertain these features as supple flowering stalks. And since the Egyptians employed the same feature in supporting their lotus stalks, in the symbolic context of supporting a regenerative life force, and often in association with winged disks and deities, we are obliged to recognize direct Egyptian influences over Assyrian sacral tree imagery.

Near Eastern sacral trees are recurrently associated with a solar motif (winged disk), just like their Egyptian homologues. And as noted by many authors and emphasized by McDonald (2002) and Parpola (1993), the Egyptian lotus and Near Eastern tree of life share close iconographic associations with winged and wingless serpents, lions, eagles, goats, humans, and bulls, often under the aura of an Egyptian-styled winged disk.

6. Roles of the Lotus in Funerary and Libation Ceremonials

Since images of Mesopotamian and Levantine sacral trees are usually encountered within closely guarded sanctums of temples, it is abundantly clear that the symbol played a critical role in the practice of religion and the assumption of kingship. The same practice applies to the ankh and sema-taui signs among Egyptian temples and burial sites, and therefore compels us to question why these vegetation symbols share so many physical characteristics and functional roles in religious expression of the Nile and Fertile Crescent. Given the common occurrence of Egyptian symbols among Mesopotamian sites, including the ankh and sema-taui, there is no question that the artistic conventions of distant Egyptian communities were responsible for several developments in the evolution of sacral tree imagery. We have yet to explain, however, why so many successive societies employed lotus symbolism so frequently or why the palm tree and other Mesopotamian plant species played limited roles in Egyptian symbolism. Perhaps more importantly, we are bound to question why the lotus plant represented so many gods and goddesses in so many different times and places and how its form and function relates to cross-cultural conceptions of immortal life and aspirations to join the gods in the afterlife.

Although most references to the divine transformation of a king into a lotus flower apply to deceased individuals, there is also substantial evidence that a divine rite of passage to paradise involved a person's metaphorical transformation into a lotus flower in a ritualistic context. The transformational process and experiences were apparently performed within the inner sanctum of Egyptian temples. Various Egyptian textual sources that span 3000 years of pharaonic history, from the Old Kingdom to the Ptolemaic period, including the Pyramid Texts, Coffin Texts, and Book of the Dead (Table 1, l. 32), describe the consumption of the solar eye of Horus by means of a libation or sacramental food ceremony. Upon performing the rite, the consumer gains passage to the sun god's riparian Fields of Felicity. Imbibing the sun god's vitalizing and immortalizing efflux (often translated as "water," "oil," "ointment," or "drippings"; Table 1, l. 33; (Piankoff 1964, p. 42, pl. 5.47)) makes little sense if we consider the eye of Horus to be a solar orb, given that the god's eye arises from the Nile's aquatic underworld (Table 1, l. 34). Moreover, the Nilotic sun has nothing but a profound desiccating, if not lethal effect on inhabitants of the Nile River. On the other hand, the allusion seems sensible if we envisage the solar eye as a lotus flower, given that lotus flowers produce copious amounts of sweet-smelling nectar on their first day of anthesis (McDonald 2002; Schneider 1982; Wiersema 1988) to wash pollen grains off their insect visitors. Countless friezes and paintings suggest that the king imbibed a fluid that was identified with an "efflux" from the eye of Horus (Figure 1c,d), otherwise associated with the solar semen or seed of Osiris-Ra and Ra (Figure 7a). Perhaps this is why the Pyramid Texts refer to the 'eye of Horus' as the sweet-smelling, sweet-tasting, blossom of Isis (i.e., blue lotus; Table 1, l. 35).

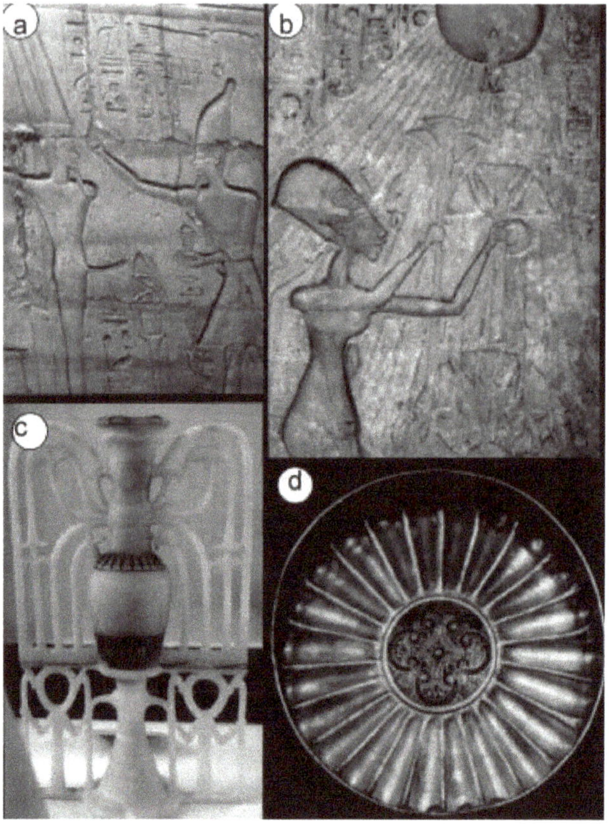

Figure 7. Lotus extracts in funerary rituals. (**a**) A lotus-libation scene at Luxor suggests that the king partook of a libation that was identified with the semen of the sun/lotus god, Min (an aspect of Amen). Karnak, 13th c. BCE. (**b**) The famous heretical sun worshipper, Akhenaten, enjoys the breath of eternal life (ankh to nose) as he upholds lotus blossoms to the sun during a libation ritual. El Amarna, 14th century BCE (Cairo Museum). (**c**) The contents of unguent vessels in the tombs of Egyptian kings were often identified with lotus stalks and flowers, life (ankh motifs), and everlasting sovereignty over Upper and Lower Egypt (sema-taui symbol). Thebes, Valley of the Kings, Tomb of Tutankhamen, 14th c. BCE (Cairo Museum). (**d**) Libation cups and goblets in Egypt and the Middle East were often decorated with, or depicted as, lotus blossoms. Tanis, Tomb of Psusennes I, 10th c. BCE (Cairo Museum).

Lotus nectar may well have been the substance to which the mythology of On alludes in a reference to the invigorating semen of the sun-god Nefertum, as we observe the king in reliefs at Luxor and elsewhere partaking of an ithyphallic god's ejaculum as it spills over lotus flowers and libation vases (Figure 7a; (Gillispie and Dewachter 1987, vol. 3, pls. 36.5, 36.6, 47.1)). Similar images occur throughout Egypt, and clearly relate to the ubiquitous associations of lotus stalks with libation vases and urns that appear first during the Old Kingdom (2649–2150 BCE) at Saqqara during around 2500 BCE. Lotus libation scenes only increase in frequency during the Middle and New Kingdoms (ca. 2050–1100 BCE) at Thebes, Abu Simbel and Abydos, and are encountered no less frequently at Kom Ombo, Edfu and Meroe from 300–100 BCE. According to various textual sources, this rite allowed priests to revive and refresh themselves with truth (maat), wisdom, and joy ((Piankoff 1968, p. 46); Table 1, l. 36).

A more personal and detailed account of a libation ceremony is described in a relatively late Demotic text (3rd c. CE; (Betz 1986, PDM xiv. 1–92)) that describes a young initiate's experience of ecstatic exhilaration upon drinking the sacramental beverage. The initiate relates that he is transported to the primeval waters and netherworld of the gods after transforming himself into a ram-lion-lotus god known as Amun. Proclaiming the secrets of the underworld have been revealed to him and that the libation has opened his eyes to the divine light of a lotus flower, his soul ascends from the netherworld into a celestial sphere of light, upon which he shouts, "Oh Lotus, open to me heaven in its breadth and height! Bring me the light which is pure" (Betz 1986, PDM xiv. 862–65). Euphoric experiences of such type lend credence to the perennial hypothesis that psychoactive principles of water lilies were possibly employed as a shamanic medium (Emboden 1979, 1981, 1989a, 1989b; McDonald 2002; McDonald and Stross 2012).

Egyptian libation scenes are commonly observed on temple and tomb walls, papyri, thrones, and coffins, suggesting that drinking lotus nectar (or perhaps extracts of water lilies, as suggested by (Emboden 1989a, 1989b)) within the inner sanctums of Egyptian temples was as common in burial rituals as it was in daily life (Lange and Hirmer 1968, Figure 226; Gillispie and Dewachter 1987, vol. 3, pl. 15). Numerous lotiform libation cups and vases were unearthed, for example, from the tomb of King Tutankhamen (Lange and Hirmer 1968, pl. xxxiii), some alluding in script to the king's achievement of immortal life (Assaad and Kolos 1979, p. 32; Fox 1951, pl. 3). One such vessel is a long-stemmed alabaster drinking cup fashioned in the image of a lotus corolla (Desroches-Noblecourt 1989, Figure xxiia), while another common vessel type is an alabaster 'oil vase' fashioned as a sema-taui symbol (Figure 7c). The central axis of this receptacle is decorated with a lotus perianth, implying that the vessel contains the essence (or semen) of the floral eye of Horus. These vessels compare closely with libation lotus cups in a ritual scene on a golden shrine of King Tutankhamen and Queen Ankhesenamen, where the convivial couple is observed sharing a libation with lotus flowers and buds in their hands (Lange and Hirmer 1968, pl. xxxiii).

Only a few centuries later, in the Tomb of Psusennes at Tanis (11th c. BCE), we encounter a distinctive lotus vessel made of gold, but this particular cup bears all the features of a Mesopotamian vessel (Figure 7d). While it is difficult to say if the vessel was obtained as a gift or spoil of warfare, the four-cornered lotus motifs in the center and the fluted walls of the vessel match closely with libation implements and lotus-cup imagery at Nimrud, Iraq and throughout the Middle East. Since we observe numerous examples of libation scenes with lotus flowers at Edfu, Kom Ombo, and Philae during the later Ptolemaic and Greco-Roman periods, we can only conclude that lotus flowers played a central role in libation ceremonies for thousands of years.

7. Lotus-Libation Scenes in the Near East

Almost identical lotus-libation scenes are observed on ivory plaques and steles at Megiddo (Palestine) and Ras Shamra (Syria) from the 16th–13th centuries BCE (Loud 1939, pls. iv.2b, xxxii.160; Keel and Uehlinger 1998, p. 65, Figures 65, 67 and 68a; McDonald 2002, Figure 7b,c), and frequently so among friezes and art objects from the Near East, Mesopotamia and Persia during the first millennium BCE (McDonald 2002, Figure 7d; Mazar 1961, vol. 2, p. 270; Roaf 1998, p. 163; Strommenger 1964, Figures 194, 195 and 241). The ritual can also be linked indirectly to the cult of Yahweh during the age of Solomon (ca. 1000 BCE), for the stone sarcophagus of the Phoenician Ahiram of Byblos, a predecessor to the Phoenician builder of Yahweh's first temple in Jerusalem, Hiram of Tyre, portrays the king in the act of drinking a lotus libation (Mazar 1961, vol. 2, p. 143) while sitting on a seraphic/sphinx throne that matches closely with biblical descriptions of Solomon's "mercy seat." A lotus bud-and-blossom motif (an Egyptian symbol of immortal life) surrounds the lid of Hiram's casket.

We can be sure that the practices of Solomon's regional allies were not discouraged in Jerusalem during this historical era, for biblical records make clear that Yahweh's first temple was constructed in part for the benefit of Egyptian, Canaanite, and Middle Eastern gods and goddesses (I Kings 11: 4), despite prior prohibitions to such practices during the Mosaic age (Exodus 34: 11–13; Deuteronomy

16: 21; Judges 3: 7; 6: 25, 28; Jeremiah 44: 3–6). Like many kings of his day, Solomon accepted female concubines from distant lands to consummate peace accords with former or potential adversaries; since these consorts were not expected to renounce the religious traditions of their homelands, Solomon promoted the offering of incense and sacrifices to Astarte (Ishtar) of the Sidonians, Chemosh (=Shamash, a Mesopotamian sun god represented iconographically as an Egyptian winged disk above sacral tree motifs) of the Moabites, and Molech of the Ammonites (1 Kings 11: 5–8). Biblical records also indicate that Yahwists participated in the worship of various Near Eastern goddesses and their vegetative symbols during and shortly after Solomon's reign (Patai 1990, p. 32; Keel and Uehlinger 1998, p. 152; Wiggins 1993, p. 30; James 1966, p. 181), along with sacred prostitution in temple complexes (1 Kings 14: 23; 2 Kings 17: 10; 23: 5–7; Jeremiah 17: 1–2; Hosea 4: 12–13), all of which were practices employed by contemporaneous religions of Mesopotamia and the Levant.

Hebraic records acknowledge that Solomon, just prior to his temple's construction, accepted into his harem the daughter of an Egyptian pharaoh (1 Kings 3: 1; presumably an offspring of Psusennes), for whom altars were established on "high places" to honor the Egyptian pantheon. In Ezekiel's vision of Yahweh's first temple, worshippers wept for Tammuz at its northern gate (Ezekiel 8: 14) and bowed before the sun at the eastern gate while "putting the branch before their noses" (Ezekiel 8: 15–17). The latter allusion can only refer to the Egyptian and Mesopotamian practice of worshipping the sun while placing an aromatic lotus flower before the nose, as we encounter frequent portrayals of such practices on scarabs and ivory etchings in ancient Canaan (Keel and Uehlinger 1998, p. 86, Figure 107). Moreover, Hebraic devotions to Mesopotamia's famous god of aquatic vegetation, Tammuz (=Dumuzi of Sumeria), a close associate of the Mesopotamian sun god, Shamash of the Moabites, is of particular interest in this connection, because this god was recognized mythically as a guardian of the blue-leaved (=blue-petalled?) tree of life, the kiskanu plant of ancient Eridu and Ur (James 1966, pp. 8–10; Langdon 1914, pp. 30, 114; Langdon 1928; McDonald 2002). It is also noteworthy that Eridu is very close to the biblical garden East of Eden in the land of Ur and that Tammuz was the wife of Ishtar, the Mesopotamian equivalent to Astarte in Sidon, where Hiram built temples in her honor (Durdin-Robertson and Durdin-Robertson 1979, pp. 53, 126).

Around the age of Solomon, we are aware that the Assyrian "Myth of Adapa" was in circulation and that this tale recognized Tammuz and his close associate, Ningizzida, as the "Lord of the Good Tree" (Black et al. 1992, p. 138). This divine pair served as guardians to the gateway of heaven, in which role they thwarted the efforts of mortal men to attain immortality by tricking the human offspring of the god Enki, Adapa, the "seed of humankind" (the equivalent of biblical Adam; (James 1966, p. 72)), into passing up an opportunity to consume the food and water of the gods (presumably from the tree of life; (Pritchard 1969, p. 102)). Obviously, similar mythic themes are echoed in the book of Genesis.

8. The Hebraic Dimension

Numerous biblical scriptures allude to the erection of wooden idols and "pillars" known as asherim and mazzeboth in the Temple of Solomon to pay obeisance to the creators of the Ugaritic pantheon, El (Baal) and Asherah (1 Kings 15: 12–15; 19: 18; 2 Kings 10: 18–24; 2 Chronicles 15: 16; 33: 1–7). According to Hebrew tradition, these customs were outlawed by Moses after his epiphany on Mount Sinai (Exodus 34: 13; Deuteronomy 12: 2–3; 16: 21; Judges 3: 7; 6: 25–28), but the prophet's divine edicts proved futile in discouraging religious tolerance and polytheistic inclinations of his tribal associates and descendants. Biblical references to the erection of idols and asherim appear to relate to sacral tree worship since, from a scriptural and iconographic point of view, the 'poles' (mazzeboth) of Baal and 'pillars' (asherim) of Asherah (whose word-roots obviously share a common origin), were undoubtedly plant symbols (Wiggins 1993, pp. 14–15, 93–97) and must surely relate to pillared sacral tree motifs in archeological records of this day. Such practices were apparently shared by the Egyptians, insofar as the famous pharaoh, Rameses II, had a pillar dedicated to Asherah's daughter, Anat, at Beth Shean during the 13th c. BCE (Cassuto 1971, p. 65). Not only did the idolizing of asherim relate to the practice of "tree worship" (Deuteronomy 16: 21; 1 Kings 14: 23; Hosea 4: 12–13), but the erection of these effigies is described in terms of a "planting" (Deuteronomy 16: 9) and their destruction as an "uprooting" (Micah 5: 14) or a "hewing down" (Exodus 34: 13; Judges 6: 25, 28, 30; 1 Kings 15: 13; 2 Kings 23: 14; 2 Chronicles 14: 2–4; 15: 16).

Art historians are justified in drawing a direct link between the proto- and stereotypical images of Near Eastern fertility goddesses and stylized images of the sacral tree (Keel and Uehlinger 1998, pp. 199, 234, Figures 9–72, 214, 215 and 233a,b); or indeed, McDonald (2002) goes so far as to identify Asherah as a lotus goddess (Patai 1990, p. 59, pls. 13, 15, 16, 27), if not the personification of the Nilotic lotus. Not surprisingly, this goddess and her daughter, Anat, as well as Kadesh (Mazar 1961, vol. 2, p. 66; Patai 1990, pl. 25) and Astarte/Ishtar (Patai 1990, p. 59), exhibit hairstyles and the general aspect of Egyptian goddesses and are frequently associated with lotus flowers and serpents, which had formerly and contemporaneously related iconographically to standard images of Isis, Nephthys and Hathor of ancient Egypt. As earlier noted, these same goddesses were assimilated into the Egyptian pantheon long before the age of Solomon. Because these effigies are conventionally executed in a columnar form and occasionally wear lotus crowns, historians justifiably draw a direct connection between the goddess Asherah and the Canaanite/Hebraic asherim. Moreover, many of these figurines are charred, recalling Hebraic records that recommend the burning of false idols as an act of penitence (2 Chronicles 15: 16).

Given that the Temple of Solomon was constructed by a Canaanite king to serve a host of Egyptian and Near Eastern gods and goddesses, it should come as little surprise that Solomon's house of worship shared features with temple constructions in Egypt and the Middle East. Detailed descriptions of the temple in the biblical books of Kings and Chronicles make clear that the rooms were filled with images that relate to the Egyptian lotus and sacral trees of the Near East. Solomon's temple entrance was framed, for example, with two large pillars whose capitals were decorated with "lily-work" (1 Kings 7: 16–22, 26; 2 Chronicles 4: 5). We can rest assured that the floral designs were based on the Egyptian water lily because the Hebrew word for the flowery capitals, shushan (=susa, shushan-eduth, shoshannim, shoshanah, (Moldenke and Moldenke 1952, pp. 41–43, 154; Walker 1957, p. 226)), is clearly cognate with Coptic shoshen and Arabic sousan, deriving from an Egyptian word for the Nile's blue water lily, sheshen (Anthes 1959; Darby et al. 1977, vol. 2, p. 633; Wilkinson 1992, p. 121). Predictably, the hieroglyph for sheshen, a logograph, is a lotus shoot. In all likelihood, pillars with lotus capitals shared a symbolic relationship with the famous asherim. In this same connection, Coomaraswamy (1935, p. 104) suggests the pillared lotus capitals of Egypt and Greece, with symbols of Heaven above and Earth below, are essentially "cognate in form and coincident in reference." And to be sure, an image that marks the entrance to the Judaic holy of holies is of paramount importance.

In addition to the vegetative symbolism in Solomon's temple, Near Eastern animal symbolism associated with sacral trees also comes into play. The antechamber of Solomon's temple contained, for example, a giant bronze basin that bore Nilotic lotus petal engravings on its outer rim and was supported by a base formed by twelve bronze bull figures. Triplets of bovine forms that faced the four cardinal points of the cosmos (I Kings 7: 23–26) suggest that early Yahwists in Jerusalem held little regard for the admonitions and warnings of Moses in the book of Exodus. Since biblical records state specifically that the bronze basin symbolized the sea, and we know that Phoenician traditionalists identified the goddess Asherah as a sea goddess and her consort, Baal, as a bull (Cassuto 1971, p. 58), it seems clear that Solomon's bath was fashioned in the image of mythic and iconographic themes that were borrowed from Ugaritic associates in Tyre (Keel and Uehlinger 1998, p. 169).

It also seems more than coincidental that the most prominent images in Solomon's sanctuary were those of the cherubim, a mythical class of heavenly creature that Yahweh appointed as the protector of Eden's tree of immortal life (Gen 3: 24). Images of these creatures dominated the inner confines of Solomon's temple, including the Holy of Holies, where the ark of the covenant was guarded from the outside world. Solomon received the voice of Yahweh directly from this mysterious container (Patai 1990, p. 82), not unlike Moses before him (Numbers 7: 89) and as Ezekiel soon thereafter (Ezekiel 10: 5). The Book of Kings emphasizes the fact that these creatures were rendered large in scale and that they touched their outstretched wings (1 Kings 6: 26–27; 2 Chronicles 3: 7–12), suggesting the Egyptian practice of portraying Isis and Nephthys, the sisters of Osiris-Ra, with their wings held together on the 'arks' of Horus and Egyptian pharaohs (Gillispie and Dewachter 1987, vol. 1, pl. 11.4; vol. 2, pl. 35.7; vol. 3, pl. 32.5; vol. 4, pl. 24.2), which were paraded around temple grounds during religious holidays. Equivalent motifs are found among Levantine ivory plaques (Frankfort 1970, Figure 378). Other scriptures note that cherubs occurred on blue curtains that shrouded the Holy of Holies (2 Chronicles 3: 14)—a feature dating from the Mosaic age, when the ark of the covenant was shielded in the tents of nomadic Hebrew tribes (Exodus 26: 1; Numbers 7: 89)—and on the ark of the covenant itself (2 Chronicles 5: 7), as well as the mysterious "mercy seat" depicted on the ark (Exodus 25: 17–22; 37: 6–9; (Mazar 1961, vol. 1, p. 162)).

Although the latter verses do not specify the physical nature of the cherub, Ezekiel's vision describes this creature in terms of a chimera that bore the "faces" (aspects) of an eagle, lion, bull, and man (Ezekiel 1: 4–11; 10: 14) or simply of a man and lion (Ezekiel 41: 18–23). Such descriptions call to mind, of course, either an Egyptian sphinx or the two massive creatures that stood guard at the entrance of Ashurnasirpal's palace (Layard 1849, vol. 2, p. 464; Mazar 1961, vol. 3, p. 159; Roaf 1998, p. 163; Ward 1910) and conventionally before the lotus-flowering boughs of cosmic trees in the Middle East, as observed on Ziwiye's lotus-trees of life (Figure 5c) and the armrests of Levantine thrones (McDonald 2002, Figure 7b). At Til Barsip (Tell Ahmar), a similar creature with blue wings is followed by a priest that upholds a blue-petalled water lily (Parrot 1961, Figure 110). Since these figures are obviously based in part on Egypt's ancient image of a sphinx and this creature's close lotus associations, we are given to identify biblical cherubs as the chimeric forms that flank lotiform trees of life, usually in pairs, throughout the Near and Middle East (Frankfort 1970, Figures 187, 196, 218, 224, 380, 381, 391).

9. Felling the Asherim

The use of lotus and cherub imagery in the temple of Yahweh, along with the worship of vegetative asherim, suggests that Hebrew communities likely employed sacral tree imagery to the same extent as their historical associates in Assyria, Babylon, and Phoenicia. Such customs came to an end in Judah, however, during the reign of Josiah (ca. 620 BCE), at which time prohibitions against the manufacture and use of graven images were more strictly enforced (II Kings 23: 3–20). The historical reason for this radical change in tradition is still a matter of debate, but the Old Testament is consistent on the issue. In the original establishment of Mosaic law, it was stipulated that Yahweh would allow no other gods be held before him, and that the Creator's protection of Hebrew tribes against the onslaughts of Amorites, Canaanites, Hittites, and Midianites would be withdrawn if they continued to pay homage to foreign gods (Exodus 34: 11–13; Leviticus 26: 1; Judah 6: 25, 28). The same general terms applied during the 7th c. BCE reformations of Josiah, and thus required of Hebrew communities the abandonment of former religious practices. Paradoxically, the enforcement of Mosaic laws resulted in the removal and destruction of the magical serpent-rod (nehustan) of Aaron and Moses (2 Kings 18: 4) "from high places." That Hebrew communities would continue to hallow Mosaic doctrine and yet destroy one of the patriarch's most significant possessions is of considerable interest, in that it demonstrates that post-exilic Hebrews were historically ambivalent to aspects of their past, some of which were deemed sacred and others profane, at least in terms of post-exilic Hebraic perspectives on Near Eastern history.

The destruction of Moses' brazen serpent is of particular relevance to the present discussion on two counts; first, the implement was likely Egyptian in origin, given that the priests of the pharaoh employed the same sort of staff when they matched their powers of magic against the powers of Moses (Exodus 7: 8–20); and second, the Egyptian staff was likely associated with the "lotus-scepter of Ra" (Piankoff 1974, spell 1090), since Egyptian kings and priests frequently upheld a lotus staff that was encoiled by a divine cobra during mortuary and religious rites (Budge [1931] 1970, p. 166; Lange and Hirmer 1968, pl. li; El-Mallakh and Bianchi 1980, p. 44). These images relate, no doubt, to the habit of associating Horus with a lotus flower and serpent (as noted in the aforementioned inscription at Denderah; Table 1, l. 37; (McDonald 2002)). In this connection, it is interesting that biblical records never state explicitly that the rod of Aaron was inherently evil, but that Jews had sinned by presenting offerings directly to the staff. This particular detail compels us to wonder if the destruction of the asherim resulted primarily from the worship of false idols instead of an aversion to lotus-tree symbolism.

However strong the resistance to Canaanite idols and symbolism during Josiah's reforms may have been, there are no overt or even implicit biblical prohibitions to the traditional use of lotus symbolism. This is somewhat surprising because the plant was widely employed as the principal symbol of many prohibited gods and goddesses of Egypt, Canaan, and Mesopotamia. Similarly, we encounter many negative references to the act of tree worship and idolatry in the Bible, but no direct references against the associated practice of libation ceremonies per se. While it is stated that the burning of incense and the pouring of libations in honor of the "Queen of Heaven" (Astarte/Anat) was sinful (Jeremiah 44: 14–22), it is abundantly clear that similar practices played an important role in Judaic ritual following the exile in Egypt. For, had not Jacob offered libations before a sacred pillar in pre-Mosaic times (Genesis 35: 14)? And had not members in the tribe of Moses celebrated similar practices in front of the ark of the covenant (Exodus 25: 29; 2 Chronicles 5: 5)?

During the advent of the post-exilic period, it is noteworthy that the famous Persian dynast, Cyrus (Koresh), was glorified by the Jews on account of his role in releasing the Jews bondage in Babylon and the repatriation of Jerusalem's cherished libation vessels (Ezra 1: 7–11). Cyrus was therefore promoted to the exalted status of an "anointed one" (messiah) of Yahweh (Isaiah 45: 1), ostensibly placing him on equal footing with Jesse, David, and Solomon. This tribute seems exceedingly generous when we consider that Cyrus did not worship Yahweh in Persia, but probably paid allegiance to Ahura Mazda, the creator of the Zoroastrian pantheon. We can be sure that Cyrus worshipped Ahura Mazda, for Cyrus had Median ancestry and sired children that bore the names of Gathic (Zoroastrian) personages: Hystaspes/Vistaspa and Atossa/Hutaosa. Moreover, Zoroastrian fire altars have been found among the ruins of Pasargade. That Hebrew communities would chastise all outsiders that held a god before their own and yet recognize a Perso-Aryan dynast as a divine personage seems to demonstrate, once again, a certain degree of compromise and ambivalence regarding the application of reformation doctrines and foreign religious practices in post-exilic Judah.

In later days, pseudepigraphal works also make reference to libation ceremonies, as evidenced by a hymn from the Odes to Solomon (number 11), which refers to a plant of the Lord that "spilt" its holy spirit and its "living" and "speaking" waters, making Solomon drunk with knowledge and filling his nostrils with the aroma of the Lord (Barnstone 1984, p. 273). Such reports appear to echo the aforementioned Egyptian notion of imbibing truth (maat) from the waters that spill from the eyes of Horus, a concept that is portrayed iconographically by streaming ankh symbols. Another song refers to a sweet cup of milk as the delight and "Son" of the Lord; those who drink of this cup are near his right hand, the traditional locus of Yahweh's tree of life (Barnstone 1984, p. 279).

It is of considerable interest, therefore, that before the last vestiges of pharaonic Egypt were eclipsed by religious and cultural traditions of Semitic origin (i.e., Christianity and later Islam) around the 2nd c. CE, vestiges of Egypt's traditional habits in ritual and symbolism persisted in a syncretistic manner for several centuries. The earliest known visual impressions of the Christian cross and tree of life derive from Coptic traditionalists along the Nile River around 200 CE and reveal a nascent school of Christian artistic expression that continues to borrow conservatively from ancient Egyptian lotus imagery and symbolism. An exemplary stele from the second century associates the cross of Christ with the Greek letters alpha and omega, a Mediterranean symbol for immortal life, and thus indicates growing European influences over Nilotic culture (Figure 8). While the symbolic relationship between the cross, tree of life and Greek letters is biblical, art historians have yet to acknowledge that a five-membered palmette that surmounts the cross derives from lotus blossom imagery and clearly establishes a transition between Egypt's traditional past and its Christian future. We note that the same five-membered perianth reappears in a radial configuration on either side of the cross, each being placed within the loop of the ankh symbols (or crux ansata = 'cross with handle'), precisely where Egyptians had traditionally placed the lotus flower (Figure 3a). In this case the two ankhs assume a quasi-personified aspect by wearing Christian robes and upholding two additional crosses and stylized grape leaves. The latter vegetative motif relates, of course, to scriptural passages that equate Christ as the grapevine of life (John 15: 1, 4–5), much as his blood is equated with wine during celebrations of the Eucharist, the imbibement of which confers immortality in the afterlife. Hence the ancient Egyptian ankh symbol, now the Latin crux ansata, was identified with the Messiah, the sacrificial cross, the Nilotic lotus, the blood of Christ (i.e., grape leaf as the source of wine), the tree of life and related concepts of attaining eternal life. The practice of the eucharist may well have seemed consonant during this age with earlier performances of lotus-libation rituals in ancient Egypt, as they both were esteemed as religious expression of the highest order and apparently served a similar religious purpose, i.e., achieving immortal life. Such possibilities must be considered hypothetical, however, until connections between the Christian concepts of the tree of life and the Nilotic lotus are explored more rigorously in both written and iconographic records from Egypt's Christian dawning. A key to such inquiries will hinge, to be sure, on a more complete understanding of the time-tested role of water lilies in libation ceremonies in ancient Egypt, Mesopotamia and the Levant.

Figure 8. Lotus, ankh, and Coptic cross. Early Christian communities in Egypt symbolized the cross of Christ with their traditional ankh symbol. Note that the cross of Jesus—here identified with the Greek letters alpha and omega—supports a five-petaled palmette, radial views of which are observed within the "handle" (the Egyptian shen loop) of the crux ansata. The quasi-personified ankh signs, apparently emblematic of Christ himself, wear robes and uphold crosses and dangling grape leaves. Cairo, 3rd c. (Coptic Museum).

10. Discussion

Mythic and artistic themes that relate to an immortalizing plant of the gods are shared throughout Egypt, the Levant and Mesopotamia. While one school of thought maintains that the biblical tree of life bears no direct relation to sacral tree imagery in Mesopotamia (Black et al. 1992, p. 171; Parpola 1993) and another admits to historical connections between mythic tree of life motifs in Egypt, the Mediterranean and Mesopotamia (James 1966), resolution of these competing views requires coherent arguments that explain both how and why so many distant human populations came to share so many mythic and iconographic conventions.

A comprehensive consideration of lotus symbolism in ancient Egypt, the Levant and Mesopotamia, in light of the plant's unique biological attributes and behaviors, serves to accentuate the profound and influential roles this iconic plant once played in early developments of ritual and religious expression on an international basis. We have long been aware that the Nilotic lotus pervaded and dominated iconographic and mythic records of ancient Egypt from 2500 BCE to the early centuries of the common era, and that the plant served as a symbol for living creation and the everlasting life of the sun, solar deities and pharaohs. But the degree to which closely related developments of lotus symbolism in the Middle East borrowed from, or paralleled those of ancient Egypt from around 1500 BCE is poorly explored. While less definitive evidence suggests that the plant played a critical role in mythic and religious traditions in the Tigris-Euphrates Valleys around 2500 BCE (McDonald 2002), the abrupt and abundant appearances of Egyptian lotus imagery among important Levantine urban centers around 1500 BCE, especially with respect to carved ivory decorations on thrones, aristocratic furniture and temple walls, seems to anticipate the widespread adoption of Egypt-inspired lotus symbolism on large scales in the guise of iconographic 'sacral trees' at Kar Tikulti Ninurta of Mesopotamia around 1200 BCE. The latter specimens exhibit features that are clearly homologous with elements of the ankh and sema-taui symbols of Ancient Egypt, and share close association of mythic animals that similarly seem to have Nilotic origins.

The ubiquity of this plant symbol and role in religious and ritualistic expression over such a broad geographical range is no less remarkable than the critical role the plant played in modelling the cosmos and defining the concepts of 'first principles' in ancient Egypt and Mesopotamia. The Egyptians identified the world's Creator, Nefertum, as a personification of this sun-like, sweet-smelling plant, and also identified the plant's flowers as the source of the sun itself. Various central members of the Heliopolitan pantheon were symbolized by the plant's continual production of sun-flowers, and were thus equated with the everlasting cycles of life. And by association, successive kings in pharaonic Egypt were equated with these divine personages in life and after death. Like most ancient cosmological concepts, these symbolic and metaphorical notions were communicated by use of various symbols of everlasting life, such as the ankh, sema-taui and shen insignias, all of which migrated and transitioned into closely symbolic forms of the Middle East that assumed the guise of a 'sacral tree,' large scale depictions of which reached a pinnacle of popularity Neo-Assyrian and Neo-Babylonian traditions. The relevance of an Egyptian plant in Mesopotamia owes in no small part to the abundance of this same plant species in marshlands of the Tigris-Euphrates River system. The transition of a herbaceous lotus plant into a sacral tree motif established one of the most pervasive and as yet enigmatic developments in early Middle Eastern iconography which continues to mystify historians and connoisseurs of ancient arts.

Present attempts to identify lotiform tree of life motifs in Mesopotamia with Hebraic concepts of pillared vegetative fetishes known as asherim during Mosaic and post-exilic ages of the Old Testament introduces a number of novel perspectives and underscores ritualistic relations between early Judaic cultures and neighboring tribes. These associations are supported by biblical references to iconography and historical images of libation ceremonies that trace from the Levant and Mesopotamia from 1500–500 BCE, often in association with lotus flowers and lotus-related mythic figures, such as sphinxes and 'cherubim' (chimeras of bulls, eagles, bulls and humans). A review of biblical scriptures emphasizes an under-appreciated role of lotus imagery in the construction and implementation of the temple of Solomon, the holy of holies, and the ark of the covenant, thus broadening our awareness of the influence and religious impacts of Egyptian traditions and rituals among Levantine and Mesopotamian peoples. These novel viewpoints pose new and compelling questions regarding the early developments of religious expression that now seem far removed from our present-day practice of religions that originated in these regions of the world. Perhaps foremost among these questions is the abandoned role of a sacred/mythic plant that formerly played a central role in libation ceremonies, the result of which culminated at times in transcendental experience.

Funding: This research received no external funding.

Conflicts of Interest: The author declares no conflict of interest.

References

Albenda, Pauline. 1994. Assyrian sacred trees in the Brooklyn Museum. *Iraq* 36: 123–33. [CrossRef]

Andrae, Walter. 1925. *Coloured Ceramics from Ashur, and Earlier Anci3ent Assyrian Wall Paintings*. London: K. Pau, Trench, Tubner & Co.

Annus, Amar. 2002. *The God Ninurta in the Mythology and Royal Ideology of Ancient Mesopotamia*. Helsinki: State Archives of Assyria Studies, vol. XVI, pp. 1–242.

Anthes, Rudolph. 1959. Egyptian theology in the third millennium B.C. *Journal of Near Eastern Studies* 18: 169–212. [CrossRef]

Assaad, Hany, and Daniel Kolos. 1979. *The Name of the Dead: Hieroglyphic Inscriptions of the Treasures of Tutankhamun Translated*. Mississauga: Benben Publications.

Atac, Mehmet-Ali. 2008. Religion as represented in the art of the ancient Near East. *Religion Compass* 2: 889–928. [CrossRef]

Babbitt, Frank C. 1936. *Moralia: De Iside et Osiride*. Plutarch's Moralia V, Loeb Classical Library. Suffolk: St. Edmundsbury Press.

Baines, John. 1975. Ankh sign, belt, and penis sheath. *Studien zur altaegyptischen Kulture* 3: 1–24.

Barnett, Richad D. 1982. *Ancient Ivories in the Middle East*. Qedem, Monographs in the Institute of Archaeology. Jerusalem: The Hebrew University.

Barnstone, Willis. 1984. *The Other Bible*. San Francisco: Harper Collins.

Betz, Hans D. 1986. *The Greek Magical Papyri in Translation*. Chicago: University of Chicago Press.

Black, Jeremy, Anthony Green, and Tessa Rickards. 1992. *Gods, Demons and Symbols of Ancient Mesopotamia*. London: British Museum Press.

Bonavia, Emanuel. 1894. *The Flora of the Assyrian Monuments*. Westminster: Archibald Constable and Co., W.

Brugsch, Heinrich. 1884. *Religion und Mythologie der Alten Aegypter*. Leipzig: J. C. Hinrichs Publ.

Budge, E. A. Wallis. 1989. *Book of the Dead*. 2 vols. London: Arkana. First published 1899.

Budge, E. A. Wallis. 1969. *The Gods of the Egyptians*. 2 vols. New York: Dover. First published 1904.

Budge, E. A. Wallis. 1989. *The Mummy*, 2nd ed. Cambridge: Constable and Co. First published 1925.

Budge, E. A. Wallis. 1970. *Amulets and Talisman*. New York: MacMillan. First published 1931.

Cassuto, Umberto. 1971. *The Goddess Anath*. Jerusalem: Magnes Press.

Chevalier, Jean, and Alain Gheerbrant. 1996. *Dictionary of Symbols*. Translated by John Buchanan-Brown. London: Penguin.

Cline, E. H. 1995. Egyptian and Near Eastern imports of late Bronze age Mycenae. In *Egypt, the Aegean and the Levant*. Edited by Vivian Davies and Louise Schofield. London: British Museum Press.

Coomaraswamy, Ananda K. 1935. E. Andrae, Die ionische Säule, Bauform oder Symbol? *Art Bulletin* 17: 103–7.

Cooper, Jerrold. 2000. Assyrian Prophecies, the Assyrian tree, and the Mesopotamian origins of Jewish monotheism, Greek philosophy, Christian theology, Gnosticism, and much more. *Journal of the American Oriental Society* 120: 430–44. [CrossRef]

Crowfoot, John W., and Grace M. Crowfoot. 1938. *Early Ivories from Samaria*. London: Palestine Exporation Fund.

Danthine, Helene. 1937. *Le Palmier-Datier et les Arbres Sacre*. 2 vols. (text and album). Paris: Librairei Orientaliste Paul Geuthner.

Darby, William J., Paul Ghalioungui, and Louis Grivetti. 1977. *Food: The Gift of Osiris*. 2 vols. London: Academic Press.

Desroches-Noblecourt, Christiane. 1989. *Tutankhamen*. New York: Penguin Books.

Durdin-Robertson, Lawrence, and Anna Durdin-Robertson. 1979. *The Goddesses of Chaldaea, Syria and Egypt*. Enniscorthy: Cesara Publ.

El-Mallakh, Kamal, and Robert S. Bianchi. 1980. *Treasures of the Nile: Art of the Temples and Tombs of Egypt*. Tokyo: Newsweek Inc. and Kodansha Ltd.

Emboden, William. 1979. *Nymphaea ampla* and other narcotics in Maya drug ritual and religion. *Mexicon* 1: 50–52.

Emboden, William. 1981. Transcultural use of narcotic water lilies in ancient Egyptian and Mayan drug ritual. *Journal of Ethnopharmacology* 3: 39–83. [CrossRef]

Emboden, William. 1989a. The sacred narcotic lily of the Nile: *Nymphaea caerulea*. *Economic Botany* 32: 395–407. [CrossRef]

Emboden, William. 1989b. The sacred journey in dynastic Egypt: Shamanistic trance in the context of the narcotic water lily and the mandrake. *Journal of Psychoactive Drugs* 21: 61–75. [CrossRef] [PubMed]

Faulkner, Raymond O. 1969. *The Ancient Egyptian Pyramid Texts*. Oxford: Clarendon Press.

Faulkner, Raymond O. 2004. *Ancient Egyptian Coffin Texts*. Oxford: Aris and Phillips.

Fox, Penelope. 1951. *Tutankhamun's Treasure*. London: Oxford University Press.

Frankfort, Henri. 1939. *Cylinder Seals*. London: Macmillan and Co.

Frankfort, Henri. 1970. *The Art and Architecture of the Ancient Orient*. London: Penguin Group.

Gardiner, Alan H. 1928. Life and death. In *Encyclopaedia of Religion and Ethics*. Edited by James Hastings. New York: Charles Scribner's Sons, vol. 8.

Gardiner, Alan H. 1950. *Egyptian Grammar*, 2nd ed. London: Oxford University Press.

Garlick, Constance. 1918. Notes on the Sacred Tree in Mesopotamia. *Proceedings of the Society of Biblical Archaeology* 40: 111–12.

Gillispie, Charles C., and Michel Dewachter. 1987. *The Monuments of Egypt: The Napoleonic Edition*. Old Saybrook: Konecky and Konecky.

Giovino, Mariana. 2007. *The Assyrian Sacred Tree: A History of Interpretations*. Orbis Biblicus et Orientalis 230. Göttingen: Vandenhoeck and Ruprecht.

Goodyear, William H. 1887. Egyptian origin of the ionic capital and the anthemion. *The American Journal of Archaeology and of the History of Fine Arts* 3: 271–302. [CrossRef]

Goodyear, William H. 1891. *The Grammar of the Lotus*. London: Sampson Low, Marston and Co.

Gordon, Andrew H., and Calvin W. Schwabe. 2004. *The Quick and the Dead: Biomedical Theory in Ancient Egypt*. Leiden: E. J. Brill.

James, Edwin O. 1966. *The Tree of Life*. Leiden: E. J. Brill.

Jones, Owens. 1995. *The Grammar of Ornament*. London: Bernard Quaritch. First Published 1856.

Keel, Othmar, and Christoph Uehlinger. 1998. *Gods, Goddesses, and Images of God in Ancient Israel*. Translated by Thomas Trapp. Minneapolis: Fortress Press.

Kramer, Samuel N. 1974. Kingship in Sumer and Akkad: The ideal king. In *Le Palais et la Royauté: archéologie et Civilization*. Edited by Paul Garelli. Paris: Geuthner, pp. 163–76.

Lang, Bernhard. 1983. *Monotheism and the Prophetic Minority*. Sheffield and Decatur: Almond Press.

Langdon, Stephen. 1914. *Tammuz and Ishtar*. Oxford: Clarendon Press.

Langdon, Stephen. 1928. The legend of the kiskanu. *Transactions of the Royal Asian Society, Great Britain and Ireland* 1: 843–48. [CrossRef]

Lange, Kurt, and Max Hirmer. 1968. *Egypt: Architecture, Sculpture, Painting in Three Thousand Years*, 4th ed. London: Phaidon Press.

Layard, Austen Henry. 1849. *Nineveh and its Remains: with an Account of a Visit to the Chaldaean Christians of Kurdistan, and the Yezids, or Devil-Worshippers; and an Enquiry in the Manners and Arts of the Ancient Assyrians*. 2 vols. London: John Murray.

Loud, Gordon. 1939. *The Megiddo Ivories*. Chicago: University of Chicago Press.

Lurker, Manfred. 1980. *The Gods and Symbols of Ancient Egypt*. London: Thames and Hudson.

Maspero, Gaston. 1913. *Egyptian Art*. London: T. Fisher Unwin.

Mazar, Benjamin. 1961. *Views of the Biblical World*. 5 vols. Jerusalem: International Publishing.

McDonald, J. Andrew. 2002. Botanical determination of the Middle Eastern tree of life. *Economic Botany* 56: 113–29. [CrossRef]

McDonald, J. Andrew, and Brian Stross. 2012. Water lily and cosmic serpent: Equivalent conduits of the Maya spirit realm. *Journal of Ethnobiology* 32: 73–106. [CrossRef]

Merhav, Rivka. 1987. *Treasures of the Bible Lands*. Tel Aviv Museum. Tel Aviv: Modan Publishing.

Moldenke, Harold, and Alma Moldenke. 1952. *Plants of the Bible*. New York: Ronald Press.

Parpola, Simo. 1993. The Assyrian tree of life: Tracing the origins of Jewish monotheism and Greek philosophy. *Journal of Near Eastern Studies* 52: 161–208. [CrossRef]

Parpola, Simo. 1997. *Assyrian Prophecies*. State Archives of Assyria. Helsinki: Helsinki University Press, vol. 9.

Parrot, Andre. 1961. *The Arts of Assyria*. New York: Golden Press.

Patai, Raphael. 1990. *The Hebrew Goddess*, 3rd ed. Detroit: Wayne State University Press.

Piankoff, Alexandre. 1964. *The Litany of Re*. New York: Pantheon Books.

Piankoff, Alexandre. 1968. *The Pyramid of Unas*. Princeton: Princeton University Press.

Piankoff, Alexandre. 1974. *The Wandering of the Soul*. Princeton: Princeton University Press.
Porada, Edith. 1945. Griffin demons, genii and griffin demons. In *The Great King of Assyria: Assyrian Reliefs in the Metropolitan Museum of Art*. Edited by Charles Sheeler. New York: Metropolitan Museum of Art.
Porter, Barbara N. 1993. Sacred trees, date palms, and the royal persona of Ashurnasirpal II. *Journal of Near Eastern Studies* 52: 129–39. [CrossRef]
Pritchard, James B. 1969. *Ancient Near Eastern Texts Relating to the Old Testament*, 3rd ed. Princeton: University Press.
Redford, Donald B. 1992. *Egypt, Canaan, and Israel in Ancient Times*. Princeton: Princeton University Press.
Roaf, Michael. 1998. *Cultural Atlas of Mesopotamia and the Near East*. Oxfordshire: Andromeda.
Schäfer, Heinrich. 1974. *Principles of Egyptian Art*. Translated by Emma Brunner-Traut. Oxford: Clarendon.
Schneider, Edward L. 1982. Notes on the floral biology of *Nymphaea elegans* (Nymphaeaceae) in Texas. *Aquatic Botany* 12: 197–200. [CrossRef]
Schweinfurth, Georg. 1884. The Flora of Ancient Egypt. *Nature* 28: 109–14.
Shaw, Ian, and Paul Nicholson. 1995. *The Dictionary of Ancient Egypt*. New York: British Museum, Harry N. Abrams Inc.
Strommenger, Eva. 1964. *5000 Years of the Art of Mesopotamia*. Translated by Christina Haglund. New York: H. N. Abrams.
Walker, Winifred. 1957. *All the Plants of the Bible*. New York: Harper and Brothers.
Ward, William H. 1910. *The Seal cylinders of Western Asia*. Carnegie Institution of Washington, Publication no. 100. Washington, DC: Carnegie Institution.
Wiersema, John H. 1988. Reproductive biology of *Nymphaea* (Nymphaeaceae). *Annals of the Missouri Botanical Garden* 73: 795–804. [CrossRef]
Wiggins, Steve A. 1993. *A Reassessment of 'Asherah*. Darmstadt: Verlag Butzon and Bercker Kevelaer.
Wilkinson, Richard H. 1992. *Reading Egyptian Art*. New York: Thames and Hudson.
Wilkinson, Richard H. 1994. *Symbol and Magic in Egyptian Art*. New York: Thames and Hudson.
Wilkinson, Richard H. 2003. *The Complete Gods and Goddesses of Ancient Egypt*. New York: Thames and Hudson.

religions

MDPI

Article

Continuity and Discontinuity in 17th- and 18th-Century Ecclesiastical Silverworks from the Southern Andes

Andrea Nicklisch

Roemer- und Pelizaeus-Museum Hildesheim, Am Steine 1–2, 31134 Hildesheim, Germany; a.nicklisch@rpmuseum.de

Received: 12 July 2018; Accepted: 15 August 2018; Published: 3 September 2018

Abstract: This article deals with interpretations of images on silver ecclesiastical objects from the Southern Andes dating from the 17th and 18th centuries. The silverworks communicate contents on a nonverbal level and are integrated into ritual acts in the context of church services; this facilitates associations with non-Christian beliefs. If the images are studied by means of a combination of various analytical levels, transcultural processes become apparent in the images on the objects studied, and meanings emerge that would not have been brought to light by simple image analysis. This applies particularly to the comparison with possible indigenous meanings of European images, which enables a much more comprehensive interpretation. Depending on the beholder, the images may be interpreted as expressing continuity, i.e., as representations of indigenous beliefs; as expressing discontinuity, i.e., as representations of Christian beliefs; or as the result of a transfer of meaning encompassing and combining both belief systems, thus enabling a new way of "reading" them. However, a transcultural process of regional relocation and use of cultural elements is not only visible in the images; it is also illustrated by the ecclesiastical silverworks in the Americas as such, given the European influence manifest in them.

Keywords: South America; colonial period; religious transfer of meaning; multiple readings of images

1. Introduction

The continuity of pre-Hispanic/indigenous religions has its basis in transcultural processes. These religions are witnessing a powerful renaissance in the context of the current political developments in Bolivia, and can be viewed as the foundation of an emerging new concept of the self.

This article deals with the ways historical actors have used new media—such as ecclesiastical silverworks of the new religious system—to configure new cultural orders and systems of meaning within colonial power relations; another question addressed is whether the ecclesiastical silverworks can be interpreted as media of a transfer of meaning.

The 17th- and 18th-century ecclesiastical silverworks from the Southern Andes region, particularly the antependia and candle banks, are decorated with a multitude of angels, angel-like beings, and birds. Hence, they are well suited for demonstrating the simultaneousness of continuity and discontinuity on the one hand, and for illustrating the concept of multiple interpretations on the other. The focus will be on two winged anthropomorphic beings on the altar of the Virgin of Guadalupe in Sucre (in colonial times also called Charcas, Chuquisaca, and La Plata), Bolivia, in the southern Andes.

2. Region and Time under Study

The objects studied date from the 17th and 18th centuries. The *Provincia de Charcas* where they come from was then a colonial contact zone that, at the same time, was also a cultural contact zone. The latter term is used by Mary Louise Pratt to refer to social spaces where cultures meet and establish spheres of action with each other.[1] These encounters are often based on unequal power relationships (Pratt 1991, p. 34). In the contact zone, transcultural processes unfold within a culture as well as in the interplay of several cultures.

3. The Altar of the Virgin of Guadalupe in Sucre, Bolivia

The Virgin of Guadalupe (Figure 1) is the patron saint of Sucre, the constitutional capital of today's Bolivia. The original picture of the Virgin was painted in 1601 by the Spaniard Diego de Ocaña, a member of the Hieronymite Order. Ocaña modeled the depiction in his painting on the sculpture of the Black Virgin in the monastery of Santa María de Guadalupe in what is now the Cáceres Province in Spain's Extremadura region. Worship of the Virgin established itself quickly in 17th-century Sucre, and believers presented her image with countless precious stones, pearls, pieces of jewelry, medals, coins, and small watches to express their veneration. These gifts were attached to the canvas. The votive gifts weighed so heavily on the canvas that the Madonna's hands, her face, and the face of the divine infant were cut out of the image and set into a cloak-shaped plate of silver and gold. The votive gifts were subsequently transferred onto the cloak too (Figure 2). In addition, this devotional picture, which is reminiscent of Byzantine icons, was given a so-called throne—a kind of frame. It has a glass front, and its sides and back are made of massive silver.

Figure 1. Devotional image of the Virgin of Guadlupe, Sucre (photo: Andrea Nicklisch).

[1] "[. . .] what I like to call the *contact zones*. I use this term to refer to social spaces where cultures meet, clash, and grapple with each other, often in contexts of highly asymmetrical relations of power, such as colonialism, slavery, or their aftermaths as they are lived out in many parts of the world today" (Pratt 1991, p. 34).

Figure 2. Detail, Virgin of Guadalupe (photo: Andrea Nicklisch).

As early as 1602, a chapel, which has since been the place where the Virgin is worshipped, was added to the cathedral of Sucre.[2] So popular was the Virgin that it became necessary to enlarge the chapel as early as 1617. Mass is held there every day. In colonial times, it was mostly the elites of Sucre who hallowed the Virgin; today, she is widely worshipped by the indigenous population as well.

Every year, nine days before the Virgin Mary's birthday on September 8, the devotional image is taken from the chapel and carried through the city in a procession, accompanied by secular and church dignitaries and the sound of music and firecrackers (Figure 3), and eventually reentering the cathedral through the main entrance. The image is then worshipped by the believers until the holiday proper, the day of the Birth of the Blessed Virgin Mary (Figure 4). On September 8, an open-air mass is held on the Plaza 25 de Mayo. After that, the Virgin is again carried through the city, this time accompanied by a motorcade. The procession temporarily expands the sacred space, and the course of the procession along various buildings of political institutions serves to conjoin and reaffirm worldly and clerical power.

The continuity of pre-Hispanic religious ideas, as well as their association with Christian religious ideas by means of winged anthropomorphic beings, becomes visible on the stairs of the altar of the Virgin of Guadalupe. The candle banks—three wooden steps beneath the devotional image of the Virgin—are decorated with silver plates of various sizes. On two steps, silver elements are mounted to the left and to the right of the tabernacle, respectively; these elements are sides, and possibly also supports and backs, of missal bookstands (Personal communication, Bernardo Gantier SJ, 15 August 2012, Sucre, Bolivia; Figure 5). The 1799 inventory of the chapel of the Virgin of Guadalupe lists altogether eight missal bookstands, three of which were faced with silver. However, the inventory merely mentions the value of the missal bookstands without giving a description of the depictions on them. It is thus not clear whether the silver parts on the candle banks are one of the bookstands listed. As a consequence, it is not possible to exactly date these plates. Judging from their decoration, however, they were probably made in the 18th century.

2 Building of the cathedral itself was begun in 1559 and completed in 1712.

Figure 3. Procession of the Virgin of Guadalupe (photo: Andrea Nicklisch).

Figure 4. Worship of the Virgin (photo: Andrea Nicklisch).

(a) (b)

Figure 5. (a,b) Tabernacle and candle banks, altar in the chapel of the Virgin of Guadalupe, Sucre, Bolivia (photo: Andrea Nicklisch).

The parts of the missal bookstands are attached to the lowermost and uppermost candle banks. The parts on the lowermost step, which are probably support surfaces, show a crown surrounded by a garland, as well as rocaille-like[3] ornaments on the former side parts. Rectangular silver plates are attached to the left and right sides of the third and uppermost steps (Figure 6).

Figure 6. Tabernacle and candle banks, altar in the chapel of the Virgin of Guadalupe, Sucre, Bolivia (photo: Andrea Nicklisch).

These are probably the backs of the missal book stands. Each of the two plates features an anthropomorphic figure; these figures are almost identical in their postures: their arms are raised, and they are holding a round object above their heads. Both figures look as if they have wings. The figure on the left side has breasts and is thus probably a woman (Figure 7a) who, in addition, has an umbilicus. From her wrists emerge two objects that look like snake heads. The figure on the right side has neither secondary sexual characteristics nor an umbilicus. Twigs with leaves on them spring from its raised arms. Like the female figure, it is holding a round object—which has a cross on top—above its head (Figure 7b). Based on their attributes, their position on the altar, and Christian iconography, the two figures can be interpreted as being Adam and Eve. According to Christian iconography, the figure on the left side would be Eve. Her depiction with breasts and umbilicus is unusual. These features were not usually present, particularly in medieval depictions, as Adam and Eve were created by God and not born as mortal humans. Hence, they often lack both sexual characteristics and an umbilicus. From the Renaissance onward, however, they were depicted with both umbilicus and sexual characteristics (Poeschel 2005, p. 38; Menzel 1854, p. 21). The round object above their heads is probably the fruit from the Tree of Knowledge.

[3] Conchiform curved ornaments that first emerged in France in the first half of the 18th century. Available online: http://www.beyars.com/kunstlexikon/lexikon_7623.html (accessed on 28 June 2013).

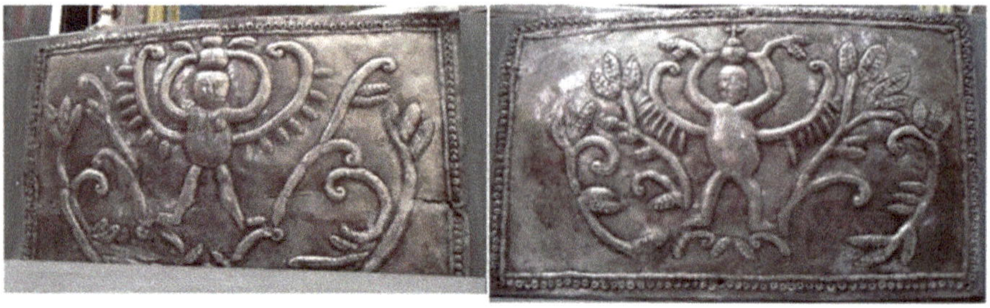

(a) (b)

Figure 7. (**a**) Silver panel with female figure on the altar of the Virgin of Guadalupe, Sucre, Bolivia (photo: Andrea Nicklisch); (**b**) Silver panel with male figure on the altar of the Virgin of Guadalupe, Sucre, Bolivia (photo: Andrea Nicklisch).

According to Christian iconography, the figure on the right side would be Adam. The leaves on his arm may allude to an apocryphal tale: Adam is said to have brought a kernel of the fruit from the Tree of Knowledge with him from Paradise to Earth. When Adam died and was buried, he had that kernel in his mouth. From it grew the tree of which the cross of Christ was made (Menzel 1854, p. 114). The round object above his head appears to be an imperial orb, a Roman symbol of sovereignty over the world that later became one of the insignia of the Christian rulers.

The Bible says that God had Adam and Eve expelled from Paradise after the Fall. They found themselves in a world where they did not have eternal life; instead, they had to suffer sorrow, pain, and death. By sinning they had destroyed the harmony and peace of nature.

After expulsion from Paradise, Adam and Eve found themselves in a world unknown to them—a disordered world like that with which the indigenous population had to cope after Conquest.

Iconographic analyses reveal the agency of transcultural processes in the images on the objects studied. However, only the combination of various levels of analysis—analysis of historical documents, and inclusion of pre-Christian European and pre-Hispanic contents of images—results in interpretations that would not have been yielded by simple image analysis. This applies particularly to the comparison with possible indigenous meanings of European images, which enables a much more comprehensive interpretation. Depending on the beholder, the images may be interpreted as expressing continuity, i.e., as representations of indigenous beliefs; as expressing discontinuity, i.e., as representations of Christian beliefs; or as the result of a transfer of meaning encompassing and combining both belief systems, thus allowing for a new way of "reading" them. However, they may also be viewed as being purely decorative.

4. Objects of Comparison

Several objects of comparison make the transfer of meaning on the silver plates visible: pre-Hispanic petroglyphs from the Sucre region; a cloak from the colonial era (probably 17th century, Roemer- and Pelizaeus-Museum Hildesheim, inv.-no. V 9.000); and contemporary textiles from the Jalq'a region near Sucre. These modern textiles, which are almost exclusively in red and black, show chaotic scenes (Figure 8a) referring to the absence of sunlight, the difficulty of seeing things clearly (both in the literal and in the metaphoric sense), and the supernatural world (exhibition text "Tejidos de Jalq'a", Fundación Antropológos del Surandino, ASUR, Sucre, Bolivia, 2010). One of the most prominent figures represented on the textiles is the so-called *supay* (Figure 8b).

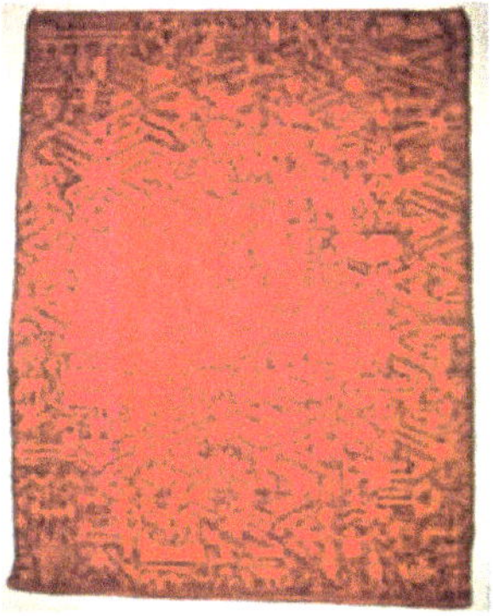

(a)

(b)

Figure 8. (**a**) Textile from Jalq'a, Bolivia (Fundación Antropólogos del Surandino, ASUR, Sucre, Bolivia, photo: Andrea Nicklisch); (**b**) Representation of the supay (Fundación Antropólogos del Surandino, ASUR, Sucre, Bolivia, photo: Andrea Nicklisch).

The *supay* is a supernatural being associated with the world beyond the human world—that is, with dangerous and disordered (i.e., noncivilized) places. The representations of the *supay* on the textiles bear close resemblance to the two figures on the altar of the Virgin of Guadalupe. This type of representation may have developed from pre-Hispanic petroglyphs showing a head with raised arms (exhibition "Tejidos de Jalq'a", Fundación Antropólogos del Surandino, ASUR, Sucre, Bolivia, 2010). The abovementioned garment, which is probably the wedding cloak of a high-ranking woman (Phipps et al. 2004, p. 194), shows a creature covered with black hair. With its arms raised and a long snout, it appears among pre-Hispanic- and European-style images (Figure 9). The textile in the collection of the Roemer- and Pelizaeus-Museum Hildesheim is only one half of the cloak; the other half is in the Textile Museum Washington (Textile Museum Washington D.C. 1968.35.I). The latter features the being covered with black hair, which can be linked to the two figures on the altar of the Virgin of Guadalupe.

Figure 9. Wedding cloak, southern Andes, 17th century(?), Roemer- und Pelizaeus-Museum Hildesheim, inv.-no. V 9.000 (photo: Shahrok Shalchi).

The pre-Hispanic *supay* ranks among the ambivalent mountain deities of the Andes, and is found in various regions under various names (Martínez 1983). Still today, the miners regard him as the "Lord of Metals", whom they need to put into a favorable mind (Salazar-Soler 1987, p. 197). This establishes a connection between the *supay* and the silver plates. In addition, Martínez refers to the mountain deities as double-gendered, "como marido y mujer", due to their characteristics (Martínez 1983, p. 98f.). This suggests that Adam and Eve, depicted separately on two matching missal bookstands as well as on the wedding cloak, do not only express that aspect of the *supay* but also one of the basic concepts of Andean dualism: the division of the world into masculine and feminine. According to Constance Classen, Adam and Eve are referred to by the Quechua term of *yanantin* ("to help each other"); they are two halves that belong together while at the same time containing within themselves elements of the respective other sex (Classen 1993, p. 13). The indigenous population may thus have interpreted Adam and Eve as the embodiment of a cosmos that, while divided by gender, is essentially one. The representation of the *supay* on the wedding cloak from the collection of the Roemer- und Pelizaeus-Museum can be seen in that context, too.

In addition, the positioning of Adam (at the right in depictions) and Eve (at the left in depictions) in Christian iconography is in accordance with the Andean principle associating the male with the right side and the female with the left (Classen 1993, p. 12).[4] Both indigenous and European beholders could thus interpret the images from the perspective of their respective faith—pre-Hispanic or Christian—, and easily incorporate them into their belief system.

Since the colonial era, the term *supay* has largely been used synonymously with "devil" or demons in general. The missionaries tried to transform the ambivalent concept of *supay* into an unambiguously Christian concept, so as to establish a contrast between the Christian God and the Andean *supay* and other deities and deified ancestors (MacCormack 1991, p. 257). A translation of the term from the Quechua language is first found in Domingo de Santo Tomás' 1560 dictionary *Lexicón o vocabulario de la lengua general del Perú*. Santo Tomás translates the term into Spanish as "good or bad angel", "demon or household spirit", and "good or bad demon".[5] Hence, his translation clearly alludes to the dual, not exclusively evil nature of the *supay*. The dictionary by Antonio Ricardo, published in 1583, gives more translations into Spanish such as "apparition of a ghost" and "shadow of a person". The lexicon by Diego Gonzalez Holguin also has the translation "apparition of a ghost", as well as "ghost" and "vision" MacCormack 1991, p. 254f.).[6] However, the term is given an exclusively negative connotation in the example sentences included in these dictionaries. That negative meaning was taken for granted by the Jesuit friar José de Acosta as early as 1577. He defined the *supay* as the antagonist of God, and the following definition is found in the *Catecismo Mayor* of the Third Council of Lima: "[. . .] chay mana alli Angelcunactam çupay ninchic" ("[. . .] these evil angels whom we call çupay") (Karlovich 2006, n.p.). Inca Garcilaso de la Vega reported in 1609 that the Inca used to distinguish between good and evil, between God and *supay*; and Guaman Poma de Ayala refers to the Inca deities in general as *supay* who had kept the indigenous population from practicing the Christian faith prior to conquest by the Spaniards (MacCormack 1991, p. 255). The advanced Christian reinterpretation of the concept of *supay* becomes apparent in both these statements.

With the figures of *supay* Adam and *supay* Eve, the altar thus features both pre-Hispanic and Christian concepts that reveal a transfer of meaning: a nondominant system can instrumentalize a dominant system unnoticed as a vehicle for its own ideas.

---

4 "Left" and "right" always refers to the position of the depictions, not to the perspective of the beholder.

5 "Çupay: Angel bueno o malo, demonio bueno o malo, demonios, trasgo de casa" (Eyzaguirre Morales, Milton. De Ancestros y Muertos a Diablos Ángeles. La Resemantización del Supay en el Contexto Andino, La Paz 2011, n.p.).

6 "Cupay could be a vision, phantasm, or ghost. [. . .] These included seeing evil phantasms or spirits, being possessed by a demon or devil; speaking with the devil; and making oneself wicked, like a demon" MacCormack 1991, p. 255.

In addition, the existence of the concept of *supay*, as well as very similar depictions of that being, can be traced from pre-Hispanic times (petroglyphs) to the colonial era (silver plates and textiles V 9.000) and into the 20th century (textiles).

5. Theoretical Approaches

As mentioned above, the *Provincia de Charcas* was a colonial contact zone and as such the scene of "transcultural processes". The underlying term "transculturation" was first introduced by Fernando Ortiz in 1940. Ortiz used the term to characterize the development of Cuban society from the pre-Hispanic era until the modern period. He held the view that "acculturation" was an inadequate term with regard to those historical events, of which European conquest was the most massive encroachment on the existing cultures, as the term merely refers to the process of adaptation of one culture to another (Ortiz [1940] 1947, p. 97). Bronislaw Malinowski supported that point of view in his preface to Ortiz's study, as he deemed the concept of acculturation an ethnocentric notion with a pronounced moral connotation. According to Malinowski, that notion implied that "the 'uncultured' is to receive the benefits 'of our culture'; it is he who must change and become converted into 'one of us'". Malinowski, in contrast, viewed cultural contacts as "a system of give and take, it is a process in which both parts of the equation are modified, a process from which a new reality emerges, transformed and complex, a reality that is not a mechanical agglomeration of traits, nor even a mosaic, but a new phenomenon, original and independent" (Malinowski [1940] 1947). Besides the encounter between cultures, the cultural process called "transculturation" includes the deculturation of all populations involved, as well as neoculturation. As defined by Ortiz, deculturation refers to people's separation from their culture of origin, which applied to all parties involved in the conquest of the Americas: while the Spaniards or Europeans were the dominant power, they found themselves in a completely different world inhabited by people whose languages they could not—and probably did not want to—understand, and by animals and plants unknown to them. The indigenous population,[7] in turn, usually continued to live in its respective region of origin but was forced not merely to arrange itself with European/Christian culture but to make it their own. The black slaves deported from Africa to the Americas were faced with deculturation as well. The next step, neoculturation, is the intentional creation of a new culture. According to Ortiz, such a culture, while having features of its predecessors, is to be viewed as a culture of its own (Ortiz [1940] 1947, p. 102f.).

The preconditions of transculturation were also found in the *Provincia de Charcas* in the time period under study. Prompted by transculturation, structures of power and rule were established and negotiated—depending on each party's room for maneuver—between the Spaniards as the secular conquering power, the Christian church as the religious power, and the indigenous population.

In the sphere of pictorial representation and its perception and interpretation, Margot Berghaus has developed a thesis based on her engagement with Niklas Luhmann's systems theory, which is applicable to the silverworks studied. Berghaus states that, in contrast to pictorial representations, language is completely defined in social terms; that is, it is socially learned and its use is subject to social control by society. Pictorial representations, in turn, are defined by Berghaus as being "partially extrasocial" (outside social systems, *partiell außersozial*) and "partially social" (inside social systems, *partiell sozial*) (Berghaus 2010, p. 179f.). "Partially extrasocial" refers to pictorial representations or parts of images that are decoded by means of cognitive potentials outside the realm of language. These cognitive potentials can take effect regardless of the prerogative of interpretation in a given society, as images defy any complete governing control; hence, they are only subject to partial interpretational control by society. It is possible to understand pictorial representations directly,

[7] This term is not to suggest that there existed a homogeneous population in the Viceroyalty of Peru. It is used here to refer to the indigenous peoples as a whole as opposed to the Spaniards who, by the way, did not view themselves as a homogeneous population either, making clear distinctions among themselves based on their respective regional origins in Spain.

without "social processes of learning, control, and translation" (Berghaus 2010, p. 180). "Partially social", in contrast, are parts of images that can only be understood from the perspective of a specific society. The beholder cannot necessarily grasp the sociocultural meaning of a pictorial representation, what it is supposed to express, and for what purpose it was made (Berghaus 2010, p. 180). This means that pictorial representations can be partly understood "extrasocially" due to visible resemblance to reality; other elements, however, are incomprehensible, and interpreting them in social terms is a painstaking process (Berghaus 2010, p. 182).[8]

The validity of Berghaus' thesis regarding the partially social and partially extrasocial character of pictorial representations becomes evident in the images on Southern-Andes ecclesiastical silverworks. The representations on antependia, tabernacles, and arches present the beholder with a definitely familiar inventory of images, and the social component of their character reveals itself. However, the setting of the depictions is a foreign cultural context, which renders it much more difficult to decipher their extrasocial component: not only early modern Spanish-European but also indigenous preconditions must be taken into account.

In addition, pictorial representations are associated with very diverse social acts or practices that are inevitably linked to actors, and assign use of the images to a specific purpose (Kramer and Baumgarten 2009, p. 21). The observations of the actors always go along with making a distinction between "referring to something as this and not as that" (Berghaus 2010, p. 28). Distinctions are thus decisive for describing reality, and any such description is inevitably constructed by the beholder. This also means that reality is constructed by the beholder, which, in turn, raises the question as to how something has been constructed (Berghaus 2010, p. 29), as it is the beholder who decides what distinction is made (Berghaus 2010, p. 46).

In their approaches, Berghaus as well as Kramer and Baumgarten (2009), describe what has been called the concept of multiple readings, or interpretations, by Margit Kern. That concept starts from the assumption that, whenever different societies get into contact, one group adopts types of images that have been handed down by the other; it then adapts these to its own realities based on its experiences, horizon of knowledge, and way of thinking, and "reads" and processes them accordingly. It is the beholder who decides on the extent of adopting or combining different visual systems. That is why there exists not only one way of reading the new visual system; there are several ways (Kern 2010, p. 251). With regard to the ecclesiastical silverworks, this implies questions such as: Do the pictures play a role in church service, and, if yes, is it possible to reconstruct that role? What role is played by which pictures for which strata of the population? What are the various possibilities of interpreting the pictures among the indigenous and Spanish-European populations? As has been mentioned above, the last point in particular raises problems, as there exist no colonial-period records of ways in which images were perceived and interpreted. Iconographies, their contents, and the resulting connections and new possibilities of interpretation are the only feasible approach to these issues.

6. Continuities and Discontinuities

One question arising in the context of studying transfers of meaning in a colonial contact zone relates to cultural continuity or discontinuity that may find expression in the transcultural processes. Cultural continuity is not identical with historical continuity. While both are often viewed as being the same, the latter is actually a characteristic of nationalist and separatist ideologies. It is based, among other things, on Johann Gottfried Herders' concept of culture, according to which cultures are closed orbs, each with its own spatial and/or linguistic territory.[9] The basic assumption of this concept is that cultures are static entities that do not enter into unions with one another. In my opinion,

[8] For Problems with interpretation see also (Nicklisch 2013, pp. 155–71).

[9] Transkulturalität: Interkulturell vs. transkulturell. Available online: http://www.ikud-seminare.de (accessed on 7 June 2018).

such a notion has at no time been applicable to cultures, as they are constantly changing and never static. The cultural concept proposed by Herder and others has mainly been employed in constructs of separatist and nationalist ideas that were far from reality. However, it has also played a role in the emergence of nation states in the 19th century. In the present article, cultural continuity is defined as the ability of cultures to change, to adapt to new conditions, to borrow, modify, or discard features of other cultures, and to undergo changes within themselves; however, cultural continuity also relates to the ability of cultures to preserve elements of themselves over long periods of time in spite of adverse circumstances. Defined that way, the notion of cultural continuity implies neither subversion of the conquered vis-à-vis the conquerors, nor agreement with Herder's concept of culture; it implies the possible continuity and, at the same time, changeability of elements of culture even in a situation of colonial contact.

George Kubler, a renowned expert in ancient American studies, has vehemently spoken out against cultural continuity (Kubler 1985). According to Kubler, continuity can manifest itself in biological and ecological phenomena; in the sphere of the symbolic, however, there is too much instability to allow for continuity over long periods of time (Kubler 1967, p. 11). Mainly using architectural features as examples, Kubler maintains that indigenous iconographies were broken down into incoherent fragments in the course of conquest. These fragments lost their content-related meaning even though their origin was, in some cases, still recognizable (Kubler 1985, p. 68). Kubler claims that while ancient European civilizations, for example, continued to exist in human memory even after their demise, such persistence cannot be found in the Americas. According to him, conquest caused an artificial "lack of culture" onto which the culture of the Spaniards was subsequently implemented (Kubler 1985, p. 72).

Jeffrey Quilter takes a basically affirmative stance towards cultural continuity, assuming that cultural elements can persist for a very long time in cultures that have supraregional concepts, as is the case in Mesoamerica and South America. In addition, he believes that it is essential to look at everyday culture, as elites are more prone than commoners to adapt to new conditions. However, Quilter argues against a priori assumptions on both continuity and discontinuity (Quilter 1996, p. 313f). He shows that, in retrospect, historical events may be interpreted as expressions of either cultural continuity or discontinuity, depending on the perspective taken. While Quilter believes that concepts are capable of surviving in societies for centuries or even millennia, he insists on considering both possibilities—continuity and discontinuity—in analyses of transcultural processes (Quilter 1996, p. 314f).

A similar conclusion is reached by Terence Grieder, who writes that "neither disjunction nor continuity can be safely assumed" (Grieder 1975, p. 852). According to him, the traditions of cultures include the latter's practice of expressing themselves by means of symbolism in their material legacy. His ethnological method starts out from the assumption that the symbolic content of a form lives on for a long time in cultures that are characterized by continuity in other spheres as well (Grieder 1975, p. 649). While Grieder believes that it is impossible to prove anything beyond doubt in this context, he states that it is legitimate to speculate, and he calls upon culture historians to engage in such speculation. According to him, analogy is the best tool, as it allows for conclusions that may reveal, or at least suggest, meanings (Grieder 1975, p. 853).

With regard to the above example of representations on the silver plates on the altar of the Virgin of Guadalupe, a continuity of the concept of *supay* can be assumed from the pre-Hispanic era until the present. At first glance, this appears implausible, given the missionary endeavors of the Spaniards in South America. However, there are arguments supporting the longevity of both iconography and the religious ideas associated with it. Christopher Donnan and Donna McClelland have studied burial rites of Moche culture by means of narrative representations on pottery. They succeeded in establishing a concordance between scenes found on the vessels and shamanic rituals described by Fray Antonio de Calancha in his 1638 *Crónica moralizada* (Donnan and McClelland 1979, p. 11f). Given that observation, Donnan and McClelland assume that the contents of the scenes were known from the first century

BC until the colonial era (Donnan and McClelland 1979, p. 12). In addition, Christopher Donnan has studied the motif of bird warriors in Moche iconography. Based on observations he made among modern religious specialists in Peru, he interprets the bird warriors as curers in a state of trance, flying in the air and combating supernatural beings (Donnan [1976] 1979, pp. 124–43). This suggests the continuity of a religious concept from the time of Moche culture until the present.

In this context, it may be noted that examples of iconographic elements surviving for centuries are found in Europe as well. The early Christian insular manuscripts (from Ireland, northern England, and Scotland), for instance, which date from the seventh to the ninth centuries AD, feature animal and spiral motifs that have their origin in Iron-Age, pre-Christian La Tène culture (Brown 2003, p. 237; Netzer 1998, p. 227) that thrived from the fifth century BC until the first century AD.

These manuscripts are also an example of the longevity of pictorial, and particularly religious, representations. In her study of the Lindisfarne Gospels, Michelle P. Brown writes that these manuscripts reflect the ethnic and cultural conglomerate of the region, which includes influences of Celtic, Pict, Germanic, Anglo-Saxon, and Mediterranean art. The latter, in turn, is composed of Roman, Byzantine, Syrian, Armenian, and Coptic traditions. Brown believes that the results of such unions survive for a very long time (Brown 2003, p. 272f).

7. Conclusions

It is essential, in my opinion, to allow for the possibility of both continuity and discontinuity; in addition, their simultaneous existence needs to be kept in mind in any interpretation of transcultural processes. This line of thought is inherent in the idea of multiple readings, or interpretations, which enables very diverse interpretations—e.g., of pictorial representations—depending on the beholder's experiences and horizon of knowledge. However, this also means that ideas or pictorial traditions that have been handed down for a long time are just as likely to exist as are new ideas that merge with older concepts into something third.

Depending on the beholder, pictures can be interpreted as expressing cultural continuity (i.e., representations of indigenous belief systems), discontinuity (i.e., representations of Christian concepts), or as the result of a transfer of meaning that includes both belief systems, combines them, and allows for a new interpretation. Any solid assessment of the way representations were perceived would require surviving records that, however, do not exist. The only viable approach is to base such an assessment on as much information as possible. In the present article, this information pertained to the respective iconographies of the Christian-Spanish and pre-Hispanic indigenous cultures, as well as to the way the objects were historically integrated in their social contexts. This results in a new interpretation of supposedly known picture contents.

In my opinion, the question of whether the transcultural transfer of meaning actually generates something new or whether there is merely a transfer of content is difficult to answer. Cultures are nonstatic entities that are constantly changing; at the same time, however, they pass down elements and contents over long periods of time, locating them in changing contexts of meaning. This means that cultural continuity and discontinuity are always parallel processes, and that not everything that seems to be new is actually new. On the other hand, seemingly traditional elements can turn out to be new, as new meanings are attributed to them over time. In addition, another fact needs to be considered: depending on the beholder, either the "indigenous eye" or the "European eye" is blind when it comes to analyzing iconography. This results in one-sided interpretations. This (in)visibility and (dis)continuity needs to be taken into account in analyses so as to get a historical reconstruction that is as accurate as possible, and to avoid essentialization.[10] If the analysis is based on written

[10] In this context, attention should also be paid to the so-called *Rashomon effect*, named after the movie directed by Akira Kurosawa. The term describes the process in which various observers have different perceptions of an approximately simultaneous reality, and describe that reality differently in retrospect (Gareis 2003, 103f). The point is not to acknowledge

sources, different perspectives on reality are taken by the various texts on a given event (or rather by their authors) and the researcher. In the case of pictorial representations on which there exist (as in the present study) no interpretative texts, the researcher needs to describe and interpret from all possible perspectives.

Conflicts of Interest: The author declares no conflict of interest.

References

Berghaus, Margot. 2010. *Luhmann Leicht Gemacht. Eine Einführung in die Systemtheorie*. Stuttgart: Böhlau Verlag GmbH & Cie.

Brown, Michelle P. 2003. *The Lindisfarne Gospels: Society, Spirituality and the Scribe*. London: British Library.

Classen, Constance. 1993. *Inca Cosmology and the Human Body*. Salt Lake City: University of Utah Press.

Donnan, Christopher B. 1979. *Moche Art of Peru. Pre-Columbian Symbolic Communication*. Los Angeles: Museum of Cultural History, University of California. First published 1976.

Donnan, Cristopher B., and Donna McClelland. 1979. *The Burial Theme in Moche Iconography*. Washington, DC: Dumbarton Oaks, Trustees for Harvard University.

Gareis, Iris Estefanía Ana. 2003. *Die Geschichte der Anderen. Zur Ethnohistorie am Beispiel Perus (1532–1700)*. Berlin: Dietrich Reimer Verlag.

Grieder, Terence. 1975. The Interpretation of Ancient Symbols. *American Anthropologist. New Series* 77: 849–55.

Karlovich, Atila. 2006. La sombra, el alma y el Diablo Supay en los Andes. *Nuevo Diario de Santiago del Estero*, January 22. Available online: http://www.adilq.com.ar/atila11.html (accessed on 17 August 2018).

Kern, Margit. 2010. Übersetzungsprozesse in der religiösen Kunst der Frühen Neuzeit: Die Mission in Neuspanien. In *Religion und Mobilität: zum Verhältnis von raumbezogener Mobilität und religiöser Identitätsbildung im frühneuzeitlichen Europa; [Ergebnisse einer internationalen Tagung am Mainzer Institut für Europäische Geschichte]*. Edited by Henning P. Jürgens and Thomas Weller. Göttingen: Vandenhoeck & Ruprecht, pp. 247–74.

Kramer, Kirsten, and Jens Baumgarten. 2009. Einleitung: Visualisierung und kultureller Transfer. In *Visualisierung und kultureller Transfer*. Edited by Kirsten Kramer and Jens Baumgarten. Würzburg: Königshausen & Neumann, pp. 11–28.

Kubler, George. 1967. *The Iconography of the Art of Teotihuacán*. Washington, DC: Dumbarton Oaks, Trustees for Harvard University.

Kubler, George. 1985. On the Colonial Extinction of the Motifs of Precolumbian Art. In *Studies in Ancient American and European Art. The Collected Essays of George Kubler*. Edited by Thomas Ford Reese. New Haven: Yale University Press, pp. 66–74.

MacCormack, Sabine. 1991. *Religion in the Andes. Vision and Imagination in Early Colonial Peru*. Princeton: Princeton University Press.

Malinowski, Bronislaw. 1947. Introduction. In *Cuban Counterpoint: Tobacco and Sugar*. New York: Duke University Press. First published 1940.

Martínez, Gabriel. 1983. Los dioses de los cerros en los Andes. *Journal de la Société des Américanistes* 69: 85–115. [CrossRef]

Menzel, Wolfgang. 1854. *Christliche Symbolik. Theil 1*. Regensburg.

Netzer, Nancy. 1998. The Design and Decoration of Insular Gospel-Books and other Liturgical Manuscripts, c. 600–c. 900. In *The Cambridge History of the Book in Britain*. Edited by Richard Gameson. Cambridge: Cambridge University Press, vol. 1, pp. 225–43.

Nicklisch, Andrea. 2013. The Seeming and the Real. Problems in the Interpretation of Images on Seventeenth- and Eighteenth-Century Silverworks from Bolivia. In *Image-Object-Performance. Mediality and Communication in Cultural Contact Zones of Colonial Latin America and the Philippines*. Edited by Astrid Windus and Eberhard Crailsheim. Münster: Waxmann Verlag GmbH, pp. 155–71.

one description as generally valid and thus as correct, but to keep in mind that various truths may be equally valid (Gareis 2003, p. 101)—that is, that multiple truths and realities may exist.

Ortiz, Fernando. 1947. *Cuban Counterpoint: Tobacco and Sugar*. New York: Duke University Press. First published 1940.

Phipps, Elena, Johanna Hecht, and Cristina Esteras Martín. 2004. *The Colonial Andes: Tapestries and Silverwork, 1530–1830*. New York: Metropolitan Museum of Art, pp. 194–96.

Poeschel, Sabine. 2005. *Handbuch der Ikonographie. Sakrale und Profane Themen der bildenden Kunst*. Darmstadt: Primus Verlag GmbH.

Pratt, Mary Louise. 1991. Arts of the Contact Zone. In *Profession*. New York: Modern Language Association, pp. 33–40.

Quilter, Jeffrey. 1996. Continuity and Disjunction in Pre-Columbian Art and Culture. *RES: Anthropology and Aesthetics* 29/30: 303–17. [CrossRef]

Salazar-Soler, Carmen. 1987. El Tayta Muki y la Ukupachu. Prácticas y creencias religiosas de los mineros de Julcani, Huancavelica, Perú. *Journal de la Société des Américanistes* 73: 193–217. [CrossRef]

religions

MDPI

Article

Prayers of Cow Dung: Women Sculpturing Fertile Environments in Rural Rajasthan (India)

Catrien Notermans

Department of Cultural Anthropology and Development Studies, Radboud University, PO Box 9102, 6500 HC Nijmegen, The Netherlands; c.notermans@maw.ru.nl

Received: 5 December 2018; Accepted: 15 January 2019; Published: 22 January 2019

Abstract: In line with the special issue's focus on material religion and ritualistic objects, this article focuses on the multi-sensory prayers that certain groups of Hindu women craft in cow dung at the doorstep of their residences during Divali. This yearly ritual of kneading and praying with cow dung is known as the *Govardhan puja* (worship of Mount Govardhan). It is generally said to be the worship of the popular cowherd god Krishna and the natural environment he inhabits. Ethnographic research into the multiple meaningful layers of women's cow dung sculptures in the rural villages nearby Udaipur (Rajasthan) reveals the ritual is more than that. The cow dung sculptures not only reflect Krishna's body and sacred landscape but also the local environment women share with families, animals and (other) gods. Therefore, the article seeks to answer the following questions: how are women's cow dung sculptures built up as ritual objects, what different images are expressed in them, and what do these images reveal about women's intimate and gendered connections with their human and non-human environment? To answer these questions the article focuses on the iconography of women's sculptures, the performance of the ritual, and the doorstep as the location where women's beautification of the cow dung takes place.

Keywords: Hinduism; India; Govardhan puja; cow dung; gender; ritual art; nature; human-nonhuman sociality; symbolic anthropology; ethnography

1. Introduction

On the fourth day of the annual Hindu festival Divali, women of the land- and cattle owning castes in the rural villages near Udaipur city in southern Rajasthan knead two-dimensional sacred sculptures out of large quantities of fresh cow dung (*gobar*) (Figure 1). The women's ritual of making and blessing the sculptures starts in the morning after sunrise and finishes about three hours later. The sculptures, which the women call Govardhan, only exist in the creative and ritual process of making them. Immediately after completion, women pray over the sculptures, take their cows from the cow shed to crush and bless them, and then abandon the material to give it time to perish. Two weeks later, they scatter it at their fields as manure and bringer of good luck. The crafting of the cow dung is a joyful event in the villages. The women occupy the village streets and do the ritual without help from temple priests. Male relatives also respect the women as ritual experts and wait for the evening when it is their turn to honour their bulls and beautify them with red paint and henna decorations (Figure 2).

This yearly ritual of kneading and praying with cow dung is known as the *Govardhan puja* (worship of Mount Govardhan).[1] It is generally said to be the worship of the popular cowherd god Krishna

1 *Puja* means Hindu ritual worship. It is often done by one person (priest or lay persons) and attended by others, in temples or in home shrines (e.g., Burkhalter Flueckiger 2015, pp. 89–93). A puja can be directed towards gods, people, ancestors,

and the natural environment he inhabits (Entwistle 1987; Lodrick 1987; Toomey 1990; Vaudeville 1980; Wadley 2000b, pp. 12–13). Mount Govardhan is a sacred hill in Braj, a region in the Indian state of Uttar Pradesh. Braj, and particularly, Mount Govardhan, are the setting for many legends relating to Krishna's life: it is where he was born and raised, grazed his cattle, and played with his girlfriends. The stony and oval shaped flat mountain is perceived as the natural form of Krishna himself and thus as a living being (Haberman 1994, p. 126).[2] Even beyond this sacred landscape, Hindus recognize in every oval-shaped stone the aniconic form of Krishna's body (Haberman 2017, p. 487). Krishna *is* Govardhan and in this manifestation the protector of cattle and cowherd populations. The oval and convex appearance of Krishna Govardhan is also the basic shape of the cow dung sculptures made by the women in rural Udaipur, at 650 km from Braj.

Figure 1. Women kneading sacred cow dung sculptures, Badi 2017 (picture by author).

Figure 2. Farmer with his decorated and venerated bulls, Havala 2017 (picture by author).

animals, landscape elements or goods. The ritual takes a few minutes: a prayer is chanted while the object of devotion is honoured with gifts of fire, smell (incense sticks), colour, pure water, food and/or sweets. After the prayer the gifts return to the devotees as blessings.

2 The actual size of Govardhan Mountain sharply contrasts with its legendary fame. It is an eight kilometres long flat rocky ridge that, at its highest, stands not more than 30m above the adjacent land. Not only the hill but also every stone or rock from this hill is seen as Krishna's natural form (Toomey 1990, p. 176 fn 11).

When doing ethnographic fieldwork during the Divali festival in 2017, I observed women creating the sculptures at the doorstep of their residences in two different villages. These women share with Krishna a deep love for cows. They raise an average of two cows and two buffalos and spend most of their (leisure and working) time in close proximity with them by sheltering them in or nearby the house and taking them back and forth to the fields for grazing. The cattle are part of the family and receive women's unremitting care and attention. When observing the Govardhan worship, I noticed that the women intensely enjoyed the kneading of cow dung. When questioning them about the form and content of the sculptures afterwards, I realised even more the ritual was not restricted to the worship of Krishna. Although it is generally said that the cow dung figure represents the Govardhan hill and thus Krishna's body (e.g., Vaudeville 1980), women's own iconography revealed many more figurative layers. The sculptures also reflect the local environment women share with families, animals and (other) gods.

In line with the special issue's focus on material religion and ritualistic objects, this article seeks to answer the questions: how are women's cow dung sculptures built up as ritual objects, what different images are expressed in them, and what do these images reveal about women's intimate connections with their human and non-human environment? Concentrating on the iconography of women's sculptures I aim to understand how the ritual—with its mythical origin in the sacred landscape of Braj—finds its local expression in rural Udaipur that is meaningful to women's daily religious and economic lives.

Women's sensory engagement with cow dung took me right into the core business of the women in the villages. Working with cow dung turned out to be daily routine rather than exceptional religious practice. What in a series of Divali rituals is festively set apart from everyday life in fact reflects women's daily operations with this material: they collect it in the cow shed, carry it on their heads to the fields to be used as manure, and process it into various products vital to their daily lives. The cow dung is not 'dirty shit' nor animal 'waste' but the most precious gift women receive from their cows. For me as a researcher it was core material too because it offered me an entrance into the realm of human–nature relationships which appeared to be crucial to women's daily lives. The focus on cow dung made me realise that women, cows and cow dung are intimately connected and constitute the vital link in the ecological equilibrium of land, humans, animals, plants and water; a link that guarantees the villager's well-being.

The cosmology women express in their cow dung sculptures challenges any nature–culture and nature–supernature divide that is recently discussed in anthropology (e.g., Descola 2014; Hastrup 2014; Ingold 2000, 2011); as well as the stereotypical domestic-public, female-male divide that is often said to characterize people's segregated social lives in North India. Wadley (1989, p. 73) for example, stated in her work on women's ritual in a North Indian rural community:

> Whereas men's rituals are aimed primarily at general prosperity or good crops and at the world outside the house itself, women's rituals focus more specifically on family welfare and prosperity within the walls of their homes. (...) Essentially, men and women in Karimpur occupy separate worlds. For the most part, women live and work in their homes and have little mobility outside of them. (...) The courtyard and the rooms around it form the women's world. (...) In many aspects of life, even in the content of songs and the way they are sung, men and women express their separate worlds. It is not surprising, then, that women's desires, as expressed in their rituals, are those of their world—the household—while men's concerns are focused primarily on the outer world.

Such a gender divide resonates in the literature on Govardhan puja in Braj. Although this may be the outcome of local research on gendered divisions of tasks and responsibilities in private and public spaces in the 1980s and 1990s, it also may reflect dominant (traditional) western and (priestly) male assumptions about Hindu women's confinement to the home. To this perspective I would like to add a gender perspective that connects with (feminist) anthropologists' scholarship challenging the stereotype image of the subordinated and secluded North Indian woman (e.g., Gold 1988; Harlan 1991; Jeffery 1979; Jeffery and Jeffery 2018; Pintchman 2005, 2007; Raheja and Gold 1994) and is based on my research in Rajasthan (e.g., Notermans and Pfister 2016). In my opinion, women's Govardhan puja in rural Udaipur today, in both its public location and its outward orientation towards the natural environment, allows a gender perspective that goes beyond women's domestic domain and values the vital contributions women make to the rural economy and the sustenance of the environment that humans and non-humans share. It also reveals a gendered view of the human–nature relationships that is part of women's cosmology.

I will first describe the fieldwork location and the research methodology employed. Then I will explain how the research connects to the existing literature on the Govardhan puja in particular, to the women–cows–cow dung connection in North India, and to women's ritual art more generally. Then I turn to the context of the Divali festival before focusing on the material form and ritual sequence of women's Govardhan worship in rural Udaipur. The description of Govardhan as a ritualistic object will follow the analytical distinction between the various meaningful layers I found to be present in women's cow dung sculptures. In addition to the iconographic layers and before turning to the conclusion I will add to the analysis two more dimensions by describing the performance and the ritual space.

2. Fieldwork in Rural Udaipur

My qualitative study of Govardhan puja took place against the background of 10 years of recurrent research in the same region. My long-term involvement in women's religious lives in Udaipur and nearby villages started in 2008 and continued with yearly revisits ever since. Studying the meaning of women's rituals and symbolic activities requires longitudinal commitment because women express their religious knowledge in a year-round cycle of festivals. During a total of 17 months of fieldwork, I studied a variety of these calendrical festivals (like Holi, Sheetala Mata, Dasha Mata, Gangaur, Raksha Bandhan, Navratri, Karva Chauth, and Divali) and often seized an additional meaning of a recurring symbol in another ritual than that under study at an earlier moment. Moreover, religion in everyday practice is often about *doing* not *saying* and, therefore, difficult to access through interviews alone, especially when the ritual (or festival) is still taking place (Pink 2009). Revisits make it possible to look back, get detailed explanations, and take multiple perspectives into account.

As the Govardhan puja occurs in a short time on one particular festival day, I focused my attention on women's ritual activity in two neighbouring Hindu villages, Havala and Badi.[3] In both villages, a vast majority of the population belongs to the land- and cattle owning castes: the Brahmin (priestly) and Sutar (carpenter) castes in Badi, and the Rajput (warrior) and Teli (oil presser) castes in Havala. In Badi, the dominant caste is Sutar (40 percent of the population). Together with the Brahmin who are almost equal in size they make up 75 percent of the village population; leaving 20 percent for scheduled tribes and 5 percent scheduled castes.[4] In Havala, the dominant caste is Rajput (75 percent of the population). Together with the Teli caste they make up 85 percent of the village population; leaving 15 percent scheduled castes. Nearly all houses in Havala have a cowshed inside their compound, right opposite or next to it. With an average of 5 people and 4 cattle per household Havala village is populated by almost an equal number of human and animal inhabitants.[5]

---

3 According to the India Census from 2011 (http://censusindia.gov.in/2011-Common/CensusData2011.html) Havala (at 8 km from Udaipur) counts 1159 inhabitants and Badi (at 10 km from Udaipur) 2712 inhabitants. In both villages the households contain an average number of five people. Havala and Badi belong to Tehsil Girwa in district Udaipur.

4 The tribal Bhil people in Badi also used to have land and cattle (mainly goats, some cows, no buffalos) but many sold their costly land to property dealers and invested the returns in luxurious housebuilding and weddings. As scheduled caste people they also profit from the job reservations offered to them by the government. Class thus not always overlaps with caste.

5 In 2018, I conducted a survey with a sample of 10 percent of the households in Havala. This revealed an average of 4 cattle and 0.5 acres land per household. The ratio between human and animal inhabitants of households is 95:80. Scheduled caste people in Havala neither had land nor cattle but seemed to live good lives due to high degrees of education and well-paid jobs in the city.

Cows occupy a vital position in women's daily lives: they are simultaneously perceived as children of the family, demanding constant care, and as mothers because they give milk and nourish the human family. In this position they are venerated as *Gaumata* (Mother Goddess Cow). The cow helps the human mother to sustain the family: by providing milk (which women process in various nutritious products like curd, butter, cheese, buttermilk, and sweets), urine (used as medicine and insecticide, and as a purifier in rituals because it is considered as pure as sacred water from the Ganges), and cow dung. Cow dung has several uses: as an organic and ecologically sound manure for the fields, or processed into cow dung cakes as fuel (for cooking or heating when temperatures get cold, and because of its pureness for sacred sacrificial fire ceremonies (*havan*)), as a disinfectant in homes, and for coating walls and floors because of its capacity to absorb malignant energies, to purify the space, and to cool the house in summer times.[6] The intimacy and good feeling people have with cow dung is also experienced when eating the most favourite local bread which is baked directly in cow dung cakes and consumed with lentils (a dish called *dahl bati*). Because of all these nourishing and life-giving capacities the cow is a symbol of prosperity and fertility, which applies, *par excellence*, to the cow dung as well.

The traditional caste occupations in the villages are largely replaced by agriculture and animal husbandry; by work in dairies oriented at the urban market, and by wage labour in Udaipur (government or tourism-related jobs). When asked about the gendered division of labour, people say both men and women engage in agriculture and cattle breeding. In practice, however, the women do most of the work: they feed, milk and care for the animals, decide about crossing their female cattle and care for the baby animals; clean the stable and collect the dung; carry water; cultivate the fields (for subsistence and marketing); and collect fodder and firewood. Men assist in the fields when necessary, help with transportation and marketing in town, and take over women's animal care mainly when running a commercial dairy (with 4–8 buffalos). Men doing wage labour commute between the village and the city, leaving the bulk of agriculture to their wives but boosting the household economy with cash money, often used for house construction and luxury goods. The women studied state that they love their work and appreciate the husband's financial contribution. Only a few women received no support from their husband; some were widowed, others complained about their husband's drinking habits. These women helped themselves out with sharecropping.[7]

Altogether, the village women appear to live a prosperous and independent life, enjoying the daily freedom to move around in the village and between their house and their field, often in cheerful company of neighbouring female friends and relatives. The villagers in general seem to be well off. They have land and cattle that secure their lives; their land is fertile and extremely valuable; there is sufficient groundwater for irrigation; and at a stone's throw from Udaipur (with half a million inhabitants and a flourishing tourist industry), a surplus of milk and vegetables is easily sold at the urban market, enhancing the household income as well.

To study Govardhan puja, I initially stayed for one month during festival time in 2017. I focused on the women of the land- and cattle-owning population (Brahmin, Sutar, Bhil in Badi; Rajput and Teli in Havala) as they have cows and fields to honour and ample cow dung for doing the puja. I made observation tours through the villages at the specific festival day of Govardhan puja. I had small talks with the women doing the ritual and recorded their activity on photos and videos. When I returned to the field in 2018 (two visits of one month each) I used this visual material for small talks about the event and during in-depth photo-elicitation interviews with 15 women I observed

6 Despite the fact that women process the cow dung into multiple products, women do not experience serious shortages of cow dung for manuring the field. Cow dung cakes for fuel are made only in the hot season (April–June) for using them in the humid monsoon season (July-September) when brushwood is too wet for being used as fuel. In the remaining nine to ten months of the year, cow dung is mainly used (and stored) as manure in agriculture. As also the dung of goats, horses and camels is used on the fields, women are generally not short of manure during the rainy season.

7 This means they make an agreement with a landowner who offers them land, water and manure to use. Together they buy the seeds. The women do the agricultural work and deliver half of the harvest to the landowner.

doing the ritual before. Walking through the rural environment as 'participant sensing' (Pink 2009) allowed me to observe people's engagement with nature from a different perspective. From the height of the mountains I saw how the connections between the different landscape elements (mountains, fields, and lakes) reflected the composition of women's cow dung sculptures. I also made grand tour observations in the villages to observe women during daily activities and to learn about the gendered division of tasks as this could deviate from the spoken information in interviews. Two male and two female local residents helped me translating between English, Hindi and the local language Mewari. As the Census of India from 2011 lacks quantitative information on land- and cattle ownership and caste composition, I conducted a survey with a sample of 10 percent of the households in Havala and interviewed the block development officer at the Panchayat in Badi. I also asked men about the meaning and stories behind women's cow dung figure but they said they could not help me because 'it was a ladies' concern'. While cattle raising and agriculture was said to be (in principle) gender neutral, praying with cow dung was unanimously defined as women's work.

3. Govardhan Puja in the Literature

Considering the fact that the Govardhan puja is said to be an 'all-Indian (although predominantly northern Indian) cult' (Vaudeville 1980, p. 1), recurring every year, and involving large numbers of female cattle farmers in North India, remarkably little scholarly attention has been paid to it. Braj scholars clearly dominate the literature on Govardhan puja (e.g., Entwistle 1987; Vaudeville 1980). They explain the ritual from the Govardhan myth, known as "govardhana-dharana" (the lifting of the Govardhan hill) (Vaudeville 1980, p. 1). This story goes that Krishna saved the cowherd people in Braj from heavy rains by lifting the Govardhan mountain with his left hand and sheltering the people together with their cows under the mountain. Putting much emphasis on the mythical and scriptural context, little attention is paid to the women doing the ritual and the social-economic context in which the ritual takes place. Braj scholars also tend to equate the Govardhan puja with the ritual of *Annakut* (mountain of food), happening at the same day of the Divali festival. During this temple ritual people offer huge amounts of cooked food to Krishna, usually under priestly supervision (Entwistle 1987, p. 283; Toomey 1990, p. 165; Vaudeville 1980, p. 1). Emphasising temple religion rather than women's lived religion, women's sacred sculptures produced in or nearby the home remain neglected. Moreover, Braj scholars found the Govardhan puja to be a private and domestic ritual, done by the women of the household in the inner courtyard of their residence (Vaudeville 1980; Toomey 1990). In rural Udaipur, however, I found today's ritual taking place in the public domain of the village streets. This made me wonder whether the Braj literature pictured a regional rather than a general North-Indian image and how a contemporary and deviant local expression in rural Udaipur relates to the classical North Indian myth.

In the Rajasthani villages, I found the ritual to be different in many aspects. Besides the Govardhan myth local stories about Krishna appeared to be meaningful. The women neither spoke about Annakut nor cooked huge amounts of food. Although Vaudeville's article 'The Govardhan myth in Northern India' (Vaudeville 1980) offers detailed information on both legend and ritual, only one of the three essential features of the ritual she raises corresponds to my observations, namely that it entails 'a cow dung anthropomorphic representation of the Govardhan hill' (1980, pp. 3–4). Although Vaudeville (1980) mentions the ritual to be an exclusively women's activity, I believe the gender perspective would deserve more attention in the literature on the Govardhan puja. In this study, I would like to focus on such a gender perspective by offering a study of lived religion. In my approach gender matters because women are the sole practitioners, the cow dung figure itself is gendered, and also the cattle and the natural environment are locally perceived in gendered terms.

I intend to show that Govardhan worship in rural Udaipur responds to the age-old myth and simultaneously integrates local realities and women's present-day matters. It is likely that the Govardhan puja varies across North India and takes its peculiar form in each specific context of oral and ritual traditions, gender relations and human–nature relationships. Lodrick (1987, pp. 109–11) confirms the variation across the country and states that the Govardhan puja varies from being strongly related to Krishna in Braj to being less associated with Krishna elsewhere, or lacking such a link altogether. According to Lodrick, when the connection with Krishna is weak and the focus more on the dung, "an alternative etymology of Govardhan sees the word being derived from *gobar* and *dhan*, meaning "dung-made," which in village usage becomes "cow-dung wealth"" (1987, p. 109). This interpretation comes close to the popular etymologies I found in rural Udaipur: "go-vur-dhan" is "cow-increase-wealth"—thus remaining true to the Sanskrit noun vardhana (increasing; bringing prosperity)—but also: "gobar-dhan" is "cow dung-wealth"—a delightful spin in which the vernacular pronunciation of v as b produces a direct association with gobar, cow dung. The local ritual involves the worship of cow dung *and* Krishna, and simultaneously honours women and cows who increase wealth in mutual cooperation.

4. The Women–Cows–Cow Dung Connection in the Literature

In contrast to the Braj literature paying explicit and extensive attention to the Govardhan puja, the (feminist) ethnographic literature on women and religion in rural North India hardly mentions women's ritual handling of cow dung. Wadley (1989, p. 75) briefly r efers to the Govardhan ritual in her study of a calendrical cycle of 20 rituals practiced by high-caste Hindu women in a rural village in Uttar Pradesh. For detailed description, however, she selects five rituals in which, she states, women's male kin (brothers, husbands and sons) are the focus of worship. In her contribution to the longitudinal study of Wiser and Wiser (2000); Wadley (2000a, p. 319) briefly mentions the Govardhan puja as one of the rituals occurring during the fall festival season but again does not pay analytical attention to it. Notable is the picture at the first page of this book's appendix showing two women kneading a cow dung sculpture for Govardhan puja (which appears to be a variation to the ones in Braj and Udaipur). Its caption provides the sole information on Govardhan puja in this extensive ethnography on the lives of rural women in North India.

In her work on women's religious rituals in Benares (Uttar Pradesh), Pintchman (2005, pp. 63–66) instead dedicates a complete section on Govardhan worship and Annakut, complemented with a picture showing two women worshipping a cow dung figure (ibid., p. 65). Although her description largely follows the Braj literature by emphasizing the importance of the Govardhan myth and Krishna, she also found that "celebrants place the image at their front gate so that Govardhannath will safeguard the home for the upcoming year" (ibid.). This is confirmed in the picture showing two women sitting on the sidewalk in front of their residence. Pintchman, however, does not analyse the positioning and iconographic content of women's cow dung figures, but focuses on the textual interpretation of women's songs and narratives accompanying the ritual.[8]

I found the most detailed elaboration of women's cow dung sculpturing in Raheja (1988) work on rituals of gift-giving and intercaste relationships in a rural village in north-western Uttar Pradesh. She describes a ritual called *godhan takkarpurat* (ibid., pp. 166–68, picture on p. 190) which she analyses in the context of Divali, the sugar cane harvest, and people's crucial relationship with cattle. She notes a link with the Govardhan myth and observes women doing the ritual in the cattle pen and placing small figurines of cow dung into the *takkarpurat* (a square frame made of cow dung) (ibid., p. 167). Both aspects of the *takkarpurat* come close to women's practice in rural Rajasthan. Even more interesting is that the *takkarpurat* would absorb the inauspiciousness of the cattle, the family and the harvest and bring auspiciousness and wealth for the upcoming year. This corresponds with the meaning of women's doorstep designs in rural Udaipur that are also meant to attract fortune and protect the home against

8 The same emphasis on women's poetic language of song and story can be found in the work of feminist scholars focusing on women's ritual practices and oral traditions (like songs, folktales, and personal narratives, and everyday talk) in North India. To reveal women's critical voices and 'poetic resistance to structures of power' (Raheja and Gold 1994, pp. xv–xvi; see also Harlan 1991; Pintchman 2005, 2007; Wadley 2008, p. 330), their work is mainly speech-oriented and makes little explicit references to women's cow dung practices or other artistic aspects of the rituals.

misfortune. In line with Raheja's emphasis on the functioning of the ritual, I will focus on cow dung as the central material that makes women's sculptures work as purifiers and bringers of good luck.

The aforementioned studies which (more or less) refer to women's cow dung ritual pay little or no attention to the cow dung material as well as its unique properties. Some descriptions of women's rituals indirectly (mainly through the pictures included; e.g., (Pintchman 2005, p. 105)) reveal that sculpturing with cow dung, and also with (river) clay, regularly occurs in women's worship (Pintchman 2005, pp. 103–4; Wadley 1989, p. 76). Pintchman says about clay that women declared the Ganges mud to be "not only readily available, but also pure, and hence an appropriate substance to use to make divine images. The Ganges is a goddess, and the mud along the river's bottom is continuously cleansed by her sanctifying presence" (2005, pp. 103–4). This aspect of being plentiful, pure and sacred applies to cow dung as well, which makes it a proper substance for ritual sculpturing. Because of its cleaning property of absorbing evil and inauspiciousness, women also use cow dung for plastering houses, floors and doorsteps (e.g., Elgood 2000, p. 223).

Taking into account the capacity of cow dung to make things clean and auspicious, I follow Ingold's plea "to take materials seriously" (Ingold 2007, p. 14). I will explore the cow dung and study its properties, "not as fixed, essential attributes of things (...) but as processual and relational" (ibid.) and study how women, in processing the material, shape and establish their relationships with their human and non-human environment. I will show that via the processual and relational properties of cow dung, women play a vital role in village economics and environmental care.

In addition to the scarce descriptions of women's Govardhan puja in the ethnographic literature on women's rituals in North India, I found relevant comparative information in the ethnography of women's ritual art in India. This art includes terracotta figurines, wall and floor paintings which are, like the cow dung figures, "largely ephemeral, made to endure the time of the ceremony and only efficacious if combined with ritual performance" (Elgood 2000, p. 188) and closely linked to people's residences. In women's artistic activities, ethics and aesthetics are closely related (ibid.; Nagarajan 2019). What looks good and is beautified (places, humans, animals, gods) entices good luck and abundant life. During Divali in particular, women purify and beautify places to attract divine attention and to invite Lakshmi and her auspicious energies into their house.

Nagarajan (2019) recently published ethnography on women's art in *kolam* rituals in the South Indian state of Tamil Nadu comes closest to my observations of Govardhan rituals in rural Rajasthan. In Tamil Nadu, women paint a kolam (ritual design made with ground white rice flour) on the front threshold of the house: the place where the private domestic world encounters the outside world. Women make this sacred drawing "to do something beautiful, to banish misery and bad luck, and to encourage the auspicious entry of Lakshmi who brings wealth and good luck" (2019, p. 4). The design also acts, Nagarajan states, "as a bridge between inner and outer world, between what can be controlled and what cannot be controlled, and between domestic and public space" (2019, p. 10). Women's doorstep rituals during Divali in rural Udaipur resemble women's daily kolam rituals in Tamil Nadu. The Govardhan, like the kolam, serves as a bridge and 'as a marker of gender' (2019, p. 33). By making the doorstep pure and beautiful with Govardhan, women celebrate their identity as auspicious wives and mark it as a crossing—not a divide—between domestic and public space; a crossing where women together with their cows play an important role as protectors of the house and providers of wealth and prosperity.

By saying that women's socio-religious and economic participation goes beyond domesticity and stretches out into the wider environment, I do not deny that the domestic domain highly matters for the women studied. Their daily orientation and activities certainly *contain* the domestic but are not *confined* to it.[9]

---

9 In this article, the public domain refers to the physical space of village streets, shops and meeting places, fields and 'jungle'. In the locations studied, women's participation in the public space does not (yet) comprise political engagement or environmental activism. As long as the women keep control of land, cattle, seed selection, and methods of irrigating and

5. Divali, a Celebration of Wealth

The Govardhan puja is one in a sequence of various rituals, each connected to a specific day of India's nationwide and biggest religious event Divali (see Burkhalter Flueckiger 2015, pp. 127–29). At new moon, on the third and main festival day, Hindus celebrate the material world, with Lakshmi, the goddess of abundance, money, and material wealth, at the centre of their devotion. Popular images of Lakshmi depict her as the provider of money and gold and as such people want her to cross their threshold on Divali evening. In the build-up to the festival, people thoroughly clean their residences (to brush away old and negative energies), renew the paintwork (and other decorations), and then shop for gold and silver coins and all kinds of consumer goods (devices, vehicles, home appliances) to beautify the house and home shrine. Women in particular shop for new furniture, kitchen utensils, clothes and golden jewellery. They also clean and paint the doorstep of their residences before decorating it with colourful geometrical designs (*alpana* or *rangoli*) to attract Lakshmi's attention (Figures 3 and 4).[10] On the main festival day they dress up nicely to welcome Lakshmi into their purified houses with *Lakshmi puja* and numerous small candle lights (*diya*).

Figure 3. *Alpana* made of cow dung-paint and chalk, at the doorstep of a residence in Havala during Divali 2017 (picture by author).

Figure 4. Young woman colouring her peacock *rangoli* design at the doorstep of her house, Badi 2017 (picture by author).

manuring their fields, it is unlikely they take political action. It is possible such a move takes place when women's balanced subsistence economy becomes threatened by the increasing and disturbing growth of urban elites purchasing rural patches of land for constructing villas, resorts, swimming pools and/or golf courses. Besides land shortage for the villagers, this change of land use in the countryside will increase the amount of non-recyclable waste and the exploitation of ground water. These businesses run on an immense water consumption that the desert area can hardly provide.

10 *Alpana* is a design of white chalk applied to the red base of cow dung paint. *Rangoli* is a brightly multi-coloured design of (mostly) synthetic paint.

In Udaipur and surroundings, the clay lamps lit for Lakshmi contain a grain of corn, a wild red stone fruit called *bor*, and cotton for fuse.[11] Together with the red earth colour of the lamps, they refer to the fact that Divali is originally a rural harvest festival, honouring the land and the wealth of food that people gain from it. The festival still demarcates the transition from harvest to sowing season. It combines people's monetary wealth—the 'harvest' of consumer goods in shops—and people's natural wealth –the harvest of crops in the fields. While Lakshmi reigns over the third day, Krishna reigns over the fourth day, the day of Govardhan puja. Together they cover people's economic life that stretches between rural and urban activities. The two festival days also publicly celebrate women's vital contributions to society: they are honoured as married women and providers of domestic happiness in their identification with Lakshmi, and as farmers and cattle raisers in their identification with Krishna.[12]

Lakshmi and Krishna are closely related to each other in their symbolic relationship with cows and cow dung, the earth and fertility.[13] While in the popular urban image, Lakshmi's gold is depicted as money, in the rural areas, the precious cow dung and sugar cane are considered to be her 'gold' (which will be explained later on). Lakshmi's reference to riches, abundance, fertility and the potency of the earth finds expression in women worshipping her in the form of cow dung (Elgood 2000, p. 76). The Divali festival thus provides, next to the age-old Govardhan myth, an important symbolic context for understanding women's cow dung rituals in their lived religious lives.

6. The Govardhan Puja

On an early morning in 2017, I observed the women of the land- and cattle owning castes doing Govardhan puja in the streets of the two selected villages. The women's main activity is kneading the sculpture. Govardhan is jointly made by the married women of a patrilineal family who together enjoy the artistic process of beautifying the cow dung. When asking both women and men why only women make Govardhan, everyone answered it was because of the beautification work: "Only ladies know how to make Govardhan beautiful. Gents don't know, they don't have the techniques to make things beautiful." Only the married women do the kneading because they enjoy the auspicious position to bring fertility and prosperity to the family.[14] The women make the Govardhan at the entrance of the house or the cattle yard, depending on whether there is only one entrance for people and animals or two separate ones. This entrance demarcates for both humans and animals the transition between inner and outer space; a transition that needs to be protected against bad energies and to be beautified to let positive energies enter.

It is the same transit space that was beautified to welcome Lakshmi in the house the day before. The beautification of Govardhan is in fact the third layer of auspiciousness that women apply to the doorstep. After cleaning the doorstep on the third festival day, women paint the floor with a mixture of cow dung, red earth and water. Cow dung thus is "the primary ritual ingredient in the creation of an auspicious and unpolluted basis, a sacred space that acts as a 'canvas' for the ritual designs that follow" (Nagarajan 2019, pp. 44–45). The second layer is the alpana or rangoli design made on the purified and sacred canvas to attract Lakshmi's attention in the evening. The next morning,

---

11 The official name for the *bor* tree is *zizyphus*. This wild tree grows in the mountains and supports high temperature and little water. The fruits mature at the time of Divali and recur in women's ritual actions during festival time because of their red color and round shape that resemble women's *bindi*: a dot of red *sindoor* powder placed on the forehead to mark women's auspicious married status.

12 The latter mainly counts for female cattle raisers in the villages. In Udaipur, I also came across (high-caste) families keeping five to six cows into their house and noticed cow dung sculptures in the streets; however, not with the same regularity as in the villages. See Wadley (2000b) for an elaborate discussion of the contested use of sacred cow dung in modern urban and global culture.

13 With Krishna being the reincarnation of Vishnu and Lakshmi being Vishnu's consort, the two gods also have an intimate divine relationship. They represent the divine connection of land and cattle as Lakshmi is the goddess of the earth and Krishna the god of cows. The connection between land, cattle and wealth counts for women in the villages as well.

14 Hindu sexual morality prescribes that female sexuality and reproduction are confined within the social institution of marriage.

the Govardhan is added as a third layer on top of the cow dung-painted and colourfully decorated doorstep (Figure 5).

Figure 5. Women kneading Govardhan on top of the cow dung-painted canvas and the brightly coloured rangoli's, Badi 2017 (picture by author).

When modelling the sculpture, women sit on the doorstep of the houses in the village streets. Tens of kilos of freshly collected cow dung are processed in the Govardhan that vary in size between a 0.5 and 2 square metres. The more cows and cow dung women have, the bigger the size of their sculpture. I often heard the expression that 'cow dung is like pure gold' which explains women's pleasure of working with big amounts of this material. The gift of 'gold' women get from their cows, is subsequently offered to the gods to beautify and please them and pray for prosperity and good luck. "Cow dung is so pure, it doesn't smell," a 35-year-old Teli woman in Havala explained to me, "that's because our cows get good and organic food, no chemicals or artificially processed food. We collect the fodder in the mountains and in our fields." When beautifying and protecting the doorstep as a transition place with Govardhan, the pureness and cleanliness of the cow dung matters because it absorbs inauspiciousness and appeals good luck.

The figure women carve in the precious and fertile cow dung material roughly shows two oval human bodies with head, nose, arms and legs. A proportionally big hole in the belly demarcates the navel and two smaller holes the eyes. On top of the body parts, there are flat round balls. The two human bodies are joint with a half circular strip of cow dung. The figures may vary in size, details, decorations, and finishing, but the two connected human figures recur in all village streets observed (Figure 6).[15] After finishing this basic figure, different natural materials, like the freshly harvested cotton, corn, sugar cane, wheat, hay, and flowers, are added to beautify the figure (Figure 7). Corn and wheat seeds are used to mark off the mouth, fingers, toes and the midriff. Tufts of raw white cotton do for dress-up, and fresh flowers and red coloured strings of spun cotton serve as jewellery. To make the design complete, two other major attributes are added to the figure: a freshly harvested sugar cane stick and an old door string made of hay. The sugar cane symbolises wealth and money. It is the main attribute of Lakshmi during Divali and refers to the natural 'gold' recently harvested in the field. An 80-year-old woman told me that in former times, before money entered the village economy, women used the sugar cane as a currency. The door string is part of the doorstep as a crossing place.

[15] This may be the case at district level as well. When I asked people living within a radius of about 100 km from Udaipur city whether the women in their village made the same designs as I had photographed in the two villages observed, they happily recognized the Govardhan and positively confirmed.

Placed above the doorway, it saves the inner space from destructive forces coming from outside. The old door string is replaced by a fresh one at Divali. When throughout the year a member of the household dies, the string is taken off and burnt with the corps on the stake. Offering the old string as an ornament to the cow dung figure, is a gesture of thanksgiving and a sign of prosperity as it shows that no one died in the household that year.

Figure 6. Two figures connected by a half circular strip of cow dung, Havala 2017 (picture by author).

Figure 7. Govardhan beautified with corn, cotton, hay, flowers and an old door string, Havala 2017 (picture by author).

The kneading and the decorating work take most of the time of the ritual. In a calm and joyful atmosphere, women work quietly though with a non-stop energy towards the end result. Only in Badi did I observe the women of the Brahmin caste singing songs while kneading (I will return to this later on). When satisfied with the result, the women worship the figure with puja. This only takes a few minutes. Some of the women then want to have their picture taken together with the beautified and blessed sculpture. The result of several hours of meticulous work is not meant to stay for exhibition. Immediately after the finishing, a cow is taken from the shed to cross the doorstep and bless the Govardhan by trampling it. This brings the event to an hilarious end as the cow often refuses to step through her own shit. She prefers to jump over it but the women insist till she crushes the figure with her hoofs, even if it is just a little part. The women then leave the sculptures behind and go inside their houses to resume their daily activities. Eleven days later, on the auspicious lunar day of *ekadeshi*, women sweep the dried cow dung aside and decorate the spot with a *swastika* (Figure 8) or rangoli.[16] Herewith, they renew the doorstep as a symbolic place where good luck enters the home. Two days later, at full moon, women bring the dried-up cow dung to the fields to scatter it as blessed manure.

Figure 8. Dried-up Govardhan, completed with a swastika: a good luck design made of flour, turmeric and *sindoor* (vermilion red powder) on the lunar day of ekadeshi, Havala 2018 (picture by Francine Jain).

Although the ritual sequence and the visual form of women's Govardhan puja is very similar across the villages, I noticed differences in performance and narrative as well. While the women in Havala brought up a shared local story behind their Govardhan, there was not such a strong narrative consensus among the women in Badi. The women in Badi, however, had a repertoire of songs for Govardhan which I did not find in Havala. While the women in Badi wore red wedding saris and excessive jewellery, and did not always involve the cows in their ritual; the women in Havala were less exuberantly dressed, did not observe a common dress code, and took their cows from the shed without exception. Even within the villages variation seemed to occur when newly married-in women from other locations brought their own habits and interpretations along.

7. Reading the Cow Dung

Women's sculptures represent many things at the same time: various images conflate to capture a complex reality. In order 'to read the cow dung' and to understand women's prayer, I will look at it from different perspectives. I disentangle five symbolic layers, each offering a different image. In explaining the five images moulded together in each sculpture, the emphasis will not be on the differences between or within the two villages nor on women's multiple voices and diverse interpretations.[17] My aim is to represent the story that these farmer women *share* about their intimate relationship with cows and land, their crucial role in the rural economy, and their cosmology. In the

---

16 This special lunar day is called *dev uthani ekadashi*, the awakening of god Vishnu, or *choti Divali* (small Divali). It is said to be a special day because Lakshmi and her divine husband Vishnu give blessings to all people that day.

17 A focus on the differences within and between different villages and castes would certainly add to our understanding of the variations in Govardhan puja in rural Rajasthan. If only with a view on the performance of Brahmin women in Badi, still more images, narratives and prayers come to the fore. However, in this article, extending the range of images would not add to the analysis of what the images together tell about women's connections with the human and non-human environment.

following description, I will mainly rely on the narrative information of the women in Havala. Women's songs from Badi will be used to interpret women's narrative performance in the next section.

7.1. Father and Son

With loving devotion and meticulous care the women knead two connected human figures. When asking them who these figures are and what they represent, the women in Havala unanimously answered: a father and his son. The story behind this is a story related to the cowherd-god Krishna and located in Braj. A 65-year-old woman told me that the story goes as follows:

> One day [about 5000 years ago], a married woman of the Gujjar caste [cattle breeders] left the house to sell curd. She was very good-looking: pretty and strong. Krishna *bhagwan* (god) noticed her, he immediately felt attracted by her and tried to snatch her. When he seized her sari, she responded: "Leave me", but he didn't let her go because he wanted to marry her. She then told him to come on Divali night. Then he could take her and marry her. This beautiful woman was married and had a little son.
>
> On Divali night, Krishna *bhagwan* came with his crown, to take her. The woman was sleeping in the cow shed while her husband and son were resting under a tree at the foot of the mountain. When Krishna *bhagwan* appeared at the top of the [Govardhan] mountain to go down and take the woman in the village, his cows were frightened that someone came out so abundantly dressed in the night. He'd put on many decorations and a huge headdress, because he wanted to enchant the beautiful woman who was waiting for him. The cows didn't expect to see him like that and, scared by his outfit, they ran down the hill in panic and trampled the two men resting there and killed them.
>
> The woman told to Krishna *bhagwan*: "You may take me but I want my husband's and my son's name to be honoured. You have to do something." Then, in the morning after Divali, Krishna *bhagwan* came to the village and told the women in the village to make the father and son in cow-dung and to worship them and remember them with puja.

With only some minor variations, the same story was told by all women I spoke to in this village. They said that in remembrance of the two men killed by Krishna's cows, and observing Krishna's instructions, they repeat the kneading and trampling every year.

7.2. Krishna Govardhan

Besides local stories, the village women recall the "govardhana-dharana" (the lifting of the Govardhan hill) myth when explaining the figure. This myth remembers the day that Krishna defeated Indra, the god of thunder and rain. Still a child, Krishna protected the people in the Govardhan area from heavy rains and floods supposedly caused by god Indra who was angry with the people for not venerating him (see also Haberman 1994, p. 111; Eck 2012, p. 359). Krishna sheltered some in a cave inside the mountain and others by lifting the entire mountain with his left hand, and holding it up like an umbrella. All inhabitants, along with their cows, took refuge under the mountain. This image of child Krishna lifting the mountain with one finger and the people and cows hiding underneath, is very popular through North India (Figure 9).

A particular manifestation of Krishna lifting the Govardhan mountain is Shri Nathji. He is very much loved and worshiped as the god of wealth in Rajasthan. According to the legend, Sri Nathji manifested himself in stone when he emerged from the Govardhan hill, first showing his arm and then his mouth (Vaudeville 1980, p. 36). Thereupon, the local inhabitants started to worship Shri Nathji and placed the stone image in a temple on the hill in 1501 (ibid., p. 37). More than a century later, this image was brought to Rajasthan to protect it from the hands of the Mughal emperor Aurangzeb who in 1665 was vandalizing Braj by destroying Hindu temples. Sri Nathji fled and went on a journey to Mewar which took several years before he reached Nathdwara near Udaipur. A temple was built in which the god took refuge in 1671 (Vaudeville 1976; Eck 2012, p. 377). When in the late 18th and early 19th century, the temple of Shrinathji was attacked, the stone image body was shifted again and protected at Udaipur. As Udaipur and its adjacent area was home to Sri Nathji for centuries, people's devotion to this manifestation of Krishna is immense. Typical iconographic characteristics of Sri Nathji are his rich headdress, his exuberant jewellery, expensive clothes, and his raised left hand (Figure 10).

Figure 9. Krishna lifting Mount Govardhan[18].

Figure 10. Shri Nathji[19].

18 http://radhanathswamiyatras.com/wp-content/uploads/2013/04/govardhan.jpg.
19 www.nathdwaratemple.org/manorath/shakghar-samagri-shriji.

Related to the Govardhan myth are thus two images of Krishna: Krishna as the convex and oval shaped natural form of Mount Govardhan and Krishna as the god child Shri Nathji lifting the mountain. Both images are visible in women's cow dung sculptures. Each of the two male cow dung figures represents the rocky hill in Braj and the abundantly dressed and decorated Sri Nathji lifting that hill. Concerning the first image, the flat round balls of cow dung put on top of Krishna's body are said to represent the stones located at the rocky hill (which again are natural forms of Krishna). The twigs of hay that women upwardly fix into the cow dung mountain give the mountain its trees and greenery. Concerning the second image, Shri Nathji emerges from the cow dung figure through its excessive jewellery (cotton strings and flower necklaces), his pronounced headdress, his raised finger, and the balls of cow dung now representing the hill he lifts up.

7.3. A Fertile Natural Environment

A striking and meaningful element of the cow dung figures is the semicircle connecting the two human/divine figures at the bottom (Figure 6). The inner arms of the two figures also often touch, creating in this way a closed space which is said to be a water basin. Some women explain this part of the figure to be 'a river' (the sacred river Yamuna) others say it is 'a lake'. Inside this river/lake basin women put small cow dung figures that represent the buffalos bathing in the water. When women, during the puja, pour water and other precious liquids like milk and curd in the basin, the image of cattle bathing in the river fully emerges.

From this perspective, the image changes from being a father and a son, and being Krishna Govardhan and Sri Nathji into the image of a fertile sacred environment: an environment of a sacred mountain and a sacred river, of earth and water. The image's orientation also turns into another direction: Mount Govardhan is on top of the figure and the river Yamuna at the foot of it. The geographical connection between the hill and the river goes back to ancient times, when the sacred Yamuna used to flow nearby the Govardhan hill. Nowadays, the sacred river Yamuna still winds her way through Braj (Entwistle 1987; Haberman 2006). Also in the imagery of Sri Nathji the Yamuna often flows at the foot of the sacred hill (Vaudeville 1980, pp. 9–10).

Besides the geo-physical connection between mountain and river, there is also an aesthetic and gender connection: mountain and river together form a good-looking, and well-balanced landscape (see Eck 2012, pp. 125–26). In view of beauty, harmony, fertility and prosperity male and female natural elements need to be joined. In India, sacred rivers are generally considered female and sacred mountains male. In addition, the Yamuna river is said to be the natural female form of Krishna (Haberman 1994, p. 14); but also Krishna's lover or bride, particularly in his form as Sri Nathji (Haberman 2006, p. 102). This means the river and the mountain are worshipped as a divine couple, with the female river being seen as a liquid form of love, and the male mountain as a condensed form of love (ibid.). The divine world includes male and female elements as fertility and prosperity are said to arise from the union of both genders. Rivers need mountains to flow and to reach the earth without damaging it; mountains need rivers to live and have green overgrowth. It is only in the complementary of male and female landscape elements that life exists.

Approaching the top of the Aravalli Hills during the observation tours, I recognized these two landscape elements carved in women's cow dung sculptures: the lakes situated in between the mountains. It is not the mountain-river couple of Braj that counts here, but the pairing of mountain and lake. Lakes are the hallmark of Udaipur's natural landscape and from the height of the mountains, I realised how vital the mountain–lake union is for the villagers. In this desert area people largely depend on ground- and rainwater for drinking, cooking and irrigating. Only once a year, during the monsoon season, the lakes are filled with rainwater. The precious water runs down the mountains by intervals, regulated by the government. Although bigger in size, the shape of the Aravalli Hills appeared to come close to the mythic form of Mount Govardhan. In fact, the sacred mountain in Braj and Aravalli mountains in rural Udaipur belong to the same mountain range (Haberman 2017, p. 486). The sacred landscape of Braj thus resonates in the villagers' natural environment: the mountain and the lake, and the cattle in the enclosure. Even the cow dung stones and the twigs of hay that women add to the cow dung mountain reflect their own environment of dry stony soils and rocky hills, covered with the hay that women collect as fodder 'in the wild' (in the mountains) right at the time of the Govardhan puja.

In the image of the sacred and fertile environment, the gender of the cow dung also matters. With the earth being female, the cow dung is said to be male; male, because of the two men and god Krishna emerging from the cow dung and because it is scattered as male seed at the female earth to make it productive (see for symbolism of seeds and earth also (Dube 1986)). Fertility results from impregnating the fields with cow dung. Both genders again need each other to produce life and food.

7.4. *The Fertile Family*

Looking more closely at the cattle in the water basin and listening to what the women tell about this image, I learnt there was another meaningful layer in the Govardhan that concerned prosperity and fertility in the family. When pointing at the small cow dung figures in the river/lake, some women said these were the bathing buffalos, others said they were the children in a mother's womb. When asked, they confirmed they could be both. Through this material visualisation of the family in the cow dung figure, we come to see different aspects that are vital to women's lives: (1) women's families include both humans and animals; (2) women consider their cows and buffalos to be their children, sharing with them the same intimate space and giving them the same amount of care; (3) women's fertility and the family's prosperity is expressed in having cattle in the yard and children in the womb; and (4) women not only work on the reproduction of the human family; as breeders of cattle, they also work on the reproduction of their livestock. Crossing cows and elevating calves are main occupations in women's daily life.

At first sight, the figures of father and son represent patrilineality. Both men and women desire having sons because male offspring carries on the family line. Sons used to stay with their wives and children after marriage while daughters will move out to their in-laws' place. The importance of male sexuality for family fertility is made visible through an often well-articulated penis (and testicles) of cow dung in between the legs of the male figures. Simultaneously, women's sexuality and reproductive power are expressed in the water basin. The babies in the womb and the cattle in the water refer to women's reproductive capacities as mothers and cattle breeders. The Govardhan, on second thoughts, thus shows that besides men's sexual power in patrilineal descent, women actively contribute to the patrilineal family by bearing children and breeding cattle, and nurturing humans, animals and land.[20]

Similar to the image of Krishna being male and female, mountain and river, the Govardhan blends male *and* female sexuality that together produce offspring. This mixing is also evident in women's ritual action when they worship the completed Govardhan. By putting (or 'sowing') seeds of grain in the basin, pouring water, milk and curd into it, and adding red sindoor powder and fire—as a ritual way of feeding, washing, and blessing the figure—the warm reproductive womb manifests herself in the blood-red and sperm-white liquid that together with the seeds fill the round space of the water basin: an image of sexuality and family fecundity that goes without saying (Figure 11).

[20] See Smedley (2004) for a comparative study in West Africa. Smedley also argues that women's active contribution to the creation and maintenance of patrilineality has generally been underestimated by ascribing to women an exclusively passive and subordinate position in patrilineal systems.

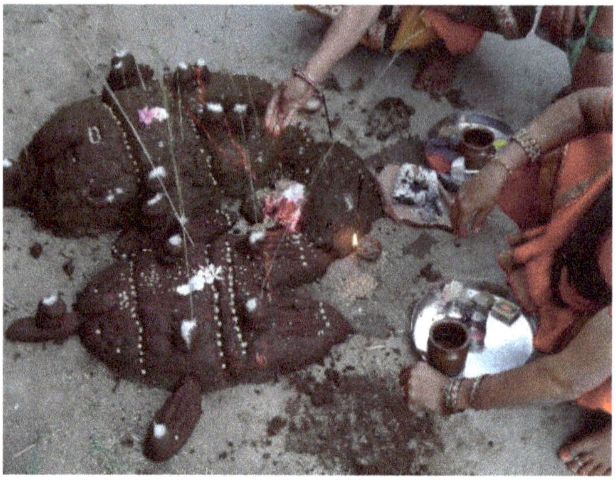

Figure 11. Mixing seeds and liquids during the ritual worship of Govardhan, Havala 2017 (picture by author).

7.5. Penis, Vagina and Navel

When elaborating on the visual image of fertility that women carve in the cow dung, we cannot ignore three Hindu key symbols present in the sculpture: the penis (*linga*), the vagina (*yoni*) and the navel (*nabhi*). Unmistakably visible in the Govardhan is the stick. When all kneading and decoration work is done, the woman go inside their house to get a tall and solid sugar cane (Lakshmi's main attribute that is offered to her at the home shrine the day before) and subsequently put it in the navel of one of the male figures (Figure 12). From a aesthetic viewpoint, the cane is disproportionally big in relation to the flat and much smaller size of the body that holds it. It fits, however, from the perspective of fertility. The sugar cane shows himself as the phallus symbol linga. The interpretation of the cane as linga is confirmed in some of the sculptures in which smaller sugar canes are put right on top of the penises of the two male figures.[21] With Lakshmi being the earth herself, her main attribute is the male sugar cane which penetrates the cow dung sculptures during Govardhan puja (see also Elgood 2000, p. 76). The red and white coloured water basin represents the vagina, yoni, another Hindu key symbol. Linga and yoni, stick and womb, associated with the colours white and red respectively, are inextricably linked to one another and together abundantly recur in the material culture of temples and home shrines, as well as in the design of allegedly profane constructions such as water pumps (Figures 13 and 14).

What is more, women do not put the tall sugar cane at a random spot in the cow dung figure but right in the middle of an equally disproportionally big navel (*nabhi*). Rising up from the navel, the cane looks like an umbilical cord, feeding and sustaining new life. Although the women did not explicitly mention this, and some even said they put the cane there for no other reason than that it was the most solid part of the cow dung figure, the navel is a recurring key symbol in Hinduism as well; it generally refers to the birth of the universe and the divine world. The navel is also one of the seven *chakra's*, energy centres in human bodies which are considered in Hindu health and yoga practices. It is significant that this particular navel chakra is linked to the goddess Lakshmi who reigns over Divali, refers to riches and abundance, and is associated with fertility and the potency of the earth (Elgood 2000, pp. 75–76). Putting the sugar cane into the navel is thus an act of visualising Lakshmi, making her strong and beautiful, and activating her as a bringer of good luck and fertility.

---

21 Gold found a similar analogy between penises and sugarcane in the songs of Rajasthani high caste women (Raheja and Gold 1994, pp. xxxi, 61). While singing about craving for sweet sugar cane and equating that craving for sweet sugarcane with a desire to have sex, women expressed in their lore a positive image of female sexuality.

The reference to fertility and family building is *explicitly* visible in the variations some women made on the figure of two male figures. Instead of two male figures, there sometimes was a male figure (with a penis) and a female figure (with breasts) with the sugar cane put in the woman's navel. One woman deviated from the two-figure composition by modelling three human figures representing a complete family: a father, mother and male child in between (Figure 15). These deviations show how women translate the mythical images of gods and landscapes into familiar images of family prosperity and fertility.

Figure 12. Sugar cane stick in Govardhan's navel, Badi 2017 (picture by author).

Figure 13. Woman's worship of linga-yoni, Udaipur 2013 (picture by author).

Figure 14. Water pump in Badi, 2017 (picture by author).

Figure 15. Govardhan representing a human family, Havala 2017 (picture by Author).

7.6. Five Images Conflating in One Cow Dung Figure

By focusing, not only on mythical or verbatim explanations of the Govardhan, but also on material forms, ritual gestures, and key symbols in the ritual, I disentangled five meaningful images. The changing faces of the figure vary in the same way as Lodrick (1987, pp. 109–11) found that the ritual varies across North India: from being explicitly associated to Krishna (the first two images described, with the first being connected to a local myth and the second to the pan-Indian myth), to being less directly associated to Krishna (the third image described), and to not at all being associated to Krishna (the last two images described). Women's Govardhan puja in Rajasthan thus entails more than 'a cow dung anthropomorphic representation of the Govardhan hill', as is argued by Vaudeville (1980, pp. 3–4). The multiple imagery also transcends the dominant explanation of the ritual being uniquely based on the myth of "govardhana-dharana." Women's lived religion does *not* exclude Sanskritic classical and authoritative texts (see also Pintchman 2005, p. 12) but it entails much more.

Taken all five images together, the constant factor is what the figure *is*: cow dung; and what the cow dung *generates*: fertility and abundant life. Women's material prayer thus is a prayer for fecundity. All that women knead in the dung are signs of prosperity: access to natural resources (cattle, land, water, mountains and forests), a healthy and beautiful family, and plenty of food. This prosperity is based on a moral economy in which the women are central actors but not the only ones. During Govardhan puja they express their dependence on cows, fields, lakes and mountains, their husbands, and their beloved gods, in attaining this prosperity. The ritual puts women's work with cow dung central and celebrates it as the vital link in the village economy. Cow dung is not just a useful crafting material, the very substance itself is divine and god-like and an object of loving care and devotion.

8. Women Performing Beauty and Solidarity at the Doorstep

After the iconographic interpretation of the visual layers of Govardhan, I want to focus on two more dimensions of the ritual to complement my analysis of women's Govardhan puja: (1) the performative dimension of women singing songs, and (2) the doorstep as the location where both kneading and singing take place. Women's prayer is not restricted to the puja at the end of the ritual (merely being a standardized ending of the ritual); it is articulated in the cow dung as well as the songs accompanying the kneading of cow dung. The songs women sing add to the kneaded prayers of 'fertile natural environment' and the 'fertile family' (described above).

8.1. Singing Beauty and Solidarity

In the process of tenderly kneading and beautifying the figures of father and son, some women sing about family beauty and prosperity and thereby confirm bonds of solidarity. In Badi, I found Brahmin women expressing unity by beautifying themselves as brides (wearing red coloured saris and plentiful jewellery) and collectively singing songs for Govardhan (Figure 16). Sitting in a (half) circle in front of the gate, each woman works on a different part of the cow dung figure and follows the (often older) woman who broke into a song. These songs are articulated over Govardhan and alternately directed to all women of the patrilineal household (those present and absent). The singing is an intimate women's affair. When women knead the two male figures with penises and testicles complete, and praise the fruits of male and female sexuality, men discretely withdraw. While creating solidarity between the women of the household, the ritual draws a spatial boundary between men and women though simultaneously celebrates their complementarity.

Figure 16. Women doing the Govardhan puja together, Badi 2017 (picture by author).

In the repertoire of songs I recorded during the event, four thematic songs recur across the different families. Together they illustrate women's view of a beautiful and fertile family. A first song directs a prayer for the fertility of fields, families, and cows and briefly runs as follows: 'may the field be full of crops, may the bullock cart leave the field full of good grain, may we have sons and daughters, may no one remain unmarried, may we have daughters-in-law and sons-in-law, and may we have good cows producing lots of milk, so we can do the churning every day.' A second song is sung for the in-married women of the family: 'Give me good fields, good cows, good wealth, my mother-in-law is doing all the work and I become the owner of the house.' A third song remembers and praises the out-married daughters of the family: 'you are far away, all alone, who cares for you, who will bring you home for festival?' This is answered by women responding: 'my younger brother will come and bring me beautiful sari and beautiful blouse, bring me colourful jewellery, and bring me back home for festival.' A fourth songs is sung for the unmarried daughters: 'Please marry me in a wealthy family so I can wear a half kilo gold and I live in a big house, all my jewellery is gold, marry me to a rich family with many cows and I become the head of that family.' Rather than deploring a subdominant position in the household, women express in their songs their ambitions and the high demands they make on their conjugal home. Although daily practice may of course deviate from these ideals, the songs express that women do not expect receiving little gold, being cut from the natal house or staying subordinate to the mother-in-law.

These songs also reveal that an auspicious house accommodates a good (=beautiful) family which means complete with humans and animals, sustained by animals and fields, and balanced by heterosexual marriage and offspring of both sexes. The absence of married-out daughters has to be balanced by the presence of married-in daughters-in-law, caring brothers travelling between the houses of parents and sisters, and sons-in-law complementing the family at a distance. While daughters-in-law aim for being the head of the family, the out-married daughters aim to return to the natal family as special guests at festive occasions. This female-centred view on the fertile and well-balanced family adds an important perspective to the visual image of father and son sculptured in cow dung and representing patrilineality. It underlines women's important position in building a patrilineal family, women's multiple belongings in houses of birth and houses of marriage, and that gender complementarity—in and outside the household—looks beautiful and entices good luck and abundant life. Women's perception of a good family thus points at the continual links of inside/domestic and outside/public domains and the need to keep them connected.

8.2. The Doorstep as Crucial Crossing

All ritual activities during the Govardhan puja occur at the doorstep which manifests itself as a crossing between the intimate interior of the household and the public space of the street and community. Like the threshold design of kolam in South India, the Govardhan "exists where the house meets the outside world, where the private and familial realm encounters the community and the shared public common" (Nagarajan 2019, p. 8). By celebrating with Govardhan the doorstep as a crucial place, women show they have multiple outward orientations—as wives, daughters, cattle raisers and farmers—and do not confine their lives to the domain inside.

During the ritual women sing about women's auspicious mobility over that crossing, leaving as out-married brides or entering as in-married brides. Also, a family's nostalgia for the out-married daughters and the daughters' wish for return visits is expressed in the songs at the doorstep. The doorstep is also a crossing of gods, cows and wealth, made possible by the women of the household. In their daily outdoor activities as farmers and cattle breeders, women cross the doorstep to procure economic security. Women and cows share the crossing as they together produce the wealth that goes out to the field in order to bring the wealth of the fields back home. During Divali women invite Lakshmi to cross the threshold on the third day and take the cows out of the shed on the fourth day. Lakshmi ritually enters the house to bring money and wealth. Cows enter the house to give birth and to give milk; their dung leaves the house to bring fertility to the fields and subsequently prosperity to the household.

Married women also share with Lakshmi their positioning at the crossing. The doorstep as transition place is dangerous and precarious and needs constant care and protection as not only positive but also bad energies may enter. As 'Lakshmi's of the house', married women master the inward flow of auspiciousness and the outward flow of inauspiciousness. Together with Lakshmi, they play a central role as gatekeepers. By doing Govardhan puja women celebrate and sanctify their roles as protectors and caretakers of the household as well as their efforts to master the erratic natural environment on which they depend.

9. Conclusions

In this article, I have analysed women's cow dung sculptures as multi-sensory prayers and showed that women craft in the sacred cow dung an affectionate intimacy with their human, natural and divine environment. By taking a material approach and looking at the figures from shifting perspectives, I found women's Govardhan to be multiform and polysemic. Depending on the perspective one takes, the Govardhan changes his face while symbols of fertility recur. The central meaning of the Govardhan puja is situated right in the cow dung and its purifying and nourishing properties, bringing fertility to land, people and animals. The figure women knead in the cow dung reveals what makes people's environment fertile: women's careful attention, their bodily and devotional work, the gods and their blessings, human sexuality, and the material gifts of the natural world. The cow dung links the human, the natural and the divine world, as well as the male and female elements of those worlds, in a continuously repeated lifecycle. Cow dung travels as a gift between the human, the non-human and the divine world and connects them to each other in order to produce wealth: from cows to women to fields to food for family and cows. It also travels in a cycle of life: the fresh cow dung has to perish and resolve in order to grow and produce life again, which is visible in the ritual sequence of the Govardhan puja.

By studying the ritual from the perspective of gender and lived religion I disclosed women's cosmology and their profound ritual and ecological knowledge that is captured in the cow dung sculpture. To date the ritual of cow dung kneading has been overlooked, either because of women mastering it, the waste material central to it, or perhaps its brief duration. My analysis points to the ritual as a gendered mode of communication. Women speak through their cow dung sculptures, not only to Govardhan and god Krishna, but also to each other and the wider society. They express their ideas about gender and human–nature relationships, and highlight the importance of their daily economic work. By embellishing the divine cow dung sculpture, women articulate how their family and natural environment should look like to be beautiful and balanced and consequently entice luck and prosperity. By jointly performing the ritual in public space, they confirm that women—together with cows—are key actors in achieving and maintaining the society's wellbeing.

Rather than a divide between private–public, female–male, or subdominant–dominant, it is the distinction between inner and outer space that matters in the Govardhan puja. This distinction is symbolically and materially captured in the doorstep. Inner and outer space are distinguished but not divided. By doing the ritual right *at* the crossing women stress their position as gatekeepers, caring for and connecting the spaces. Both spaces are occupied by women and men, animals and gods. What matters is *not* that in one of these spaces certain genders are excluded or subjugated, but that in *both* inner and outer spaces negative forces and bad luck need to be expelled and positive energies and good luck introduced. To achieve this, men and women, animals and gods need to unite, not divide, in the balanced and ethical ways that are expressed in women's cow dung sculptures.

Funding: This research received no external funding.

Acknowledgments: I thank Francine and Dinesh Jain, Narani Gameti, Fateh Lal Choubisa, and Christine d'Rozario for supporting me in this research. Without their willingness to interpret my constant questions and conversations and respond to my ceaseless need for additional information, the research would not have been possible.

Conflicts of Interest: The author declares no conflict of interest.

References

Burkhalter Flueckiger, Joyce. 2015. *Everyday Hinduism*. Chichester, Malden and Oxford: Wiley-Blackwell.

Descola, Philippe. 2014. *Beyond Nature and Culture*. Chicago: University of Chicago Press.

Dube, Leela. 1986. Seed and Earth: The Symbolism of Biological Reproduction and Sexual Relations of Production. In *Visibility and Power: Essays on Women in Society and Development*. Edited by Leela Dube, Eleanor Leacock and Shirley Ardener. Delhi: Oxford University Press, pp. 22–53.

Eck, Diana. 2012. *India: A Sacred Geography*. New York: Three Rivers Press.

Elgood, Heather. 2000. *Hinduism and the Religious Arts*. London and New York: Cassell.

Entwistle, Alan W. 1987. *Braj: Center of Krishna Pilgrimage*. Groningen: Egbert Forsten.

Gold, Ann Grodzins. 1988. *Fruitful Journeys: The Ways of Rajasthani Pilgrims*. Long Grove: Waveland Press.

Haberman, David. 1994. *Journey through the Twelve Forests: An Encounter with Krishna*. New York: Oxford University Press.

Haberman, David. 2006. *River of Love in an Age of Pollution: The Yamuna River of Northern India*. Berkeley and Los Angeles: University of California Press.

Haberman, David. 2017. Drawing out the Iconic in the Aniconic: Worship of Neem Trees and Govardhan Stones in Northern India. *Religion* 47: 483–502. [CrossRef]

Harlan, Lindsey. 1991. *Religion and Rajput Women: The Ethic of Protection in Contemporary Narratives*. New Delhi: Munshiram Manoharlal Publishers.

Hastrup, Kirsten, ed. 2014. *Anthropology and Nature*. New York: Routledge.

Ingold, Tim. 2000. *The Perception of the Environment: Essays on Livelihood, Dwelling and Skill*. London: Routledge.

Ingold, Tim. 2007. Materials against Materiality. *Archaeological Dialogues* 14: 10–16. [CrossRef]

Ingold, Tim. 2011. *Being Alive: Essays on Movement, Knowledge and Description*. New York: Routledge.

Jeffery, Patricia. 1979. *Frogs in a Well: Indian Women in Purdah*. London: Zed Press.

Jeffery, Patricia, and Roger Jeffery. 2018. *Don't Marry Me to a Plowman! Women's Everyday Lives in Rural North India*. New York and London: Routledge. First published 1996.

Lodrick, Deryck. 1987. Gopashtami and Govardhan Puja: Two Krishna Festivals in India. *Journal of Cultural Geography* 7: 101–16. [CrossRef]

Nagarajan, Vijaya. 2019. *Feeding a Thousand Souls: Women, Ritual and Ecology in India—An Exploration of the Kolam*. New York: Oxford University Press.

Notermans, Catrien, and Sina Pfister. 2016. Water and Gender in Recreating Family Life with Maa Ganga: The Confluence of Nature and Culture in a North Indian River Pilgrimage. *AIMS Geosciences* 2: 286–301. [CrossRef]

Pink, Sarah. 2009. *Doing Sensory Ethnography*. London: Sage.

Pintchman, Tracy. 2005. *Guests at God's Wedding: Celebrating Kartik among the Women of Benares*. Albeny: State University of New York Press.

Pintchman, Tracy. 2007. *Women's Lives, Women's Rituals in the Hindu Tradition*. New York: Oxford University Press.

Raheja, Gloria Goodwin. 1988. *The Poison in the Gift: Ritual, Prestation, and the Dominant Caste in a North Indian Village*. Chicago and London: The University of Chicago Press.

Raheja, Gloria Goodwin, and Ann Grodzins Gold. 1994. *Listen to the Heron's Words: Reimagining Gender and Kinship in North India*. Berkeley, Los Angeles and London: University of California Press.

Smedley, Audrey. 2004. *Women Creating Patriliny: Gender and Environment in West Africa*. Walnut Creek: AltaMira Press.

Toomey, Paul. 1990. Krishna's Consuming Passions: Food as Metaphor and Metonym for Emotion at Mount Govardhan. In *Divine Passions: The Social Construction of Emotion in India*. Edited by Owen Lynch. Delhi: Oxford University Press, pp. 157–81.

Vaudeville, Charlotte. 1976. Braj, Lost and Found. *Indo-Iranian Journal* 18: 195–213. [CrossRef]

Vaudeville, Charlotte. 1980. The Govardhan Myth in Northern India. *Indo-Iranian Journal* 22: 1–45. [CrossRef]

Wadley, Susan. 1989. Hindu Women's Family and Household Rites in a North Indian Village. In *Unspoken Worlds: Women's Religious Lives*. Edited by Nancy Auer Falk and Rita Gross. Belmont: Wadsworth Publishing Company, pp. 72–81.

Wadley, Susan. 2000a. The Village in 1984; The Village in 1998. In *Behind Mud Walls: Seventy-Five Years in a North Indian Village*. Edited by William Wiser and Charlotte Wiser. Berkeley, Los Angeles and London: University of California Press, pp. 279–338.
Wadley, Susan. 2000b. From Sacred Cow Dung to Cow 'Shit': Globalization and Local Religious Practices in Rural North India. *Journal of the Japanese Association for South Asian Studies* 12: 1–28.
Wadley, Susan. 2008. In Search of the Hindu "Peasants"' Subjectivity. *India Review* 7: 320–48. [CrossRef]
Wiser, William, and Charlotte Wiser. 2000. *Behind Mud Walls: Seventy-Five Years in a North Indian Village*, Updated and extended edition. Berkeley, Los Angeles and London: University of California Press.

religions

MDPI

Article

Bare Feet and Sacred Ground: "Viṣṇu Was Here"

Albertina Nugteren

Department of Culture Studies, Tilburg School of Humanities and Digital Sciences, Tilburg University, PO Box 90153, 5000 LE Tilburg, The Netherlands; a.nugteren@tilburguniversity.edu

Received: 29 June 2018; Accepted: 16 July 2018; Published: 23 July 2018

Abstract: The meaning of a symbol is not intrinsic and should best be seen in relation to the symbolic order underlying it. In this article we explore the ritual complexities pertaining to the body's most lowly and dirty part: the feet. On entering sacred ground persons are admonished to take off their footwear. In many parts of Asia pointing one's feet in the direction of an altar, one's teacher or one's elders is considered disrespectful. Divine feet, however, are in many ways focal points of devotion. By reverently bowing down and touching the feet of a deity's statue, the believer acts out a specific type of expressive performance. The core of this article consists of a closer look at ritualized behavior in front of a particular type of divine feet: the natural 'footprint' (*viṣṇupāda*) at Gayā, in the state of Bihar, India. By studying its 'storied' meaning we aspire to a deepened understanding of the 'divine footprint' in both its embodiedness and embeddedness. Through a combination of approaches—textual studies, ritual studies, ethnography—we emplace the ritual object in a setting in which regional, pan-Indian, and even cosmogonic myths are interlocked. We conclude that by an exclusive focus on a single ritual object—as encountered in a particular location—an object lesson about feet, footsteps, foot-soles, and footprints opens up a particular 'grammar of devotion' in terms of both absence and presence.

Keywords: Hinduism; India; material culture; ritual; Viṣṇu's footprint; place of pilgrimage; sacred geography; imaginative embodiment

1. Sacred Ground

1.1. The Object and Its Emplacement

The object is an octagonal basin, encased in silver. It stands on a low pedestal in the center of the shrine. Pilgrims flock around it and obscure my view. Some devotees make gestures of reverence, touch the basin, hold out a baby to receive a blessing, and scatter rose petals. Mourners throng around it and have their priest perform ancestor rituals. He pours milk in a conch-shell, then empties the conch-shell container in a longish dent in the middle of the basin. More flowers. Powdered sandalwood. Emerald-green basil leaves. White rice. A tray of fruits. Garlands strung of delicate white jasmine buds. Balls made of dough. Sesamum seeds. *Kuśa* grass. Brass water vessels. Marigolds.

It is only when temple assistants briskly remove all the stuff that for a moment the inside of the basin becomes visible and shows, vaguely, an uneven rock surface with a slight indentation in the center. It is perceived as a footprint. Lord Viṣṇu's footprint: Viṣṇu Himself was here and left a tangible trace around which pilgrims and mourners gather. With the Lord Himself in their midst, would not all prayers, all wishes, all vows be successful?

The place is the Viṣṇupāda temple in Gayā, in the eastern state of Bihar, India. The location is known from ancient times, and is glorified in a wide range of literature, from appropriated references in the *Ṛgveda* to personal comments in TripAdvisor. Although it must be said that today the eyes of most international travelers are focused on its neighbor, traveler-friendly Bodhgayā with which it shares part of the name. A Google search will almost always redirect to the Buddhist complex, and *Lonely Planet India* (Lonely Planet 2015, p. 520) admits: 'Truth be told, the whole of this region is off the beaten track. Outside Bodhgaya, foreign tourists are almost nonexistent, so if you are looking up to sidestep mainstream travel, this unfashionable pocket could be an unexpected highlight.'

It may be true that Gayā for foreign tourists merely serves as a transit point on the way to its Buddhist neighbor, 'Destination Enlightenment' (Geary 2008), but the town of Gayā, as one of the main ritual centers of Hinduism, on a normal day draws a steady stream of visitors who go there to perform ancestor rituals for the recently deceased. In special calendrical moments huge crowds of locals and pilgrims alike flock to the river to bathe at the most auspicious time, pour out water offerings to the Sun, perform simplified or elaborate ancestor rituals, and visit one or more of the sacred places in and around the town: particularly the 'immortal tree', the ponds, the hills, and of course Viṣṇu's footprint (see Figure 1).

Figure 1. Gayā—the footprint with traces of milk, petals and *piṇḍas* (Albertina Nugteren).

1.2. Introduction

The narratives told about places of pilgrimage in India have a variety of sources. These may consist of (1) written references made to a particular event or place in ancient texts. Although these may be no more than cryptic fragments, they are cherished as authenticating perspectives on myths, miracles, divine agency, and the special power with which a specific location is said to be imbued. (2) On a secondary level a place of pilgrimage may be mentioned and 'storied' in the great epics, *Rāmāyaṇa* and *Mahābhārata*. One of the epic heroes or heroines may have visited this place, or better still, may have had a life-changing experience here. (3) On a tertiary level a long laudatory poem may have been composed, a *māhātmya* or *sthalapurāṇa*, in praise of the sacred geography and glorifying its merits for anyone who visits such a place with a pure heart.[1] Although these panegyrics are often in Sanskrit, locally available copies in cheap print tend to be abridgments in vernacular languages. (4) And fourthly there are the local experts, ranging from long-established brahmanic families who tend to keep themselves aloof from the pilgrims' bustle but are excellent storytellers, to a special

1 Of this genre, Glücklich (2008, p. 146) wrote: 'The earliest promotional works aimed at tourists from that era were called mahatmyas.'

class of priests who serve as *paṇḍas*. *Paṇḍa* is a shortened form of *paṇḍita*, a learned person. Together they form a class of hereditary religious guides (and ritual fixers) at the major north Indian places of pilgrimage (Lochtefeld 2011, 2017). Their exclusive rights to serve certain families in the wider region are often protected by detailed genealogical records and the hand-written so-called *paṇḍa*-ledgers. They facilitate any necessary ritual actions, particularly rituals intended to help the transition of the recently dead to the state of ancestors.

Although Gayā's track record is richly established in all four types of sources mentioned above, in this article we will only briefly touch upon them, as our focus is not on the archaic pilgrims' town as such, but on one of its main features, the footprint. In Section 2.1 we introduce the fascinating world of feet, foot-soles, and footsteps in the Indian subcontinent. In section two (Section 2.2), we follow a particular form of divine embodiment, the rare footprint of the divine. In Section 2.3 we wonder how to qualify such an alleged footprint and discuss footprints (and their derivatives) as relics, representations, and reminders. In doing so we have crossed over from human-made objects to the naturally sacred, or, as ancient Indian custom has it, the self-born (*svayambhū*), self-existing, self-revealed theophany of a divine manifestation. In section four (Section 2.4), we trail—literally, in this case—Viṣṇu's footsteps through cosmogony, mythology and sacred topography, and stop in Gayā, where his divine footprint on a natural rock has become a center of devotion and ancestor rituals. By selecting three textual passages (Sections 2.4.1–2.4.3) a patchwork of 'storied' evidence and local appropriation of pan-Indian myths unfolds. We began this article with a brief sensory impression of the bustle around the footprint and pick up the trail anew by describing, analyzing and categorizing the ritual behavior in the direct presence of the footprint (Section 2.5.1). We further structure this section by zooming out to include its wider setting: a natural ensemble of sacred river (Section 2.5.2), tree (Section 2.5.3) and hills (Section 2.5.4), and, on another level, solar alignment. Finally, in part 3, we use the object lesson we learned from feet and the ritual behavior displayed around the footprint—both in its direct presence and in the sense of its narrative meaning—to discuss the embodiedness and embeddedness of a divine footprint in what we found to be a vast, layered and interlocked cultural complex.

2. Bare Feet

2.1. Of Feet and Footsteps

In Indian literature, performance art, religious life, and everyday social etiquette the human foot is both ambiguous and polyvalent. Generally, feet are humble, impure and even polluting (Moss 2016). In a hierarchically ordered society, feet both literally and figuratively are the human body's most modest and dirty part. This is particularly true in India where an ancient body symbolism—of the First Man, Puruṣa—once connected the social order with the human physique, and vice versa. The division of the First Man's physical body into a hierarchy of *varṇas* (hereditary classes) is one of the first delineations of the Hindu social body. Its four castes or classes (*caturvarṇa*) were said to correspond, in descending order, both literally and symbolically, to the four domains of the human body: the head; the shoulders and arms; the stomach area; and the legs, including the feet (cf. Smith 1994).

India may long have been a barefoot country but also has a strong culture-specific etiquette concerning feet and footwear. Putting off one's footwear before entering a home or a temple has many grounds. The first is a basic one: hygiene. The second is: a sign of respect. Crossing the threshold between the streets or fields and the house, while leaving one's footwear outside, denotes an acknowledgement of traversing from one domain to another. From the public and potentially dusty and dirty ambiance of the outside world one crosses over and steps into the domestic domain, where more subtle and possibly more rigid etiquette is required. Some may see this as an acknowledgement of the feminine domain where cleanliness and ritual propriety should rule, others simply refer to it as 'this is our custom.' In another way, home is supposed to be a more relaxed place than work or traffic, and it may be a relief to let one's shoes outside and free the feet from their day-long captivity. In some Hindu households, leather shoes and sandals are not allowed, and it is seen as a sign of respect when one leaves any offensive leather article outside, be it shoes or belt or briefcase. For some, home is traditionally also the place where one's elders live. Entering their presence in most cases no longer requires the 'touching of their feet' as a gesture of respect, humility, and submissiveness, but entering their premises may still trigger the act of leaving one's shoes outside. In some households there are, almost imperceptible to the outsider, zones of 'foot etiquette'. Families who can afford to do so may prefer to have a zone in which behavior is liberal—including footwear, smoking, eating non-vegetarian food and sitting with one's feet up—whereas there is a more private zone behind this where such things are rejected if not strictly prohibited (cf. Lamb 2005).

While in the domestic domain many traditional rules regarding feet and footwear may have disappeared, this is rarely so in temples and at other sacred sites. The threshold experience—indeed liminal in both a literal and a symbolic sense—of shedding one's footwear and walking on bare feet into the cool and shaded interior of an ancient temple may be an effective way to leave the glaring sunlight and bustle of the street behind. On the other hand, the receptiveness to another dimension may be counteracted by the feelings of vulnerability or downright helplessness upon entering 'modern' temples: slippery tiles wet with oblations, wilting petals, rotting fruit peels and sacrificial leaves. Walking around barefooted, especially in the form of a *pradakṣiṇa* (ritual circumambulation) before one enters the sanctum (*garbhagṛha*), may be a prolonged liminal experience. It prepares the devotee, through the senses—a clair-obscur for the eyes, ages of incense in the air, and bare feet grounded on stone—as well as inwardly by surrender and anticipation, for the encounter with the divine (cf. Eck 2007; Vidal 2006; Huyler 1994). Many are the temples and shrines where one devoutly touches the feet of the deity—or the living guru, for that matter. Full prostrations may not be possible because of the pressing crowds, but most of the faithful at least try to touch the *mūrti* (icon). The feet of a statue are often elaborately hennaed, circled with ankle-bells, and decorated with toe-rings; they thus invite the flow of emotions (*rasa*) and visitors may respond by laying gifts of flowers and incense at the divine feet. Moreover, as in many temples devotees find themselves at eye level with the feet of the Lord, this is the level where they can ritualize privately, intimately, without the need for a priest. In other moments of the daily ritual procedure devotees witness how the image of the deity is washed, including its feet, and subsequently dressed, decorated and fed. It should come as no surprise that this bath-water is feverishly collected as reputedly having healing and protective properties.

In some shrines, however, there may be no iconic deity or image of the revered guru or the local ruler, but merely an empty seat carrying a pair of divine feet, or a glass case holding a pair of used shoes or sandals. When asked about the origin and meaning of such objects and the ritualized behavior they evoke, some devotees refer to passages in the *Rāmāyaṇa* where the rightful ruler, Rāma, was replaced by his brother Bhārata and sent into exile. When Bhārata unsuccessfully begged his elder brother to return, he took Rāma's pair of 'paduka' with him and placed them on the king's throne in Ayodhyā, to serve as his proxy. A saint's sandals, especially the toe-knob sandals popularly known as 'paduka' (Hindi *pādikā* or *pādukā*)[2], are particularly popular in the visualization of the sacred, so much even that they may be carried around in a garland-covered palanquin (*pālkhī*), such as is the case with the saint Dnyaneswar (Jñāneśvara) whose 'padukas' are carried in a silver bullock cart from Ālandi to Paṇḍharpūr or reverse (cf. Shima 1988; Stanley 1992; Glushkova 2015).[3] A beautifully detailed depiction of 'paduka' on a stone sculpture's feet is to be seen in the Odisha State Museum in Bhubaneswar. Here the deity, Kṛṣṇa—easily recognizable by his flute-playing pose (*natavarāsana*)—is

[2] In this article, in which Indo-ethnography (a combination of ethnographic, textual and comparative approaches) moves between the Sanskrit of ancient texts, written Hindi, anglicized spelling inherited from the colonial era, and vernacular pronunciation, I use spelling suited to the particular contexts. This implies that I need to alternate, such as in the case of 'paduka', used along with *pādakā*, or Vishnupad Temple along with *viṣṇupāda*.

[3] One of the other regional Sants for which this may be performed is Tukaram (Tukārām, 1568/1608–1649/1650), the saint-singer whose deeply devotional songs are still sung during Mahārāṣṭrian pilgrimages. A relevant fragment from verse 1165 goes: 'God [is] a stone; a step [is] a stone/the one [is] worshipped, the other is trodden under a foot' (Tukaram 2003).

wearing the typical platform shoes. Not only are the 'paduka' intricately detailed, as if the 'stilts' are placed on lotus-petalled standers, his feet and ankles are covered with jewelry. A dwarfish devotee (possibly a *gopāla* or *gopī*, cowherd) reverently touches the soles of Kṛṣṇa's high-heeled sandal and looks up at him in ecstatic fervor.[4]

One often finds a pair of divine feet chiseled in stone, and resting on a round lotus pedestal, sprinkled with yellow kunkum (curcumin) and red sindur powder (vermilion, cinnabar), and covered with flowers and coins, in front of temples inside which the deity is portrayed in full iconic splendor. Feet or footwear replacing statues may symbolize both presence and absence, form and formlessness, and evoke gestures of devotion as intense as the human or divine figure would have done.[5] Perhaps even more so, since such stone feet are approachable, within reach of one's hands and eyes, free-standing so that one may make a reverent circumambulation, without priests rushing the devotee through.[6] The touching of divine feet is experienced as a full encounter, a tactile 'cross-over' possibly even richer than mere seeing (darshan; *darśana*) since this reaching out, kneeling and touching includes various physical gestures of devotion involving multiple senses and the entire human body (cf. Howes and Classen 2014).

Another way of weaving the divine into embodied acts of devotion is the common practice of making *raṅgolī* (*raṅgāvalī*), respectively *ālpanā* (*ālimpana, ālepanā*) or *kōlam* or any other regionally specific name for colorful intricately patterned designs on temple floors and at one's doorsteps.[7] This is mostly done by women, who may have a large repertoire with patterns and colors fitting the seasons and calendrical occasions (Nagarajan 1993; Tadvalkar 2015). Or their repertoire may consist of one single intricate pattern they apply anew every morning. It is an art form practiced in the belief that these decorative paintings—applied directly to the earth, Bhūdevī (Nagarajan 1998)—keep the dwelling, the village, or the city safe and prosperous. The making of these 'painted prayers' (Huyler 1999) may be a ritual in itself, or may accompany specific ritual vows (*vrata*). Such decorative patterns may be made with paint, ground flour, rice powder or colored chalk. Intricate floral-geometrical designs mostly have a dot or a series of dots in the center but some may instead have a pair of divine feet in the middle. On special days richly decorated feet (*pagla, pagliya*) may appear, especially on festival days associated with goddess Lakṣmī, who is considered the deity that protects the home. The painted feet may be in pairs, statically positioned in the center of a rich decoration, but some women produce feet that seem to be moving, ushering the goddess into the house where she will bring happiness and prosperity to the family. At night, especially during Diwali (Dīpavāli) the series of footsteps may be lighted with oil lamps. Goddess Lakṣmī may also be represented together with her consort Viṣṇu. Both symbolize happiness, auspiciousness, and prosperity. They are painted in the form of plants, creepers, and flowers, especially the lotus, or cornucopias and vases of plenty and other symbols of prosperity and domestic happiness. The divine couple may also be represented by their feet, sometimes in juxtaposition, as in southern India. Another type of moving feet belongs to Bāla-Kṛṣṇa, baby-Krishna, lovingly produced on the occasion of his birthday, *janmāṣṭamī* (or *gokulāṣṭamī*). Small

---

4 A study of Indian footwear (Jain-Neubauer 2000) may easily detract us from our main topic. Yet it is worth noting here that the 'paduka' is mostly associated with mendicants and an ascetic lifestyle. This may have its roots in the non-violent origin of the material (it is usually made of wood, not leather), and its special construction. Although these platform shoes may be very impractical for walking—let alone dancing, as Kṛṣṇa does—they are designed in such a way that they prevent accidental trampling on insects and vegetation. As both ambiguity and polyvalence are key concepts in our analysis of feet and footprints it is worth pointing out that a pair of 'paduka' used to be part of a bride's trousseau, hinting at the eroticism of the foot and the length high-heeled shoes add to the lady's legs.

5 For a more systematic discussion of this, especially in the light of the iconicity and non-iconicity debate, see further on, Section 2.3 (Of relics, representations, and reminders).

6 The term 'defiant religiosity' (Larios and Voix 2018) may be too strong here, but obviously two of the affective qualities of pavement shrines, tree shrines and foot-pedestals right at the entrance of temples are their accessibility and informality.

7 Anyone who happens to have been caught in pre-wedding frenzy in India may be aware of the 'haldi' (Bengali: *holud*) ceremony traditionally held for the bride. Turmeric paste is applied to her face and body in sensuous patterns akin to *raṅgolī* and especially her feet are objects of artistic attention: intricate decorations made of henna (*mehendi, mendi*) covering the entire foot and ankle (cf. Huyler 2008).

footsteps made of rice flour may be drawn on doorsteps but also inside the house, especially leading from the domestic altar to the kitchen, where baby Krishna is invited to gorge on butter and sweets.

Another type of divine feet we need to mention here are reproductions of deities' feet as portable devotional articles. They may be made of any material: carved in wood or stone, plastic, or paper, painted or left bare. They may come as cheap paper reproductions merely showing simple outlines of a pair of anonymous feet—as a tentative empty container, to be filled in with whatever divine name one imagines—or with the foot-soles filled, literally to the brim, with auspicious symbols pertaining to a particular deity. In the case of Viṣṇu, such foot-soles would contain his four major attributes: the conch shell (shankh; *śaṅkha*), war discus (chakra; *cakra*), mace (gada; *gadā*), and lotus flower (Hindi: kamal; Sanskrit: *padma, puṣkara, puṇḍarikā*). In addition, one can typically find the ammonite, a fossilized spiral shell (*śālagrāma*), or the primeval serpent (Nāgarāja, Śeṣanāga, Ādiśeṣa, popularly referred to as Shesh). Such foot-soles, inscribed with his most evocative attributes, may be museum pieces, but may also be sold as cheap prints or amulets in any street stall (cf. Bhatti and Pinney 2011). As we will see below, visitors of Viṣṇu's footprint in Gayā sometimes make use of such plastic forms to deploy them as bright and conspicuous overlays covering the rather indistinct 'real' footprint (Figure 2). Of a special type of mobile (and marketable!) footprints are those facsimiles reproduced on textile or strong fibrous paper (such as the handcrafted lokta paper from Nepal) by rubbing the original footprints off. By affixing a piece of paper or thin cloth over the stone footprints, and rubbing the contours of the feet with wax, paint or charcoal, a close copy of the minuscule elevations and depressions is produced. It may serve as an easily portable relic.[8]

Figure 2. Gayā—the footprint decorated for evening worship (Albertina Nugteren).

2.2. *Of Divine Footprints*

Whereas so far we have introduced man-made representations of feet and footsteps, there is a crucial distinction to be made between those manufactured ones (*mānuṣa*) on the one hand, and divine (*daivya*) footprints supposedly left on natural rocks by the gods themselves, on the other.

[8] A photograph of a Tibetan monk preparing a colorful copy of the sacred footprints of the Buddha impressed on stone in front of the Mahābodhi temple in Bodhgayā is shown on p. 131 of (Leoshko 1988).

With self-manifested 'footprints' we emphatically mean 'imprints'—perceptibly sunken, concave (hollow) impressions made on a surface by the pressure of body weight—in order to distinguish them from manmade depictions of foot-soles and feet in whatever material, which are raised, carved and convex (cambered). South Asia's topography, in the experience of believers, is brimming with such material traces of epic heroes, Hindu gods, Buddha's footprints and foot-soles (Kinnard 2000, 2014) and even footprints of the Prophet Muhammad (Hasan 1993; cf. Schimmel 1980). They are mostly natural holes, dents, and depressions more or less in the form of a foot imprint, with or without distinct indications of toes. Some of them are huge, but their size is normally not experienced as crucial; that gods supposedly leave giant footprints is normally not a barrier for believing in their authenticity. The size of the footprint in Gayā is not gigantic, a 'naturalistic' divine size of about 40 cm.[9] Our main interest here is in divine footprints—hollow imprints—in their natural and 'original' state. The confusion, even among scholars, about what is imprecisely referred to (and lumped together) as footprints, is obvious. This lack of precision and categorical fuzziness made us decide to use the term 'footprint' exclusively for the hollow indent in natural rock, of which it is claimed that a god or the Buddha made this with his foot.

2.3. *Of Relics, Representations and Reminders*

In a composite culture (Alam 1999; Mohamed 2007) we find innumerable salvific spaces woven into a web of myths, stories, and sacred topographies. Objects like divine footprints confirm the presence of the gods and goddesses (or of the historical Buddha, as in Sri Lanka, cf. Skeen 1870) not only in national history but also through personal encounter in pilgrimage.[10] Hyperbolic sayings about local icons being considered absolutely and completely Viṣṇu should be seen in the perspective of the Vaiṣṇava theological tradition. Moreover, oral traditions of popular piety ascribe a cumulative significance to their 'own' icon (*arcā*): not only is it interwoven with 'puranic' origin, the image has its own personality and is treated as a distinct person (Narayanan 2011, p. 569). Such images may also be cumulative in another way; it is often believed that an iconic statue of a deity, a half-figurative and half-non-figurative 'relic' such as a footprint, or an aniconic object such as a *śālagrāma* fossil, collects 'energy' over the years, absorbing not only layers of grease, milk, soot, turmeric, and vermilion, but also the waves of devotion radiated by generations of pilgrims. Having been the object of intense devotion 'for as long as one can remember' is considered to have charged both the material object and the place of pilgrimage with an almost tangible power and spiritual magnetism (Preston 1992, p. 33).[11]

In contrast to what is prescribed in sacred texts about images of the divine 'properly' housed in temples (Kramrisch 1976) many representations of the divine are found elsewhere, such as beneath trees, at the outer edges of religious compounds, on kitchen shelves and in wildernesses. Whatever rules there are about formal consecration of buildings and statues, believers also have a tendency to build intimate relationships with organically grown (i.e., self-revealed, *svayambhū*) embodiments of the

---

9 There is considerable confusion and contestation about the *viṣṇupāda* qualifying as (1) either a natural footprint; as (2) a manmade sunken foot-sole; (3) an 'engraving of his right foot in the basalt' (Vidyarthi 1978, p. 4); (4) a reproduction (Asher 1988, p. 74); (5) a 'replica in stone' (idem); (6) a 'sculptured impression'(idem); (7) a man-made raised foot or foot-sole; (8) or a carved pair of feet, in plural. Yet it seems safe, based on its present appearance, to copy the term Glücklich (2008, p. 3) used, 'a footprint-like indentation'. See further footnotes 10, 19, and 20. This confusion may be partly due to (possibly) later replacements, partly to the situation that most of the time the silver-coated basin is filled with offerings all over, obscuring any view one might need 'to see for oneself.'

10 Although it might seem more relevant here to refer to the many forms in which Buddha's feet occur in neighboring Bodhgayā (about intricate relations between the footprint in Gayā and the sculptured pairs of feet in Bodhgayā, see Paul 1985; Asher 1988; Kinnard 2000), the allusion to his footprint on natural rock at the summit of Mount Sumanala (Adam's Peak in Sri Lanka) is deliberate. Based on morphological considerations these two single depressions in natural rocks are much more on a par; on the same footing, as it were.

11 I borrow this term from James Preston (1992, p. 33), but find that his scholarly caveat ('It is not an intrinsic "holy" quality of mysterious origins that radiates objectively from a place of pilgrimage; rather, spiritual magnetism derives from human concepts and values, via historical, geographical, social, and other forces that coalesce in a sacred center.') should not obscure the literal meaning of *śakti*-power-energy attributed to devotional objects in India. Or, as Preston adds: 'Folk explanations of the spiritual magnetism attributed to a sacred center are valid from the participant's point of view.'

divine. Natural forms of divinity have this innate appeal, and as 'representational modes' and markers of divine presence such objects combine a visual-tactile encounter with a natural element. This poses the question of iconicity versus aniconicity. Gaifman (2017, p. 338) defines 'aniconic' as indicating 'a physical object, monument, image or visual scheme that denotes the presence of a divine power without a figural representation of the deity (or deities) involved.' It appears that divine footprints are neither completely anthropomorphic nor completely non-figural. Allowing the notion of a range or spectrum between the strictly iconic and the strictly aniconic may allow us to reflect on what Hindus experience as a god's divine pervasiveness. Hinduism is known for its unabashedly figural materiality but also has a rich and profound tradition in aniconic—or, rather, semi-iconic—imagination and representation of the divine. In popular cults aniconic and anthropomorphic elements blend and co-exist easily. A pair of anthropomorphized footsteps—originating as holes, dents, or hollows in natural rock, but adapted to look like imprints of 'real' feet—may tell us a different story of the footprint than those man-made cultic feet and foot-soles used in regular worship. These, in their turn, should be distinguished from portable second-order 'facsimiles' produced by rubbing off the original form onto a piece of paper or textile.

The scholar may make a distinction between hollow imprints, however shapeless, as more authentic than 'imitative' representations, being artifacts and clearly the work of an artisan. But in a spiritual sense both are signs of a transitive exchange: it is man who sees the divine in a stone (cf. Aktor 2017a) or in a light indent in a rock, and it is man who chisels out a pair of divine feet from stone after having imagined the feet as pre-existing in the stone. The index of divine presence may be higher in the first form, lower in the second form, and still the devotional tendency to anthropomorphize aniconic or half-iconic objects is ubiquitous. We may also speak of the co-existence of various modes, as in a spectrum (Aktor 2017b): divine feet are found to be present in this world as non-figural, semi-figural, and fully figural. In Hinduism, feet may function as recognizable embodied forms of divinity, but the extent to which they are literally or figuratively embodied (i.e., anthropomorphized in form or 'merely' in the mind) may vary. One might logically expect that naturally revealed (*svayambhūta, svarūpi, ekibhūta-rūpi*) objects are accorded a higher mode of denoting divine presence, but this is not necessarily so. The purely non-figural often invites and draws out the iconic from the aniconic (Haberman 2017): devotional practices of worship tend to transform an aniconic object into an iconic one, or at least a half-iconic one, as is the case with footprints. Naturally manifested footprints, however storied and celebrated, are 'barely there': a vague outline, an indication of toes, merely a heel. In the experience of the devout, such footprints, being merely what they are, invite being ritualized, and in that process receive reconfiguration: an emphasized outline here, a slight impression hollowed out to more effect there, and toes tend to become neatly compartmentalized.[12] What on one scale may count as an act of devotion—lovingly helping the divine to manifest more clearly—may, on another scale, count as a lack of faith. Or, as Gaifman (2017, p. 350) aptly concludes: 'the realia of practice and worshippers' perspectives may not fit scholarly paradigms.'

Another pressing question is: are they relics? In Buddhism, with its long-lasting discourse on the early aniconicity of the Buddha image (Tanaka 1998; Kinnard 2000), there appears to be a consensus that the existing natural footprints[13] of the Buddha, among which we merely mention the Śrī Pāda

---

[12] In this regard the antiquity of Viṣṇu's central footprint at Gayā was argued by Paul (1985, p. 140) as follows: '[...] indicated by a simple outline the sacred object is neither encumbered with conventional auspicious marks nor entangled by inscriptional paraphernalia.' Since the objective of Paul's discussion was the comparison with Buddha's neatly carved-out slightly hollow pair of feet on a lotus pedestal by the side of the Mahābodhi Temple in Bodhgayā, her argument is only partially relevant here. But there is no denying that, once bared of its decorations and the plastic overlay (bearing Viṣṇu's emblems for the evening worship), the silver-enshrined imprint in the nucleus of the Vishnupad Temple looks archaic, even if only as a result of the frequent anointings and rubbings. See also what O'Malley wrote more than a century ago, in 1906 (O'Malley 2007, p. 63): 'The outline of these footprints [sic] are still to be seen [...] on a large granite stone with an uneven top, which is much worn with the frequent washings it daily undergoes.'

[13] In some sources we read that Gautama Buddha left three footprints: two in what is now Afghanistan (or Pakistan?), and one on the Samantakūṭa of Samanala Mountain. In Sri Lanka it is speculated that he left his left footprint on the Samanala

in Sri Lanka, are *pāribhogaka* relics. Such relics are objects that are sanctified by having been used or owned by the historical Buddha. An imprint of his foot thus counts as a relic-of-use, or rather, a relic-of-touch. Could we likewise consider the *svayambhū* footprint ascribed to Viṣṇu as a relic testifying to the god's physical presence in this particular place, once in primeval times, and the footprint as a depression that had been produced by the pressure of his (anthropomorphic even if in some cases of giant proportions) foot on rock? Whatever dialogic imagination (Bakhtin 2008, p. 276) we may use, we enter a tension-filled discourse in which Hindu theology, Hindu on-the-ground devotionalism, and possibly our own distanced position 'brush up against thousands of living dialogic threads, woven by socio-ideological consciousness around the given object'. Or, as Kinnard (2000, p. 36) writes: 'On the one hand, a footprint[14] is considered to be the actual mark left by Viṣṇu or the Buddha and thus has been regarded as a kind of corporeal extension, even an actual embodiment. On the other hand, a footprint is not a foot but rather simply the empty mark left by a foot.'

At the very least, for the faithful it acts as a contact zone. In Hinduism the gods can be highly visible, tangible, and audible, and especially the ritual interaction with objects evokes anthropomorphic aesthetics. Yet also the formless (*nirguṇa*) is highly revered, and exists in a parallel relation with the explicit form (*saguṇa*).[15] On the other hand, Vaiṣṇava Hindus conceive the *pādas* as the actual abode of Viṣṇu. According to the *Gayāmāhātmya* (109.20, pp. 43–5) Viṣṇu is *vyaktāvyakta*, both manifest and unmanifest, in the footprint. Any artisan-produced footprint, properly inaugurated, is, essentially, a *mūrti*. A *mūrti* is a man-made image in which, through ritual consecration, the deity is invited to dwell. A *svayambhū mūrti* is more: it is a mark created by Viṣṇu himself.

2.4. How a Divine Footprint Became Embodied and Embedded

After this long prelude we now look more closely at the footprint in Gayā. Its pedigree is impressive, well-attested, and traceable through all four categories of sources (see above, page 2). Just as we may need a vivid imagination to see a footprint in a dented piece of rock, we need a narrative gaze (Morgan 2012, p. 67) to intuit what the faithful see. Accordingly, we first follow the track of three different textual motifs that are often presented as explaining, justifying as well as adding the prestige of antiquity to the existing cult. The scenes are patchworks of various text passages. We begin (Section 2.4.1) with a Vedic creation scene in which the world was created by sacrifice. The sacrifice took place in primeval (empty, unordered) space. A mysterious footprint was all there was. It was this shallow pit that served as the first sacrificial altar around which the gods gathered. Then, in Section 2.4.2 we see Viṣṇu taking three giant steps, thus ordering space. In scene three (Section 2.4.3), we see a ritual re-enactment of both, at Gayā.

2.4.1. Scene One: The First Footprint, the Place of Sacrifice

In the beginning, when the earth was still soft, someone left a first footprint: was it the footprint of a cow, of goddess Iḷā, or of Speech? They were triple and one. Together they ensured the flow of abundance, of milk, of the cosmic order (*ṛta*). Or was it Viṣṇu's footprint (*Viṣṇoḥ pada*), whose three strides had resulted in a footprint on Earth? His footprints are containers of sweetness and

---

summit (also known as Adam's Peak) and his right footprint in Anurādhapura, a feat that may well be an intended parallel to Viṣṇu's wide strides (cf. Paul 1985, p. 140). Both Myanmar and Thailand claim to have real footprints in natural rock too (cf. Sailer 1993; Sailer's website on www.dralbani.com/buddhafootprint; Guerney 2014; and various entries on 'Buddha's footprints' or 'buddhapāda' in Encyclopedias, such as in Keown and Prebish (2013, p. 113) and Buswell and Lopez (2014, p. 154)). For a categorization, see my unpublished paper presentation 'Of feet, footsteps, foot-marks, foot-soles and footprints of the Buddha', EASR annual conference, Bern, 17–21 June 2018 (www.easr2018.org/program/session S37 'Plurality and Materiality').

14 Kinnard seems to speak deliberately of footprints without distinguishing between feet, foot-soles, footsteps and footprints.

15 See, for instance, verse 33 in the popular *Viṣṇucālīsā*, the forty couplets written in praise of Viṣṇu by Sundardās: 'agaṇit rūp anup apārā/nirguṇ saguṇ svarūp tumhārā //' ('your forms are countless, incomparable and infinite; you are both personal and impersonal', or translated in a more philosophical vein: 'with and without qualities/attributes').

abundance. This is how the gods used 'ghee-dripping' Iḷā's footprint or wide-reaching Viṣṇu's footprint as an altar into which oblations were poured.[16] Man knows this because seers and poets, as 'knowers of the track', told them so. A *pada-jña* knows that footprints serve as trails, to be traced by them and their descendants; it is they who show the newly deceased their way. In the words of Gonda (1969, p. 176), Iḷā's hands and feet drip with butter, and leave a trail of footprints, a track of goodness; or of Sandness (2010, p. 519) who concludes: 'A footprint is a trace, a track or sign by means of which one has visible evidence of an invisible presence.' And both have ghee-dripping feet (*ghṛtapada*) for it is through sacrifice that the living and the dead find their way beyond by following the ancient footsteps.[17]

2.4.2. Scene Two: The Division of Primeval Space, Viṣṇu's Three Steps

Creation myths in Hinduism are practically innumerous, but here we select a single motif, that of Lord Viṣṇu creating the cosmos by dividing it into three distinct realms. Although in the disguise of a dwarf, by taking three giant steps he could claim the space he had covered with his three strides as his own. He thus brought order in empty space by his strides. This is how Viṣṇu became the god of ordered space:

> From the *Ṛgveda*: '*I will proclaim the heroic deeds of Viṣṇu, who measured apart the earthly realms, who propped up the upper dwelling place, when the wide-striding one stepped forth three times. [. . .] All creatures dwell in his three wide steps. [. . .] he alone has supported three-fold the earth, the sky, and all creatures.*'
>
> From the *Śatapathabrāhmaṇa*: '*[. . .] the demons thought, 'All this world is ours.' They said, 'Let us divide this earth, and when we have divided it let us live upon it.' Then they set out to divide it [. . .]. The gods heard about this and said, [. . .] Let us go where the demons are dividing it, for who would we be if we did not share in it?' They placed Viṣṇu [. . .] at their head and went there and said, 'Let us also share in this earth; let a portion of it be ours.' The demons, rather jealously, replied, 'As much as this Viṣṇu lies on, so much we give to you.*'
>
> From the *Vāyupurāṇa*: '*[. . .] O king, you should give me the space covered in three strides.' 'I grant this,' answered the king, [. . .] and since he thought him to be just a dwarf he himself was very pleased about it. But the dwarf, the lord [i.e., Viṣṇu in his dwarf incarnation] stepped over the heaven, the sky, and earth, this whole universe, in three strides [. . .]. He revealed that the whole universe was in his body; there is nothing in all the worlds that is not pervaded by the noble one.*' [18]

---

16 The sacrificial altar (*vedi*) traditionally is not a raised altar as such, but a sacrificial pit—a shallow depression in the ground—around which the gods were invited to sit down. In Gayā most of the places where mourners are to offer *piṇḍas* to their ancestors are referred to as *vedis*. Both footprints and *vedis* share the same symbolic order as the navel, a parallel we find in *Ṛgveda* 3.29.4 (the footprint as the 'navel of the Earth'). In Gayā one of the parallel stories told of the giant Gayāsur, and sometimes portrayed in popular colorprints sold to pilgrims, is that the fire sacrifice referred to in scene three (Section 2.4.3) had taken place in the *asura*'s navel (*nabhi*).

17 This summary is based on various cryptic passages in the *Ṛgveda*, mainly ṚV 3.23-29. See also *Śatapathabrāhmaṇa* 1.8.1.

18 These translations are taken from chapter five (on Viṣṇu) in Wendy Doniger O'Flaherty's *Hindu Myths. A sourcebook translated from the Sanskrit* (Doniger 1978, pp. 176–9). The locus classicus for 'the three strides of Viṣṇu' (*trīṇi padāni viṣṇoḥ*) is *Ṛgveda* 1.22.17–21; additionally 1.154.1–5. Although these three text passages are wide apart in time and context they are selected on the basis of their narrative strands, together forming a fabric that is locally told and retold, as well as used to authenticate the ritual practices. From a text-historical perspective the key question would be: when were such myths revolving around Viṣṇu woven into the fabric of Gayā as a place of pilgrimage famous for its *śrāddha* rites? Text passages such as *Viṣṇusūtra* 85.40 and *Viṣṇupurāṇa* 3.45, where the *viṣṇupāda* is casually mentioned, may provide links between narrative motifs and the specific location, but a full study in which the third key textual element, Gayā testified as a famous *śrāddhatīrtha*, would nicely fit in, is far beyond the scope of this article.

2.4.3. Scene Three: Viṣṇu's Footprint on Earth: Gayā

Viṣṇu's divine footsteps may spiritually be traced in every place where the sacred is encountered, but in the perception of many there is one particular footprint that is in precise alignment with the celestial path: Viṣṇu's footprint (*viṣṇupāda*) at Gayā, in the contemporary state of Bihar, eastern India. According to myth (*Vāyupurāṇa* chapters 105–106; *Gayāmāhātmya*) it is here where Viṣṇu touched Earth in his three strides, and left the imprint of his right foot on natural rock.[19] That alone would make it a formidable place, but the ancient cosmogonic myth, in which the global term 'earth' had not been specified or made geographically-topographically explicit, got blended with place-specific myths and local lore. We thus have a universal cosmogonic myth, that of Viṣṇu's three giant steps, on the one hand, and two versions of a local myth, on the other.[20] The most basic version of the local narrative tells us of a demon (*asura*) by the name of Gaya (m.) who had been engaged in such extreme austerities that this interfered with the power of Yama, the deity who presides over death. The three main gods, Brahmā, Viṣṇu and Śiva, were willing to intervene and came down in the guise of brahmans. They asked the *asura* for a sacred place where they could perform *yagya*, sacrifice. As a boon it was agreed that they could use the body of Gayāsura (Gaya the *asura*) as the location for a sacrificial fire-pit. For this, the demon had to lie completely still, without moving, for a full seven days. It was in fact a plot to kill him. At the beginning of the final day Lord Śiva took the form of a rooster and crowed already at midnight. Immediately, the demon, deluded by the 'false dawn', got up and disturbed the *yagya*. The three brahmans-in-disguise revealed their true identity and told Gayāsura he now had to be killed. Accordingly Viṣṇu stepped his foot on the demon's chest and subdued him. In an alternative version they had placed a heavy piece of rock on him in order to keep him immobilized. This large stone could also serve as a fireplace to make the sacrificial fire. To make sure that he would not get up, Viṣṇu kept his foot firmly on the stone's surface.[21] The powerful demon had thus been tamed into immobility forever, but compassionate and fair Lord Viṣṇu still granted him his boon: his giant body would become the eminent sacred place, Gayā (f) where the dead would gain salvation and would never need to return in another incarnation. And indeed, the town of Gayā grew into one of the main places of pilgrimage, especially famous for its ancestral rites (*śrāddha*). In its centre is the awe-inspiring trace, enshrined in silver: the footprint.

2.5. Rituals around the Viṣṇupāda in Gayā[22]

In this way, the contemporary town is linked into a chain of ancient text passages, myths, and sacred geographies. As a town it has a documented history that goes back to the Enlightenment of

---

19 Some authors refer to Viṣṇu 'planting his foot at the Vishnupada on the Gaya *peak*' (emphasis added, AN) (Jaiswal 1964); Bhattacharyya (1964, p. 91) writes: 'Some natural crevices in the rocks which were originally fetishistic objects of worship were *later* recognized as the footmarks [sic] of Vishnu.' [emphasis added, AN]. Anil Kumar maintains that the practice of 'footprint worship' started with the worship of the footprint of Viṣṇu at the Vishnupad Temple *since the fourth century* (emphasis added, AN) (Kumar 1987). None of these authors are able to establish full chronological evidence for the rise of *viṣṇupāda-pūjā or viṣṇucaraṇa-pūjā* in Gayā. This matter of footprint-worship is further complicated by the historically sensitive and area-specific issue which was first: reverence to Viṣṇu's footprint in Gayā or to Buddha's feet in Bodhgayā.

20 In association with the remarks made in notes 18 and 19 the Gayāsura legends form yet another narrative strand. According to O'Malley (2007) the legend of Gayāsura was invented around the fourteenth or fifteenth centuries. See also the sixteenth-century text on pilgrimage *Tristhalīsetu* (Salomon 1985); and *Gayāmāhātmya* (Jacques 1962), a pilgrimage guide to Gayā replacing some older chapters of the *Vāyupurāṇa*.

21 This alternative version is based on locally available pilgrim's documentation, such as found in illustrated bazaar booklets. In informal conversations and on Internet one finds further variations. For an impression of public relations found in digital media, such as of online services ('Online Services for After Death Rituals of Pinddaan'), a list of *paṇḍas*, photos, or services to be reserved online, see www.pinddaangaya.in. For local and regional maps, see Singh 2009 (as well as some other of his publications on Gayā).

22 This part is based on various field visits since 1979, the most recent being in 2016 (see Figures 1 and 2). Because of the crowds of worshippers, the solemn nature of the *sapiṇḍikaraṇa*, but particularly because officially 'non-Hindus are not allowed', I had to avoid making myself conspicuous and refrained from photographing people. More recently, Deborah de Koning, MA, managed to make a picture of ritual activities going on around the *viṣṇupāda* (Figure 3). I gratefully acknowledge her permission to use it here.

Gautama Buddha who may have been drawn there because of the fame of its ascetics. One of the most frequently given references to Gayā as a place where *śrāddha* was performed is based on a passage in the *Rāmāyaṇa* (2.99) where Rāma, Sītā, and Lakṣmaṇa are said to have gone to Gayā for *piṇḍa-pradāna*, the offering of food to the ancestors, after the death of King Daśaratha. Gayā's fame additionally rests on having received one of the drops of *amṛta* (the immortality drink), and partly on its locational 'topomorphic' significance. The main elements of this local fame consist of the sacred river on its way to join the Ganges; of having an 'immortal' banyan tree, the Akṣayavata; and of being surrounded by sacred hills in a meaningful astrological alignment with Sūrya, Sun.[23] When exactly the cosmogonic myth about Viṣṇu's strides and about the very first footprint that served as a sacrificial pit began to be connected with this place is uncertain. Today it is emphasized that the present *viṣṇupāda* has always been in the place where it is now, and that the present eighteenth-century temple was built around the much older footprint—whether that footprint be the result of the act of subduing the demon Gayāsur, with Viṣṇu's foot holding the piece of rock in place, or of Viṣṇu's right foot firmly stepping on Earth in his three all-encompassing cosmogonic strides (*trivikrama*).[24] But for most, the various elements, interlocking multiple traditions, form the composite culture on which the fame of the town is based.

2.5.1. The Footprint

From a spatial and ritual perspective, the divine footprint at Gayā has to compete with many other objects and other centers of attention. Formally, those who come to Gayā to perform ancestor rituals have to start close by or in the Vishnupad Temple. In fact, in preparation they should have fasted for a day, undergone ritual shaving, taken a bath in the river Phālgu and donned ritual garments. Directed by their *paṇḍa* and his assistant(s), relatives come to the Vishnupad Mandir and the cluster of other shrines with the offerings they have freshly prepared, especially the *piṇḍas*, balls made of wheat and oat flour, rice powder, sandalwood, sesame and water or milk. The offerings, representing the paternal and maternal ancestors, are offered to the deities, the sages, Yama (the god of Death) and the manes in various places in town. The encounter with the footprint is given form in the ritual that is popularly called charan pooja[25] (*caraṇapūjā*): paying respect to the footprint. Traditionally, the fixed formula with which the footprint is greeted is from *Ṛgveda* 1.22.17:

> 'We bow to this, thou Viṣṇu's circular basement, Chakra.'

In its most basic form, this ritual consists of circumambulation, gestures of respect, a fixed form of greeting, and a statement of what one's intentions for worship and offering are, such as health and prosperity. Devotees can also make a vow or state their gratefulness after the fulfillment of a vow. People may come with specific problems for which they seek healing. More elaborate rituals, apart from the usual ancestor rituals, may be in the form of other life-cycle rituals such as a child's first hair-shaving (*muṇḍana*) or initiation (*upanayana*). In a place like Gayā many people may come in order

---

23 The town's connection with the sun (in relation to the four hills) would deserve a research of its own. Here it should suffice to refer to authors such as Paul (1985) and Singh (2009). It has been stated that Viṣṇu's three strides not only spanned the universe, they also symbolize the three positions of the sun throughout the day: dawn, noon and dusk. Paul (1985, p. 84) added: 'The single footprint of Vishnupad, as opposed to an immobile pair of prints, suggests that Vishnu *was indeed moving* [emphasis added, AN] sun-like across the cosmos and placed his (right) foot momentarily on the head of the demon Gaya.'

24 The late-Pāla period saw a great popularity of the Viṣṇu cult in Bihar, and the Trivikrama-Viṣṇu became one of the 24 icons (*caturviṁśatimūrti*). Even as the 'wide-strider' the god is mostly depicted standing firmly on two legs, and holding four attributes in his hands. There is a variation, however: when he is depicted stretching his left leg to an almost straight line with his right leg, in 180○. Such an image is often part of a *daśāvatāra* temple representing his ten incarnations. Among those I saw being the center of lively worship was one in the ancient part of Bhaktapur, Nepal. Typically, while stepping wide, he has his right foot firmly planted on a pedestal surrounded by adorants.

25 Viṣṇu's footprint has an astonishing number of parallels in other local shrines. I counted at least 18 deities whose shrines are listed as 'Rudra pad', 'Brahma pad', Surya pad', 'Indra pad' etcetera. As I have made no further study of those, I leave them out of my article here; also because I assume they are not footprints but artifacts. Traditionally, these 'pad' shrines should all be visited for *piṇḍapradāna*. Together with other sacred places these constitute a full pilgrimage circuit numbering 45, 48, 51 or 54 '*vedis*', including a pipal tree (and sometimes Buddha's foot-soles as well) in the Mahābodhi Temple compound in Bodhgayā (cf. Barua 1975).

to earn merit for the next life, as all kinds of scriptures promise that the site brings many blessings, ablution of sins, liberation for the recently deceased, and even immortality. At night and during festival time there may be recitation of sacred texts (*kathā*) and sankirtan (saṁkīrtana), the collective singing of devotional songs in local dialects and the regional language. At festival times there may even be artistic and dramatic performances, mostly in the form of *līlās*, plays re-enacting episodes from the lives of the epic heroes and deities such as Rāma. Gifts offered at the footprint, and given into the hands of officiating priests, may include water, milk, ghee (*ghṛta*, clarified butter), flowers, sandalwood powder, fruits, sindur, kunkum, garlands, oil lamps, and money. Similar to the iconic deities the footprint is accorded the usual sixteen services (*upacāra*), such as offering a symbolic seat, water, garments, camphor, and a sacred thread; the footprint is anointed and offered flowers, food, betelnuts, money, and lighted lamps.

Viṣṇu's footprint, like other sacred marks, serves as an 'omphalos', the navel of the universe—or at least of the entire territory, the sacred landscape of Gayā, encompassing the other shrines, the river, the sacred trees, the cremation *ghāṭs*, the hills and even the wider pilgrimage circuit (*pañcakrośi-gayākṣetra*). This serving of the footprint as a ritual 'navel' (or in other versions, 'head', Gayāśīra) becomes evident especially on days or nights of a particular astrological constellation, such as during the winter solstice, the vernal equinox, on full moon days (especially during *pitṛpakṣa-melā*, October-November), on new moon days and during eclipses. There is a special connection between Viṣṇu and the solar order. He is imagined to have established the threefold division of space and thus determines the journey of the sun across the firmament. This becomes manifest during the annual sun festivals when offerings of water, milk, flowers, and flour cakes (*pakvan*) are made around the Sūryakuṇḍ, the well (often referred to as a 'water tank' or pool) named after Sūrya, the sun god. Ritual baths in the river include *arghya*, offerings of water to the sun, to be distinguished from *tarpaṇa*, the elaborate libations of water for the manes.

2.5.2. The River

The river Phālgu (Falgu, Falguni; Sanskrit Nairañjanā) is sometimes, to add to its sacredness, called a tributary of the Ganges, but the regional reality is quite different. The Phālgu empties itself in the Ganges flowing through the Gangetic plain further to the north-east. The river is formed by the confluence of the Niranjan (Nilanjan, Nilajan) and the Mohanā rivers. At Gayā the river reaches a considerable breadth. Here it passes high banks consisting of a rocky outcrop from which paved stairs, the *ghāṭs*, lead down to the riverbed. The Vishnupad Temple thus stands high above the river, surrounded by countless minor shrines and narrow alleys. The river is sacred to Hindus, and it is traditionally[26] in the river that pilgrims performing *śrāddha* make their first offering. However, since the riverbed is almost completely dry in the winter months, it may at times be no more than a wide expanse of sand and mud. Locally it is said that this state is due to a curse made by Sītā, when she had visited Gayā to perform ancestor rituals for her father-in-law king Daśaratha. This incident is relevant for our topic for at least two reasons. First, it refers to a passage in the *Rāmāyaṇa* and various *Purāṇas* that is used to explain the lack of water today from an ancient curse instead of natural causes or anthropogenic impact. Secondly, it indicates that at the times these ancient texts were written the town of Gayā already functioned as an eminent place where the threesome had gone in order to perform ancestor rituals. The *piṇḍas* are preferably offered in a circular movement from *vedi* to *vedi*, starting from the Punpun river bank, and ending beneath the Akṣayavat. Although today many use shortcuts, the final donation to the overseer priest at the Gāyatrī *ghāṭ* is inescapable.

---

[26] Although in some special cases the entire traditional sequence may still be followed, most *śrāddha* performances today are shortened to last merely a single day. Through e-ethnography (see, for instance, comments on TripAdvisor) we learn that some families now travel to Gayā in their own vehicle, have the rituals done with in less than two hours, and return in time to post online comments from home. As could be expected, these middle-class visitors tend to complain about the fees demanded by the priests and the squalor of the place.

Figure 3. Gayā—rituals around the footprint (picture made by Martijn Stoutjesdijk and Deborah de Koning, 10 July 2018).

The town and most temples are facing the river. The river serves as their point of orientation in many ways. This becomes especially obvious during festival days, when additional platforms are constructed in order to serve as tempory *ghāṭs*. On such occasions the river banks are teeming with people, both locals and pilgrims from far and wide. Many stand in the water, performing their water rituals. Although there is a constant use of the river in all kinds of lifecycle and calendrical events in which the river is the central point, Chhath Pooja (*chathā/śāṣṭī pūjā*) should be mentioned as a special case, indicated already in the *Mahābhārata* (3.16.31). People even refer to it as Mahaparv (*mahāparva*), the great festival. Especially women throng to the river (as well as to the Sūryakuṇḍ) and perform ablutions and water offerings (*arghya*) for the sake of children, skin diseases in particular. The four-day festival, during which devotees fast and subject themselves to other forms of austerities, is dedicated to the life-giving powers of the sun. It takes place twice a year, in October-November and March-April, following the luni-solar calendar. Interestingly, no icons are used, and the sun is worshiped directly. Some may direct themselves to a goddess, lovingly referred to as Chhathi Ma or Chhathi Maiya ('Mother Sixth', 'Mother Sun'), but there is no form of *mūrti* or *mūrti-pūjā* at all. This is part of the reason why this festival has been called the most eco-friendly festival of India: no polluting stuff floating in the river, no waste on the river banks.[27]

2.5.3. The Tree

In archaic places of pilgrimage sacred trees are often part of an ensemble, along with water bodies such as a well, a pond, a river, or the ocean; and in many cases there are hills or a mountain, or at least a central temple of which the towering form provides the vertical element. Gayā is one of those ancient places where we find not merely sacred trees in abundance, it hosts a tree with a special reputation, the Akṣayavata, or as tourist-pilgrim literature calls it, 'Immortal Banyan Tree'. It is a sacred fig tree (botanical name: *ficus indica*), characterized by its feature of sending down aerial roots, which over the course of time may become massive trunks of their own. It is commonly referred to as banyan (a name from the colonial era: 'the tree beneath which merchants used to do business'), *vata* ('surrounded' by its own aerial roots), and in literary sources as *bahupada* ('having many feet', this being an apt epithet in an article on feet). According to myth, legend, and pilgrims' lore, it was this tree that could be seen as the only point of reference above the water level when in primeval times a cosmic flood (*pralaya*) had covered the entire world. It is stated that this tree has always been there, and will always be: it is truly indestructible.[28] Other famous *akṣayavatas* are found in ancient pilgrimage towns such as Prayāg (today's Allahabad), Kurukṣetra, Varaṇasī, Gayā and Purī. Needless to say that quite a few places all over India claim that their banyan is also an *akṣayavata*.

In some esoteric circles it is said that these trees symbolize the eternal regeneration cycle of the universe and that human bodies are the reverse image of that tree, with its roots above and tip below (*ūrdhvamūlavṛkṣa*). India's geography is particularly blessed, in this regard, as its upper half is stated to be formed by one gigantic banyan tree, with its roots in Prayāg, its trunk in Varaṇasī, and its tip in Gayā (cf. Bharati 1963; Eck 1981, 1998). The Akṣayavata in Gayā is thus seen as the crown, and this is especially relevant for those who come to perform ancestor rituals and offer their final *piṇḍas* at the feet of the great banyan. Its crown, with branches 'reaching out to heaven', is said to point the newly deceased their way to the world of the ancestors.[29] Famously, it was under a banyan like this that Savitrī tricked the god of death, Yama, into bringing her husband back to life.[30] The tree is likewise associated with all kinds of 'family problems' (*pitṛ-doṣa*), such as finding a marriage partner, progeny, and other aspects of family life. In this way it attracts not only mourners but many others who come

---

[27] See Piyush Tripathi's article in the *Times of India* (Patna edition), 6 November 2016 (https://timesofindia.indiatimes.com/city/patna/Chhath-the-most-eco-friendly-festival-Environmentalists/articleshow/55266563.cms) (last accessed 22 May 2018).

[28] See *Bhagavatapurāṇa* 12.9. Although the banyan in general is often associated with Śiva, the *akṣayavata* is mythologically linked with Viṣṇu in various ways as well. It is the tree in which Viṣṇu sleeps during the cosmic dissolution, safely tucked away in one of its strong leaves (*Naradapurāṇa* 47.6–8; *Matsyapurāṇa* 167.31–67). The detail that Viṣṇu, in the form of a sleeping child, was perched on a branch of this tree, rolled into one of its leaves while sucking his toe—a charming detail in an article on feet—is found in *Brahmapurāṇa* 49.53 and 54.14–18.

[29] A verse in the *Matsyapurāṇa* (106.11) promises that anyone who dies beneath an *akṣayavaṭa* (literally: at the root of this tree, *vaṭamūle*) goes to Lord Śiva's abode. Compare this to *Brahmapurāṇa* 54.17–18 where merely worshipping the tree will lead the devotee to Lord Viṣṇu's abode.

[30] *Matsyapurāṇa* 208.14. Although in this passage the type of tree is not identified, in a much-quoted work on the banyan, *Vata-Savitrī-vratakaṭhā*, a Sanskrit guideline to vows undertaken in relation to the banyan, particularly by wives for the long life of their husbands, is specific about the type of tree.

here to make a vow or pay tribute to the tree after a prayer has been successfully answered.[31] In that sense, the tree is a wishing tree (*kalpavṛkṣa*),[32] certain to fulfill its promises. Ancestor offerings are often made on banyan leaves (sold to mourners by the priests). Visitors—mourners and other pilgrims alike—are instructed to circumambulate the tree three times, chanting softly

> 'OM Śrī Kara-Akṣayavata-Vṛkṣaya Namaḥ' or more elaborately 'O banyan tree, you are immortal, surviving all throughout time. You are Viṣṇu's abode. O banyan tree, take away my sins. O wish-fulfilling tree, obeisance to you'.

On the wall behind the tree another promise is written: 'The Lord makes immortal that place where the Immortal Tree/Tree of Immortality is praised by the priests and food is given to the ancestors.'

According to the *Gayāmāhātmya* (a portion of the *Vāyupurāṇa*):

> 'Whatever is given to the ancestors at the Vata tree in the pilgrimage town Gayā will be indestructible (*akṣaya*). By looking at, bowing to, and making obeisance to the Lord of the Banyan (Vateśa), with a calm and composed mind, that pilgrim will guide his ancestors to the indestructible eternal World of Brahmā.' [33]

2.5.4. The Hills

Hills are plentiful in and around Gayā. Although Bihar in general is a flat and flood-prone state, it has hills in various regions. The town of Gayā is enveloped by temple-crowned hills on three sides and the river flowing by the fourth (i.e., eastern) side. For some, these rocky hills are the mythical body of Gayāsura whose body became locked in the landscape as it served as an altar for the gods' sacrificial offerings. Pilgrims and sacrificers may opt for a visit to merely some of them, whereas others are determined to make the full round, an itinerary already referred to in ancient sources such as the *Gayāmāhātmya*, and today available in abridged form in vernacular languages. Although the hills may be important destinations for all types of visitors, for the purpose of this article it may suffice to include the hills merely because they are considered to form a natural ensemble of sacred tree, river and hills, of which Viṣṇu's footprint is the gravitational center. Just as the Akṣayavata is considered to symbolically, with its branches, point the way for the departing souls of the newly deceased, so the surrounding hills (being linking ladders between earth and heaven) are considered as assisting the departure to the great beyond. Especially the hills form a spatial symbolic order of transcendence. More practically, it is crucial that souls successfully make the transition from the unsteady and potentially harmful state of *preta* (ghost) to that of ancestor (*pitṛ*). Rana P.B. Singh even spoke of Gayā not only as a 'sacredscape' and a 'ritualscape' but also as a 'manescape', 'ancestorscape', and even 'ghostscape' (Singh 2009; Marshall et al. 2009). The entire complex of *antyeṣṭi* rituals, traditionally lasting thirteen days from the moment of death, is meant to ease that transition, and metaphorically the hills, in their vertical dynamics, are perceived as assisting this process. On the eleventh day, Viṣṇu is requested to liberate the dead person. On the twelfth day sixteen *śrāddhas* are performed, with the express purpose of the incorporation of the deceased with the previously departed ancestors: *sapiṇḍīkaraṇa*. The hill Pretashila (Pretaśīla, the rock of the 'ghosts') expresses this concern vividly.

---

31 The first impression of the Akshayavat is often determined by its many almost horizontal branches from which colorful strips of cloth are suspended, often in shades of red, pink and yellow.

32 Although '*kalpavṛkṣa*' (*Naradapurāṇa* 52.66–67) is commonly translated as 'wishing tree', it gets a deeper meaning here, since *kalpa* also means 'eon' or vast stretch of time; after a period of dissolution a new *kalpa* will set in. Since an *akṣayavata* is said to survive the period of dissolution, the 'wish' expressed in front of such a tree may be considered to either go beyond the present *kalpa* or may be an explicit prayer for immortality.

33 In various *Purāṇas* there are slight variations of this passage, cf. *Vāyupurāṇa* 49. 93 and 96–97 and *Naradapurāṇa* 47, 3–4. This latter passage promises the abode of Brahmā for the ancestors. Although there may be a pre-eminence of Viṣṇu in Gayā, and the local narratives around Gaya (the *asura*) may even be perceived as establishing the position of Viṣṇu over the other two gods involved in the deception, Brahmā and Śiva, the tree is impartial and promises a variety of heavenly abodes.

3. Discussion: Embodiedness and Embeddedness

In this article we have explored a particular place-specific cultic object and traced its embodiedness by first focusing on feet, footwear, foot-soles, footsteps, and footprints. We tracked its embeddedness by following some elusive trails through myth and tradition. In all instances we found ourselves dealing not with biology in itself but with symbolic classification. We witnessed ritual practices and browsed through online travel reports. We found that divine feet are objects of devotion in a special dynamic between nature and manufacture, between presence and absence, between actual topography and elusive traces of divine embodiment, between this-wordly needs and the great beyond after death. There may be cognitive ambiguity, but the faithful seem to find a third space, where they ritually interact with things seen and unseen. Their narrative gaze envelops the footprint in a ritual choreography that spans from the minuscule empty space of the footprint to the universe through which Lord Viṣṇu strode with his three cosmogonic steps.

The sacred footprint in Gayā does not stand alone. It appears to be woven into a rich fabric of textual references; ancient recommendations of Gayā as the eminent place to perform rituals for the dead; place-specific myths and topographical-geographical features; special veneration for Viṣṇu in the state of Bihar; and long-lasting associations with its twin sister, Bodhgayā. This fabric, in fact, is so rich that the pilgrim may easily lose track and forget about the footprint itself. Although the footprint may appear dis-embodied—being merely a slight depression on a rocky surface—it appears to be both embodied and embedded. It is embedded in ancient scriptures, cosmogonies, geographies, a number of overlapping symbolic orders, and a grammar of devotion. And it is embodied in elaborate systems of iconography, symbolism, esoteric interpretations, and narrative traditions of divine embodiment. In a way, ancient text passages about a mysterious primeval footprint serving as the sacrificial altar around which the gods gathered, are ritually re-enacted in the *viṣṇupāda* until today, fulfilling the ancient promise that the place will always be 'dripping with ghee'.[34]

First of all, we found feet to be both dirty and divine; both disgusting and erotic; both directly physical and highly elusive. They are not only staggeringly ambivalent, they are confusingly polyvalent. They are objects of hygiene, aesthetics, social ordering mechanisms, material culture and spiritual techniques. What would Indian classical dance be without the tapping of bare feet? How different would be the disembodied experience of Indian temples with one's shoes on, or a temple in which one would not be allowed to reverently touch the feet of the deity. Would not the world be a darker, heavier place without that light and almost imperceptible footfall of the divine? The bare calloused feet of a peasant; exquisite footwear worn by royals; delicate patterns applied to the feet of a bride; an empty throne carrying Rāma's sandals during the years of exile, serving as his proxy. All these indicate a rich culture of the senses and imaginative embodiment.

Secondly, there are footsteps. All over the subcontinent people go on pilgrimage in the footsteps of the great ones. The devotional traffic is immense. But divine footsteps are not merely for following them. Footsteps can be imagined and actively shaped, such as in expressive webs of painted prayers, in the uninterrupted lines of *raṅgolī*, in intricate patterns of auspicious symbols on the foot-soles of deities. Footsteps can invoke: come, Lakṣmī, come, bless this house, this family, with your presence. Come, baby Kṛṣṇa, enjoy sweets in my kitchen. Artisans are constantly at work, chiseling away at blocks of stone, carving out pairs of divine feet, covering foot-soles with the god's emblems. Whose feet? Does it matter? Feet and footsteps and foot-soles are empty containers, to be filled in with longings and projections. Devotees literally pour out their feelings over them, envelop

---

[34] There are even three ancient and partly interrelated associative clusters here: the hands and feet (of Ṛgvedic Iḷā or Viṣṇu) dripping with ghee; the ancient place Gayā where in the course of the cosmogonic fight between deities and demons a drop of ambrosia fell down; and Gayā as the spot where Gaya the demon-cum-ascetic was given the promise, by Viṣṇu himself, that food offerings—dripping or solid—would be continuous. Whether this implies, in the perception of both priests and mourners, an equation (ghee equals *amṛta* equals *tarpaṇa* water offerings) deserves further study.

them in enigmas of absence and presence, form and formlessness, here and there. Feet and footsteps indicate mobility; transitions and transformations. They are also transient: hands and minds try to grasp them, hold them, fix them in place, yet they are elusive, as their very nature is movement. Finally, wet footsteps on the *ghāṭs*: how long do they last? And where do the footsteps of the dead go, once they are cremated and beyond the reach of the living? Just like the smoke of the cremation pyre, their footsteps vanish in thin air.

Thirdly, there are footprints, however rare. Humans may fabricate feet and footsteps, but they cannot manufacture natural footprints. Yes, they can help, and fake. They can produce facsimiles. They can outline and decorate. They can theologize and devotionalize. But it is their imagination of the divine that sees a footprint in a piece of rock, and it is the devotee's sensory and synaesthetic experience that continues to make the chunk of rock into a relic. Generations of priests may earn their livelihood from such an imprint. Entire pilgrims' towns may be based on it, oblivious of the finer distinctions between concavities and convexities. How much water, clarified butter, milk, oil, herbal substances are poured into it, how many flowers and sacred leaves are scattered over it? How many words of praise are spoken in front of it, how many prayers silently expressed, how many vows taken with the footprint as witness? And then, who today continues to believe that the gods actually have feet, feet that walk this earth and leave footprints, feet that look suspiciously very much like our own, only perhaps just a tiny bit bigger?[35]

On the human body as a symbol of society Douglas (1976, p. 115) wrote:

> 'The body is a model which can stand for any bounded system. Its boundaries can represent any boundaries which are threatened or precarious. The body is a complex structure. The functions of its different parts and their relation afford a source of symbols for other complex structures. We cannot possibly interpret rituals [. . .] unless we are prepared to see in the body a symbol of society, and to see the powers and dangers credited to social structure reproduced in small on the human body.'

This may be true and valid but let us reverse it for the sake of this article: humans may use their own body as a symbol and cipher for the social values a society wishes to inscribe on it, but they obviously ascribe more or less the same body to the gods. *Pāda* veneration, in Hinduism, may thus cynically be regarded as an all-too-human all-too-anthropomorphic projection, yet it could also be seen as a transitive encounter, an exchange. Especially when such a footprint is ascribed to Viṣṇu, whose name literally indicates his 'all-pervading' nature, to devotees the elusive imprint may rightfully remind of the god's divine pervasiveness. And, indeed, the empty mark left by his foot, thus implies both absence—he was here, once, but is gone now—and all-pervasive presence.

Funding: This research received no external funding.

Conflicts of Interest: The authors declare no conflict of interest.

References

Aktor, Michael. 2017a. Grasping the Formless in Stones: The Petromorphic Gods of the Hindu Pañcāyatanapūjā. In *Aesthetics of Religion: A Connective Concept*. Edited by Alexandra Grieser and Jay Johnston. Berlin and Boston: Walter de Gruyter, pp. 59–73. ISBN 978-3-11-045875-6.

Aktor, Mikael. 2017b. The Hindu Pañcāyatanapūjā in the Aniconism Spectrum. *Religion* 47: 503–19. [CrossRef]

Alam, Javeed. 1999. The Composite Culture and its Historiography. *South Asia: Journal of South Asian Studies* 22: 29–37. [CrossRef]

[35] In our search for proper categorization of 'divine footprints', distinguishing them from the proliferation of feet, foot-soles, footsteps and footmarks, two parallel terms from European art history are worth considering: (1) the divine footprint on natural rock could, in a way, be called 'not made by human hands' and thus be classed among the 'acheironpoièta'; (2) as a parallel to the phenomenon of (wrongly) perceiving forms in natural phenomena divine footprints could likewise be classed among the 'paradeilia'.

Asher, Frederick M. 1988. Gaya: Monuments in the Pilgrimage Town. In *Bodhgaya: The Site of Enlightenment*. Edited by Janice Leoshko. Bombay: Marg Publications, pp. 73–88. ISBN 81-85026-05-x.

Bakhtin, Mikhail M. 2008. *The Dialogic Imagination*, 17th ed. Edited by Michael Holquist. Translated by Caryl Emerson and Michael Holquist. Austin: Austin University of Texas Press, ISBN 978-0-292-71534-2.

Barua, Beni Madhab. 1975. *Gayā and Buddha-Gayā: Early History of the Holy Land*. 2 vols. Volume One, Book One: 'Pre-Buddhistic history of Gaya'. Reprint Varanasi: Bharatiya Publishing House.

Bharati, Agehananda. 1963. Pilgrimage in the Indian Tradition. *History of Religions* 3: 135–67. [CrossRef]

Bhattacharyya, Dipakchandra. 1964. An interesting image of the goddess Marici. *Indian History Congress* 26: 91–94.

Bhatti, Shaila, and Christopher Pinney. 2011. Optic-Clash: Modes of Visuality in India. In *A Companion to the Anthropology of India*. Edited by Isabella Clark-Decès. Chicester and Malden: Wiley-Blackwell, pp. 1965–83. ISBN 978-1-4051-9892-9.

Doniger, Wendy. 1978. *Hindu Myths: A Sourcebook*. Translated from the Sanskrit. Harmondsworth UK: Penguin Books, ISBN 0-14-044.306.1.

Douglas, Mary. 1976. *Purity and Danger: An Analysis of Concepts of Pollution and Taboo*. London and Henley: Routledge Kegan Paul, ISBN 0415291054.

Eck, Diana L. 1981. India's Tīrthas: 'Crossings' in Sacred Geography. *History of Religions* 20: 323–44. [CrossRef]

Eck, Diana L. 1998. The Imagined Landscape: Patterns in the Construction of Hindu Sacred Geography. *Contributions to Indian Sociology* 32: 165–88. [CrossRef]

Eck, Diana L. 2007. 'The Deity: The Image of God'. In *The Life of Hinduism*. Edited by John Stratton Hawley and Vasudha Narayanan. Berkeley: University of California Press, pp. 42–52. ISBN 10-0520-24914-3.

Encyclopedia of Buddhism. Keown, Damien, and Charles S. Prebish, eds. Abingdon and New York: Routledge, 2013, ISBN 978-0415556248.

Gaifman, Milette. 2017. 'Aniconism: Definitions, Examples and Comparative Perspectives.' Introduction to Thematic Issue on Exploring Aniconism. *Religion* 47: 335–52. [CrossRef]

Geary, David. 2008. Destination Enlightenment: Branding Buddhism and Spiritual Tourism in Bodhgaya, Bihar. *Anthropology Today* 24: 11–14. [CrossRef]

Glücklich, Ariel. 2008. *The Strides of Vishnu: Hindu Culture in Historical Perspective*. New York: Oxford University Press, ISBN 978-0-19-971825-2.

Glushkova, Irina. 2015. From Constant Yearning and Casual Bliss to Hurt Sentiments: An Emotional Shift in the Varkari Tradition (India). In *Historicizing Emotions: Practices and Objects in India, China and Japan*. Edited by Barbara Schüler. Leiden and Boston: Brill, pp. 71–99. ISBN 978-90-04-35296-4.

Gonda, Jan. 1969. *Aspects of Early Viṣṇuism*, 2nd ed. Delhi: Motilal Banarsidass, Available online: https://archive.org/details/JanGondaAspectsOfEarlyVisnuismMotilalBanarsidassPublishers1969/ (accessed on 18 May 2018).

Guerney, Jacques de. 2014. *Buddhapada*. Bangkok: Orchid Press, ISBN 9745241636.

Haberman, David L. 2017. 'Drawing out the Iconic in the Aniconic: Worship of Neem Trees and Govardhan Stones in Northern India'. *Religion* 47: 483–502. [CrossRef]

Hasan, Parveen. 1993. The Footprint of the Prophet. *Muqarnas* 10: 335–43. [CrossRef]

Howes, David, and Constance Classen. 2014. *Ways of Sensing: Understanding the Senses in Society*. London and New York: Routledge, ISBN 978-0-415-69714-9.

Huyler, Stephen P. 1994. *Meeting God: Elements of Hindu Devotion*. New Haven and London: Yale University Press, ISBN 0-300-07983-4.

Huyler, Stephen P. 1999. *Painted Prayers: Women's Art in Village India*. New York: Rizzoli, ISBN 0847818098.

Huyler, Stephen P. 2008. *Daughters of India: Art and Identity*. New York: Abbeville Press Publishers/University of California, ISBN 978-0-7892-1002.

Jacques, Claude. 1962. *Gayā Māhātmya: Edition Critique, Traduction Française et Introduction*. Edited by Claude Jojoin. Pondichéry: Institut français d'Indologie.

Jain-Neubauer, Jutta. 2000. *Feet & Footwear in Indian Culture*. Toronto: Bata Shoe Museum Foundation, Ahmedabad: Mapin Publishing, ISBN 10-1890206202.

Jaiswal, Suvira. 1964. Foot Print of Vishnu (Summary). Proceedings of the Indian History Congress 26, Part I: 90–91. Available online: http://www.jstor.org/stable/44133096/ (accessed on 2 June 2018).

Kinnard, Jacob N. 2000. The Polyvalent Pādas of Viṣṇu and the Buddha. *History of Religions* 40: 32–57. [CrossRef]

Kinnard, Jacob N. 2014. *Places in Motion: The Fluid Identities of Temples, Images, and Pilgrims*. New York: Oxford University Press, ISBN 9780199359660.

Kramrisch, Stella. 1976. *The Hindu Temple*. Delhi: Motilal Banarsidass, vol. I, ISBN 81-208-0223-3.

Kumar, Anil. 1987. Faith, Ritual and Feudal Order: World of Early Medieval Women in Lower Ganga Valley. In *Kusumāñjali: New Interpretations of Indian Art and Culture*. Edited by Jeannine Auboyer. Delhi: Agam Kala Prakashan, chp. 8. pp. 49–61.

Lamb, Sarah. 2005. The Politics of Dirt and Gender: Body Techniques in Bengali India. In *Dirt, Undress and Difference: Critical Perspectives on the Body's Surface*. Edited by Adeline Masquelier. Bloomington: Indiana University Press, pp. 213–32. ISBN 978-0-253-11153-1.

Larios, Borayin, and Raphaël Voix. 2018. Introduction to 'Wayside-Shrines in India: Prosaic and Defiant Religiosity'. *SAMAJ-EASAS*. forthcoming. [CrossRef]

Leoshko, Janice. 1988. *Bodhgaya: The Site of Enlightenment*. Bombay: Marg Publications, ISBN 81-85026-05-x.

Lochtefeld, James. 2011. 'Pandas'. In *Brill's Encyclopedia of Hinduism: Society, Religions, Specialists, Religious Traditions, Philosophy*. Edited by Knut A. Jacobsen, Helene Basu, Angelika Malinar and Vasudha Narayanan. Leiden and Boston: Brill, vol. III, pp. 240–44. [CrossRef]

Lochtefeld, James. 2017. Pandas/Pilgrimage Priests. *Oxford Bibliographies of Hinduism*. [CrossRef]

Lonely Planet. 2015. *India*. Singapore: Lonely Planet, ISBN 978-1-74321-676-7.

Marshall, Anne L., John M. Malville, and Rana P.B. Singh. 2009. Death and Transformation at Gaya: Pilgrimage, Ancestors, and the Sun. In *Pilgrimage, Sacred Landscape and Self-Organized Complexity*. Edited by John M. Malville and Baidyanath Saraswati. Delhi: DK Printworld (for IGNCA), pp. 110–21. ISBN 81-2460-454-1.

Mohamed, Malik. 2007. *The Foundations of the Composite Culture in India*. Delhi: Aakar Books, ISBN 978-81-89833-18-3.

Morgan, David. 2012. *The Embodied Eye: Religious Visual Culture and the Social Life of Feeling*. Berkeley: University of California Press, ISBN 9780520272231.

Moss, Candida. 2016. Why Do Religions Have a Foot Fetish? *The Daily Beast*. March 27. Available online: https://www.thedailybeast.com/why-do-religions-have-a-foot-fetish (accessed on 2 May 2018).

Nagarajan, Vijaya R. 1993. 'Hosting the Divine: The Kōlam in Tamil Nadu'. In *Mud, Mirror, and Thread: Folk Traditions in Rural India*. Edited by Nora Fischer. Albuquerque/Santa Fe: Museum of New Mexico Press, Ahmedabad: Mapin Press, pp. 192–203. ISBN 8-185822-18-2.

Nagarajan, Vijaya R. 1998. The Earth as Goddess Bhū Devī: Toward a Theory of "Embedded Ecologies" in Folk Hinduism. In *Purifying the Earthly Body of God: Religion and Ecology in Hindu India*. Edited by Lance Nelson. Albany: State University of New York Press, pp. 269–95. ISBN 0-7914-3923-2.

Narayanan, Vasudha. 2011. 'Śrīvaiṣṇavism'. In *Brill's Encyclopedia of Hinduism*. Edited by Knut A. Jacobsen et al. Leiden and Boston: Brill, vol. III, ISBN 978-90-04-17894-6.

O'Malley, L.S.S. 2007. *Bengal District Gazetteers: Gaya*. New Delhi: Logos Press, ISBN 81-7268-137-2.

Paul, Debjani. 1985. 'Antiquity of the Viṣṇupāda at Gayā: Tradition and Archeology. *East and West* 35: 103–41. Available online: http://www.jstor.org/stable/29756715/ (accessed on 22 May 2018).

Preston, James J. 1992. Spiritual Magnetism: An Organizing Principle for the Study of Pilgrimage. In *Sacred Journeys: The Anthropology of Pilgrimage*. Edited by Alan Morinis. Westport and London: Greenwood Press, pp. 31–46. ISBN 0-313-27879-2.

Princeton Dictionary of Buddhism. Buswell, Robert E., Jr., and Donald S. Lopez, Jr., eds. Princeton: Princeton University Press, 2014, ISBN 9780691157863.

Sailer, Waldemar C. 1993. Chronology of Buddha Footprints. In *Exhibition Catalogue: Buddha Pada Lakkhana/ Footprints in Thailand*. Bangkok: Fine Arts Department, Ministry of Education, pp. 27–35.

Salomon, Richard. 1985. *The Bridge to the Three Holy Cities: The Sāmānya-praghaṭṭaka of Nārāyaṇa Bhaṭṭa's Tristhalīsetu*. Critically edited and translated. Delhi: Motilal Banarsidass, ISBN 0895816474-9780895816474.

Sandness, Adéla. 2010. In the footprint of Iḷā: An Early Image of Sacrificial Cosmology in Vedic Tradition. *Studies in Religion/Sciences Religieuses* 39: 509–21. [CrossRef]

Schimmel, Annemarie. 1980. *Islam in the Indian Subcontinent*. Volume 4 of Handbuch der Orientalistik/zweite Abteilung: Indien. Leiden: Brill, ISBN 9004061177.

Shima, Iwao. 1988. The Viṭhobā Faith of Mahārāṣṭra: The Viṭhobā Temple of Paṇḍharpūr and its Mythological Structure. *Folk Religion and Religious Organizations in Asia* 15: 183–97. Available online: http://www.jstor.org/stable/30233385/ (accessed on 22 May 2018).

Singh, Rana P. B. 2009. Death and Transformation at Gaya: Pilgrimage, Ancestors and the Sun. In *The Sacred and Complex Landscapes of Pilgrimage*. Edited by John M. Malville and Baidyanath Saraswati. Delhi: DK Printworld, pp. 110–21. ISBN 81-2460-454-1.

Skeen, William. 1870. *Adam's Peak: Legendary, Traditional, and Historic Notices, or the Samanala, and Sri-Pada: with a Descriptive Account of the Pilgrims' Route from Colombo to the Sacred Footprint*. Colombo: Skeen & Co., Available online: https://archive.org/stream/adamaspeaklegend00skeegoog#page/ (accessed on 3 June 2018).

Smith, Brian K. 1994. *Classifying the Universe: The Ancient Indian Varna System and the Origins of Caste*. New York: Oxford University Press, ISBN 0-19-506054-7.

Stanley, John M. 1992. The Great Maharashtrian Pilgrimage: Pandharpur and Alandi. In *Sacred Journeys: The Anthropology of Pilgrimage*. Edited by Alan Morinis. Westport and London: Greenwood Press, pp. 65–87. ISBN 0-313-27879-2.

Tadvalkar, Nayana. 2015. A Language of Symbols: Rangoli Art of India. In *Traditional Knowledge and Traditional Cultural Expressions of South Asia*. Edited by Sanjay Garg. Colombo: SAARC Cultural Centre, pp. 173–86. ISSN 2012-922x.

Tanaka, Kanoko. 1998. *Absence of the Buddha Image in Early Buddhist Art; Toward its Significance in Comparative Religion*. New Delhi: D.K. Printworld, ISBN 81-246-0090-2.

Tukaram. 2003. *Says Tuka—1. Selected Poems of Tukaram*. Translated from the Marathi with an Introduction by Dilip Chitre. Pune: Sontheimer Cultural Association.

Vidal, Denis. 2006. Darshan. In *South Asian Studies Keywords*. London: SOAS, Available online: www.soas.ac.uk/southasianstudies/keywords/file24803.pdf (accessed on 14 May 2018).

Vidyarthi, Lalita Prasad. 1978. *The Sacred Complex of Hindu Gaya*. Second edition with a new introduction. Delhi: Naurang Rai.

MDPI
St. Alban-Anlage 66
4052 Basel
Switzerland
Tel. +41 61 683 77 34
Fax +41 61 302 89 18
www.mdpi.com

Religions Editorial Office
E-mail: religions@mdpi.com
www.mdpi.com/journal/religions

www.ingramcontent.com/pod-product-compliance
Lightning Source LLC
Chambersburg PA
CBHW041137120626
46547CB00020B/3016